teach yourself...

Lotus 1-2-3
Release 5 for Windows

Meredith Fein
Andrew Sussman

A Subsidiary of
Henry Holt and Co., Inc.

First Edition—1994

ISBN 1-55828-400-1

Printed in the United States of America.

10 9 8 7 6 5 4 3

Publisher, *Brenda McLaughlin*
Development Editor, *Michael Sprague*
Production Editor, *Marni Tapscott*
Copy Editor, *Jo Anna Arnott*
Assistant Production Editor, *Anthony Washington*

Dedication

*For Caroline, my love, who stood by me and
made the long nights seem not so long.*

Acknowledgments

The publisher would like to thank Judi Fernandez without whom this book would not have been possible.

Table of Contents

Preface   **xix**

Chapter 1

Introduction to Lotus 1-2-3 Release 5   **1**

What Is a Spreadsheet? 1

Taking a Guided Tour 2

Using the QuickStart Tutorial 3

The Lotus 1-2-3 Window 4

Window Features 6

    Title bar 6

    Menu bar 7

    Edit line 7

    SmartIcons 11

    Worksheet Tabs 11

    Worksheet Window 12

    Column Headings 12

    Row Headings 13

Cells 13

Status Bar 14

What You Learned 14

Chapter 2

Worksheet Fundamentals 15

File Basics 16

Creating a New File 16

Opening an Existing File 17

Saving a File 21

Working with Multiple Worksheets 27

Creating New Worksheets 28

Inserting New Worksheets 28

Deleting Worksheets 29

Working with Worksheet Tabs 31

Viewing Multiple Worksheets 32

Referencing Across Worksheets 33

Working with Multiple Files 34

Window Menu 34

Cascade Windows 35

Tile Windows 36

Minimize Windows 36

Taking Advantage of SmartMasters 37

To Sum Up 42

What You Learned 43

Worksheets Continued 47

Chapter 3

Worksheets Continued 47

Selecting Worksheet Areas 48

Selecting a Range 49

Should You Select Before or After? 51

Selecting a Collection 53

Selecting a 3D Range 57

Naming Ranges 59

Go To Command 60

Using Navigator 62

Splitting Views 64

    Synchronized Scrolling 66

    Changing Split Size 66

    Clearing Splits 66

Freezing Views 67

Entering Data 71

Values versus Labels 72

How to Enter Data 72

Confirming and Canceling 75

Entering Numbers 76

Entering Text 78

Entering Dates and Times 80

Filling a Range with a Series 81

Range by Example 83

Editing Data 85

Moving Data 86

Copying Data 88

Inserting and Deleting Rows, Columns, and Selected Cells 90

Find & Replace 93

Spell Checking 97

Practice 99

Saving a Particular Range 100

Combining Files 101

To Sum Up 104

What You Learned 104

Chapter 4

Formatting Worksheets   115

Changing Fonts and Attributes 116

Group Mode 122

Changing Number Formats 124

Changing Cell Alignment 127

Changing Column Width and Row Height 131

Adding Borders 134

Changing Colors 137

The Right Mouse Button 138

Using Named Styles 138

Creating a Named Style 139

Applying a Named Style 140

Using the Gallery 140

Hiding Cells 142

Practice 142

To Sum Up 143

What You Learned 143

Chapter 5

Spreadsheet Calculations   149

Using Formulas 150

Types of Formulas 150

    Numeric Formulas 151

    Text Formulas 151

    Logical Formulas 152

Guidelines for Creating Formulas 153

    Always begin your formula with an equal (=) sign. 153

    Use parentheses in numeric formulas. 154

    Don't put spaces in your formula. 154

A cell that you reference in a formula will receive a
value of 0 if it is empty. 154

An error in a formula will return the result ERR. 155

If the result of the formula is too large to fit in the cell,
1-2-3 displays asterisks (*). 155

Entering a Formula 155

Relative versus Absolute References 164

Moving Formulas 166

Using @ Functions 167

What Is an @Function? 169

Function Arguments 169

@Function Selector 171

@Function List 172

Nested @Functions 175

Practice 176

To Sum Up 177

What You Learned 178

Chapter 6

Printing 181

Quick Printing 182

Printing All Worksheets 185

Printing a Selected Range 186

Print Preview 189

Page Breaks 192

Page Setup 194

Print Orientation 196

Margins 197

Headers and Footers 199

Hiding Row and Column Headings and Gridlines 201

Scaling 202

Print Titles 204

Saving and Retrieving Settings 205

To Sum Up 206

What You Learned 207

Chapter 7

Charts   211

What Is a Chart? 212

Chart Types 213

Creating a Chart 219

Using Quick Chart 222

Creating a Chart Manually 224

Naming Charts 224

Finding Chart By Name 226

Changing Chart Type 226

Formatting Chart Appearance 229

Chart Headings 229

    Moving Chart Headings 230

    Chart Notes 230

    Legend 230

    Legend Placement 231

Axes 232

    Changing Axis Units 233

Scale 234

Fun with Pie Charts 234

Frames 236

Printing Charts 237

Practice 238

To Sum Up 238

What You Learned 239

Chapter 8

Graphics   245

What Is a Drawn Object? 246

Creating Drawn Objects 247

    Lines 247

    Arrows 249

    Arcs 251

    Rectangles and Ellipses 252

    Polylines and Polygons 253

    Freehand Drawing 256

Text Blocks 257

    Creating Text Blocks 258

    Editing Text Blocks 259

    Formatting Text Blocks 259

Importing Pictures 260

Working with Objects 260

    Selecting Objects 261

    Resizing Objects 262

    Copying Objects 263

    Moving Objects 264

    Arranging Objects 264

    Fastening Objects 266

    Grouping Objects 268

    Locking Objects 269

    Deleting Objects 270

Changing Objects 270

    Changing Lines and Arrows 270

    Adding Frames 271

    Changing Colors and Patterns 273

Flipping Objects 273

Rotating Objects 273

Practice 275

To Sum Up 275

What You Learned 276

Chapter 9

Analyzing Data   283

Version Manager 283

Create a Version 288

Working with Multiple Versions 291

Version Manager Index 299

    Showing Versions in the Version Manager Index 301

    Selecting more than One Version at the Same Time 301

    Sorting versions 302

Version Reports 305

Scenarios 309

What-If's 314

Backsolver 317

What-If Tables 320

    One-Variable Table 320

    Two-Variable Table 323

    Three-Variable Table 326

To Sum Up 328

What You Learned 329

Chapter 10

Lotus 1-2-3 Database Fundamentals   333

What Is a Database? 334

Records 335

Fields 335

Queries 336

Creating A Database Table 336

Creating Field Names 336

Enter the Data 337

Name the Database Table 338

Using Queries 339

Creating Queries 339

    Select a Database Table 340

    Selecting Fields and Records 341

    Selecting the Location for a New Query Table 341

Choosing Fields 342

Setting Criteria 346

    Using One Criteria 347

    Using Multiple Criteria 350

    Sorting 353

To Sum Up 357

What You Learned 358

Chapter 11

Using Macros   **361**

Understanding Macros 362

Creating a Macro 362

Macro Syntax 363

Planning a Macro 365

Where to Create a Macro 366

    Transcript window 366

    Worksheet cell 368

    A macro library 370

How To Create a Macro 370

Recording a Macro 372

Analyzing and Editing a Macro 378

Running a Macro 381

Naming a Macro Range 382

Running a Named Macro Range 384

Creating a Macro Button 387

Assigning a Macro to a Button 387

Running a Macro Button 390

Practice 390

To Sum Up 391

What You Learned 392

Appendix A

Installing Lotus 1-2-3   395

System Requirements 395

Starting the Installation 396

Default or Minimum Installation 400

Customized Installation 403

Appendix B

Customizing Lotus 1-2-3   411

View Preferences 412

Worksheet Defaults 416

User Setup 418

International Settings 421

Recalculation Settings 423

Appendix C

Introduction to SmartIcons   425

List of SmartIcon Sets 426

Creating New SmartIcon Sets 427

Saving a SmartIcon Set 429

Position of SmartIcon Bar 429

Editing Icons 430

Icon Size 431

List of SmartIcons 432

Appendix D

Common @ Functions   435

@ABS(X) 435

@AVG(List) 436

@BINOMIAL(Trials;Successes;Probability;[Type]) 436

@COLS(Range) 436

@COUNT(List) 436

@DATE(Year;Month;Day) 437

@DATEDIF(Start_Date;End_Date;Format) 437

@DATEVALUE(Text) 437

@DB(Cost;Salvage;Life;Period) 437

@DDB(Cost;Salvage;Life;Period) 438

@EVEN(X) 438

@EXACT(Text1;Text2) 438

@EXP(X) 439

@FACT(N) 439

@FV(Payments;Interest;Term) 439

@GRANDTOTAL(List) 439

@IF(Condition;X;Y) 440

@INT(X) 440

@ISERR(X) 440

@ISNA(X) 440

@ISNUMBER(X) 441

@ISSTRING(X) 441

@LARGE(Range;N) 441

@LEFT(Text;N) 441

@LENGTH(Text) 442

@LN(X) 442

@LOG(X) 442

@LOWER(Text) 442

@MAX(List) 443

@MEDIAN(List) 443

@MID(Text;Start_Number;N) 443

@MIN(List) 443

@NOW 444

@NPV(Interest;Range) 444

@ODD(X) 444

@PI 444

@PMT(Principal;Interest;Term) 444

@PRODUCT(List) 445

@PROPER(Text) 445

@PV(Payments;Interest;Term) 445

@QUOTIENT(X;Y) 445

@RAND 446

@RANGENAME(Cell) 446

@RATE(Future_Value;Present_Value;Term) 446

@REPEAT(Text;N) 446

@REPLACE(Original_Text;Start_Number;N; New_Text;TR8) 447

@RIGHT(Text;N) 447

@ROUND(X;N) 447

@ROUNDDOWN(X;[N;Direction]) 447

@ROUNDUP(X;[N;Direction]) 448

@ROWS(Range) 448

@SIGN(X) 448

@SLN(Cost;Salvage;Life) 448

@SMALL(Range;N) 449

@SQRT(X) 449

@STD(List) 449

@STRING(X;N) 449

@SUBTOTAL(List) 450

@SUM(List) 450

@SUMSQ(List) 450

@SUMXMY2(Range1;Range2) 450

@TERM(Payments;Interest;Future_Value) 451

@TRUNC(X;[N]) 451

@UPPER(Text) 451

@VALUE(Text) 451

@VAR(List) 452

Appendix E

Working with Windows   453

Window Components 453

Using Your Mouse 454

Window Features 454

Menus 458

Dialog Boxes 459

Scrolling 459

Undo 460

The Help System 461

Program Manager 462

Index   467

Preface

You have chosen Lotus 1-2-3 Release 5 as your spreadsheet. You'll be working with one of the most sophisticated applications in today's PC world. It offers features that weren't even dreamed of five years ago. In fact, it no longer merely responds to commands, but instead frequently predicts what you want to do next. For example, if you name your first worksheet January, it automatically names the next ones February, March, and so on.

All that power makes your job much easier, but you must learn how to take advantage of it, control it, and tailor it for your own spreadsheet tasks. The purpose of this book is to help you do that.

Designed with You in Mind

In designing Release 5, Lotus set four major user-oriented goals:

- To make Lotus 1-2-3 the easiest spreadsheet to learn and to use

- To help users become more productive

- To enable users to easily share data in a work group environment

- To implement Lotus' Working Together strategy so that all your Lotus products work well with each other

With these goals in mind, Lotus developed a wide range of state-of-the-art features for this latest release of their famous 1-2-3 spreadsheet.

Easy to Learn and Use

Release 5 is chock full of learning aids, from an animated Guided Tour and an on-screen Tutorial to an exceptionally thorough Help library. To save you learning time as well as design time, a number of professionally designed worksheets called SmartMasters are built into the system. All you have to do is select a design and fill in your own data, and you have a sophisticated looking sales invoice, expense report, or profit and loss statement.

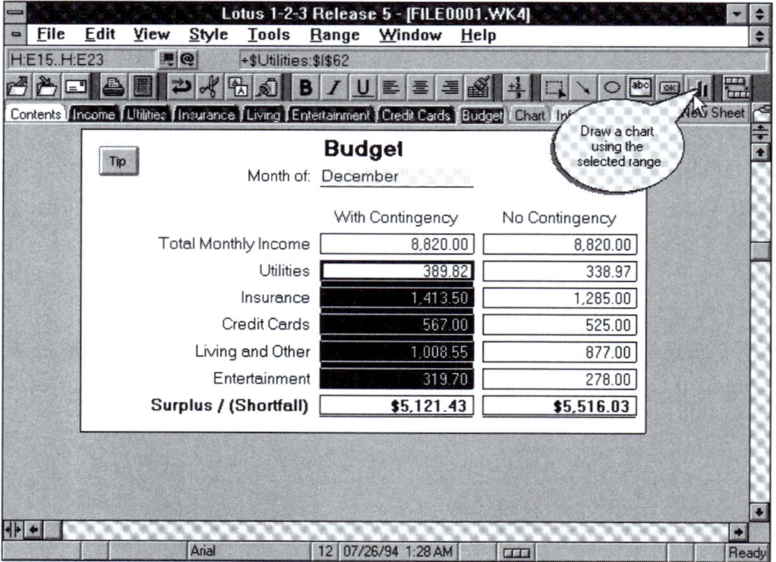

Figure P.1 *Using a SmartMaster such as this, you can produce a professional looking expense report on your first day.*

To make the spreadsheet even easiexxr to use, Lotus has moved away from menus (although they still are available) and toward direct manipulation of objects such as data cells, charts, and drawings. As an example, if you enter "Week 1" into a cell, then drag that value through the next nine cells, Lotus 1-2-3 Release 5 fills those cells with "Week 2" through "Week 10."

Dozens of icons, called SmartIcons, are available to make very advanced functions available with a single mouse click. The Button bar near the top of the window displays the SmartIcons you are most likely to use right now. It changes automatically as you work on different parts of your worksheet. (So do the menus.) But you don't have to stick to the SmartIcon bars provided by Lotus; you can create your own bars to contain any icons you wish. And so you don't have to memorize all those SmartIcons, when you pass your mouse over an icon, a cartoon-like balloon pops up to explain its function.

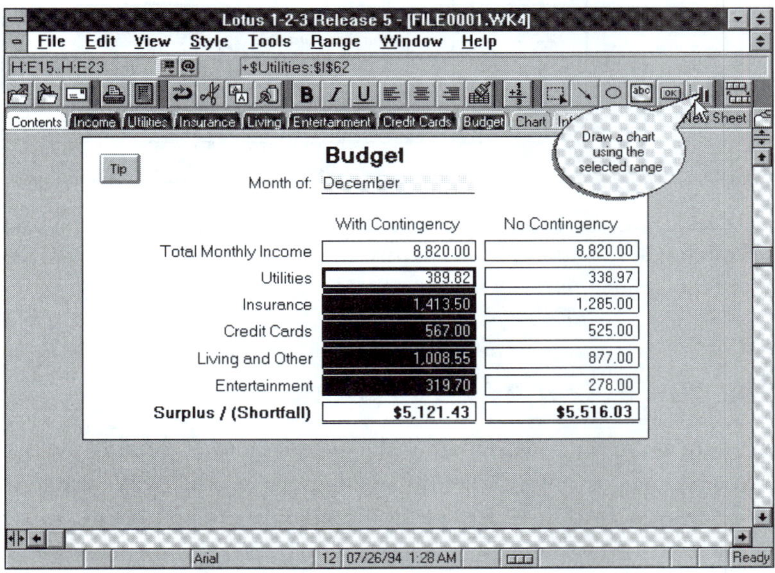

Figure P.2 *Pause the mouse pointer over an icon and a balloon pops up to explain it.*

Many areas of the screen are "alive" to the mouse pointer. Functions such as font changes can be done by clicking the status bar at the bottom of the window. Specially tailored menus called quick menus pop up when you click the right mouse button anywhere in the window. You get a different menu if you click , a cell, a chart, a drawing, a map, and so on. Each quick menu contains the most likely commands for the object that you're working on.

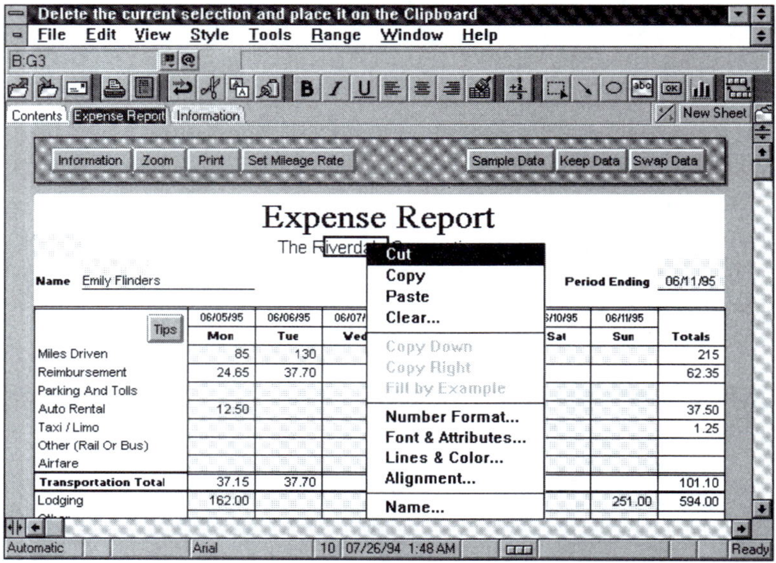

Figure P.3 *QuickMenus pop up anywhere on the screen and provide the commands you are most likely to want for that area.*

Helping You Become More Productive

Features such as SmartIcons, SmartMasters, and QuickMenus all help to make you more productive, but you'll find even more productivity oriented feature with this release. A feature called Version Manager lets you create and compare different versions of the same worksheet so that you can, for example, examine a best case and worst case scenario of next year's budget. What's more, several people in a workgroup can create their own versions of the same worksheet, such as a proposed project timeline, and Lotus 1-2-3 will keep track of them all, as well as who created them.

Databases and spreadsheets go hand-in-hand, and you can not only create your own databases within Lotus 1-2-3 Release 5, you can also access existing databases developed by other applications quickly and easily. And if you have the Lotus Approach database, you can perform some of its functions, such as printing mailing labels, from data in your spreadsheet without even leaving Lotus 1-2-3.

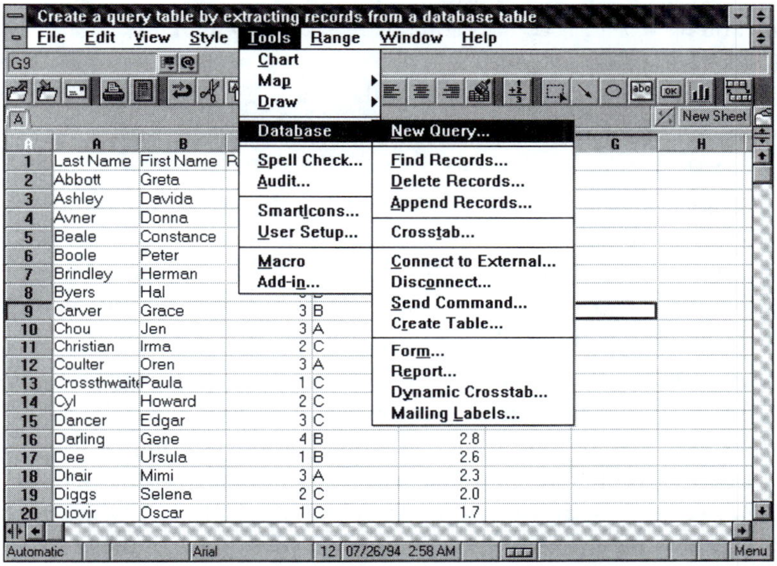

Figure P.4 *The Tools menu includes commands to access external databases and pull the data into your spreadsheet.*

Sharing Data with Your Work Group

If you're a member of a work group that shares data, Lotus 1-2-3 Release 5 offers several facilities that make everyone's life easier. You've already read about Version Manager, which keeps track of the differing scenarios that your work group develops so that there's less confusion about who did what, when, and why. And of course, you can create your own version of a budget or schedule without overwriting someone else's data. Version Manager actually flags changes made by others since the last time you viewed a worksheet, so you're immediately aware that you need to review new work.

Release 5 is also mail enabled. It takes a few simple commands to route all or part of a worksheet to others in your work group via a mailing system such as cc:Mail or Lotus Notes. The Release 5 status bar includes an indicator to notify you when you have received new mail from someone; all you have to do is click the indicator to launch into your mailing system and read the new mail.

Lotus' Working Together Strategy

Lotus' strategy of Working Together means that all the Lotus products—Lotus 1-2-3, the AmiPro word processor, Lotus Notes, the Approach database, Freelance Graphics, and so on—work well together. They all have the same look and feel, so that, if you know one, you know them all. They all, for example, offer SmartIcons, QuickMenus, and direct manipulation of objects. You can easily copy or link objects from one to the other. All are mail-enabled.

All the Lotus products share facilities such as the spell checker and its dictionaries, which are installed on your hard drive only once. This means, first, that you're not wasting hard disk space storing five different spell checkers. Second, if you add a word to a dictionary from one application, that same word becomes available to all your Lotus applications.

Working Together also means that Lotus products work well with other vendor's Windows products. Although other products don't have the same level of integration as Lotus products do, the Lotus products comply with the latest Windows standards for Open Database Connectivity (ODBC), Object Linking and Editing (OLE 2.0), and Dynamic Data Exchange (DDE), which permits the exchange of data between applications that also comply with these standards.

About This Book

This book is designed to help you get started with Lotus 1-2-3 Release 5. You'll learn how to create new worksheets, format them to create attractive and readable presentations, print them, save them on disk, and revise them. You'll see how to generate charts, such as line charts and pie charts, based on a worksheet data, and to add simple drawings to highlight details.

Then you will go on to some of the more advanced features such as Version Manager and database access. You'll learn how to create and use macros to facilitate repetitive tasks.

This book is intended for readers who have some experience with Windows but have not yet learned how to use Lotus 1-2-3 Release 5. If you don't know how to use Windows, Appendix E shows you the basics. If you already know how to use earlier versions of Lotus 1-2-3 for Windows, you might want to skip the earlier chapters that deal with spreadsheet basics and concentrate on some of the new features such as Version Manager.

If you haven't yet installed Lotus 1-2-3 Release 5, be sure to consult Appendix A for guidance in that process.

Conventions Used in This Book

Certain conventions are used in this book to make the program easier to learn. Following is a list of them that you can refer to as a key:

Menu Commands—if the program requires you to select a menu item, the command is listed in small capital letters in boldface type. For example, to open a document (as discussed in Chapter 1), you will need to go to the File menu and select **Open.**

Special Keys—if you must use one of the keyboard's special keys, such as Enter or Shift, that key will appear in bold letters. For example, in Chapter 4, you'll learn that if you want to select multiple cells, you must hold down the **Shift** key while clicking the mouse.

Indicates an alternative method that will make your life easier.

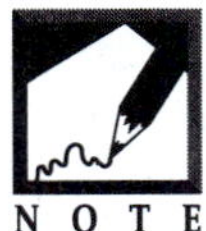

Indicates a piece of information to which you should pay particular attention, like a reminder of something covered in a previous chapter.

Indicates to proceed with caution. For example, it is used to alert you to be careful when erasing data.

Chapter 1

Introduction to Lotus 1-2-3 Release 5

This chapter begins by discussing the concept of a spreadsheet, what it is used for, and the basic features that distinguish it from other Windows programs.

You learn how to view the Lotus 1-2-3 Guided Tour and to use the Tutorial. Next, you learn about the different components of the Lotus 1-2-3 window, such as the title bar, the edit line, and the menu bar. By the end of this chapter, you will begin to understand the Lotus 1-2-3 interface and you will be ready to learn about the worksheet area.

What Is a Spreadsheet?

A spreadsheet program is an application, like a word processing program, that makes your life easier. We use spreadsheets to calculate numbers and formulas, create graphs, and help manage and present numerical data. Just as a word processor is infinitely more sophisticated than a quill and inkwell, spreadsheet programs calculate and present numerical data far more quickly and more easily than doing it manually.

You can use spreadsheets for many purposes. First of all, they are a clear and comprehensible way to organize and present data of any kind (even text data) in tabular form. Whether you are preparing a list or comparing items side-by-side, you can arrange your information in a lucid way on a spreadsheet.

But beyond simply displaying your data, spreadsheets are capable of altering numerical data to create new information, by performing calculations. Because of this feature, you can use a spreadsheet to create a financial statement to analyze statistical data. Also, Lotus 1-2-3 Release 5 has built-in charting capabilities that enable you to create graphical representations of your data. Because the worksheets you use are in tabular form, the possible uses for a spreadsheet are virtually limitless[md]from balancing your company's budget to listing all your friends and their annoying habits.

Taking a Guided Tour

The Lotus 1-2-3 Release 5 program is quite user friendly because it makes use of the Windows environment. When you open the Windows Program Manager, you will notice that the installer automatically created a program group containing program items for Lotus 1-2-3 Release 5. Double-click the Lotus 1-2-3 group icon to open the group window, as shown in Figure 1.1.

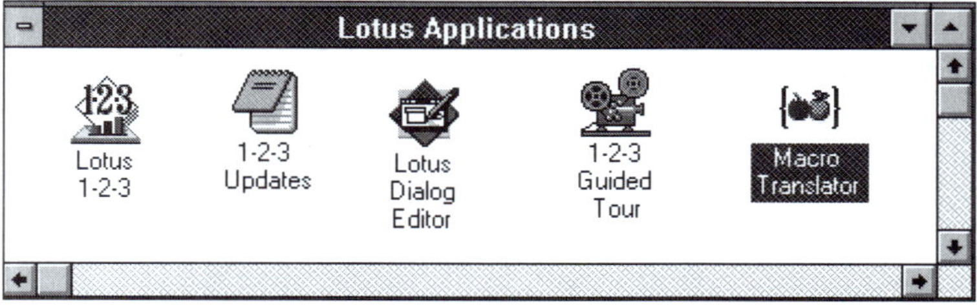

Figure 1.1 *Lotus 1-2-3 program items.*

Notice that one of the program items is called Guided Tour. Run this program (by double-clicking the icon) for an animated overview of the Lotus 1-2-3

Release 5 features. The whole tour takes just a few minutes, and you can control how much of it you want to see.

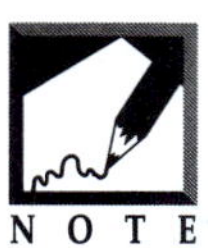

We recommend that you take the tour before continuing in this book. It's not required, but it will make you more comfortable with the Lotus 1-2-3 features. (It's also a lot of fun.)

N O T E

Using the QuickStart Tutorial

When you're ready to start Lotus 1-2-3 itself, double-click the Lotus 1-2-3 program icon (see Figure 1.2).

Figure 1.2 *Lotus 1-2-3 program icon.*

The first window you see looks like the window shown in Figure 1.3. A Welcome dialog box opens automatically, asking whether you want to open an existing worksheet, start a new worksheet, or use the QuickStart tutorial.

The QuickStart tutorial is different from the Guided Tour. It actually walks you through your first experiences at creating a simple worksheet, creating a chart, printing, and so on, using sample data provided with the tutorial. When you click the QuickStart Tutorial button, the screen shown in Figure 1.4 appears. You can select from among the eight lessons or click **Exit** to end the tutorial.

When you select a lesson, you see the Tutorial window (see Figure 1.5). The standard Lotus 1-2-3 window is on the left, and the Tutorial window is on the right. All you have to do is follow the instructions in the Tutorial window. The buttons just above the text area give you some control over what happens in the tutorial. The short dark arrow pointing to the right, for example, causes the tutorial to perform the current task for you (instead of waiting for you to perform it) and go on to the next page. To see an explanation of all the buttons, click the button that contains a question mark in a circle.

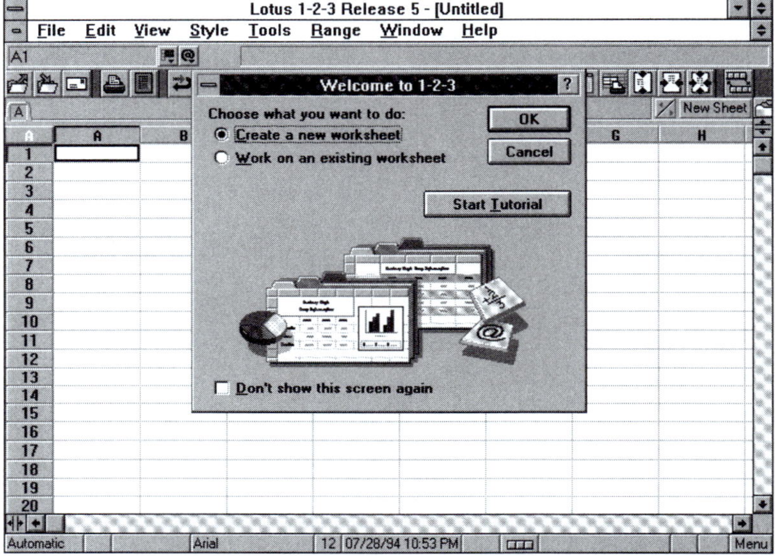

Figure 1.3 *Initial Lotus 1-2-3 window.*

After you begin working with a worksheet, the Welcome dialog box disappears from your screen. If you decide then that you want to see the tutorial, click Help to pull down the Help menu, and then click **Tutorial**.

The Lotus 1-2-3 Window

When you exit the tutorial, you see the screen shown in Figure 1.6. You also see the same screen if you bypass the tutorial and choose **Cancel** in the Welcome to 1-2-3 dialog box. (The other options in the Welcome dialog box are explained in later chapters.)

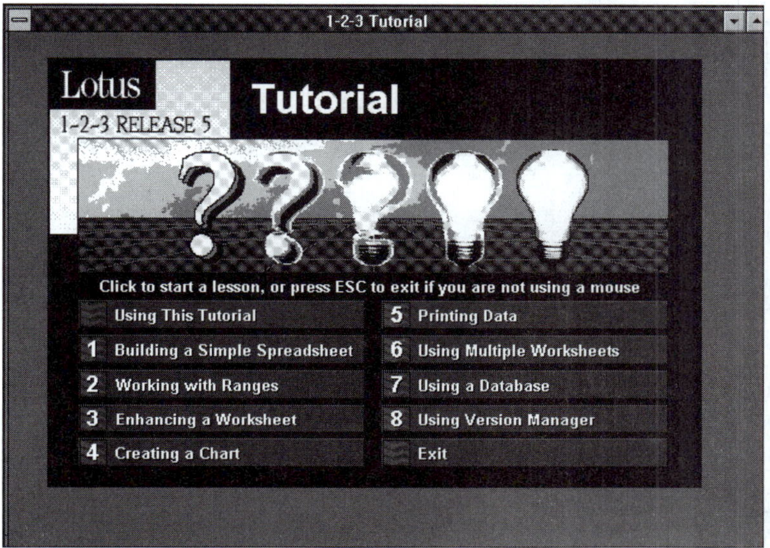

Figure 1.4 *Tutorial contents.*

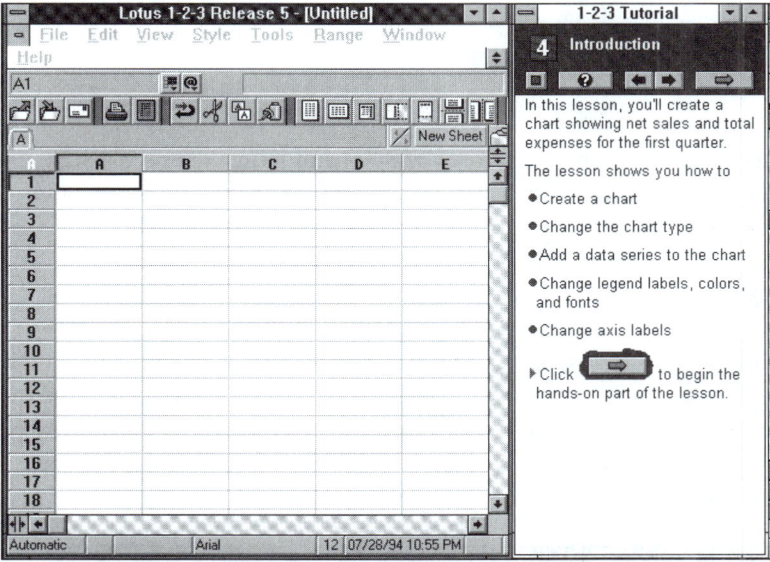

Figure 1.5 *Tutorial window.*

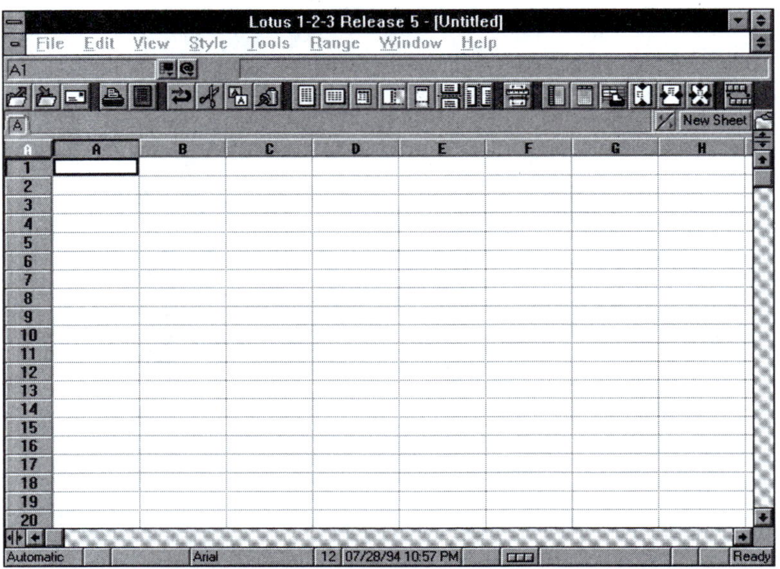

Figure 1.6 *Lotus 1-2-3 untitled worksheet.*

Window Features

The window contains many features and several icons. Like road signs that have pictures with no words, you will easily recognize them in a short time, and you will appreciate the fact that they take up less space than words..

Title bar

At the top of the window is the title bar (see Figure 1.7). This bar initially reads *Lotus 1-2-3 [Untitled]*. The word in brackets is the file name or title of the worksheet. Right now it says Untitled because you have just begun the program and have opened a new worksheet. When you save this worksheet or open an old worksheet, this bar displays that worksheet's name.

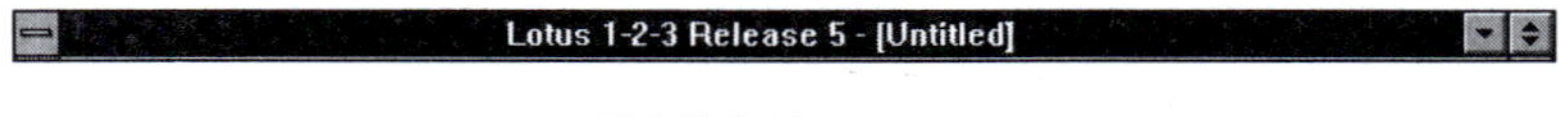

Figure 1.7 *Title bar.*

Menu bar

The next bar down is the menu bar (see Figure 1.8). If you click on a particular menu name, the menu drops down so that you can see its contents. You can use the mouse to select and click on an item from the menu to execute that function. To save a file, for example, you would click on File. When the File menu appears, you click on Save.

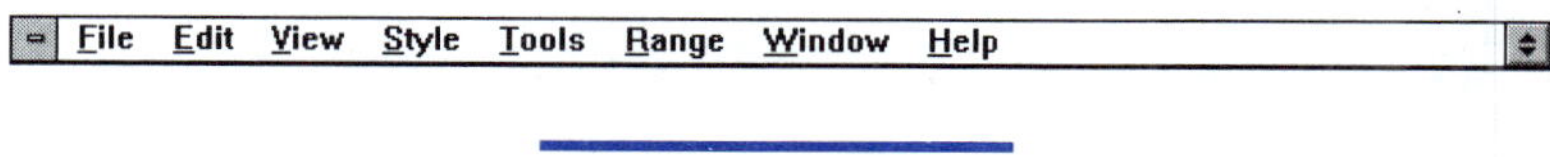

Figure 1.8 *Menu bar.*

Each menu name has a letter underlined. If you want to use the keyboard instead of the mouse, you can pull down a menu by pressing the **Alt** key and then the underlined letter. To choose a particular item from the menu, type its underlined letter (with or without the **Alt** key).

Experiment a little by playing with the mouse to examine the items in the menus. Notice that when you highlight a menu item, the title bar describes that item. This can come in handy if you have forgotten an item's function (and for some unknown reason this book is not by your side)!

If you accidentally click a function in error, don't worry! You can select **Cancel**, or go to Edit and select **Undo** to get rid of a mistake.

The Lotus 1-2-3 window includes a work area that displays the worksheets you have opened. At first, the untitled worksheet is maximized in the work area. The restore icon (to un-maximize the worksheet) appears at the right end of the menu bar. Clicking the restore button reduces the size of the worksheet and gives it a separate title bar (see Figure 1.9). When you are working with multiple worksheets, restoring their unmaximized size lets you see them all at once.

After you have restored a worksheet by unmaximizing, you can minimize it by clicking the minimize button on the side of the menu bar. Notice the minimized worksheet icon in the lower left corner of Figure 1.10. If you have several worksheets open at once, minimizing the ones that you are not currently using (but don't want to close) helps to reduce clutter in your work area.

Edit line

The next section in the window is called the Edit Line (see Figure 1.12). This area has four main parts.

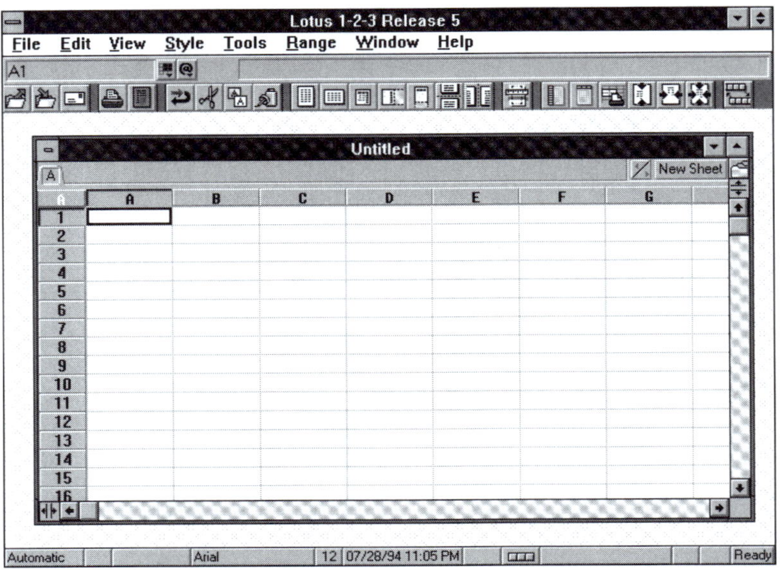

Figure 1.9 *Unmaximized worksheet.*

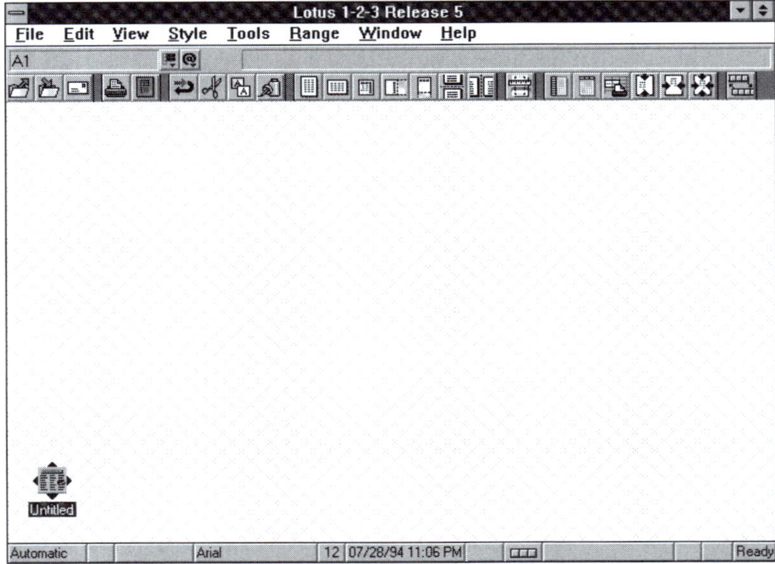

Figure 1.10 *Minimized worksheet.*

Figure 1.11 *Edit Line.*

1. On the left side of the Edit Line is the selection indicator (see Figure 1.12), where Lotus 1-2-3 lets you know what cell the cursor is on. The selection indicator displays the name of each cell as you move around the worksheet.

Figure 1.12 *Selection indicator.*

When you have more than one worksheet in a file, the selection indicator prefaces the cell location with the letter name of the worksheet you are on (see Figure 1.13). If, for example, you have worksheets A and B in a file and you are on cell A1, the indicator shows either A:A1 or B:A1, depending on which worksheet you are on. If you have a third worksheet, the indicator might show C:A1.

Figure 1.13 *Selection indicator with multiple worksheets.*

Even if you change the worksheet name to something other than a letter, Lotus 1-2-3 Release 5 still uses the A:A1 format to identify the current worksheet. Working with more than one spreadsheet is discussed in Chapter 2.

2. The next item in the Edit Line is the navigator (see Figure 1.14). This item is a drop-down box that enables you to go to a specific area in the worksheet. You learn how to use the navigator in Chapter 3, when you learn how to create and use worksheet ranges.

3. Next on the Edit Line, is the @ Function selector (see Figure 1.15). This is a drop-down menu that lets you select @ functions from a list (see Figure 1.16). These are discussed in Chapter 4.

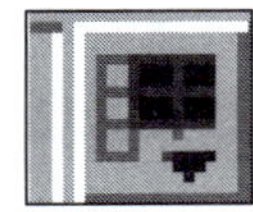

Figure 1.14 *Navigator.*

Figure 1.15 *@ Function selector.*

Figure 1.16 *@ Function menu.*

4. Finally, on the right side of the Edit line is the Contents Box. This area displays the contents of a particular cell as you enter it or when you select that cell with the mouse or keyboard. If you are entering data, a check box and an x-box appear to the left of the contents box. These boxes enable you to accept or reject what you entered into the cell. These items are discussed further in Chapter 3.

SmartIcons

Moving down the Lotus 1-2-3 window, the next things you see are the SmartIcons (see Figure 1.17). These are buttons that perform Lotus 1-2-3 functions. The button that looks like a folder with an arrow pointing up, for example, opens files. The folder with an arrow pointing down saves files.

Figure 1.17 *SmartIcons.*

Some SmartIcons perform functions that can also be found on the menu bar. But it takes less time to use a SmartIcon than a menu. Once you know what the icons represent, you will be able to use them as shortcuts to get certain things done. Appendix B explains more about using and customizing the SmartIcons palette.

You don't have to memorize the meaning of the SmartIcons. When you place the mouse pointer over an icon, a balloon appears and tells you what that icon does. If, for example, you place the pointer over the leftmost icon, the balloon says Open an existing file. But because the SmartIcons represent the functions graphically, you soon will learn the meaning of all the icons without waiting for the balloon to appear.

Worksheet Tabs

The next item down is the Worksheet Tab (see Figure 1.18). When you are using Lotus 1-2-3 Release 5, you can have more than one worksheet open at once in a file. Each worksheet is represented by a tab; the tabs look like tabs on file folders. Your worksheets are initially labeled A, B, C and so on. You can, however, change the names to whatever you like. If you are working with more than one worksheet, the letter identifying the current worksheet appears in the selection indicator. This way, if you are entering data into cell J18 on worksheet T, you will not become confused and enter the data for J18 of worksheet R.

Figure 1.18 *Worksheet tabs.*

In the same section is a button called New Sheet. This button creates new worksheets in the current file. The folder to the right of the New Sheet button hides or shows the current tabs. The arrows to the left of the New Sheet button enable you to scroll to the right or left if you are working with more tabs than fit on the screen. Using worksheet tabs is discussed in Chapter 2.

Worksheet Window

The Lotus 1-2-3 window has a work area in which the worksheets appear (see Figure 1.19). This area is where Lotus functions come into action; it is where you enter data and create charts.

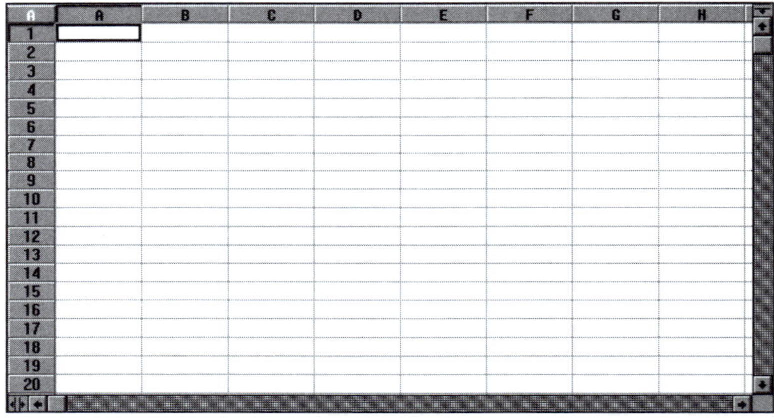

Figure 1.19 *Worksheet area.*

Lotus 1-2-3 Release 5 operates in a Windows environment. If you have used other Windows applications, many of the features will be familiar to you. The first notable difference, however, is that the worksheets in Lotus 1-2-3 look like an inverted L (see Figure 1.20).

Column Headings

Across the top of the inverted L are column headings (see Figure 1.21). The columns are identified by letters of the alphabet. The number of columns is almost limitless. After you reach column Z, the titles of the columns continue with AA, AB, AC, going on to BA, BB, BC after that.

Figure 1.20 *Column headings.*

Row Headings

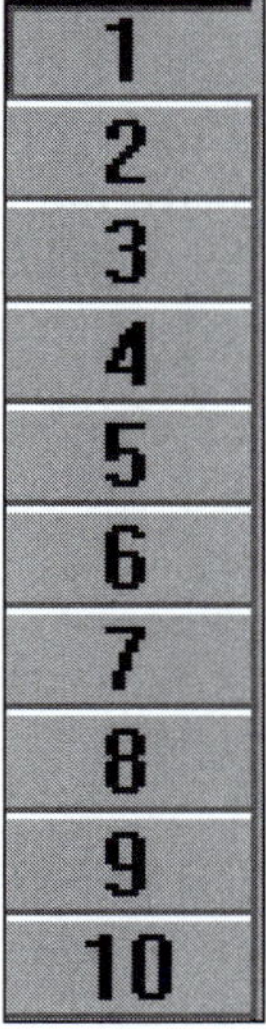

Going down the left side of the inverted L are row headings (see Figure 1.22). These are also limitless and are identified by numbers.

Figure 1.21 *Row headings.*

Cells

The columns and rows create a grid of cells. As you work with the program, you enter data into these cells. To refer to a particular cell, you first reference its column, and then its row. For example, the first cell in the upper left corner of Figure 1.21 is called A1. The cell immediately to its right is B1. The cell directly below A1 is called A2.

Status Bar

The final section of the Lotus 1-2-3 Release 5 window is the status bar (see Figure 1.23). This bar, located at the bottom of the screen, gives you information about your current selection.

Figure 1.22 *Status bar.*

There are several subsections on the status bar. Most of them are pop-up menus containing common features you can apply to your worksheet. You will learn about each of these features as you learn more about using Lotus 1-2-3.

There are several subsections on the status bar. Most of them are pop-up menus containing common features you can apply to your worksheet. You will learn about each of these features as you learn more about using Lotus 1-2-3.

What You Learned

In this chapter you learned how to:

- View the Lotus 1-2-3 Release 5 Guided Tour.
- Explore the Lotus 1-2-3 Release 5 QuickStart tutorial.
- Recognize the features of the Lotus 1-2-3 window.

Chapter 2

Worksheet Fundamentals

In this chapter, you teach yourself some of the fundamentals of a worksheet. This chapter first covers file basics. You learn to do the following:

- Create a new file.
- Open a pre-existing file.
- Save files, using special features, such as
    - Saving your whole file.
    - Using a password to protect your file.
    - Changing a file name or location.

After learning about files, you learn how to work with more than one worksheet. Then you will be able to do the following:

- Create and delete worksheets.
- Name them.
- Work with and view many worksheets at once.

After that, we return to the subject of files and discuss the different ways in which you can use and view multiple files.

File Basics

Now that you are getting a basic grasp of the fundamentals of Lotus 1-2-3 Release 5, you can begin to create worksheets. To do this, you must create a file. This file will be where you do your work and, later, where your work will be stored. To work on a file, you must first make it active. You can activate a file either by creating a new file or by opening an existing one. Either way, Lotus 1-2-3 Release 5 enables you to work with multiple files at the same time. But before we get to that, let's walk through the simple steps to create a new file and open an old one.

Creating a New File

When you start Lotus 1-2-3 Release 5 and select **Cancel** in the Welcome dialog box (or view the Tutorial), a new file is automatically created for you. As mentioned in the previous chapter, this file is called Untitled. (Remember, you can tell the name of the file by looking at the title bar.)

Now, suppose that you are working on a file and you need to create a new one. You could, of course, exit Lotus 1-2-3 and restart it to have the program create a new file, but there is a simpler way. You can create a new file by following these steps:

1. Go to the **File** menu.
2. Select **New**.
3. The New File dialog box opens (see Figure 2.1).
4. Click **Create a Plain Worksheet** or press **Alt-C** so that an X appears in the box next to it. (SmartMasters is discussed later in this chapter.)
5. When you select **Create a Plain Worksheet**, the OK button becomes available (it is no longer dimmed). Click **OK** or press **Enter** to open the worksheet.

You have just created your own new file. If you look at the title bar, you see that the new file is called FILE0001.WK4. Whenever you create a new file, the program starts it with the file name FILEnnnn.WK4, where nnnn is a four-digit number.

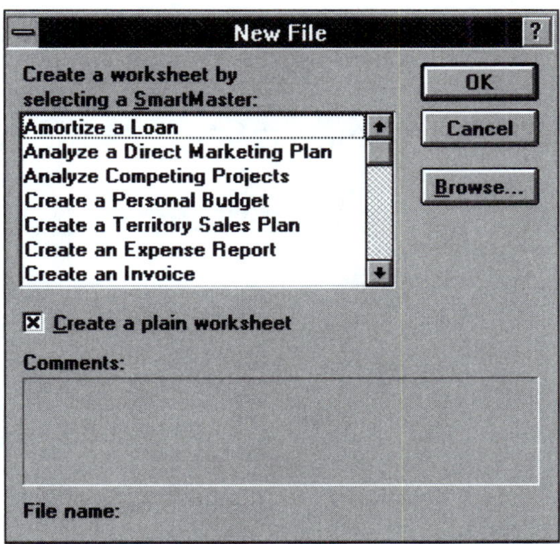

Figure 2.1 *New File dialog box.*

Opening an Existing File

Suppose that you have already created a file, saved it on your disk, and closed it. Now you want to go back to it and work with it. You have to open it in order to use it again. To open an existing file, follow these steps:

1. Go to the **File** menu.

2. Select **Open**.

   The ellipses (...), after Open in the File menu indicates that selecting this option will display a dialog box asking for more information.

3. The Open File dialog box appears (see Figure 2.2).

SHORTCUT

When you pull down the **File** menu, you will see that next to Open it says **Ctrl+O.** This means that you can hold down the **Ctrl** key and press O to bypass the File menu and go straight to the Open function. Or you can click the **Open File** SmartIcon instead of using the File menu to display the Open File dialog box.

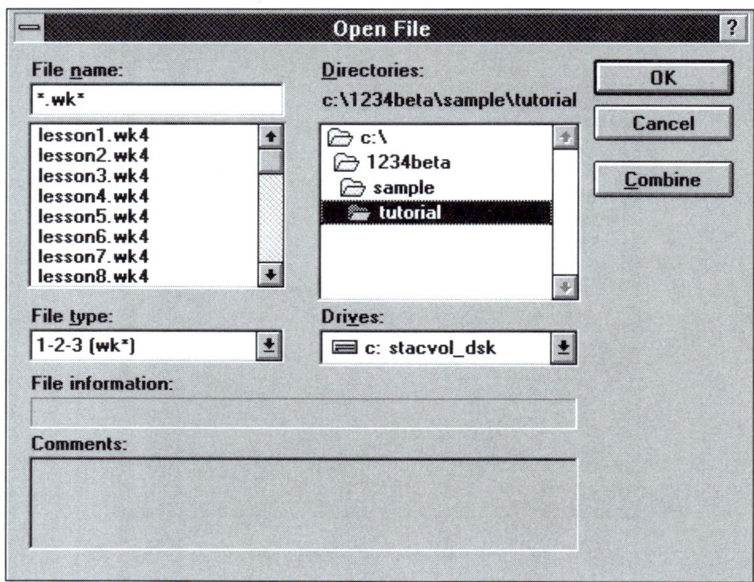

Figure 2.2 *Open File dialog box.*

A dialog box is a window that appears on top of other windows asking you to provide information. A dialog box appears when the program needs more information to clarify the task you want it to perform. Whenever you see an ellipses, get ready—a dialog box is coming!

In this case, the dialog box asks you for information about what kind of file you want to open. The information you enter tells the computer where to find the file you seek. You must select the appropriate directory, drive, file type, and filename.

The top of the window tells you the directory in which you are currently working. The box beneath the directory name shows a graphical representation of your directories. Remember that directories are like file folders. You can see the folders within folders, or subdirectories, in an outline form. In Figure 2.2, for example, the directory is C:\1234BETA\SAMPLE\TUTORIAL. The folders of the active drive and directories are all shown as open. To select a different directory, double-click the mouse on any folder. If you want to move backward (that is, move from the Tutorial subdirectory to the Sample directory or even to C:\), just double-click on that folder. Any open subdirectories will automatically close. Do not be afraid to open and close whatever folders you like to get the hang of this. Remember that you are just opening and closing folders, not changing the material within them.

Underneath the Directories section of the Open File dialog box is a Drive Selector (see Figure 2.3).

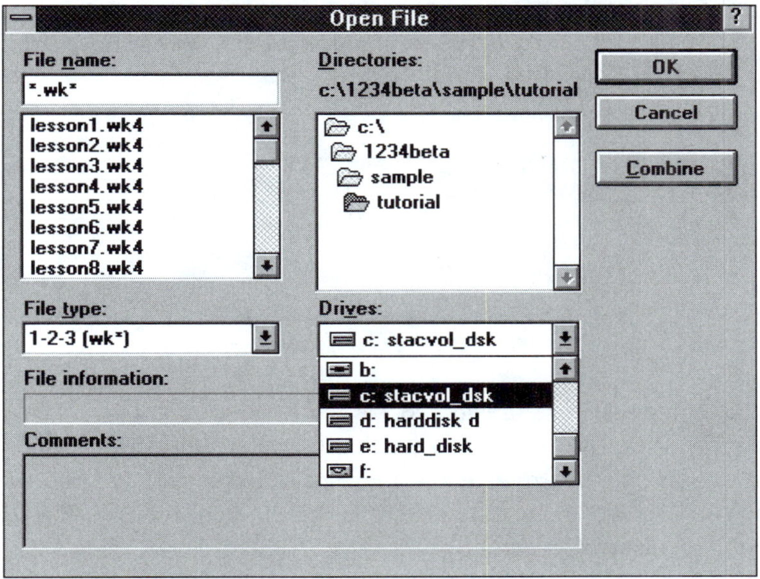

Figure 2.3 *Drive selector.*

If you have more than one hard drive or if you want to select a file that is on a floppy disk, you must select the appropriate drive to locate your file. To select a drive location, follow these steps:

1. Click on the down arrow with the mouse.

2. Select the drive you want.

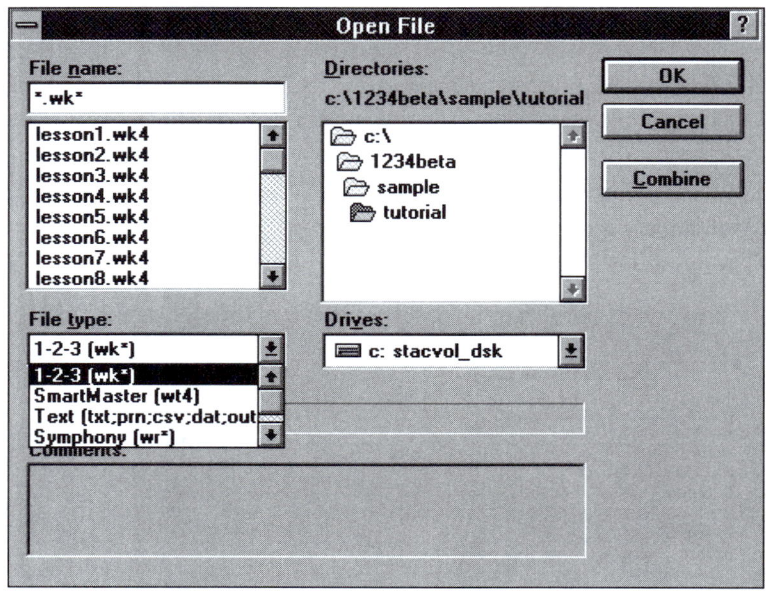

Figure 2.4 *File Type selector.*

Next to the Drive selector is a File Type selector (see Figure 2.4).

The type of file is shown in the three-character file extension of your file name. If you click the arrow in the file type selector box, a drop-down box appears. You can use the scroll bar to see the different types of files that exist and the three-character extensions that go with them. For a Lotus 1-2-3 file, for example, the extension is WK*, and for Symphony it is WR*.

The file extension for Lotus 1-2-3 is WK* because previous versions of the program did not have WK4. The asterisk is like a wild card; used this way, it specifies any file that has WK as the first two characters of the extension. Normally, the only files with WK extensions are Lotus 1-2-3 files, so WK* really means any Lotus 1-2-3 file.

To search for all file types, you can use an asterisk for the entire extension. You need only one asterisk. If, for example, you recall having created a file called Colorado, but you don't remember what type of file it was, you could search for it by typing **colorado.***. The program interprets the asterisk to mean any set of characters, including blanks.

If the directory, drive, and file type are correct, you can just type the name of the file you seek in the Filename box. Alternatively, you can search for a list of all your file names and use the mouse to select the one you want.

You can search for all the files you have by typing the default option ***.wk***. If you enter this, you are saying to the computer, "Within the drive, directory, and file type I have chosen, show me all the files that have the suffix WK*. That is, show me any Lotus 1-2-3 file." If you select the default option, the program will look for any file name with a Lotus 1-2-3 extension in the directory that is running. The names of any files that exist will appear in the box below the file name line. In Figure 2.6, for example, there are three files that fit the *.WK* format in the directory C:\.

If you highlight one of the files in this list, the program will provide you with information about that file at the bottom of the dialog box. In Figure 2.5, you can see that the chosen file, FILE1.WK4, was created on July 5, 1994 at 5:23 P.M. and it is 2,620 bytes in size. This information might help you to remember what is in a file. Even more helpful is the description in the Comments box provided by the person who created the file.

Instead of using the mouse, you can use the **Alt** key to navigate through the different areas of a dialog box. In this particular dialog box, you can change the drive by typing **Alt+V**, because the "v" is underlined in Drives.

Once you have found the file you want to open, you can either double-click on the name, or select the name and click on **OK**.

If you know the name of the file you are looking for, it is fastest to select the drive and directory, and then type the full name and extension into the file name line without using the asterisks or looking through the list. Click **OK** or press **Enter** to open the file.

Lotus 1-2-3 Release 5 has a feature that displays recently opened files at the bottom of the File menu. If you want to reopen a file that was used recently, click **File** to pull down the File menu, and then click the file name at the bottom of the menu.

Saving a File

Once you have worked on a file you will want to save it on a disk. The process of saving is very similar to opening files.

No matter how careful you are, computers sometimes crash. That is, they lose the information that was to have been stored. It is very important to save your work often! Nothing is more frustrating than putting in hours of effort, and then losing all your work because of a power surge or blackout. If you save often, your information will be safe on disk and you will not have to redo as much work.

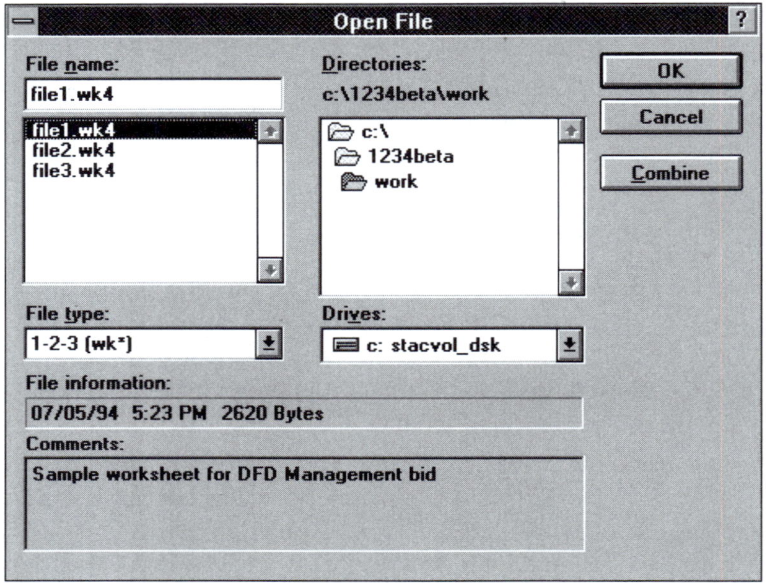

Figure 2.5 *File list.*

SAVING A FILE FOR THE FIRST TIME

There is no rule for when to first save your file. You may want to do some preliminary work on it first, or save it before you do any work. A good method is to save before you begin working. That makes saving as you go along much easier.

To save for the first time, follow these steps:

1. Go to **File** menu.

2. Select **Save**.

You can use the keyboard to press **Ctrl+S** or use the mouse to click the **Save File** SmartIcon (see Figure 2.6) instead of selecting **Save** from the File menu.

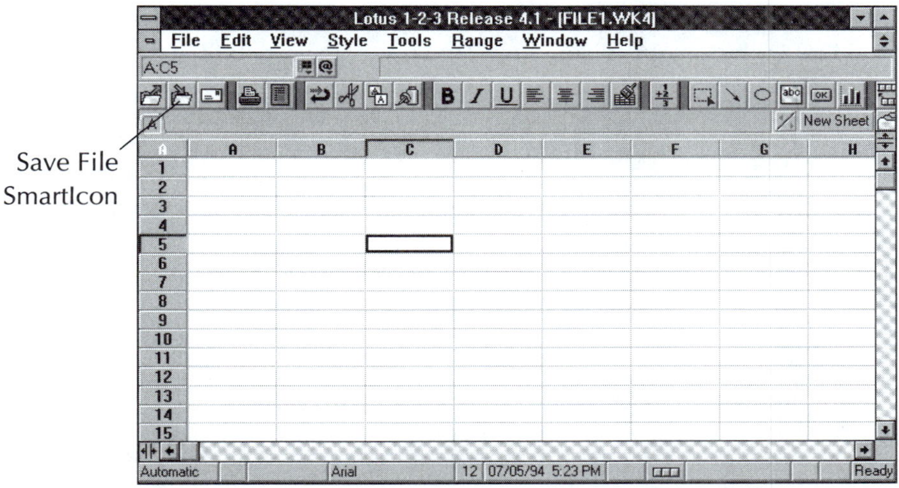

Figure 2.6 *Save File SmartIcon*

When you choose Save for the first time, Lotus 1-2-3 Release 5 opens the Save As dialog box (see Figure 2.9). This dialog box is quite similar to the Open dialog box.

3. You must select the drive and directory in which you want to save the file. You cannot, however, use asterisks in the file name. Instead, you must type a specific name unique to that file. If you do not specify a name, the program will use the default name it gave to the file when you created it (FILEnnnn.WK4). Click the **Comments** box or press **Alt+C** to place the typing cursor into that box, and then type a description of the file. The Comments box is not required, but you'll always be glad you included it.

4. Press the **OK** button to save the file.

You do not need to specify the WK4 extension when you specify a new file name. If you type just the first part of the name (without the period), Lotus 1-2-3 will fill in the correct extension for you.

PASSWORD PROTECTION

Another feature you can incorporate when saving your files is password protection. This feature enables you to afford a measure of security to your file by limiting access to only those who know the password. This is also an option you will find in the Save As dialog box. To use a password, follow these steps:

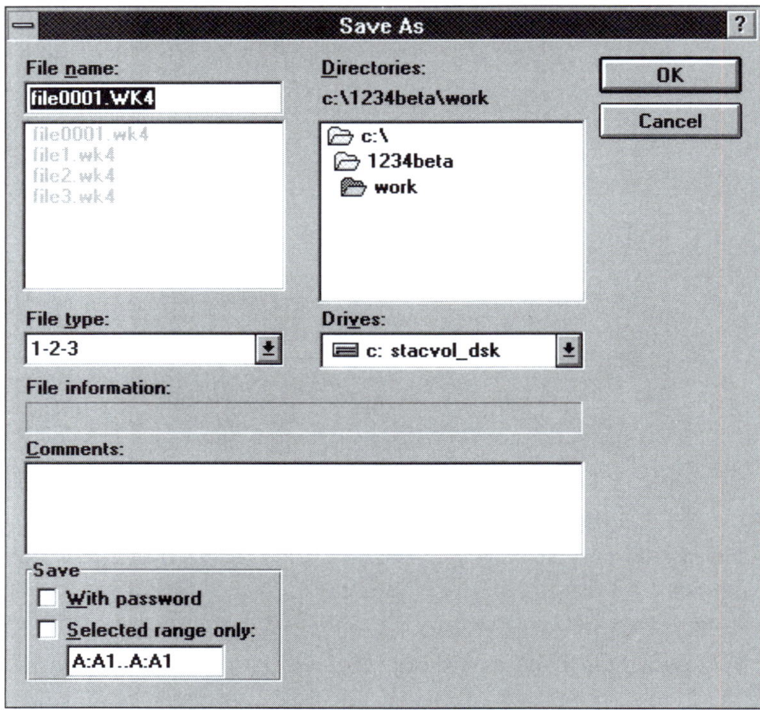

Figure 2.7 *Save As dialog box.*

1. Click on **With Password** or press **Alt+W**.

2. When you click **OK**, a Set Password dialog box appears (see Figure 2.8).

3. Type your password into the line for Password.

    As you type your password, the characters you type don't appear on your monitor. Instead, for further security, you see only asterisks.

4. Retype your password into the Verify line.

5. Click **OK**.

If you try to open a file that was saved with a password, you will be prompted to provide that password (see Figure 2.9).

Figure 2.8 *Set Password dialog box.*

Figure 2.9 *Get Password dialog box.*

TO REMOVE A PASSWORD

To remove a password, follow these steps:

1. Open the file. Remember, you need to use the password to do this.
2. Go to **File**.
3. Select **Save As**.
4. Deselect the **With Password** item by clicking it to remove the X.
5. Click **OK**.
6. The next dialog box tells you that the file already exists and displays three buttons: Replace, Backup, and Cancel. Click **Replace** to replace the password-protected version with the non-password protected version.

Password protection method ensures that anyone who does not know the password cannot access the file. Only file users who have access to the password can remove the password feature.

Lotus 1-2-3's password protection is not foolproof. Knowledgeable people will be able to find ways to access your data. A password blocks only people who don't know much about DOS and Windows.

Saving Later On

After you have given your file a name and a location, saving the changes you make to the file is easy. Follow these steps:

1. Go to the **File** menu.
2. Select **Save**.

Saving an existing file replaces the previously saved version with the new version. You no longer will be able to get back to the earlier version (unless you have a backup copy of it somewhere).

That's it! Because Lotus 1-2-3 knows where to save the file and what to call it, it does not need to open the Save As dialog box to ask any more questions. It just saves the file to disk.

Press **Ctrl+S** or click the **Save** SmartIcon (see Figure 2.8) to save the current file. If the file has not yet been saved, the Save As dialog box opens. Otherwise, the file is saved under its current name and location.

Lotus 1-2-3 Release 5 has an automatic save feature. If you want the program to automatically save your file at a designated time interval, read the appendix on Customizing Lotus 1-2-3.

Save As

Sometimes you need to save the current file under a new name or location, even though it already has a name. You might want to save a second copy of it in a different location; for example, you might want to put it on a floppy disk so that you can send it to someone. Or you might want to save the changes you are making under a different name so that the original is not changed. To save a second copy of the current file, follow these steps:

1. Go to **File**.

2. Select **Save As**.

   1-2-3 displays the Save As dialog box (see Figure 2.7).

You can also use the **Save As** command if you want to add a password to, or remove a password from, a file (as discussed earlier) or if you want to save only a portion of your file to a new file.

Working with Multiple Worksheets

Now that you have taught yourself how to create a new file, you can begin to work with one. If you do not have a new file on your screen, go ahead and create one now. Throughout this book we will be working on an exercise to create a monthly personal budget. Although this probably is not the exact project for which you intend to use Lotus 1-2-3 Release 5, the processes you follow and the skills you learn can be applied to any purpose.

The file you have just opened currently contains only one worksheet, labeled A. You can find the A tab on the left side of the worksheet tab bar (see Figure 2.10).

Suppose that you want to rename this tab as Budget to fit the example. To rename a worksheet tab, follow these steps:

1. Double-click with the mouse on the tab name (in this case, A).

2. The letter disappears, and a cursor in the form of a blinking vertical line appears (see Figure 2.11).

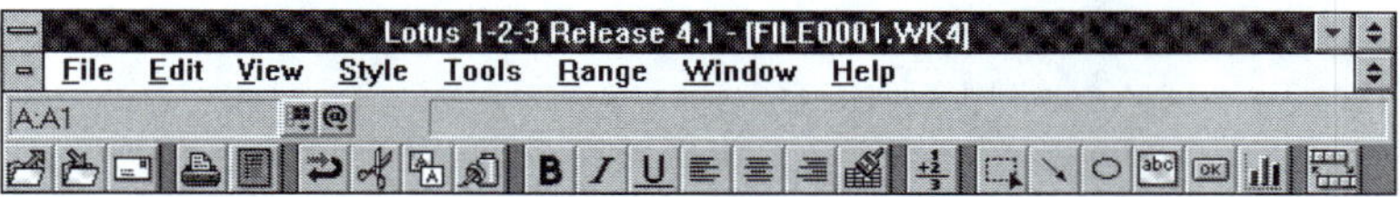

Figure 2.10 *Worksheet A tab.*

3. Type **Budget** (or whatever you want to call the new worksheet).

4. Press **Enter** or click the mouse on your worksheet.

Any time you need to change the name of a worksheet you can follow these same steps.

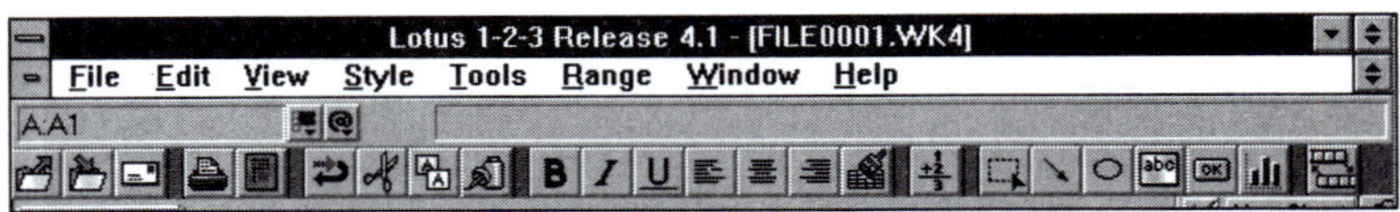

Figure 2.11 *Change tab name.*

Remember that although you changed the worksheet name to Budget, Lotus 1-2-3 Release 5 still refers to it by its original name, A.

Creating New Worksheets

Sometimes you need to use more than one worksheet in the same file. 1-2-3 enables you to create as many worksheets as you like in one file, so that you can go back and forth to the different worksheets without having to open and close your files. For this example, create a second worksheet called Actual. The first worksheet will contain the budgeted monthly values for a number of items. The second worksheet, B, will contain the corresponding actual values for each month, so that you can compare your budget to your actual expenses.

To create a new worksheet, follow these steps:

1.   Click on **New Sheet** on the tab bar.

     Notice that a new tab appears on the tab bar (see Figure 2.13). The file name on the title bar is still the same, but you now have a second worksheet in that same file. The first worksheet, A or Budget, is in the background, behind the new worksheet, B, or Actual.

     Now change the name of tab B to Actual.

Inserting New Worksheets

Suppose that you were working on your budget and you decided to compare your budget to someone else's. You could easily create a new tab between Budget and Actual.

To insert a new worksheet, follow these steps:

1.   Click on the **Budget** tab, making it the active worksheet.

2.   Click on **New Sheet** in the tab bar.

3.   Change the tab name to **Budget2**.

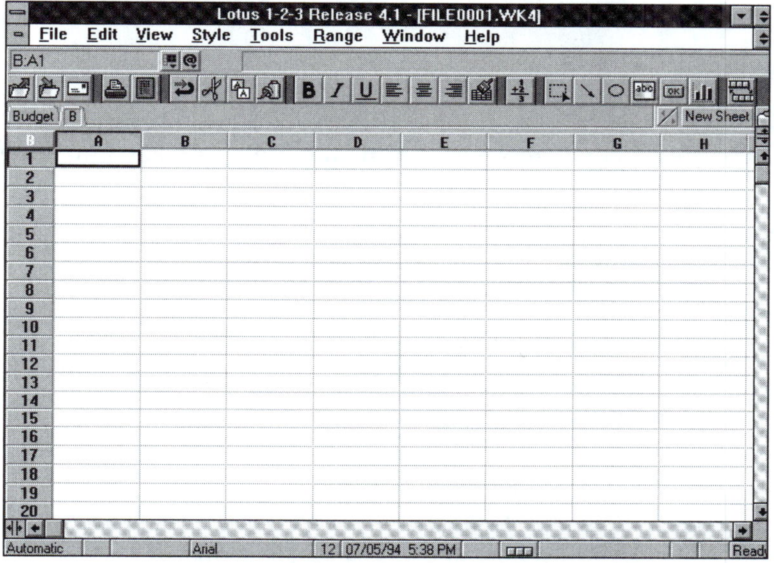

Figure 2.12 *New tab in tab bar.*

You have now placed a new sheet called Budget2 between Budget and Actual.

Whenever you create a new worksheet, it appears directly after the active worksheet. Make sure that you have the correct worksheet open when you are adding a new one.

Deleting Worksheets

Suppose that you decided to compare your budget to that of the federal government, but after creating a new worksheet and getting started, you realized it was too complicated and not helpful at all. You could delete the entire worksheet.

For this exercise, click on New Sheet. If you want to practice renaming worksheets, you can do so, calling this one Federal. You can delete this item just as easily as it was created.

If you delete a worksheet, you will lose the information stored in it. Delete a worksheet only if you are sure that you are deleting the correct item.

To delete a worksheet, follow these steps:

1. Go to the **Edit** menu.

2. Select **Delete**.

SHORTCUT

It's faster to press **Ctrl+-** (Ctrl with the minus key from the numeric keypad) instead of using the Edit menu.

You see the Delete dialog box, as shown in Figure 2.13.

4. Click in the circle (called a radio button) next to Sheet, or press **Alt+S**.

5. Click on **OK**.

Now the current worksheet has been deleted.

If you delete a worksheet that is not the last worksheet in your file (for example, if you delete Budget2 instead of Federal), the rest of the worksheets will remain in order, moving up as necessary. In other words, if you had worksheets A through T and you decided to remove J, worksheet K would become J, L would become K, and so on to the end of the list; the last worksheet would be S.

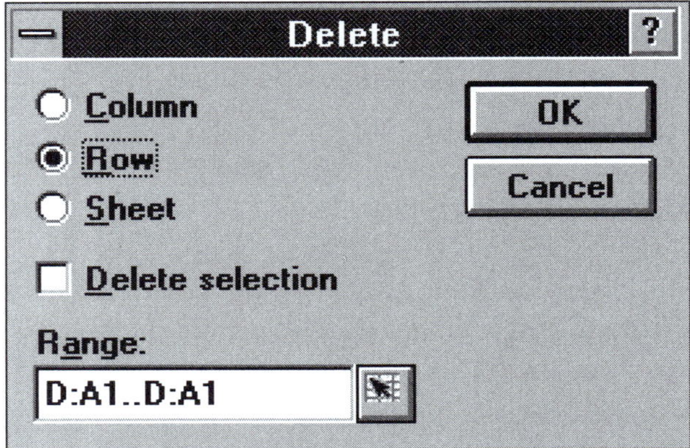

Figure 2.13 *Delete dialog box.*

Working with Worksheet Tabs

Worksheet tabs are just like folder tabs in a file cabinet. If you want to look at the contents of a particular folder, you can pull it out by its tab. Similarly, to switch between worksheets, you just click on the worksheet tab. This makes it the active worksheet.

If your work gets really complicated, you may end up with oodles of worksheets. If there are too many tabs to fit across your screen, you can use the arrows in the box next to New Sheet to scroll left and right to display the missing tabs.

Figure 2.14 shows a file that has too many worksheets to be displayed on the screen. You can see only 21 worksheets (A through U).

If you want to scroll to the right so that you can see more worksheets, click on the Right Arrow of the tab bar (see Figure 2.15).

Notice that you can now see tab V. If you were to click again or hold down the button, you could see more tabs.

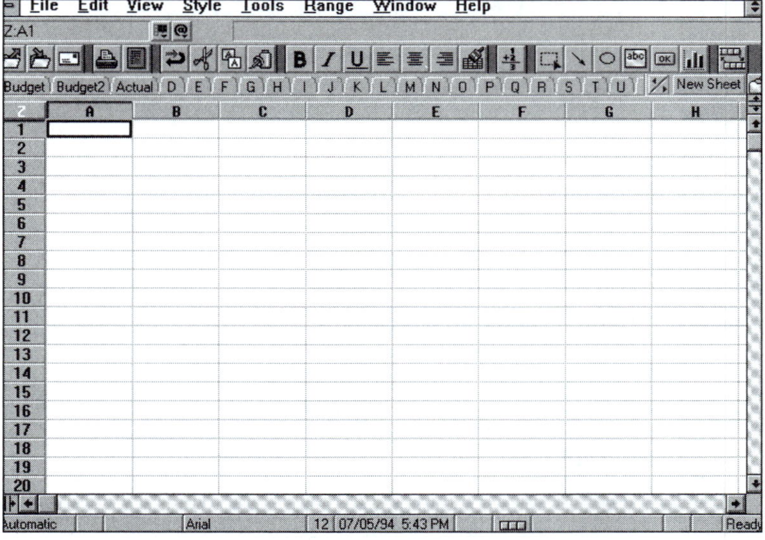

Figure 2.14 *Too many tabs to fit into the window.*

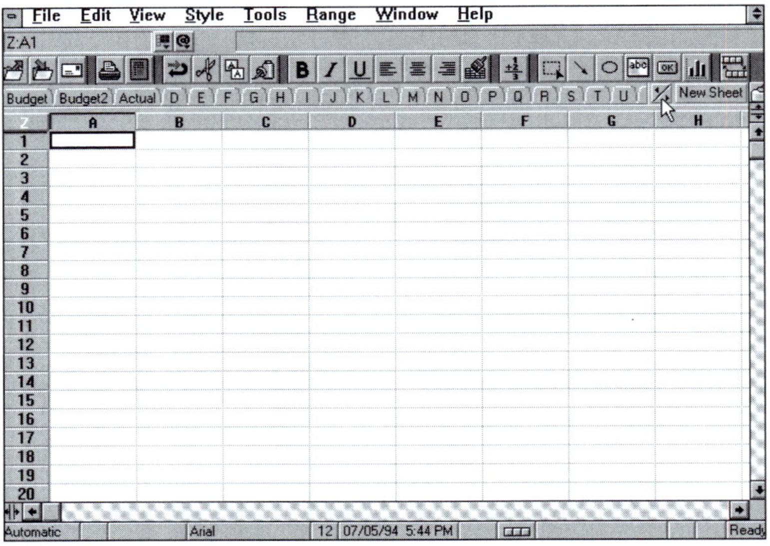

Figure 2.15 *Scroll right in the tab bar.*

Viewing Multiple Worksheets

Sometimes you may want to look at multiple worksheets at the same time. Instead of clicking on the worksheet tabs to display one at a time, Lotus 1-2-3 Release 5 enables you to show multiple worksheets at once.

To display multiple worksheets, complete the following steps:

1. Go to the **View** menu.

2. Select **Split**.

   You will see the Split dialog box (see Figure 2.16).

3. Select the **Perspective** button and click on **OK**.

Now you will see that all three worksheets are displayed in a three-dimensional perspective view. Notice that the top left corners of the worksheets have their letter names. The program does not display the names you gave to these worksheets.

To move another worksheet into view, press **Ctrl+PageUp** to move the cursor to the next higher worksheet; the worksheets scroll in the window as necessary so that you can always see the one containing the cursor. You can press **Ctrl+PgDn** to move down through the worksheets. You can also press **Ctrl+Home** to jump the cursor to the first worksheet, or press **End** followed by **Ctrl+Home** to jump the cursor to the last worksheet.

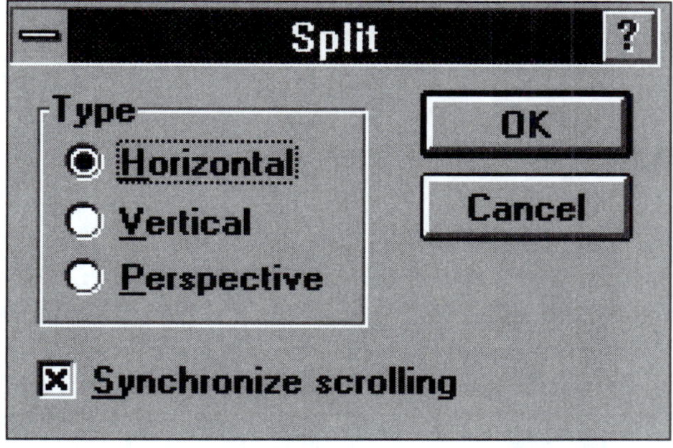

Figure 2.16 *Split dialog box.*

To return the display to the original tab bar, follow these steps:

1. Go to the **View** menu.
2. Select **Clear Split**.

Now you can see one worksheet with the tab bar above it.

Referencing Across Worksheets

It is worth pointing out here that Lotus 1-2-3 Release 5 has the capability to perform calculations involving cells from other worksheets. If, for example, you wanted to calculate the difference between a budgeted amount and your actual amount, you could have a formula that referenced cells on your budget worksheet and your actual worksheet. Chapter 7 discusses calculations that will refer to cells in other worksheets.

Working with Multiple Files

You now know that you can work with many worksheets in a file at the same time. Lotus 1-2-3 Release 5 also lets you work with multiple files at the same time. For the purposes of this exercise, create three new files and save them with the names File1, File2, and File3. For help with creating a new file, refer to the beginning of this chapter.

Window Menu

There are a variety of ways to view multiple files in this program. If your files are maximized, you can view only one file at a time. If you want to have the flexibility to switch between files, you can do this by using the Window menu (see Figure 2.17).

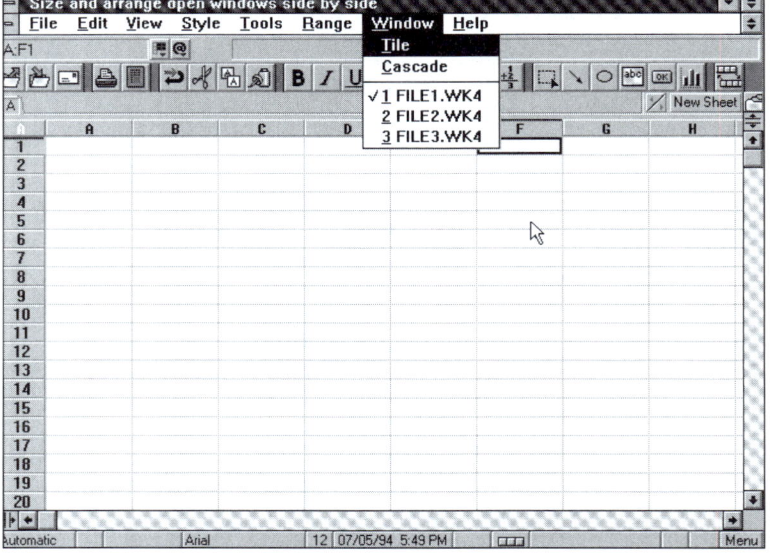

Figure 2.17 *Window menu.*

Notice that this menu lists three files at the bottom. FILE1.WK4 has a check mark next to it because it is the active file. If you want to switch to File2 or File3, all you have to do is select its name from the menu.

Each file is numbered, so you can switch between them with keyboard shortcuts. To switch from File1 to File2, for example, you would type **Alt+W+2**.

Cascade Windows

If you want to view more than one file at a time, you can use the Cascade command under the Windows menu. To cascade windows, follow these steps:

1. Go to the **Window** menu.
2. Select **Cascade**.

Notice that the windows are reduced in size and laid down on top of each other with their title bars visible (see Figure 2.18). If you want to do so, you can manually move these windows to any location, or change their size to see more or less of a particular file.

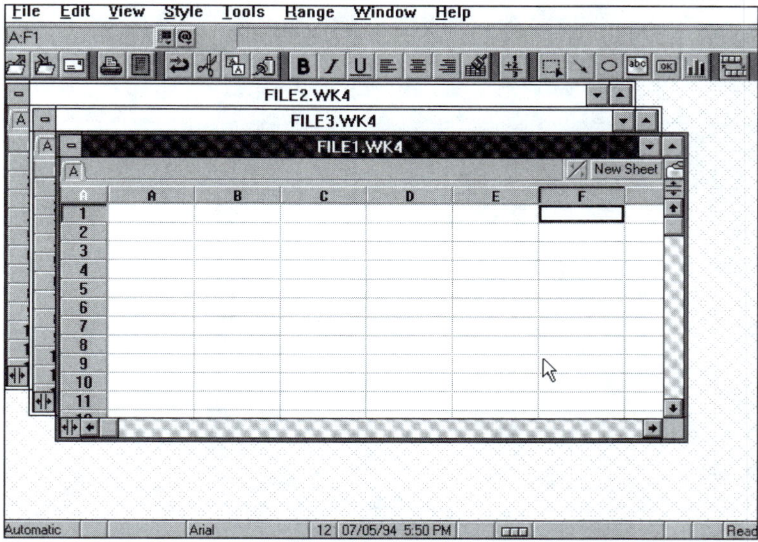

Figure 2.18 *Cascade windows.*

Do not confuse cascading with perspective view of worksheets. One involves multiple files; the other involves multiple worksheets in one file. Of course, you could have a perspective view of multiple worksheets at the same time you displayed several files in cascade. If you want to see what this looks like, you can try it. With all these windows open, however, there is hardly any work space. In most instances, it is unlikely that you will need to see all of these variables at once.

Tile Windows

Another way to view multiple files is to use the Tile command. To tile windows, follow these steps:

1. Go to the **Window** menu.

2. Select **Tile**.

The windows are now resized to fit in the screen (see Figure 2.19). They are laid down next to each other like tiles in a bathroom.

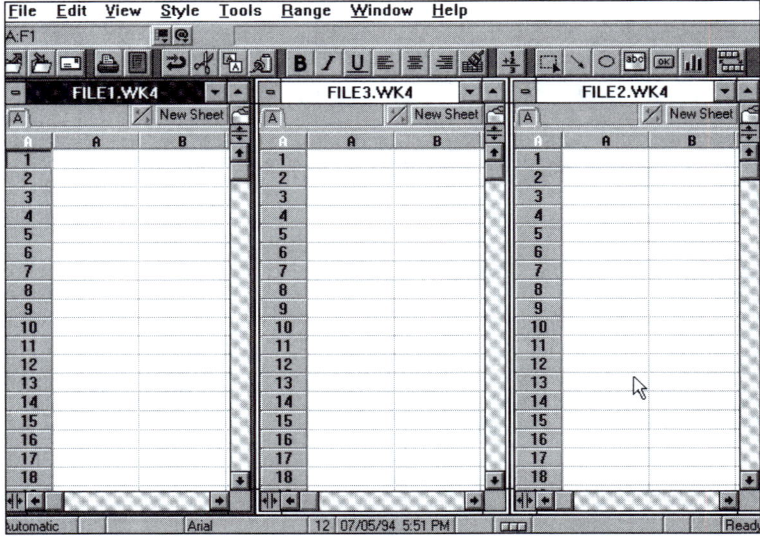

Figure 2.19 *Tile windows.*

Minimize Windows

A third way to see multiple windows is to minimize them. To do this, click on the minimize button of the window. When you minimize file windows in Lotus 1-2-3

Release 5, their icons are displayed at the bottom of the screen (see Figure 2.20). Although you cannot see the cells or the actual worksheets of these files, the icons indicate that the files are still open. All you have to do is double-click to get the worksheet on the screen. This method is especially useful when you are working with a large number of files. You can work on a file, minimize it, switch to a different file, and so forth.

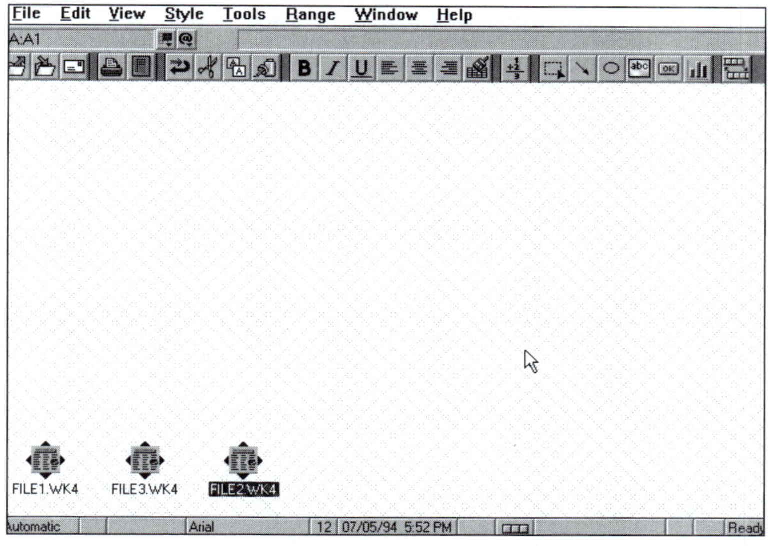

Figure 2.20 *Minimized file windows.*

Taking Advantage of SmartMasters

What if you don't have time to learn everything about Lotus 1-2-3 Release 5 before you start to use it? What if you need to start producing sophisticated and effective worksheets right now? Relax, you can, by using SmartMasters. Each SmartMaster is a worksheet file that has been professionally designed and for-matted. It even comes with sample data so that you can see how the final prod-uct will look. All you have to do is open the file, enter your data in the right places, and save and print the results.

To use a SmartMaster, start a new file, either by starting Lotus 1-2-3 Release 5 or by choosing **New** from the File menu. Either way, the New File dialog box displays a list of all the SmartMasters. Select the SmartMaster you want and click **OK** to open a new file based on that SmartMaster.

You can read a brief description of each SmartMaster by highlighting it in the list called Create a Worksheet by Selecting a SmartMaster. The Comments box displays a short description of the highlighted SmartMaster.

Let's look at how you would use a typical SmartMaster. For this example, use the SmartMaster called Fill Out a Time Sheet. To create a new file based on this SmartMaster, follow these steps:

1. From the File menu, choose **New**.

2. Click **Fill Out a Time Sheet**.

3. Click **OK**.

It takes a few moments for Lotus 1-2-3 Release 5 to load the SmartMaster. You'll see some information flash on your screen. Don't worry, it's just the various parts of the worksheet being loaded. When it's all loaded, it will look like Figure 2.21.

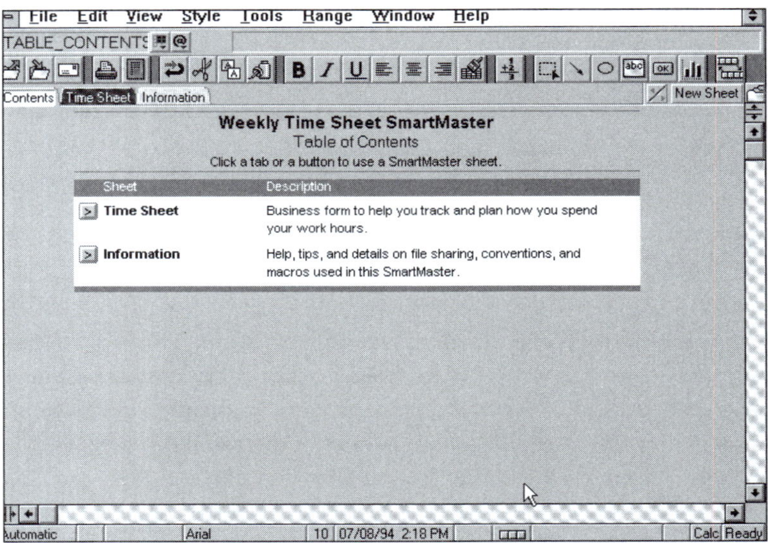

Figure 2.21 *Weekly Time Sheet SmartMaster, Contents Sheet.*

Every SmartMaster starts with a Contents page (which is actually a worksheet, although it doesn't look much like one). From the list of Contents, you can choose **Information** (to read more about the SmartMaster) or the **Time Sheet** itself. Every SmartMaster has similar choices, although some of the more complex ones have several worksheets to choose from. To choose one of these topics, click the button containing a greater-than sign. For now, click the button next to **Information** so that you can find out more about the Weekly Time Sheet SmartMaster. Your screen will look like the one shown in Figure 2.22.

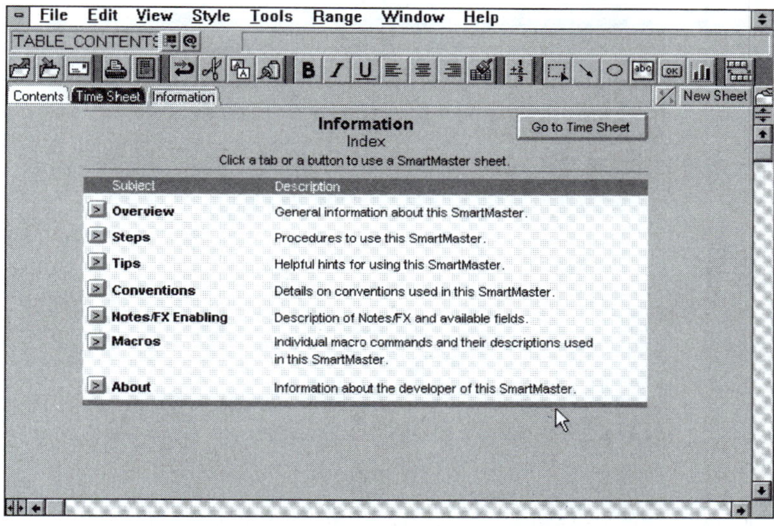

Figure 2.22 *Weekly Time Sheet SmartMaster, Information Index.*

These same seven topics are available for most of the SmartMasters; some have a few more. To view a topic, click the button containing the greater-than sign next to Overview. Your screen should look like Figure 2.23.

Notice the three buttons above the text box. You can print the overview by clicking the **Print** button. The Information Index button takes you back to the first page of the Information sheet (see Figure 2.22) so that you can select another topic. If you're ready to start working on the time sheet, the **Return to Time Sheet** button takes you there. Almost every page in the SmartMaster includes similar buttons so that you can travel around to the various parts of the worksheet.

For now, click the **Information Index** button. Then try out a few more of the Information topics, such as Tips and Conventions. When you're ready to look at the time sheet itself, click **Go To Time Sheet** to display the screen shown in Figure 2.24.

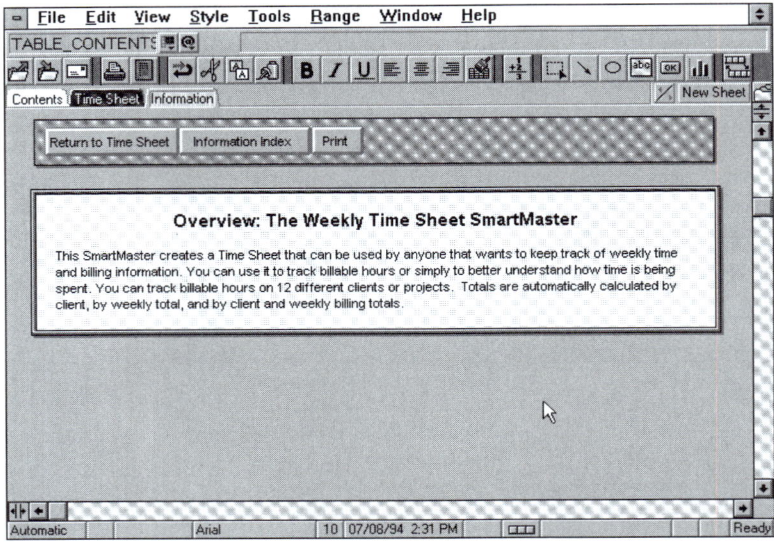

Figure 2.23 *Weekly Time Sheet SmartMaster, Overview.*

The shaded areas (which are light yellow on a color monitor) indicate where you enter data. Lotus 1-2-3 Release 5 calculates all other data. When you enter the Starting Date, for example, Lotus 1-2-3 immediately inserts the Ending Date and adds dates to the days of the week in the lower part of the screen.

Each SmartMaster includes some sample data that can act as a guide to help you fill out the form, but you need to save the file once to make the sample data available. To see the sample data, follow these steps:

1. Click the **File Save** SmartIcon.

   The Save As dialog box opens.

2. Click **OK** to save the file with the default name in the default location.

3. When the Time Sheet reappears, click **Sample Data**. Your worksheet should now look like Figure 2.25.

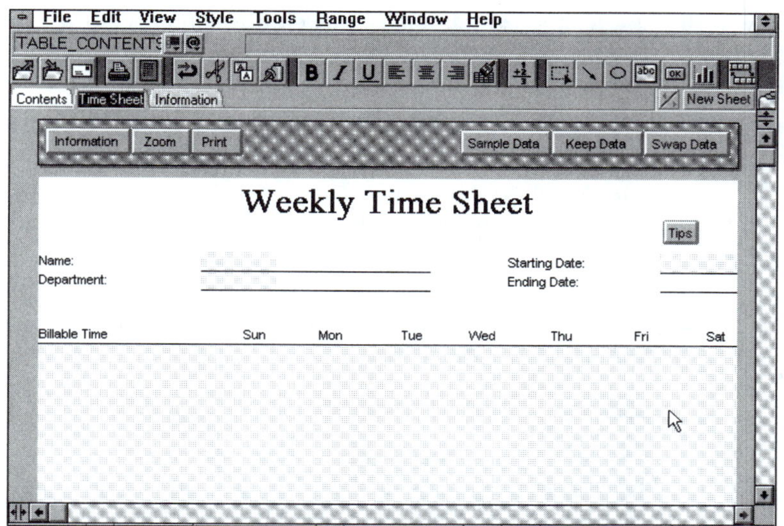

Figure 2.24 *Weekly time sheet.*

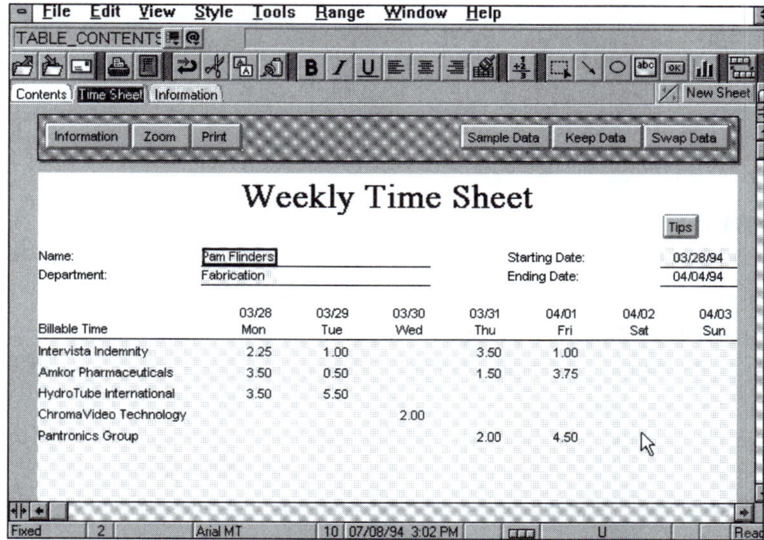

Figure 2.25 *Weekly time sheet with sample data.*

You can work right over the sample data, replacing it with your own. Just click a field and type your data (or press Delete to blank out the sample data). There is more data in the bottom of the time sheet. When you have the top half filled out, scroll down and fill out (or delete the information from) the bottom half (nonbillable hours). Notice that Lotus 1-2-3 Release 5 is calculating the totals as you enter your hours. When you're ready, click Print to print your time sheet. You might also want to save it again now that it contains the correct data.

Now that you know where the data is supposed to go in the time sheet, you don't have to use the sample data any more. You can work from the blank time sheet.

Although the other SmartMasters do different things, you use them in much the same way. Open the SmartMaster as a new file, explore the Information topics, and perhaps view the sample data (but you usually have to save the file first). Then, enter your own data in the shaded fields, save it, and print it. It's as simple as that.

Click the **Print** button in the worksheet (not the Print SmartIcon) to print the current worksheet. Lotus 1-2-3 sets up the Print dialog box to print just the important part of the worksheet. Don't make any changes in the Print dialog box; just click **OK**.

To Sum Up

You have learned how to create a file, open an old one, and save files. You can use a password or change a file name or location. You can create and use multiple worksheets and view as many as you want. You know how to use the window function to display several worksheets or several files. And you can use a SmartMaster to produce an professional-looking worksheet with very little effort or knowledge. Now that you are comfortable using these features of Lotus 1-2-3 Release 5, you can go on to teach yourself about the meat of the program, the worksheet area.

What You Learned

Create a new file:

> Turn on Lotus 1-2-3 Release 5 and a new file is automatically created, or
>
> Select **File**, **New**, or
>
> Press **Alt+F+N**

Open a file:

1. Select **File**, **Open**, or

   Press **Alt+F+O**, or

   Press **Ctrl+O**, or

   Click the **File Open** SmartIcon.

2. A dialog box opens. Choose the appropriate directory, drive, file type, and file name.

Save files:

1. Select **File**, **Save**, or

   Press **Alt+F+S**, or

   Press **Ctrl+S**, or

   Click the **File Save** SmartIcon.

2. A dialog box appears. Choose the drive, directory, file type and name you want to save.

Save with a password:

1. Select **File**, **Save**, or

   Press **Alt+F+S**, or

   Press **Ctr+S**, or

   Click the **File Save** SmartIcon.

2. In the dialog box, use the mouse to click with password or press **Alt+W**.

3. A new dialog box appears. Type in the password, and then verify the password.

Remove a password:

1. Open the file.

2. Select **File**, **Save As**.

3. In the dialog box, use the mouse to click with password or press **Alt+W**.

Save a previously saved file:

Select **File**, **Save**.

Change the way a file is saved:

1. Select **File**, **Save As**.

2. A dialog box appears. Select or enter new information.

Name a worksheet:

1. Use the mouse to double-click on the true (letter) name of the worksheet.

2. Type the new name.

Create a new worksheet:

Click on **New Sheet** in the tab bar.

Delete a worksheet:

1. From the Edit menu, select **Delete**, or

   Press **Ctrl+-** (Ctrl plus the minus sign on the numeric keypad).

2. A dialog box appears. Click on the button next to Sheet, or press **Alt+S**.

View multiple worksheets:View multiple worksheets:

1. Select **View**, **Split**.
2. In the dialog box, select the **Perspective** button.

Use a SmartMaster:

1. Select **File**, **New**.
2. In the dialog box, select the desired SmartMaster and choose **OK**.
3. On the Contents page, click **Information**.
4. Click whatever Information topics you want to explore.
5. Go to the worksheet itself.
6. Save the file once to make the sample data available.
7. Click **Sample Data** to see the sample data.
8. Type over the sample data with your own data. (If you didn't display the sample data, fill in your own data on the blank form.)
9. Click the **Save** SmartIcon to save the worksheet.
10. Click the **Print** button in the worksheet to print the worksheet. Don't make any changes in the Print dialog box.

Chapter 3

Worksheets Continued

This chapter continues to discuss worksheets and the fundamentals of how to use them. The chapter is divided into three parts.

First, we talk about selecting worksheet areas. You will teach yourself to do the following:

- Select a range of cells using the mouse or the keyboard:
    - Select a range before or after performing a command.
    - Select a collection of cells that are not all in the same place.
    - Select a collection of cells across multiple worksheets.
- Name the range you select.
- Go to a selected range using the **Go To** and **Navigator** functions.
- Split a screen to see more of your data:
    - Synchronize scrolling in a split screen.
    - Change the size of a split screen.
    - Freeze views of the titles on your screen.

Next, you learn about entering data. Once you understand that there are two different types of data—values and labels—you go on to learn how to do the following:

- Enter data into a cell or into the edit line.
- Use the **Confirm** and **Cancel** buttons to check on the data you entered.
- Enter numbers.
- Enter text.
- Enter dates and times.
- Enter a series.
- Create a custom-made series.

Finally, we discuss how to alter the data you have entered. You will learn to:

- Edit data.
- Move data in two ways.
- Copy data in three ways.
- Insert and delete rows, columns and cells.
- Find terms anywhere in your worksheet or replace them with new terms.
- Check spelling on a file.

Selecting Worksheet Areas

As you know, a spreadsheet is composed of individual cells. But often you will want to work with more than one cell at a time. This section helps you teach yourself how to travel around the worksheet to select and activate the cells you want to use.

A group of cells is called a range (see Figure 3.1). As you learn to identify and select ranges of cells, keep in mind that an individual cell is referred to by its column letter and row number. For example, the cell one to the right of A1 and three down is B4. This is the cell's address.

When you are using multiple worksheets, remember that the cell address is preceded by the letter for the worksheet you are on, as in A:B4.

Because a range is composed of a number of cells, the address is determined by the first and last cell in the range. The first cell is the upper left cell and the last is the lower right. The range address shows the first cell and the last cell separated by two (or more) dots. If, for example, you select a range that begins at B4 and extends three columns across and eight rows down to cell D11, the range is called B4..D11. This is like saying to the computer, "I want cells B4 and D11 and everything that lies between them."

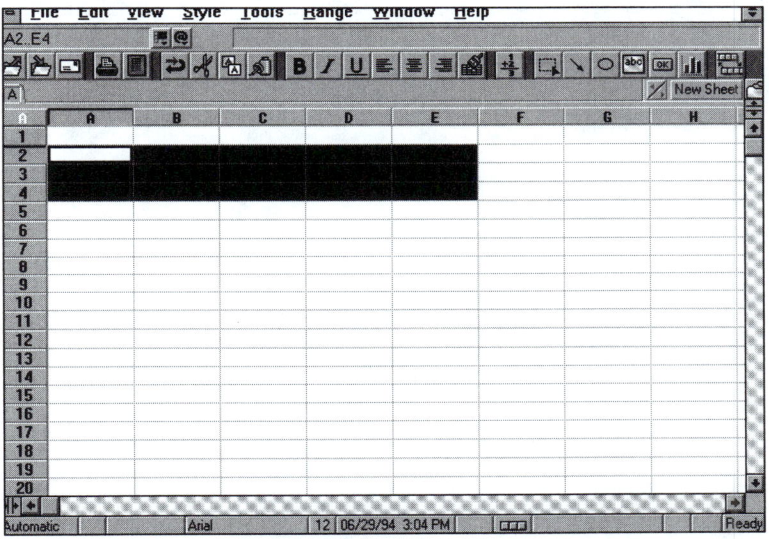

Figure 3.1 *A range of cells.*

Selecting a Range

It is easy to select a range of cells. When you click with the mouse on a cell, that cell becomes active. You can identify an active cell by looking at the indicator on the edit bar or by looking for a cell that is white with a dark outline (see Figure 3.2).

To select a range of cells instead of just an individual cell, hold down the mouse button and drag the mouse from the first cell to highlight the other cells to be included in the range. Notice that when you select a range, the cursor changes. Also, when you select a range, the first cell in the range continues to be the active cell (see Figure 3.3).

While you are dragging the mouse, the range indicator on the edit line continues to show the active cell. When you release the mouse button, it changes to display the entire range. In the example, the edit line changes from B4 to B4..D11.

If you no longer need the range you selected, simply click anywhere else on your worksheet. The highlighting disappears and range no longer is selected.

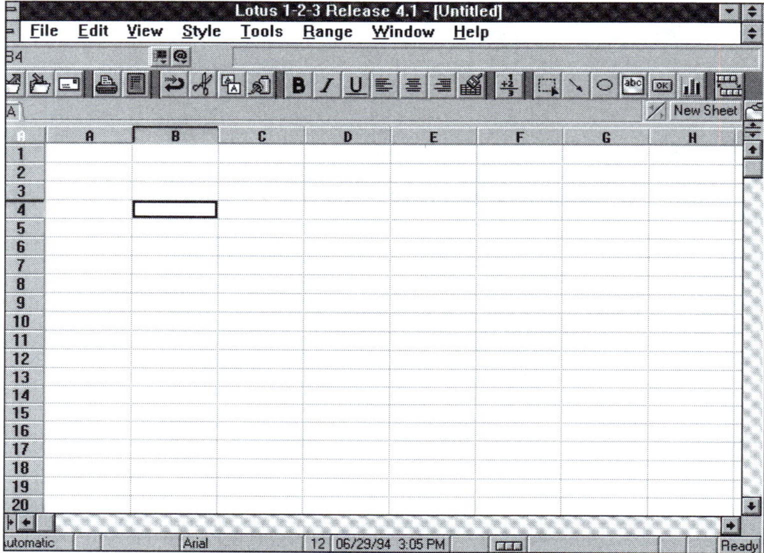

Figure 3.2 *An active cell.*

You do not need to use the mouse to select a range. Instead, you can follow these steps, using the arrow and Shift keys to select a range using the keyboard:

1. Use the arrow keys to position the active cell where you want to begin your range.

2. Hold down the **Shift** key.

3. Use the arrows to expand the range up or down, to the left or right of the active cell.

Notice that the cursor changes again when you select a range.

If you are working with a very large range, it may be helpful to use both the mouse and keyboard. Instead of holding down the mouse button and dragging for the entire range, you can click the mouse at the beginning of the range, hold down **Shift** and click the mouse at the end of the range. Follow this example:

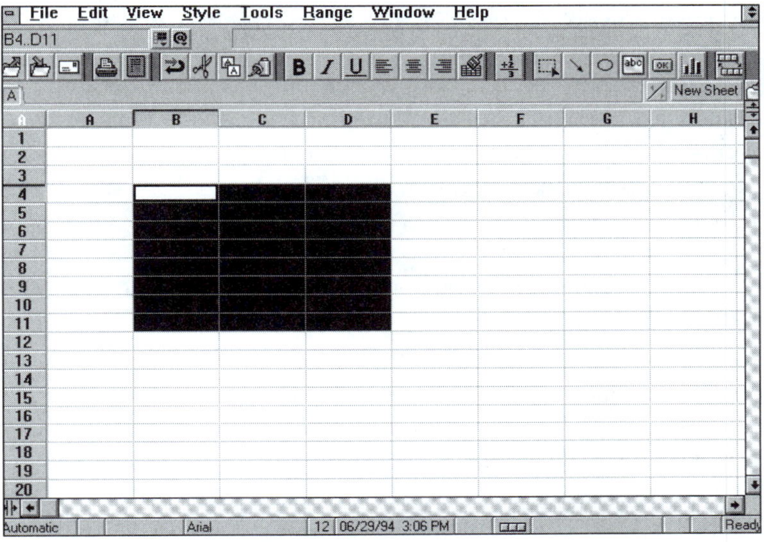

Figure 3.3 *Selecting a range of cells.*

1. Click the mouse on cell **B4**.

2. Hold down the **Shift** key.

3. Click the mouse on cell **D11**. The range B4..D11 is selected.

The Shift key is like a "hold" button. Suppose that you select a range, say B4..D11, and you want to extend that range further to E11. Instead of starting over, you could extend the range by holding down the **Shift** key and using the arrows or clicking to continue the range where you left off. In this way, the Shift key acts to hold your place.

If you want to select an entire column or an entire row, click the mouse on the column letter or row number. Similarly, to select an entire worksheet, click the mouse on the upper left corner of the worksheet, between the letter A and the number 1.

Should You Select Before or After?

As you learn Lotus 1-2-3 Release 5, you will encounter tasks that you can perform a task in a number of ways. After you experiment with the different possibilities, you will decide which way you like the best. For example, you will decide when it is more comfortable to use the mouse or keyboard commands. Similarly, there is more than one way to perform a function on a range of cells. You can select a range of cells, and then choose a command or, in many cases, you can choose the command, and then select the range of cells to which it applies. If a function does not involve a dialog box, as in the Copy or Clear function, then it acts immediately on whatever cell or range is currently selected and you must be sure to select the correct cell or range before choosing the command. But if a function involves a dialog box, you can select the desired cell or range after the dialog box opens.

You may, for example, want to change the font used in a range of cells in your worksheet. (Fonts, also called typefaces, are discussed in detail in Chapter 4.) There are two ways to perform this task. First, you can select a range of cells, and then choose the command:

1. Click the mouse on cell **B4** and drag to cell **D11** to select the range B4..D11.

2. From the **Style** menu, choose **Font & Attributes**.

    Notice that the dialog box indicates that the range is B4..D11 (see Figure 3.4).

3. Alter the font to whatever you like.

The second way to do the same thing is to choose the command, and then select the range from the dialog box:

1. From the **Style** menu, select **Font & Attributes**.

2. The Font dialog box appears. The Range box indicates whatever cell happens to be currently active. In Figure 3.5 it is cell G12.

3. Click the button next to the Range box that has an arrow over it (see Figure 3.6). This button is the range selector. Or you can press **Alt+A** to activate the Range box, and then press any cursor-movement key, such as left arrow.

4. The dialog box disappears and you are returned to your worksheet with the range selection cursor (see Figure 3.7).

5. Now click on cell **B4** and drag to cell **D11** to select this range (see Figure 3.8). Or use the cursor-movement keys to position the cursor at the beginning of the range, press the period key **(.)**, and use the cursor-

movement keys to move the cursor to the end of the range; press **Enter** to signal the end of the range.

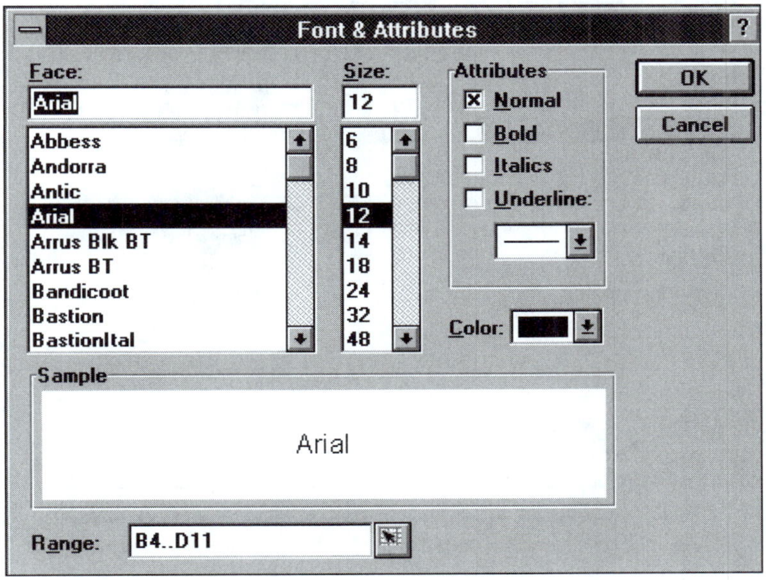

Figure 3.4 *Font & Attributes dialog box for selected range B4..D11.*

6. When you release the mouse button or press **Enter**, the dialog box returns. The range box now shows that the range is B4..D11 (see Figure 3.9).

7. Now you can set the font attributes that you want to apply to this range.

You can cancel the range selection function and return to the dialog box without selecting a range by pressing **Esc**.

Selecting a Collection

Sometimes you will want to perform a function on a group of cells that are not next to each other. A group of cells that are to be treated together, but are not all in one place, is sometimes called a *discontiguous range,* or more simply, a collection of cells.

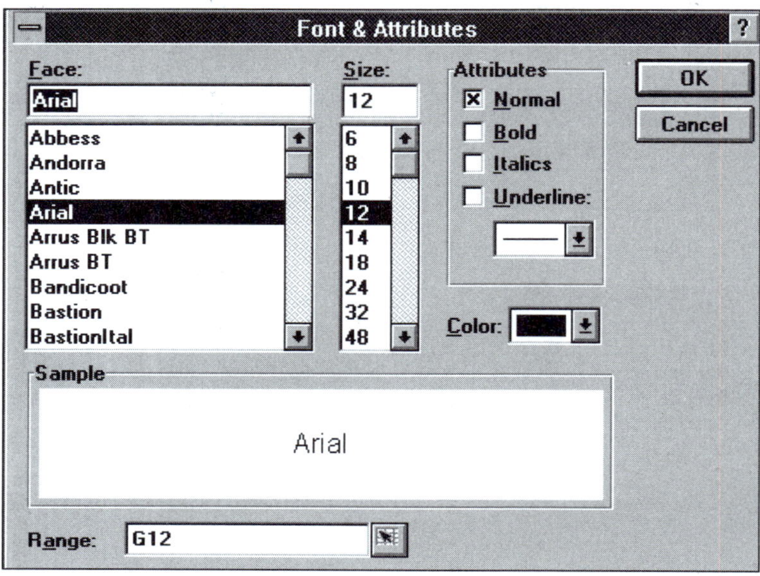

Figure 3.5 *Font & Attributes dialog box for no selected range.*

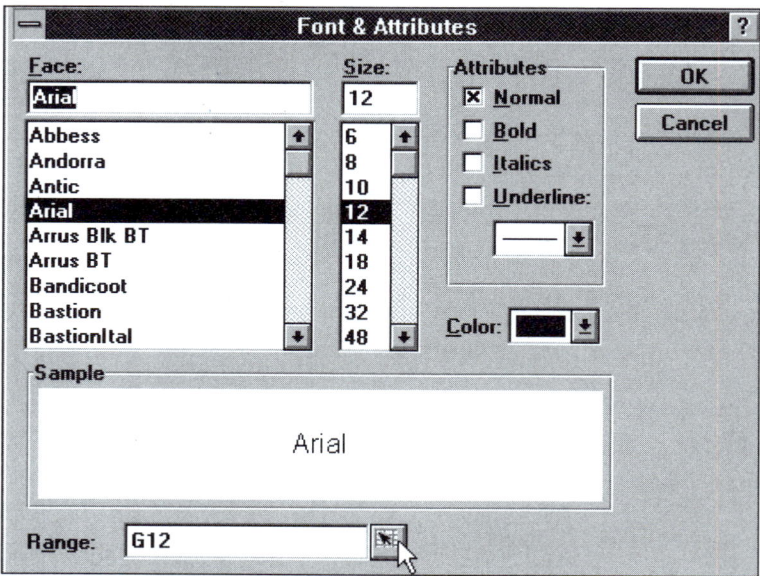

Figure 3.6 *Click on the range selector.*

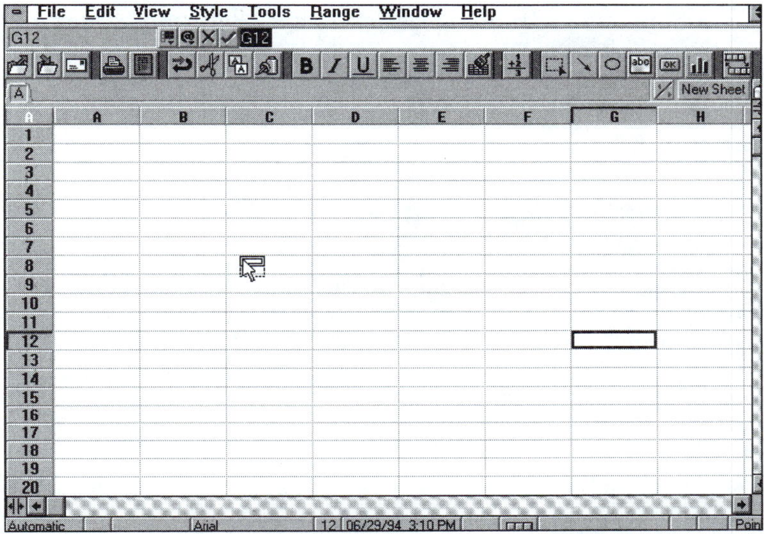

Figure 3.7 *Range selection cursor.*

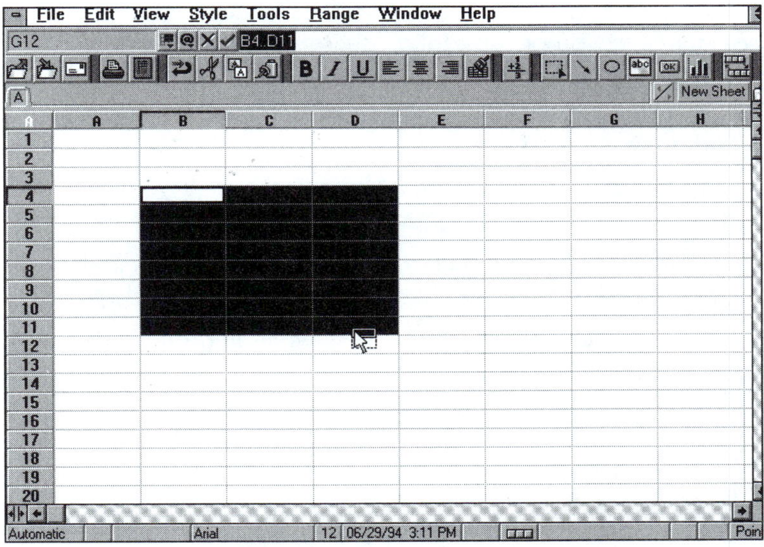

Figure 3.8 *Select range B4..D11.*

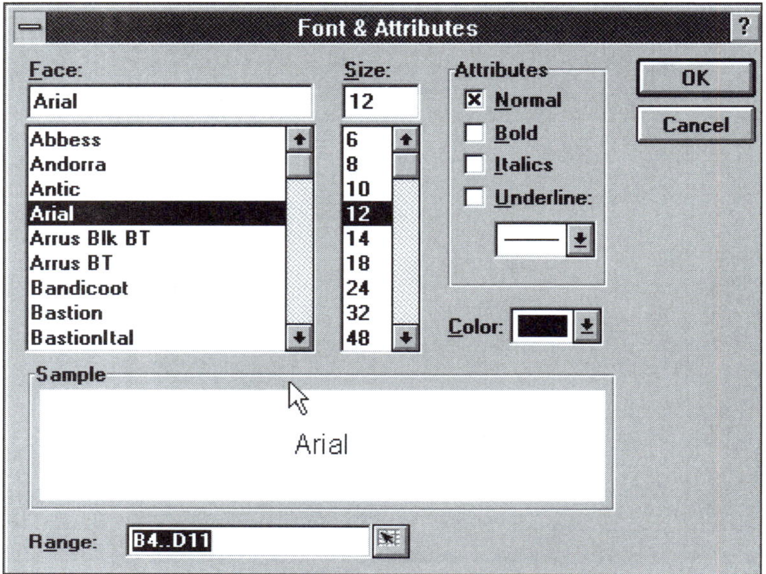

Figure 3.9 *Back to the dialog box.*

To select a collection of cells, follow these steps:

1. Select the first cell or range.

2. Hold down the **Ctrl** key.

3. Using the mouse, select the next cell or range you want (see Figure 3.10).

4. Continue holding the **Ctrl** key to select as many cells and ranges as you want by using the mouse.

   Notice that the last cell you select is white and outlined; it is the active cell. If you select a range last, the first cell of the range is the active cell. The other cells are highlighted (see Figure 3.11).

To deselect a cell, continue to hold down the **Ctrl** key and click on the selected cell that you do not want selected.

1 3 0 7 0 2

Via

Ship To

Market ID: 76524136
Order ID: 1307027
Order Date: 07/06/2026
Shipping Method:

oris APEX DC 76524136-11
EX
AVONDALE AVE.
ANDVIEW HEIGHTS, OH 43212-3473, US

SKU	QTY	TITLE	TOTAL
SM.165HF	1	Microbiology: a Centenary Perspective	42.1
SM.16RU2	1	Teach Yourself...Lotus 1-2-3 Release 5 for Windows	10.1

Order Total: $52.32

ur order has been packaged and created with great care. Enjoy! Bay State Books

7027

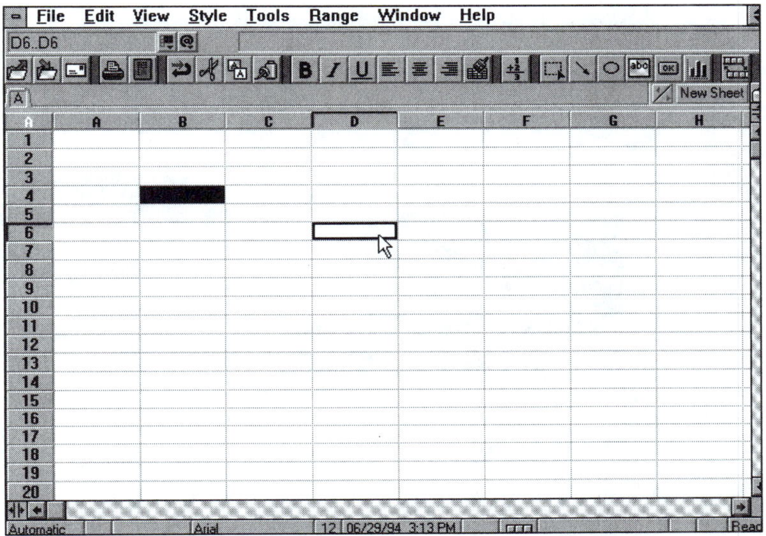

Figure 3.10 *Two discontiguous cells.*

Selecting a 3D Range

If you are working with more than one worksheet in a file, you can select a collection of cells across the different worksheets. This is called a 3D range. You can do this while viewing worksheet tabs or while viewing the worksheets in perspective mode. For these purposes, it will generally be easier to see what you have selected when you use the perspective mode.

To select a 3D range, follow these steps:

1. Select the desired cells and ranges from the first worksheet.

2. Hold down the **Ctrl** key.

3. Select the desired cells and ranges from the next worksheet, and so on. Figure 3.12 shows an example of a 3D range.

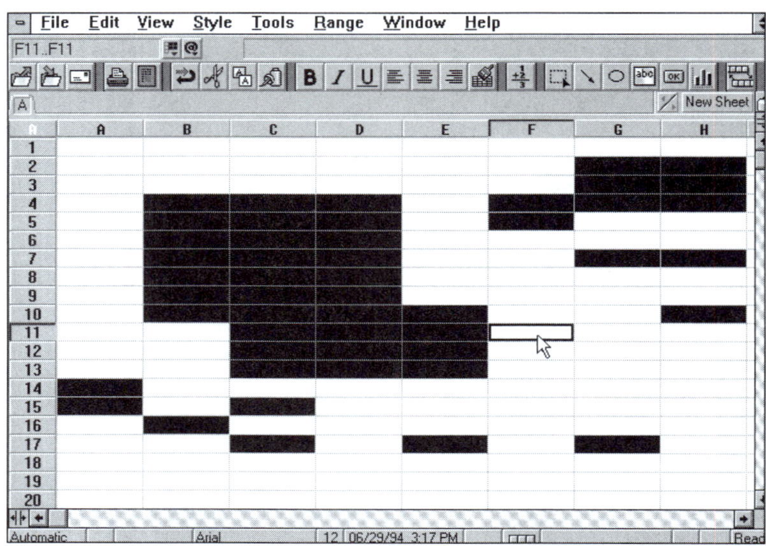

Figure 3.11 *A collection of cells with the last one active.*

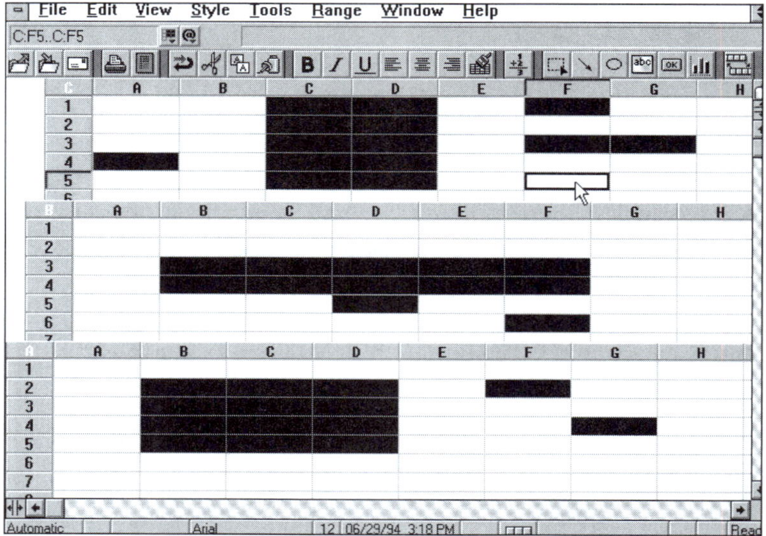

Figure 3.12 *3D range.*

Naming Ranges

If you repeatedly use a particular range of cells, it may be helpful to name the range. Once a range is named, you can go to it and select it quickly by choosing the name you assigned.

For this example, name **B4..D11** as **Range1**. Follow these steps:

1. Select the range **B4..D11**.

2. From the Range menu, select **Name**.

   The Name dialog box opens (see Figure 3.13).

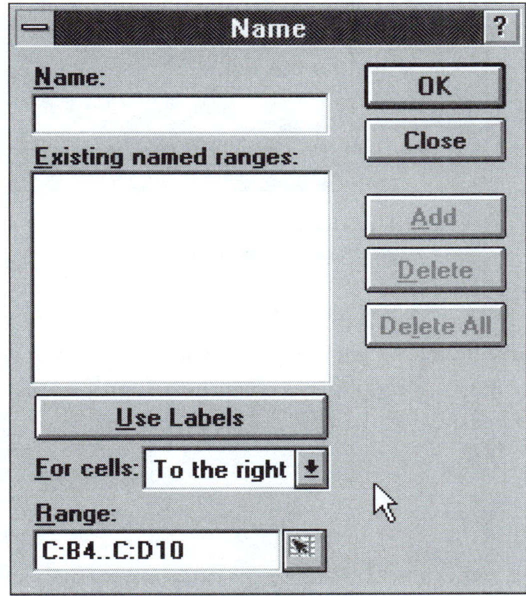

Figure 3.13 *Name dialog box.*

Notice that the dialog box says B4..D11 for the range. If you did not select the range first, you could click on the range selector, and then select the range. Again, this is just a question of which order you prefer.

3. Type **Range1** into the Name box and click **Add** (see Figure 3.14).

4. Click **OK**.

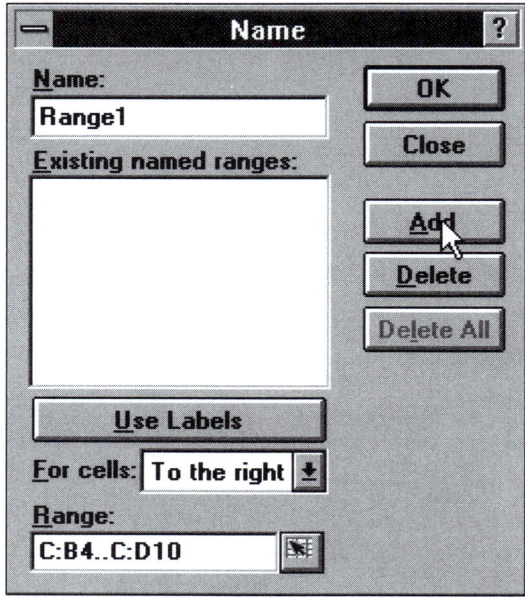

Figure 3.14 *Naming Range1.*

Now the range B4..D11 is called Range1.

You do not have to name ranges using the word Range. We did it just for simplicity. Your ranges should have more meaningful names, such as August Income or 1999 Forecast.

Go To Command

If you know exactly where you want to go on your worksheet, you can use the **Go To** command, which allows you to go directly to any range, chart, drawn object, or query table in any file on your computer.

To go to a particular range, follow these steps:

1. From the Edit menu, select **Go To**.

    The Go To dialog box appears (see Figure 3.15).

2. Type the desired range into the box that now displays your current cell address (in this case, type A:B4..A:D11, which is the range in the example).

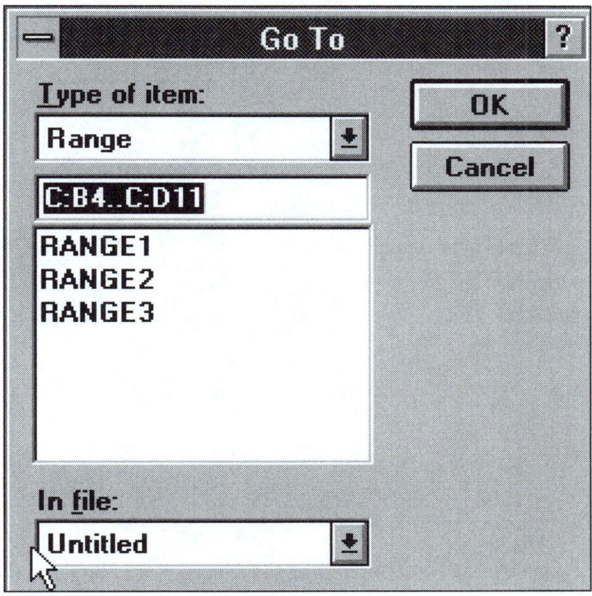

Figure 3.15 *Go To dialog box.*

3. Click **OK**.

You also can use Go To to go to any one cell on your worksheet, whether or not that cell is in a particular range.

To go to a named range, follow these steps:

1. From the Edit menu, select **Go To**.

   The Go To dialog box is displayed (see Figure 3.16).

2. Click the name **Range1**, in the box below the range line. Notice that the cell address changes to the name Range1 (see Figure 3.17).

3. Click **OK**.

Now Lotus 1-2-3 Release 5 automatically takes you to the range defined as Range1.

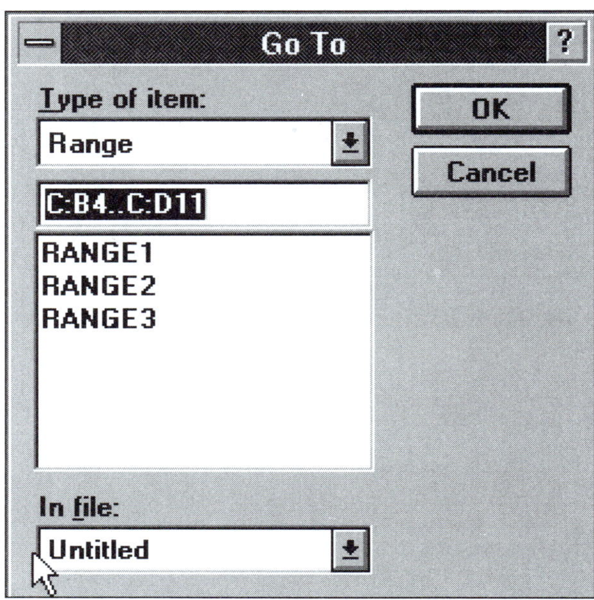

Figure 3.16 *Go To dialog box.*

Using Navigator

There is an even easier way to go automatically to a named range in your work-sheet. Notice the Navigator item on the edit bar (see Figure 3.18).
The Navigator is a drop-down list of the ranges you named. You can select one of them to easily go to that range.

To use the Navigator, follow these steps:

1. Click on the **Navigator** icon on the edit bar.

2. Select the named range you want from the drop-down list (see Figure 3.19).

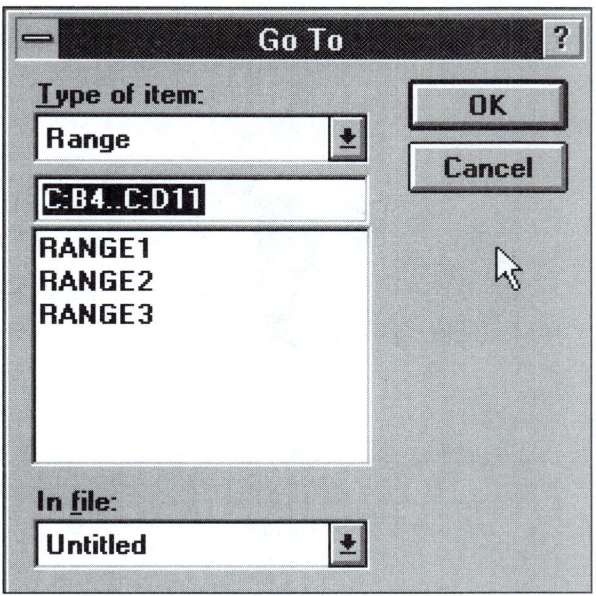

Figure 3.17 *Go To named range.*

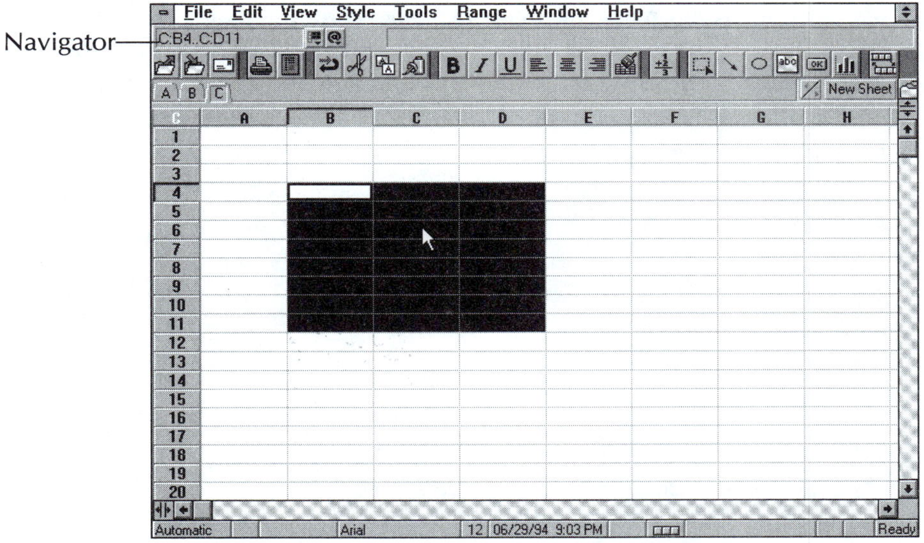

Figure 3.18 *Navigator.*

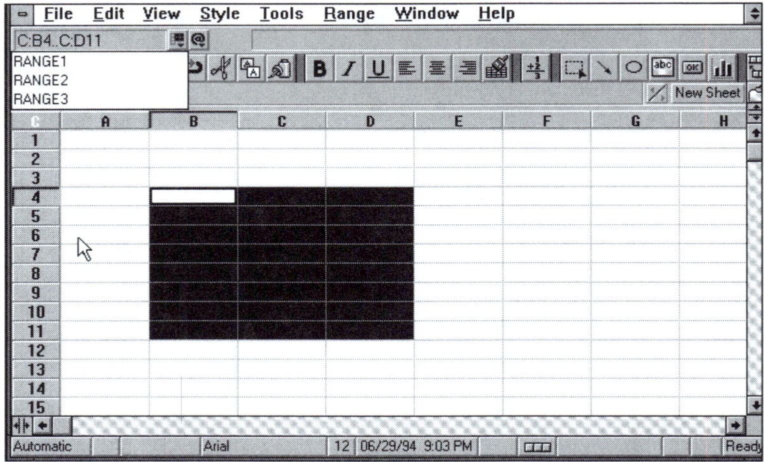

Figure 3.19 *Navigator drop-down list.*

Splitting Views

If you need to work on a very large spreadsheet, you might expect some frustration because of the need to work on cells at either end of the worksheet. Instead of having to constantly scroll back and forth or up and down, however, Lotus 1-2-3 Release 5 enables you to split the worksheet view, revealing different parts of the worksheet at the same time.

You can split a worksheet vertically (see Figure 3.20) or horizontally (see Figure 3.21).

Notice that when the screen is split vertically, you can see columns B and Z at the same time. Similarly, when the screen is split horizontally, you can see rows 2 and 55 at the same time.

To split a worksheet, follow these steps:

1. From the View menu, select **Split**.

    The Split dialog box appears (see Figure 3.22).

2. Choose either **Horizontal** or **Vertical**.

3. Click **OK**.

Figure 3.20 *Vertical split.*

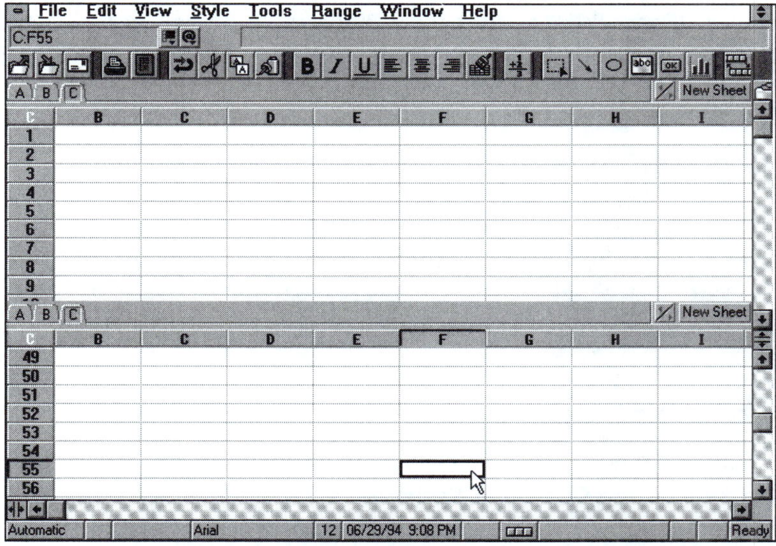

Figure 3.21 *Horizontal split.*

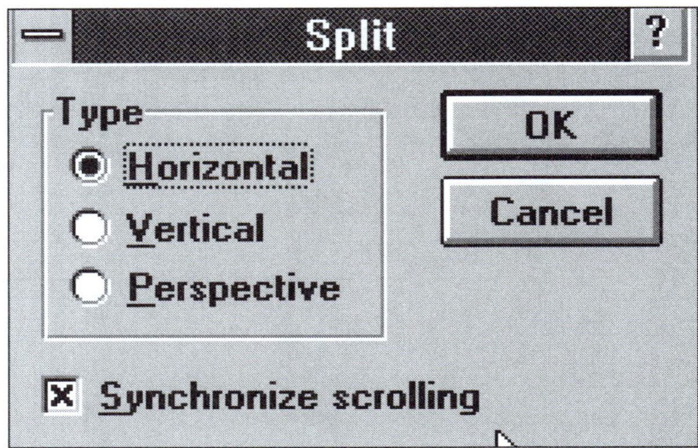

Figure 3.22 *Split dialog box.*

Synchronized Scrolling

When you split the screen, Lotus 1-2-3 Release 5 gives you the option of synchronized scrolling. When this option is checked (as in Figure 3.22), if you scroll up or down or left or right, the program does the same thing on both halves of the worksheet. If you do not select this option, only the half of the screen containing the active cell scrolls. To scroll the other half of the window, you must activate a cell in that window, and then scroll.

Changing Split Size

Once you split the screen, you can change the size of the split. At the top of the vertical scroll bar (see Figure 3.23) and at the right of the horizontal scroll bar (see Figure 3.24) are split panel sliders. If you click on one of the split panel sliders and drag, you can manually split the worksheet or change the size of the splits.

Clearing Splits

When you are finished using a split window, you can return to a full window. From the View menu, select **Clear Split**.

You also can remove splits manually by dragging the vertical split panel slider to the far left or by dragging the horizontal split panel slider to the top.

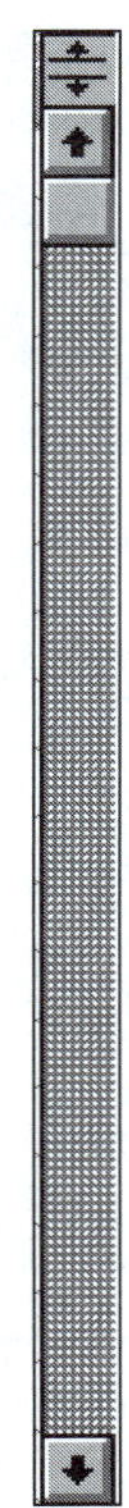

Figure 3.23 *Vertical scroll bar with horizontal split panel slider.*

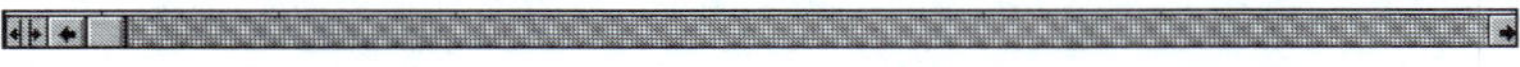

Figure 3.24 *Horizontal scroll bar with vertical split panel slider.*

Freezing Views

When you are working on a large worksheet, you may not always need to split the window to know precisely where in the spreadsheet you are working. The Freeze View option of Lotus 1-2-3 Release 5 enables you to freeze the rows and columns that run along the edges of the spreadsheet. This way, you can see the titles of the columns and rows no matter which cell is currently active. Figure 3.25 shows an example of a worksheet with frozen titles in both the rows and columns.

	A	Jan	Feb	Mar	Apr	May	Jun	Jul
5	A	$371	$728	$1,085	$1,442	$1,799	$2,156	$2,513
6	B	$320	$357	$461	$990	$1,360	$1,397	$1,434
7	C	$365	$402	$506	$1,035	$1,405	$1,442	$1,479
8	D	$313	$350	$454	$983	$1,353	$1,390	$1,427
9	E	$368	$405	$509	$1,038	$1,408	$1,445	$1,482
10	F	$420	$457	$561	$1,090	$1,460	$1,497	$1,534
11	G	$332	$369	$473	$1,002	$1,372	$1,409	$1,446
12	H	$351	$388	$492	$1,021	$1,391	$1,428	$1,465
13	I	$355	$392	$496	$1,025	$1,395	$1,432	$1,469
14	J	$376	$413	$517	$1,046	$1,416	$1,453	$1,490
15	K	$399	$436	$540	$1,069	$1,439	$1,476	$1,513
16	L	$387	$424	$528	$1,057	$1,427	$1,464	$1,501
17	M	$391	$428	$532	$1,061	$1,431	$1,468	$1,505
18	N	$321	$358	$462	$991	$1,361	$1,398	$1,435
19	O	$303	$340	$444	$973	$1,343	$1,380	$1,417
20	P	$366	$403	$507	$1,036	$1,406	$1,443	$1,480

Figure 3.25 *Example of frozen worksheet.*

Across the top are the months of the year. Down the left side are letters of the alphabet. When you freeze the views, you can scroll down to a letter at the end of the alphabet and still see the month at the top of the column. Also, you can scroll all the way to December and still see what row letter you are on.

To freeze the column and row titles:

1. Select the first cell that should not be frozen (see Figure 3.26). If, for example, you want to freeze rows 1 and 2, select a cell in row 3. If you want to freeze column A, select a cell in column B. If you want to freeze rows 1 through 4 and column A, select cell B5, as shown in the example.

2. From the View menu, select **Freeze Titles**.

   The Freeze Titles dialog box appears (see Figure 3.27).

5. You can freeze titles for either rows or columns, or both. For this example, you should freeze both, so select the **Both** radio button.

6. Click **OK**.

Figure 3.26 *Select first cell that should not be frozen.*

Figure 3.27 *Freeze Titles dialog box.*

If you scroll down (see Figure 3.28), the months remain at the top of the screen while the rest of your worksheet scrolls down. Additionally, if you scroll to the right, as shown in Figure 3.29, the letters stay along the left side of the work-sheet while the rest scrolls to the right.

	Jan	Feb	Mar	Apr	May	Jun	Jul
L	$387	$424	$583	$1,416	$1,787	$2,129	$2,648
M	$391	$428	$587	$1,420	$1,791	$2,133	$2,652
N	$321	$358	$517	$1,350	$1,721	$2,063	$2,582
O	$303	$340	$499	$1,332	$1,703	$2,045	$2,564
P	$366	$403	$562	$1,395	$1,766	$2,108	$2,627
Q	$212	$249	$408	$1,241	$1,612	$1,954	$2,473
R	$245	$282	$441	$1,274	$1,645	$1,987	$2,506
S	$413	$450	$609	$1,442	$1,813	$2,155	$2,674
T	$321	$358	$517	$1,350	$1,721	$2,063	$2,582
U	$323	$360	$519	$1,352	$1,723	$2,065	$2,584
V	$344	$381	$540	$1,373	$1,744	$2,086	$2,605

Figure 3.28 *Scrolling down with frozen titles.*

	Aug	Sep	Oct	Nov	Dec
B	$2,804	$3,720	$728	$728	$728
C	$2,849	$3,765	$728	$728	$728
D	$2,797	$3,713	$728	$728	$728
E	$2,852	$3,768	$728	$728	$728
F	$2,904	$3,820	$728	$728	$728
G	$2,816	$3,732	$728	$728	$728
H	$2,835	$3,751	$728	$728	$728
I	$2,839	$3,755	$728	$728	$728
J	$2,860	$3,776	$728	$728	$728
K	$2,883	$3,799	$728	$728	$728
L	$2,871	$3,787	$728	$728	$728
M	$2,875	$3,791	$728	$728	$728
N	$2,805	$3,721	$728	$728	$728
O	$2,787	$3,703	$728	$728	$728
P	$2,850	$3,766	$728	$728	$728
Q	$2,696	$3,612	$728	$728	$728

Figure 3.29 *Scrolling across with frozen titles.*

Frozen titles cannot be selected or edited. You must unfreeze them first.

To remove frozen titles, from the View menu, select **Clear Titles**.

Entering Data

By now you are familiar with the components of a spreadsheet and you know how to find your way around the worksheet area. You can now start to enter the data and use Lotus 1-2-3 Release 5 to accomplish a real task: the monthly budget. In the last chapter, you created a file with three worksheets named Budget, Actual, and Difference. This file was saved on disk under the name BUDGET.WK4. Now you can call up this file (or create it if you did not do so before). As you go along, you can refer to this file and use it to learn about and try out the different functions and features of Lotus 1-2-3 Release 5.

Let's begin with the basics: entering and editing data. To start, open your file and look at the screen. It should look like the one shown in Figure 3.30.

Figure 3.30 *File BUDGET.WK4.*

Values versus Labels

As you can imagine, there are several types of data you could enter into a spreadsheet program. There are numbers, words, formulas, @ functions, and more. But Lotus 1-2-3 Release 5 divides any information you enter into two categories: values or labels.

Value is the name the program gives to numerical items. Numbers, formulas, amounts of money, @ functions, dates, and times are all values. In the budget, the amount you enter to represent the income and expenses are values. The other type of data, labels, are text entries. Any words or notes are labels. In the budget example, the words that describe the income and expenses are labels.

If you think about what the words really mean, values are the things that represent the numerical data, whereas labels describe some aspect of the data. The number 80 might be the value of your total income, and the words *total income* are a label to describe that value. Keep in mind that some data, such as information regarding dates and times, could be a value or a label, depending on the context in which it is used.

You can identify whether your data is a value or a label by looking at the bottom right corner of the status bar, which usually displays **Ready**. When you enter data, this area will display whether your entry is a label, as shown in Figure 3.31, or a value, as shown in Figure 3.32.

When you are finished entering data, the status returns to its normal **Ready** setting.

How to Enter Data

Suppose that you have a piece of data and you want to insert it into a cell. There are two ways to enter all data, whether the content of the data is a label or a value.

The first way, shown in Figure 3.33, is to type the data directly into the cell. To enter data this way follow these steps:

1. Click the mouse or use the arrow keys to select the cell you want.

2. Type the data into the space provided.

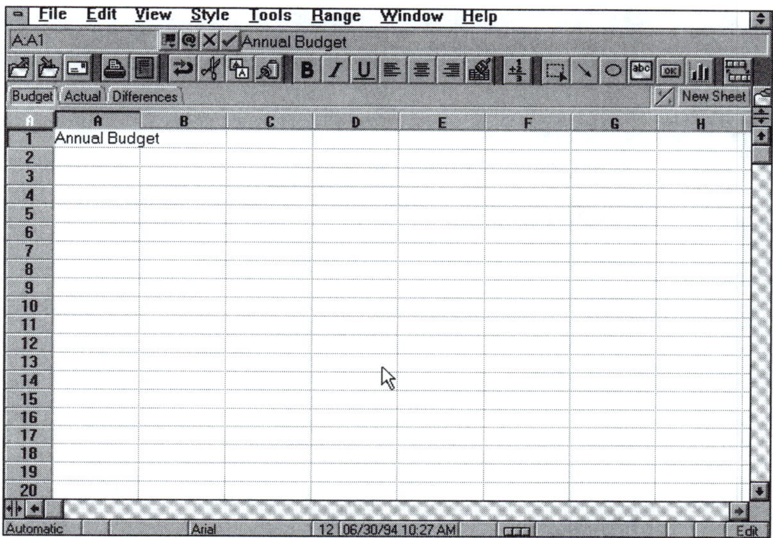

Figure 3.31 *Label entry.*

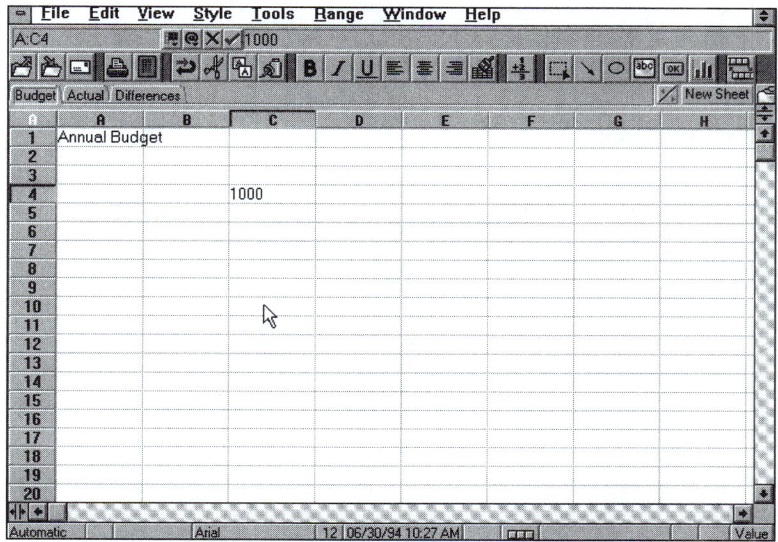

Figure 3.32 *Value entry.*

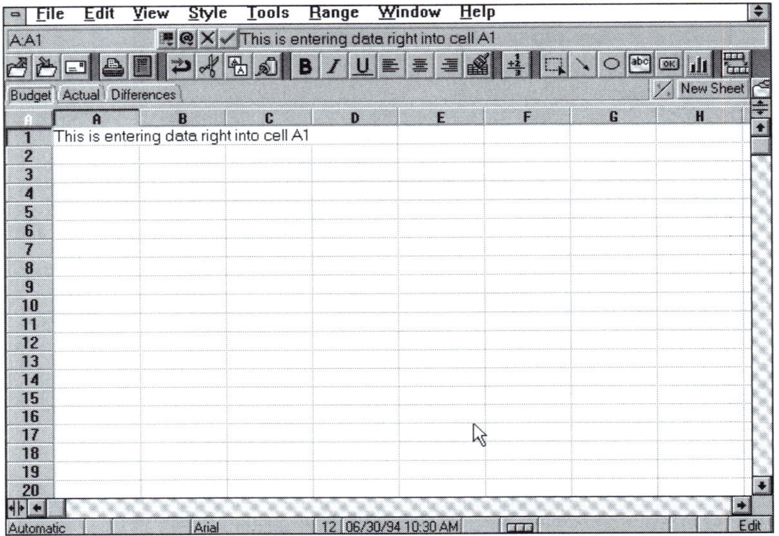

Figure 3.33 *Entering data directly into a cell.*

Before you start, double-check to be sure that you have selected the correct cell. After you type the first character, notice that the insertion marker, which is a vertical line (|), is in the worksheet cell and the edit line is gray. This indicates that you are editing the cell.

You can place the insertion marker in a cell before typing the first character by double-clicking the cell.

N O T E

Sometimes when you type directly into a cell in this manner, the data entered takes up more space than exists in the cell width. Never fear! If this happens, the data isn't cut off, but extends past the right edge of the cell. It will look as though the too-long data is taking up the space of the neighboring cell, but actually the program stores it in just the one cell. No matter how long your data is, it will not be cut off or take up space in another cell. In Chapter 4, you learn how to adjust the cell size to accommodate this too-long data.

The other way to enter data is to type it into the edit line (see Figure 3.34).

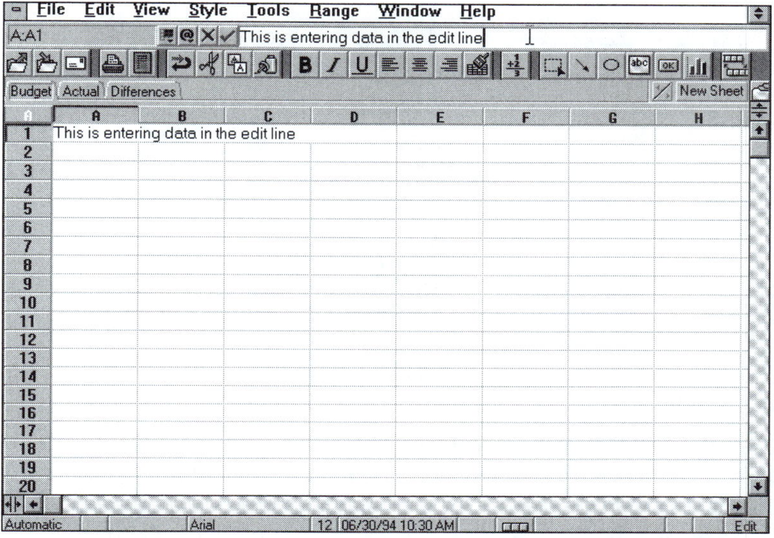

Figure 3.34 *Entering data into the edit line.*

Notice that in this figure, the insertion marker appears in the edit line, instead of in a cell. Also, the edit line is white, indicating that it is ready. To enter data in this way, follow these steps:

1. Select the cell into which you want to enter data.
2. Click the mouse in the edit line.
3. Type the data in the space provided.

Whichever way you choose to enter data, Lotus 1-2-3 Release 5 will display the information both in the cell and on the edit line.

The alternative methods of entering data are equally effective. Whichever is more comfortable for you is fine; they perform exactly the same functions.

Confirming and Canceling

No matter which data entry method you choose, when you begin to enter data, two buttons will appear (see Figures 3.35 and 3.36).

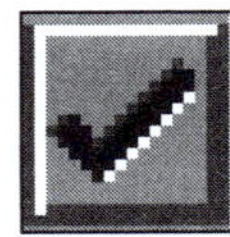

Figure 3.35 *Confirm button.*

Figure 3.36 *Cancel button.*

The check mark, or Confirm button, tells Lotus 1-2-3 to accept the data you entered. The X, or Cancel button, tells Lotus 1-2-3 to discard your entry. These buttons give you the chance to look over what you have entered and confirm that it is correct before you move on. You can confirm or cancel the entry in the current cell by clicking one of these buttons, or you can press Esc to cancel the entry or Enter to confirm it. Selecting another cell also confirms the current entry.

Once you have started entering data into a cell or have clicked the edit line to place the cursor there, you must confirm or cancel the entry before you can do anything else. You cannot, for example, use a SmartIcon or pull down a menu. Lotus 1-2-3 simply beeps if you try to perform a function while editing a cell. After you confirm or cancel the entry in the cell and the Confirm and Cancel buttons have disappeared from the edit line, all other functions are available again.

Entering Numbers

Entering numbers is the most common procedure in spreadsheet programs. Lotus 1-2-3 Release 5 makes this task very easy. You simply go to the cell you choose and type in the number you want. Figure 3.37 shows a sample worksheet with numbers entered as data.

To practice entering data this way, follow these steps:

1. Go to cell **A:C4**.

   Remember that this is cell C4 on the A worksheet. In your file, this worksheet is called Budget.

2. Type the number **1400**. Remember, you can do this either by clicking the mouse on the edit line or clicking directly on the cell and typing there.

3. Confirm the entry by clicking the mouse on the **Confirm** button or by pressing **Enter**.

4. Now move to cell **A:C5** and enter **20**.

5. Continue to enter the numbers into their respective cells as they appear in Figure 3.37.

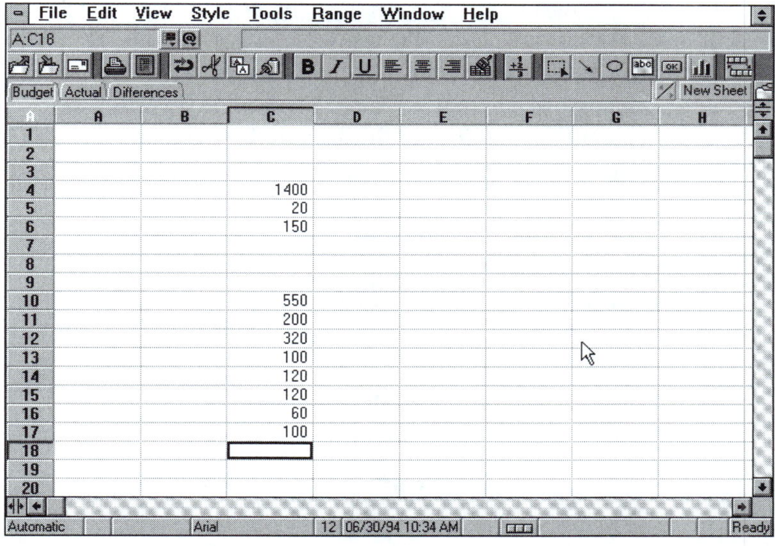

Figure 3.37 *Budget worksheet with numbers.*

SHORTCUT

You can confirm the entry and make the next cell active in one move simply by moving the cursor to the next cell. You can do this by clicking the next cell or by pressing one of the cursor-movement keys. To type the data in Figure 3.37, simply press the down-arrow key after typing each value. (If you are working on the edit line, however, the left and right arrow keys move the insertion point in the line. You must press one of the other cursor-movement keys, such as up arrow, to select another cell.)

Lotus 1-2-3 Release 5 has a feature called Auto Format. This recognizes numbers in a certain category. If, for example, you entered **$1400,** Lotus 1-2-3 Release 5 would recognize this as a sum of money. Similarly, **14%** would be recognized as a percentage. You learn more about formatting data in Chapter 4. For now, the numbers are just entered in General Format. They represent just numbers, with no specific format designated.

Entering Text

It is a bit more complicated to enter text into cells. When you are entering labels instead of values, you have to consider label-prefix characters. These characters tell the program how to align the text in the cell. You might, for example, want the text centered instead of aligned to the left side. If you want to use a label-prefix, you type it at the beginning of the line, before the first character of the label. Table 6.1 displays the various label-prefix characters.

Table 6.1 *Alignment characters.*

Character	Type of Alignment
'	Left Alignment
"	Right Alignment
^	Center Alignment
\	Label Repeats to Fill the Cell

Of course, you can just enter the text into the cell and not worry about the label-prefix character. If you do this, Lotus 1-2-3 automatically assigns a left-aligned label-prefix character as a default option. You may find it easier to enter all your data first, and then go back and change the label prefix, or you may like to enter the prefix for each cell as you go along. Either way, if you want to change the label prefix, you can do so by typing it into the cell or the edit line or by using a feature called the Alignment command, which is discussed further in Chapter 4. One of the most comforting attributes of Lotus 1-2-3 Release 5 is that it allows for human error. You can always go back and change the formatting later, so it is not necessary to memorize the label-prefix characters.

Let's enter some sample text labels. Follow these steps:

1. Go to cell **A:A1**.

2. Type **Caroline's Budget**.

You are not assigning a specific label-prefix character because you will format the worksheet later. Lotus 1-2-3 automatically aligns the entry with the left edge of the cell. When you look at the edit line, you can see that the symbol to align to the left (') appears before the words *Caroline's Budget*. If you changed the alignment, one of the other marks appearing in table 6.1 would appear here.

Notice that the words *Caroline's Budget* take up more space than is provided in the cell. You see that the text label extends beyond the right cell edge. For now, this is fine, but later if you enter data into the adjacent cell (cell A:B1), you will not be able to see the words that are extending out of cell A:A1. Lotus 1-2-3 will display as much of the entry as possible to show in a cell this size. Later, in Chapter 4, you learn how to change the size of the cell.

Figure 3.38 shows the rest of the text entries on the sample worksheet. Practice entering this kind of data by filling in the text as shown in the figure. Again, don't worry about label-prefix characters or the width of the cells; you will format the entire worksheet later.

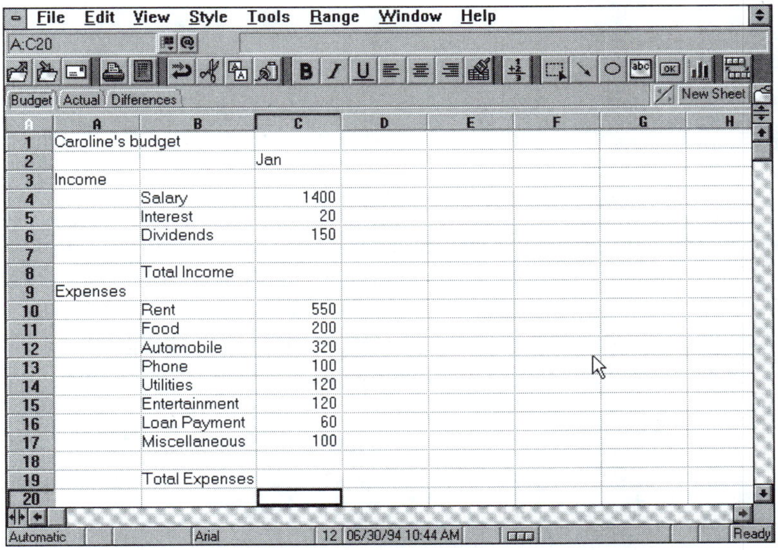

Figure 3.38 *Your text entries should look as follows.*

Entering Dates and Times

Sometimes you will need to enter data in the form of dates and times. This is the trickiest type of data to work with because dates and times could be values or labels. You could, for example, enter a date as a value to use in a calculation, say, to calculate the time between two dates.

Alternatively, you may use a date as a label for a text entry. This way, the program thinks of it as text and not as a value for calculation. The purpose for which you plan to use a particular piece of data, as indicated by the way the data is entered, will determine the way the program records that data.

To enter a date as a value:

1.   Go to the cell you have chosen.

2.   Enter the date in number form, for example **10/14/75**.

Lotus 1-2-3 Release 5 treats a date as a value if you enter it in any of these formats:

10/14/75

10/14

14-Oct

14-Oct-75

Oct-75

Lotus 1-2-3 Release 5 recognizes and can calculate dates between January 1, 1900 and December 31, 2099. Dates outside that range are treated as labels. Dates between 1900 and 1999 can be expressed using two or four digits for the year, as in 10/14/75 or 10/14/1975. Dates after 1999 must use four digits for the year, as in 1/13/2000.

Similarly, a time entry is treated as a value and can be used in calculations if you enter it in one of these formats:

3:15 PM

3:15:25 PM

15:15

15:15:25

NOTE Every cell has a format. When you first create a worksheet, every cell has the Automatic format, and any dates and times you enter are treated as described here. But if you change the format of a cell before entering a date or time, the value in the cell appears as described, but the value on the edit line will be a number between 0 and 73050 (for a date) expressing the numbers of days after 1/1/1900, or a fraction between 0.000000 and 0.999988 (for a time) expressing the number of seconds after midnight.

You also can enter dates and times as labels. One way of doing this is to type the date using letters. You could, for example, enter **October 14, 1975** instead of writing the date in numerical form. If you enter the date this way, it is stored as a label automatically.

But if you don't want to go through the hassle of typing the words for each date, you can store dates as labels even if they are in numerical form. Doing so involves using the label prefixes discussed earlier. To enter the date 10/14/75 and have it stored as a label, first type a label prefix from table 6.1.

If you don't insert the label prefix for a date that is entered in numerical form, Lotus 1-2-3 Release 5 will store it as a value. You can change the date to a label by inserting a label prefix into the cell or edit line.

Filling a Range with a Series

One of the most significant benefits of Lotus 1-2-3 Release 5 is that it can generate a series of numbers, dates, or times. If you needed to insert numbers down a column from 1 to 80,000, Lotus 1-2-3 could enter them for you, so you don't have to do it manually. As you work with 1-2-3, you will appreciate its capability to understand and extend a series.

This function uses the Fill command. You can select the range before or after you select the command. Be sure to select an empty range, because Fill will overwrite any data that's already in the selected cells.

To fill a range of cells with a series, follow these steps:

1. Select the range in which you will enter the series.

2. From the Range menu, select **Fill**.

   The Fill dialog box is displayed (see Figure 3.39).

4. If you are filling with dates or times, select the interval first. If, for example, you want a series of Mondays, select the **Week** interval. If you want a series of times a minute apart, select the **Minute** interval.

5. In the Start box, enter the starting number, date, or time. If the starting value is contained in a cell, you can enter the address of the cell. If, for example, you enter **C10** and cell C10 currently contains a 6, the starting value will be 6. You can also enter a formula, such as **=C10+10**, which would result in a starting value of 16. (Formulas are explained in Chapter 5.) For dates and times, you must use one of the valid formats that Lotus 1-2-3 recognizes.

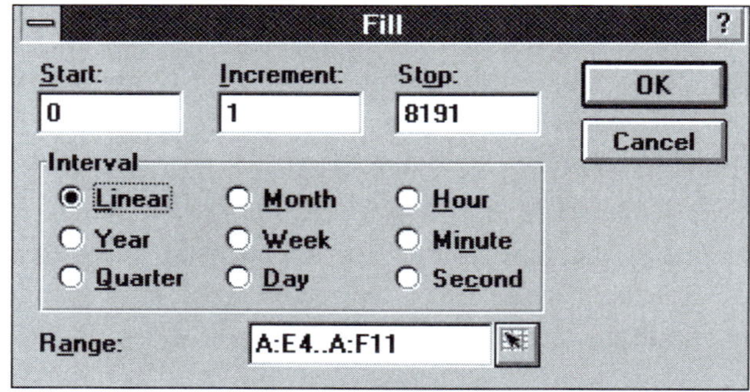

Figure 3.39 *Fill dialog box.*

6. In the Increment box, enter the amount by which the value should be increased in each succeeding cell. To fill in the series 10, 20, 30, …, for example, the increment is 10. The increment can be expressed as a number, a cell address, or a formula. For dates and times, both the increment and the interval determine the succession of numbers. If, for example, you want every fourth Monday, the interval should be Week and the increment should be 4. If you want a series of 15 minute time periods, the interval should be Minute and the increment should be 15.

7. In the Stop box, enter the highest value that should be generated. If you

don't feel like calculating this value, enter a ridiculously high number. The Fill function stops automatically when it reaches the last cell.

8. Click **OK**.

The Fill function fills from top to bottom in the first column of the range, and then moves to the top of the next column and fills down that column, and so on.

You don't need to use the Fill command in the Budget example. Instead, you will be filling data in a different way. If you experimented with this function in your BUDGET.WK4 file, erase the data you entered using this command. You can do this by selecting Undo from the Edit menu, or by clearing the values you entered. To clear a value, select the cell and press the Delete key.

Range by Example

Sometimes you may have data in a series that is not strictly numeric. In that case, you will be happy to know that the program has the capability to learn a series. If, for example, you have a range of cells selected and the first two cells contained entries of "toolbox 1" and "toolbox 2," you could use the Fill by Example function to complete the rest of the range as "toolbox 3," "toolbox 4" and so on, without having to type those words over and over. This way, you can use series that are not listed in the Fill command, but are your own, customized series.

If your customized series is fairly simple, you can establish the pattern of the series even if only a few cells contain values. For example:

1. Go to cell **A:C2** (notice that it contains the word Jan).
2. Select the range A:C2..A:H2.
3. From the Range menu, select **Fill by Example**.

Notice that Lotus 1-2-3 Release 5 fills the range with Jan, Feb, Mar, Apr, May, and Jun (see Figure 3.40).

There's an even easier way to fill by example. You can drag and fill a range. Click the **Undo** SmartIcon to remove the month names you just filled. Then try entering them using the drag and fill function.

To drag and fill by example, follow these steps:

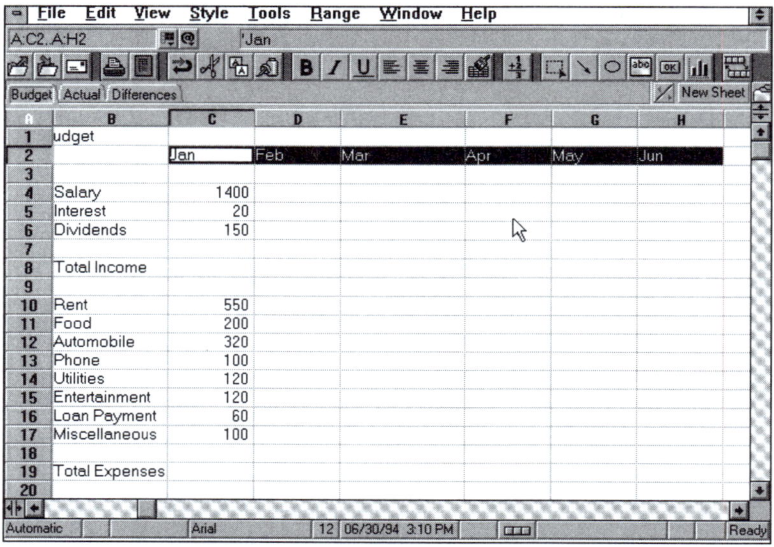

Figure 3.40 *Range filled by example.*

1. Select cell **A:C2**, as before. (The Jan value should still be in this cell, to act as the example for the fill.)

2. Move the pointer near the bottom right corner of the cell, until it becomes a drag-and-fill pointer (see Figure 3.41).

3. Press and hold the mouse button and drag to the right until cells C2 through H2 are selected.

4. When you release the mouse button, the range is automatically filled.

Similarly, if the information in the first cell had not been abbreviated but had been entered as **January**, the series would have continued with the full names of the months of the year. Lotus 1-2-3 Release 5 determines the series based on the values already entered in your range.

Sometimes you will need to use a series that is more complex than the months of the year. If so, the program will need several initial values to determine the pattern of the series.

Suppose, for example, that you entered the series **10101**, **10102**, **10103**, and so on. In this case, you would need to provide at least two cells of the range for the program to be able to determine the pattern.

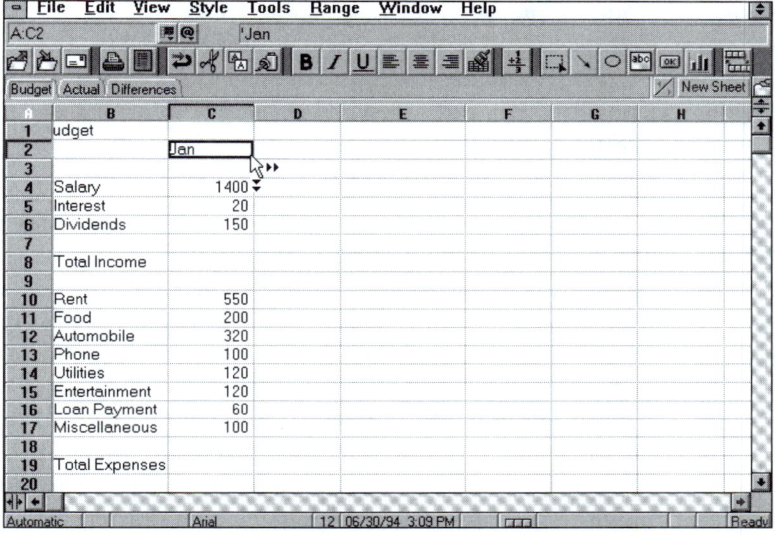

Figure 3.41 *Drag-and-fill pointer.*

Editing Data

Sometimes you will enter some data and, when you come back to it or print it out later, you notice an error or just want to change some of the information. Lotus 1-2-3 Release 5 enables you to go back to a cell and edit the information in that cell.

To edit data in a cell, follow these steps:

1. Double-click with the mouse on the cell to activate it.

    The cursor appears at the end of the data currently in the cell.

3. Use the mouse or the arrows to alter your data.

You can perform the same function by following these steps:

1. Click on the cell with the mouse.

2. Click on the edit line.

    The cursor appears on the edit line at the end of your entry and you can edit your data.

If you single-click with the mouse and begin typing before you click on the edit line, your data in the cell will be replaced with the new value. Don't worry; you can retrieve the old value by immediately pressing **Esc** or clicking the **Cancel** button. If you accidentally confirm the new value before realizing your mistake, you can still retrieve the old value by going to the Edit menu and choosing **Undo** (or by clicking the **Undo** SmartIcon or pressing **Ctrl+Z**). Phew!

If you decide that you no longer need any of the information in a cell or range, you can delete the whole thing easily by pressing the **Delete** key.

The **Delete** key removes the data from the selected cells without further ado. You can restore the data by immediately choosing the **Undo** function. If you don't choose **Undo** immediately, you won't be able to retrieve the data. If, however, the data was saved on disk, you can still get back to it. Save the current file under a different name, and then open the older version, which contains the data you're trying to retrieve. Copy the missing data from the old version to the new version. Then save the new version again under its original name.

Moving Data

After entering data, you may decide that the contents of one cell really belong elsewhere on the worksheet. Moreover, you may decide a whole range of cells needs to be moved. You can accomplish this in two ways. The first way is to select a range, cut it to the clipboard and paste it to a new location. In the following example, you move the data from A:C4..A:C6 (the January values for Salary, Interest and Dividends) to A:D4..A:D6.

To move a cell or a range in this way, follow these steps:

1. Select the range (in this case, **A:C4..A:C6**).

2. From the Edit menu, choose **Cut** (or press **Ctrl+X** or click the **Cut** SmartIcon).

3. Move the cursor to first cell of the new location (in this case, **A:D4**).

4. From the Edit menu, choose **Paste** (or press **Ctrl+V** or click the **Paste** SmartIcon).

Be careful when using the Cut function, as it immediately removes all data from the selected cells. If you cut by accident, you can restore the data by immediately choosing the **Undo** function. Or, because the data has been cut to the clipboard, you can paste it back into its original location, which doesn't have to be done immediately. The data stays on the clipboard until you cut or copy something else to the clipboard. Once you do that, the former data is gone from the clipboard and cannot be recovered. (The Undo function does not affect the clipboard.)

The other way to move a cell or range is to select it with the mouse and drag it to its new location.

To move a range or cell, follow these steps:

1. Select the range (in this case, you chose **A:D4..A:D6**).

2. Position the mouse so that the cursor is on one of the edges of the range. Notice that the cursor changes shape and now looks like a hand (see Figure 3.42).

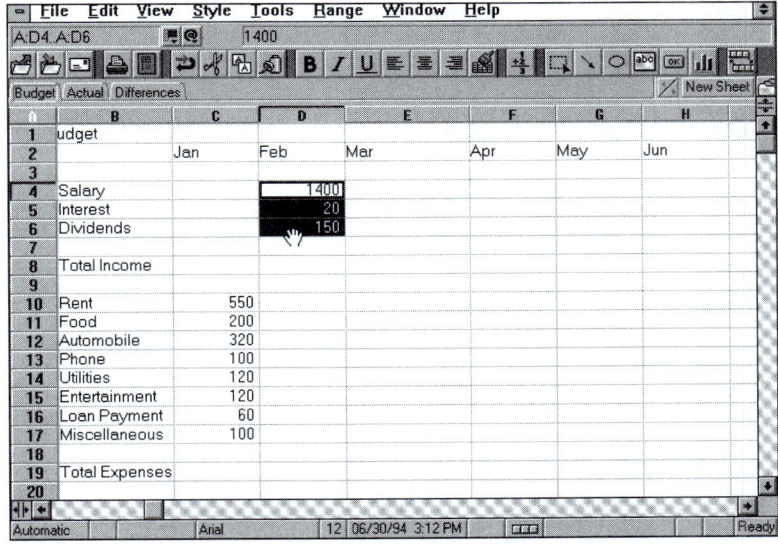

Figure 3.42 *The Move cursor.*

3. Click and hold the mouse while you drag the range selected to the new location, which is **A:C4..A:C6** (where you originally took it from). Notice that the hand drags an outline of your selected range as you move it (see Figure 3.43).

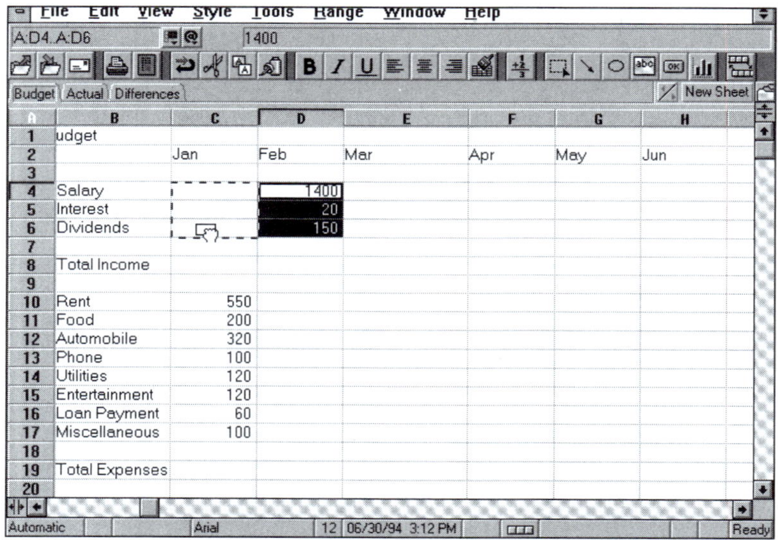

Figure 3.43 *Moving a range.*

This helps you to see the area that will be covered by your range when you move it.

If the new area in which you place your range already contains data, that data will be lost as it is overwritten by the newly moved information. A warning box appears so that you can confirm or cancel the move. Be sure that you don't accidentally move a range on top of pre-existing data unless you want to replace it. You can undo the move and recover the former data by choosing the **Undo** function immediately afterward.

Copying Data

Suppose that you enter data into a cell, and then realize you need the very same data in another cell somewhere else. Instead of retyping the data into the new cell, you can copy the data in one cell and paste it in another cell in three different ways. The first two methods are very similar to moving data.

First you can copy it to the clipboard, and then paste it somewhere else. For example:

1. Select range **A:C4..A:C6**.

2. From the Edit menu, choose **Copy** (or press **Ctrl+C** or click the **Copy** SmartIcon).

3. Move the cursor to cell **A:D4**.

4. From the Edit menu, choose **Paste** (or press **Ctrl+V** or click the **Paste** SmartIcon).

When you copy or cut to the clipboard, Lotus 1-2-3 Release 5 stores a copy of the data until the next copy or cut. Because of this, you can paste and repaste and repaste as many times as you want until you perform another copy or cut.

The second way to copy data is to drag a copy of the range to a new location. To copy by dragging, follow these steps:

1. Select range **A:D4..A:D6**.

2. Move the cursor over the edge of the range so that the cursor changes into a hand.

3. Hold down the **Ctrl** key while clicking on and dragging the mouse to move the selection to a new location. Notice that the hand has a + sign in it this time (see Figure 3.44). This tells you that Lotus 1-2-3 Release 5 is copying your selection to the new location instead of moving it.

WARNING

Be sure to release the mouse button before releasing the **Ctrl** button. If you release **Ctrl** first, you will move the data instead of copying it. You can choose the **Undo** function to restore the data to its original location.

The final way to copy a selection is to use the Copy Right or Copy Down commands. For example:

1. Select range **A:E4..A:H6**, starting with E4.

2. From the Edit menu, select **Copy Right**.

   Notice that Lotus 1-2-3 took the contents of the left-most cell and copied it to all cells to the right in the selected range.

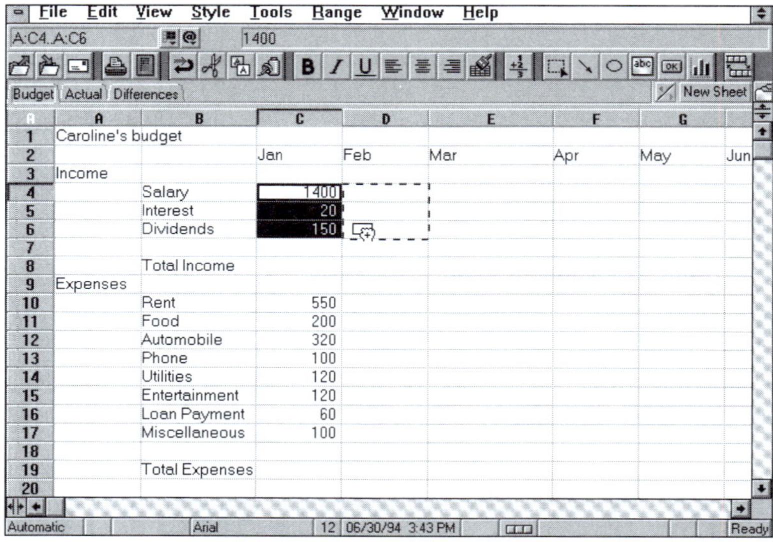

Figure 3.44 *Copy a range by dragging the selection.*

Copy Down performs the same kind of function, except that it copies the upper-most cell to all the cells below it in the selected range.

Inserting and Deleting Rows, Columns, and Selected Cells

Lotus 1-2-3 Release 5 lets you add a row or column, or, alternatively, to delete a row or column. These functions, which employ the Insert or Delete commands, are useful for updating your files to accommodate new data.

To insert an entire column:

1. Click on the column heading **C** to select the entire column.

2. From the Edit menu, select **Insert**.

   In this case, a dialog box does not appear even though the Insert command is followed by three dots.

   Notice that Lotus 1-2-3 has inserted a column at column C and shifted everything else to the right.

The program inserts a column to the left of your selection. The data that was in column C is now in the column called D, and D's information is in column E. When you insert a column, all of the data of your old columns is preserved, but relocated. Any formulas that you have entered into these cells are transferred to their new locations. If, for example, the value of cell K5 is equal to 18 percent of the value of cell C5, when you insert a new column C, the program will know to change the formula to make K5 equal to 18 percent of cell D5. If you delete the new column, the formula will return to 18 percent of C5. Chapter 5 discusses formulas in greater detail. For now, it is only important that you understand that inserting columns will not throw off the rest of the data in your worksheets.

To delete an entire column, follow these steps:

1. Click on the new column heading **C**, to select the entire column. This is the column you are deleting.

2. From the Edit menu, select **Delete**.

    Notice that Lotus 1-2-3 has deleted the new column you had created.

When you delete a column, you are erasing all the data in that column. Always make sure that is what you want to do. You can undo the action by selecting **Undo** immediately.

The same procedures apply to insert or delete rows. You may want to insert or delete a range of cells, rather than a whole column or row. To insert a range of cells, follow these steps:

1. Select the range, in this case **A:C4..A:C6**.

2. From the Edit menu, select **Insert**.

    The Insert dialog box appears (see Figure 3.45).

3. If you want the current cells to move down, select **Row**.

    If you want the current cells to shift to the right, select **Column**. This is what you will select in the example.

4. In either case, make sure that you choose **Insert Selection**.

5. Click **OK**.

Notice that Lotus 1-2-3 Release 5 inserted a blank selection where January's numbers used to be. The original numbers have all shifted to the right.

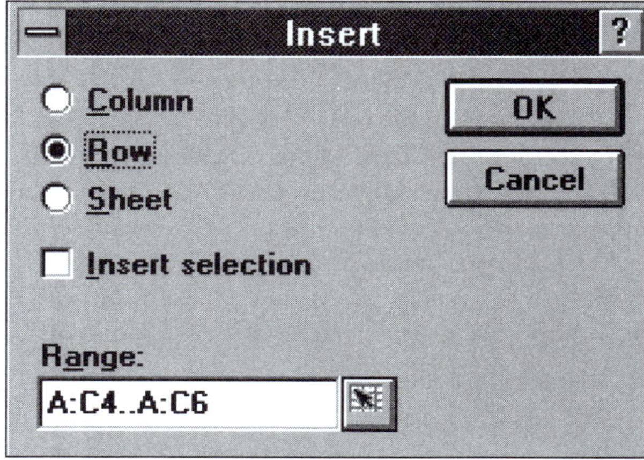

Figure 3.45 *Insert dialog box.*

To delete a range of cells, follow these steps:

1. Select the range, in this case, **A:C4..A:C6**.

2. From the Edit menu, select **Delete**.

   The Delete dialog box appears (see Figure 3.46).

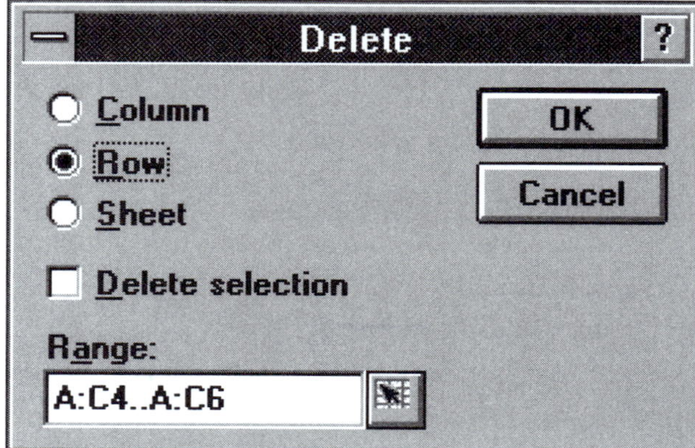

Figure 3.46 *Delete dialog box.*

4. Select Column, and **Delete Selection**.

    This function erases any values in the selected range. Always make sure that you want to delete this selection. You can undo the deletion by selecting the **Undo** function immediately.

5. Click **OK**.

Notice that the old data is back in its original place.

Find & Replace

Sometimes when you are working on a long and complicated worksheet, you will remember having typed something, yet will not be able to find it. Or you may want to change all occurrences of a particular word to a different word. Ordinarily, these would be annoyances, but Lotus 1-2-3 Release 5 has a Find & Replace function that enables you to do both.

The Find & Replace dialog box, located in the Edit menu, is shown in Figure 3.47.

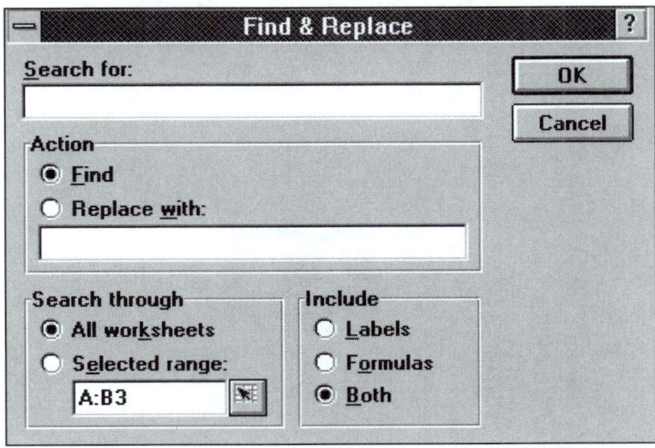

Figure 3.47 *Find & Replace dialog box.*

The top of this dialog box has a space for you to enter the term you want to search for. Once you have done this, tell Lotus 1-2-3 Release 5 whether it should **Find** that term or **Replace** it with a different term. If you choose **Replace**, insert the new term in the box provided. Next, choose a location for the search. You can have Lotus 1-2-3 Release 5 search through **All Worksheets** or through a **Selected Range**. Once the location is chosen, you tell Lotus 1-2-3 Release 5 whether to search **Labels, Formulas**, or both for the designated search term.

Suppose that you want to find all occurrences of the word automobile; follow these steps:

1. From the Edit menu, select **Find & Replace**.

   The Find & Replace dialog box appears.

2. Type **automobile** in the Search For box.

3. Check that the Action is set to Find.

4. Select **All Worksheets**.

5. Choose to search through both **Labels and Formulas**.

6. Click **OK**.

   The Find dialog box appears (see Figure 3.48.)

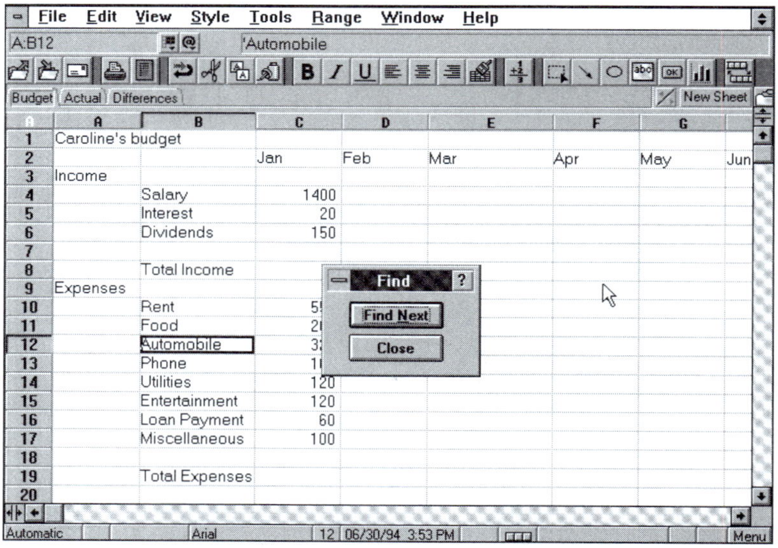

Figure 3.48 Find dialog box.

9. Lotus 1-2-3 Release 5 selects the cell where it found your search term. You either can click on the **Find Next** button to move to the next occurrence or you can click on **Close**.

10. After 1-2-3 finds the last occurrence of your search term, you see the message shown in Figure 3.49.

Figure 3.49 *No More Matching Strings Message.*

11. Click **OK.**

Now, suppose that you wanted to find all occurrences of automobile and replace them with car.

To replace text with different text, follow these steps:

1. From the Edit menu, select **Find & Replace**.

   The Find & Replace dialog box appears.

2. Type **automobile** in the Search For box.

3. Click with the mouse to activate **Replace With**.

4. Type **car** into the Replace With box.

5. Select **All Worksheets**.

6. Make sure that Lotus 1-2-3 Release 5 is set to search both **Labels and Formulas**.

7. Click **OK**.

   The Replace dialog box appears (see Figure 3.50).

8. 1-2-3 selects the cell in which it found your search term. You have the option to **Replace** it with the new term, **Replace All** occurrences with the new term, **Find** the next occurrence without replacing this one, or close the dialog box.

   If you choose **Replace All**, Lotus 1-2-3 Release 5 replaces all occurrences of your search term without asking you for approval. If you chose **Replace All** by mistake, immediately select **Undo** from the Edit menu.

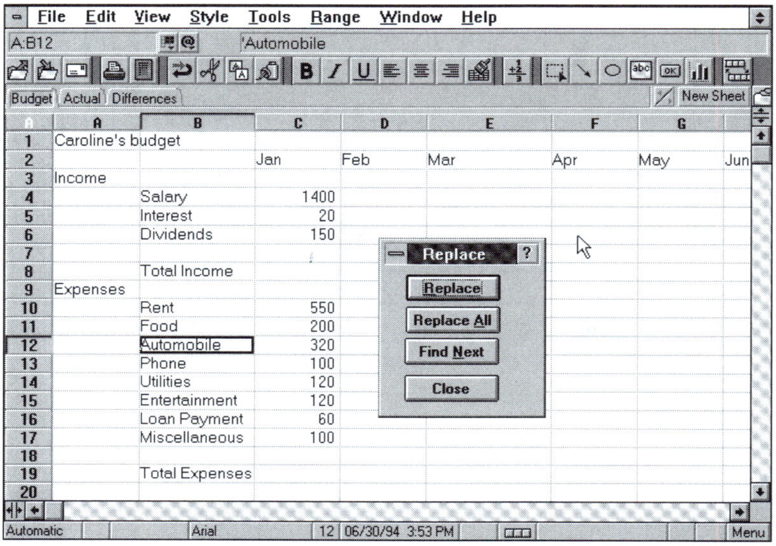

Figure 3.50 *Replace dialog box.*

You are alerted when the last occurrence of your search term is found. 1-2-3 displays the **No More Matching Strings** message. (If you choose **Replace All,** Lotus 1-2-3 Release 5 doesn't display the **No More Matching Strings** Message.)

9 Click **OK**.

Now, for practice, go back and replace all occurrences of *car* with *automobile*. By doing this, you will return Caroline's Budget to the way it looked at the beginning. But don't use the **Replace All** feature. If you do, 1-2-3 will replace *Caroline* with *automobileoline* because her name begins with *Car*. Instead, use the **Replace** feature and skip the Caroline occurrences.

When you seek to replace a term, the exact characters you type into the **Replace With** box will become the new item. Therefore, make sure that you capitalize letters and punctuate, paying close attention to detail. On the other hand, when you are searching for a word, Lotus 1-2-3 Release 5 does not consider the case of the letters.

Spell Checking

Even the world's best typist makes a few typographical or spelling errors now and then. And even the world's most careful proofreader can miss a spelling mistake. To accommodate this human error, Lotus 1-2-3 Release 5 has a built-in spell checker. You can use it to go through your worksheets and find misspelled words or repetitions, such as "the the." The Spell Check Settings dialog box is shown in Figure 3.51.

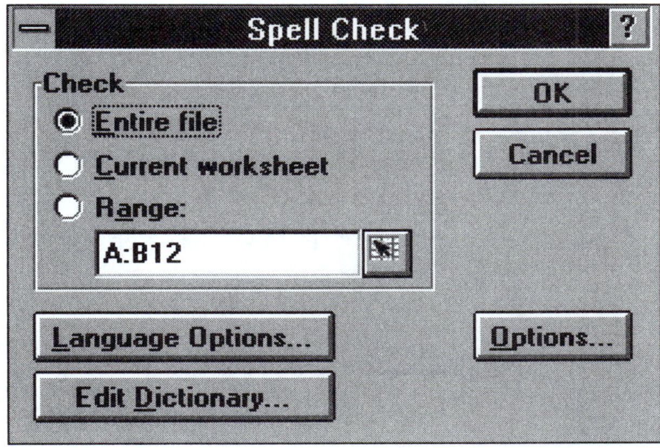

Figure 3.51 *Spell Check Settings dialog box.*

In this dialog box you have to tell Lotus 1-2-3 Release 5 where to check the spelling (the entire document, the current worksheet, or a specified range). You also can set the Language Options. Depending on which language dictionaries are installed in your system, you can switch the language in which Lotus 1-2-3 Release 5 checks the spellings.

The Spell Check also lets you edit the user dictionary. This dictionary is a storage place where you can enter words you use often that might not be in Lotus 1-2-3 Release 5's normal dictionary, such as names you use in your worksheets. If you click on the Edit Dictionary button, a dialog box appears that enables you to add new words or delete words you have already added.

Finally, there is an Options button. If you click on this button, the Spelling Options dialog box appears (see Figure 3.52).

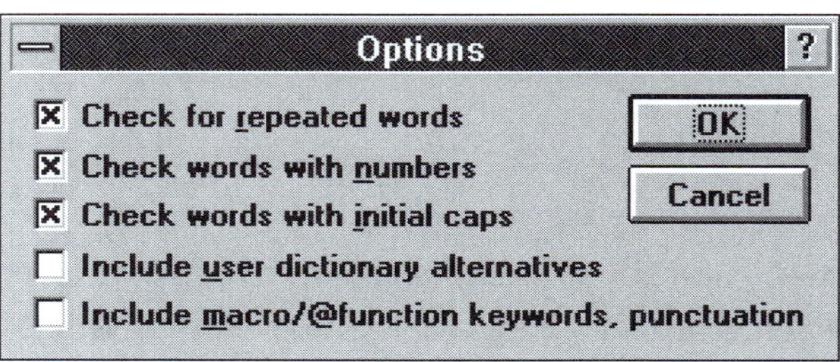

Figure 3.52 *Spelling Options dialog box.*

In this box you can select whether 1-2-3 should search for repeated words (such as "the the"), whether it should search for words with numbers or with capital letters, whether it should include alternative spellings found in your user dictionary, or whether it should search using macro and @Function keyword punctuation. When you have the settings you want, click **OK**.

To check the spelling in a document, follow these steps:

1. From the Tools menu, select **Spell Check**.

2. Choose where you want Lotus 1-2-3 Release 5 to check (in this case, the entire file).

3. Click **OK**.

    The Spell Check dialog box appears (see Figure 3.53).

    The first unknown word (in this case, "Feb") appears at the top of the dialog box.

    Below, Lotus 1-2-3 Release 5 suggests alternative spellings for this selection, based on what it thinks are the closest matches to what you typed.

    Sometimes the alternatives will not be the correct spelling. This is okay; Lotus 1-2-3 Release 5 simply had difficulty matching the word.

4. Either select an alternative from the list or type one yourself on the **Replace With** line.

5. You can either **Replace**, **Replace All**, **Skip** or **Skip All**. If you choose Replace, Lotus 1-2-3 Release 5 replaces this occurrence and move on. It will not, however, replace it again if the same mistake occurs. The Replace All option replaces every occurrence of this mistake in the document. The Skip option skips this word and moves on to the next one. Skip All skips every occurrence of this word in your document.

Figure 3.53 Spell Check dialog box.

If you choose **Replace All**, Lotus 1-2-3 Release 5 changes every occurrence of this word without asking for your approval. This may replace text that you didn't want changed.

6. You can also **Add** the unknown word to your user dictionary. If you click the **Add to Dictionary** button, Lotus 1-2-3 Release 5 does this for you.

When Lotus 1-2-3 Release 5 has completed the Spell Check, you see the message shown in Figure 3.54.

Figure 3.54 Spell Check Complete message window.

Practice

Now that you have explored the various ways to enter and edit data, look at Figure 3.55 and edit your data to add the new entries shown.

Also, enter the values shown in Figure 3.56 into worksheet B, called Actual.

	A	B	C	D	E	F	G	H
1	Caroline's budget							
2			Jan	Feb	Mar	Apr	May	Jun
3	Income							
4		Salary	1400	1400	1400	1400	1400	1400
5		Interest	20	20	20	20	20	20
6		Dividends	150	0	0	0	0	0
7								
8		Total Income						
9	Expenses							
10		Rent	550	550	550	550	550	550
11		Food	200	200	200	200	200	200
12		Automobile	320	100	100	100	100	100
13		Phone	100	100	100	100	100	100
14		Utilities	120	120	120	120	120	120
15		Entertainment	120	80	80	80	80	80
16		Loan Payment	60	60	60	60	60	60
17		Miscellaneous	100	50	50	50	50	50
18								
19		Total Expenses						
20								

Figure 3.55 *Update your worksheet to look like this one.*

Finally, enter the same text labels you have for worksheets A and B into worksheet C, called Difference. You will be entering formulas into this worksheet later.

Saving a Particular Range

Let's say you want to save a range as a separate file, perhaps in addition to keeping it as part of the current file. The Save As dialog box contains an option labeled Selected Range Only. To save only a particular range of your file, follow these steps:

1. Select the range you want to save.

2. From the File menu, select **Save As**.

    The Save As dialog box opens (see Figure 3.57).

3. Click in the square next to **Selected Range Only** or press **Alt+S**. Notice that an X appears in the box, indicating that it has been chosen.

4. Fill out the rest of the Save As dialog box appropriately to identify a new name and location for the file.

	A	B	C	D	E	F	G	H
			Jan	Feb	Mar	Apr	May	Jun
1	Caroline's Budget							
2			Jan	Feb	Mar	Apr	May	Jun
3	Income:							
4		Salary	1438	1438	1438	1438	1438	1438
5		Interest	22	22	22	22	22	22
6		Dividends	150	0	0	200	0	0
7								
8		Total Income						
9	Expenses:							
10		Rent	550	550	550	550	550	550
11		Food	220	195	207	202	198	200
12		Automobile	330	50	80	110	120	120
13		Phone	130	117	120	100	105	109
14		Utilities	125	100	97	90	110	122
15		Entertainment	100	98	90	80	80	100
16		Loan Payment	60	60	60	60	60	60
17		Miscellaneous	67	25	40	50	90	60
18								
19		Total Expenses						
20								

Figure 3.56 *Enter these values into worksheet B, Actual.*

5. Click **OK** to complete the job.

You also can select the range after opening the dialog box if you prefer.

To deselect this option, just repeat step 3. The X disappears from the box, indicating that it is no longer a selected feature.

Combining Files

You may have noticed that the Open File dialog box contains a button labeled Combine. This option enables you to combine the data from another file into the current file. You can combine selected ranges or the entire files. Three combine actions are available: Replace, Add, and Subtract. Replace overwrites the values in the current file with the values from the other file. You might, for example, want to replace your Automobile expenses for April, May, and June with more accurate ones from a different accounting file. The Add function adds the values from the other file to the comparable values in the current file. You might, for example, have compiled some additional automobile expenses in another worksheet; you can add them to the current worksheet's figures by selecting both ranges and using the Add function of the Combine command. The Subtract function is much like the Add function except that it subtracts the other file's values from the current file's.

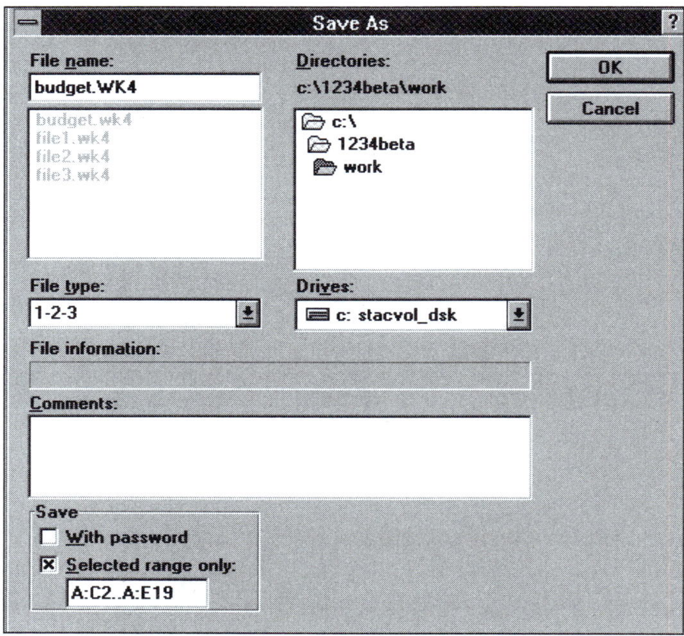

Figure 3.57 *Save As dialog box.*

When you select this function, the data in your current file is changed. Data from the file you select will replace, be added to, or be subtracted from the values in your current file. Plan to be especially careful when using the Combine function. If you discover that you made a mistake, you can undo it immediately by choosing the **Undo** command from the Edit menu. If you don't undo it immediately, you might be able to get back to your old data by closing the file without saving it. If that fails, you may have to fall back to a backup version of the file. (See your backup program for instructions on how to do that.)

To combine files, follow these steps:

1. Position the cursor in the first cell of the current file that you want to be replaced with the combined data.

2. From the File menu, select **Open**.

3. Choose the file you want to combine with your current active file by confirming the drive, file type, and name information (this is the same way you select a file to open).

4. Click the **Combine** button. The Combine dialog box is displayed (see Figure 3.57).

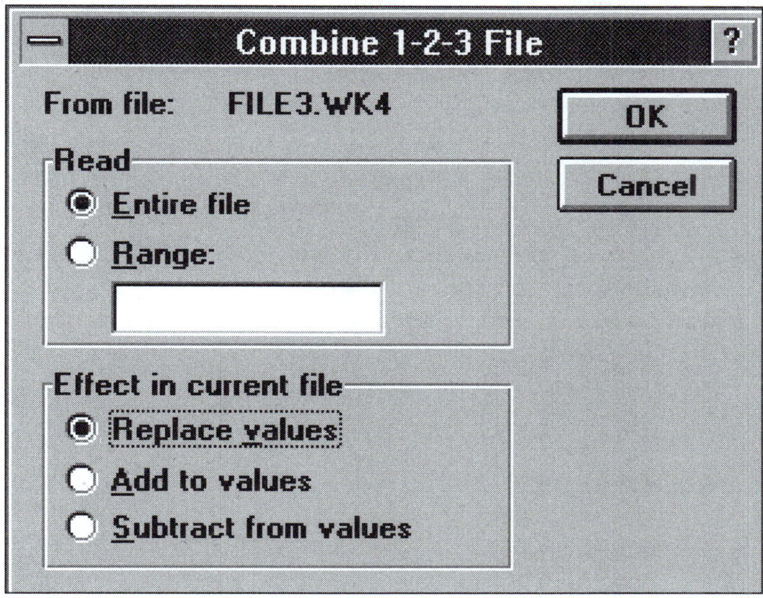

Figure 3.57 *Combine dialog box.*

5. Select the range of cells from the second file that you want to combine into the current file.

6. Select whether you want Lotus 1-2-3 to replace, add to, or subtract from the current values.

When adding or subtracting values, text values are ignored.

7. Click **OK**.

To Sum Up

You have covered a great deal in this chapter about using worksheets. You have learned to identify a cell, a range of cells, and a cell collection, whether they are all in one worksheet, on different worksheets, or even in different files. You also learned to name these ranges and collections.

You have taught yourself to use keyboard commands or the mouse to go to a range or a collection, and also can locate cells using special functions, such as Go To and Navigator. Finally, you can alter the way your screen looks, to see more or less of your worksheet, or to see both ends of it at once.

We discussed the issues relating to traveling around the worksheet and the task of entering data, noting the different kinds of data and how each different type of data is entered. You also learned how to get the program to enter a series.

Finally, you learned about editing the data you entered, by changing it, moving it, or copying it. You learned to edit your worksheet by inserting or deleting areas, finding terms and automatically replacing them with new terms, and checking your spelling. And you have learned to save a range as a separate file and to combine the values in two files.

What You Learned

Select a range with the mouse:

> Hold down the mouse button and drag the mouse from the first cell to highlight the other cells to be included in the range.

Select a range with the keyboard:

1. Use the arrow keys to position the active cell where you want to begin your range.
2. Hold down the **Shift** key.
3. Use the arrows to expand the range up or down, to the left or right of the active cell.

Extend a range:

> Hold down the **Shift** key and use the arrows to continue the range where you left off.

Select a range before choosing a command:

1. Click the mouse to select a desired range.

2. Go to the menu bar and select the command you want to perform. (The dialog box indicates the range you just selected.)

3. Follow the directions in the dialog box to execute that function. It will apply to the selected range.

Select a range after choosing a command:

1. Go to the menu bar and select the command you want.

2. The Font dialog box appears. The Range box indicates the currently active cell.

3. Click the button next to the **Range** box that has an arrow over it. This button is the **Range Selector**.

    When you click on the button, the dialog box disappears and you are back in your worksheet with the range selection cursor.

4. Select the range.

    When you release the mouse button or press **Enter**, the dialog box returns. Notice that the range box now reveals that the range is B4...D11.

5. Now you can choose the command that you want to apply to this range.

Select a collection of cells:

1. Click the mouse on the first cell you want selected.

2. Hold down the **Ctrl** key.

3. Click on the next cell you want to select.

4. Continue holding the **Ctrl** key to select as many cells as you want.

5. To deselect a cell, continue to hold down the **Ctrl** key and click on the cell you don't want selected.

    Notice that the last cell you click is white and outlined—it is the active cell. The other cells are highlighted

Select cells in a 3D range:

1. Select the desired range or collection from the first worksheet.
2. Hold down the **Ctrl** key.
3. Select the desired range or collection from the next worksheet, and so on.

Name a range:

1. Select the range or collection you want.
2. From the Range menu, select **Name**.

    The Name dialog box opens. Notice that the dialog box indicates the range you have just chosen.
3. Type the name you choose into the Name box and click **Add**.
4. Click **OK**.

Find cells using Go To:

1. From the Edit menu, select **Go To**.

    You will see the Go To dialog box.
2. Type the desired range into the box that now displays your current cell address.

    You also can use **Go To** to go automatically to one cell instead of a range.
3. Click **OK**.

Find cells using the Navigator:

1. Click on the **Navigator** icon on the edit bar.
2. Select the named range you want from the drop-down list.

Split Views of the screen:

1. From the View menu, select **Split**.

    You will see the Split dialog box.
2. Choose either **Horizontal** or **Vertical**.

3. Click **OK**.

Clear a Split screen:

> From the View menu, select **Clear Split**.

Freeze titles on a screen:

1. Select the first cell that should not be frozen.
2. From the View menu, select **Freeze Titles**.
   You will see the Freeze Titles dialog box.
3. You can freeze titles for either rows, columns, or both by selecting the appropriate button.
4. Click **OK**.

Clear frozen titles:

> From the View menu, select **Clear Titles**.

Enter data into a cell:

1. Click the mouse or use the arrow keys to select the cell you want.
2. Type the data into the space provided.

Enter data into the edit line:

1. Select the cell into which you want to enter data.
2. Click the mouse in the edit line.
3. Type the data in the space provided.

Fill a range with a series:

1. Select the range in which you will enter the series.
2. From the Range menu, select **Fill**.
   You will see the **Fill** dialog box.
3. Choose the desired interval by clicking on the radio button next to the name.

4. Enter a starting point, an increment, and, if necessary, a stopping point.

   If your selected range is less than the stopping point, Lotus 1-2-3 will automatically stop when your range ends.

5. Click **OK**.

Fill a range by example:

1. Go to a cell in a range that contains the beginning of a pattern.

2. Select that range.

3. From the Range menu, select **Fill by Example**.

Drag and fill a range by example:

1. Select the cell that contains the beginning of the pattern.

2. Move the pointer to the lower right corner of the selected cell(s), until it turns into the drag-and-fill pointer.

3. Drag to select the range.

Edit data in a cell:

1. Double-click with the mouse on the cell to activate it.

   The cursor appears at the end of the data currently in the cell.

3. Use the mouse or the arrows to alter your data.

Edit data on the edit line:

1. Click on the cell with the mouse.

2. Click on the edit line.

3. The cursor appears on the edit line at the end of your entry, and you can edit your data.

Clear data from a cell or range:

1. Select the cell or range.

2. Press **Delete**.

   This operation deletes data from your worksheet. Make sure that you really want to delete the specified range of data. Choose Undo to retrieve the data if you need to.

Move data using cut and paste:

1. Select the cell or range.
2. From the Edit menu, choose **Cut** (or press **Ctrl+X**).
3. Move the cursor to the new cell or range in which you want the old data.
4. From the Edit menu, choose **Paste** (or press **Ctrl+V**).

Move data with the mouse:

1. Select the cell or range.
2. Position the mouse so that the cursor is on one of the edges of the range. The cursor changes shape and now looks like a hand.
3. Click and hold the mouse while you drag the selection to the new location. The hand drags an outline of your selected range as you move it.

Copy data using cut and paste:

1. Select a cell or range.
2. From the Edit menu, choose **Copy** (or press **Ctrl+C**).
3. Move the cursor to the new location for the data.
4. From the Edit menu, choose **Paste** (or press **Ctrl+V**).

Copy data using the mouse:

1. Select a cell or range.
2. Move the cursor over the edge of the range so that the cursor changes into a hand.
3. Hold down the **Ctrl** key while clicking on and dragging the mouse to move the selection to a new location. Notice that the hand has a + sign in it this time. This tells you that Lotus 1-2-3 Release 5 is moving a copy of your selection to the new location.

Copy data using Copy Right and Copy Down:

1. Select a range. The first cell in the range should contain the data to be copied.

2. From the Edit menu, select **Copy Right**.

    1-2-3 takes the contents of the left-most cell and copies it to all cells to the right in the selected range.

    Copy Down performs the same kind of function, except that it copies the uppermost cell to all the cells below it in the selected range.

Insert a column or row:

1. Click on a column heading to select the entire column.

2. From the Edit menu, select **Insert**.

    The program inserts a column to the left of your selection.

Delete a column or row:

1. Click on the column heading you want to delete to select the entire column.

2. From the Edit menu, select **Delete**.

    When you delete a column, you are erasing all the data in that column. Always make sure that is what you want to do.

Shift cells:

1. Select a range.

2. From the Edit menu, select **Insert**.

    The Insert dialog box appears.

3. If you want the cells to move down, select **Row**.

    If you want the cells to shift to the right, select **Column**. In either case, make sure that you select **Insert Selection**.

5. Click **OK**.

Delete cells and their data:

1. Select a range.

2. From the Edit menu, select **Delete**.

   The Delete dialog box appears.

3. Select **Column** and **Delete Selection**.

   This function erases any values in the selected range. Make sure that you want to delete this selection.

4. Click **OK**.

Find a term:

1. From the Edit menu, select **Find & Replace**.

   The Find & Replace dialog box appears.

2. Type the term to find into the **Search For** box.

3. Check that the Action is set to **Find**.

4. Select the places to search: **All Worksheets** or **Selected Range**.

5. Choose the type of cells to search: **Labels**, **Formulas** or both.

6. Click **OK**.

   The Find dialog box appears. 1-2-3 shows the cell where it found your search term.

7. Either click on the **Find Next** button to move to the next occurrence or click on **Close**.

   You will be alerted when the last occurrence of your search term is found.

8. Click **OK**.

Replace a term:

1. From the Edit menu, select **Find & Replace**.

   The Find & Replace dialog box appears.

2. Type the term to find in the **Search For** box.

3. Click with the mouse to activate **Replace With**.

4. Type the term to replace with into the **Replace With** box.

5. Select the places to search for the original term.

6. Select the type of cells to search: **Labels**, **Formulas** or both.

7. Click **OK**.

   The Replace dialog box appears. 1-2-3 selects the cell where it found your search term.

8. Use the mouse to **Replace** it with the new term, **Replace All** occurrences with the new term, Find the Next occurrence without replacing this one, or close the dialog box.

   If you choose **Replace All**, 1-2-3 replaces all occurrences of your search term without asking for your approval. If you select **Replace All** accidentally, immediately go to Edit and select **Undo**.

   You are alerted when the last occurrence of your search term is found.

9. Click **OK**.

Check spelling:

1. From the Tools menu, select **Spell Check**.

2. Select the location for the spell check.

3. Click **OK**.

   The Spell Check dialog box appears. The unknown word will appear at the top of the dialog box. Below, 1-2-3 suggests alternative spellings for this selection.

4. Either select an alternative from the list or type one yourself on the **Replace With** line.

5. Select **Replace**, **Replace All**, **Skip**, or **Skip All**.

   If you select **Replace All**, every occurrence of this word will be replaced.

9. If you want, click with the mouse on **Add Dictionary** to teach the word to Lotus 1-2-3 Release 5.

   You are alerted when the Spell Check is complete.

Save a range:

1. Select a range.

2. From the File menu, select **Save As**.

3. Click **Selected Range Only**.

4. Fill out the rest of the dialog box to identify the file name and location.

5. Click **OK**.

Combine files:

1. Position the cursor in the first cell to be combined.

2. From the File menu, select **Open**.

3. Choose another file and click **Combine**.

   The Combine dialog box opens.

4. Choose the range to be combined, if any, and select **Replace** values, **Add to Values**, or **Subtract from Values**.

5. Click **OK**.

Chapter 4

Formatting Worksheets

Now that you have learned how to enter and edit your data on a worksheet, you can teach yourself to do all sorts of things that will give your worksheet a professional look. This chapter covers formatting functions that personalize your worksheet and make it clear and easy to read. As we go through the various options available, you will see that there are many functions to choose from. After you experiment with the different fonts, styles, colors, and lines, you will find attributes that you like best. As you read this chapter, you learn how to:

- Change fonts, font styles, and the color of your text.
- Format in a way that affects all your worksheets at once.
- Alter the number and date formats.
- Change the cell alignment to
    - Align horizontally or vertically
    - Extend the text across columns
    - Wrap text that would not otherwise fit in a cell
    - Change the text orientation

- Change column width and row height.

- Add borders, outlines, and designer frames to your cells.

- Change the colors of your cells.

- Use a pop-up menu to save time.

- Create and apply named styles to format worksheets the way you like.

- Choose from a variety of pre-formatted Gallery templates to format worksheets.

- Hide areas of the worksheet that are private.

Changing Fonts and Attributes

One of the ways that you can improve the look of your worksheet is to change the fonts and attributes that you use to create it. The fonts are the typefaces of the characters that you see on the screen[md]the way the letters look. Depending on your computer and printer, you may have any number of different fonts available. But in general, there are two main categories of fonts: serif and sans-serif. A serif font is a typeface that has tiny hanging edges on each of the letters. For example, the fonts called Times and Courier, shown in Figure 4.1, are serif fonts.

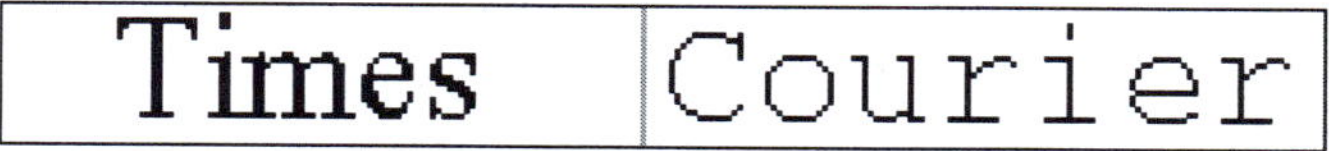

Figure 4.1 *Serif fonts.*

If you look at the edges of the letters, you will notice that they have little extensions that hang off the edges. By contrast, fonts that are sans serif (which means without serifs), like Helvetica and Arial, do not have those hanging edges. Some sans serif fonts are shown in Figure 4.2. Notice that these fonts have smooth edges.

Each font can also appear in different styles. A font style is a particular formatting, such as bold, italic, underline, and so on. These attributes can be applied to any font (see Figure 4.3).

Figure 4.2 *Sans-serif fonts.*

Figure 4.3 *Different styles on a font.*

Deciding which font to use is a matter of personal preference. You may like the appearance of a certain font, or decide that a particular font is most appropriate to the task at hand. One guideline may be helpful: If your spreadsheet contains many numbers, it is usually considered easier to read if a sans serif font is used. Because this type of font has smooth edges, the characters do not "run together." Sans serif fonts are especially useful when the font size is small.

You can use one typeface for a particular set of data and choose another for the rest of the worksheet. If you like, you can use multiple fonts and styles on your file. You could even have all your cells display different fonts, or even change fonts within one cell. But we recommend that you do not go wild with the fonts. The more fonts you use, the more complex your document becomes when it is time to print. For some printers, using many fonts creates difficulties or slows down the print job. This can be annoying, because you'll think you're almost done with a file, but it seems to take forever to print the job. Limiting your fonts usually speeds along the printing.

Another reason to limit your use of fonts is that readers of your spreadsheet may become confused by an abundance of different fonts as they try to decode what the different fonts signify. We suggest that you use only a handful of fonts in any particular worksheet. To create differentiations in your characters, you can use different styles of a particular font. This function is discussed later in this chapter.

Furthermore, as you adjust fonts, try to group them into categories. You can use one font for all your headings, another for all numbers, and so on, thus creating the font conventions that will apply to your entire file. If you do otherwise, you risk confusing the reader.

Now that you know about dialog boxes and selecting ranges and cells, it will be easy to change fonts. In fact, the examples used at the beginning of Chapter 3 also cover how to change a font and attribute.

All the formatting aspects for fonts are located in the Font & Attributes dialog box, located in the Style menu (see Figure 4.4).

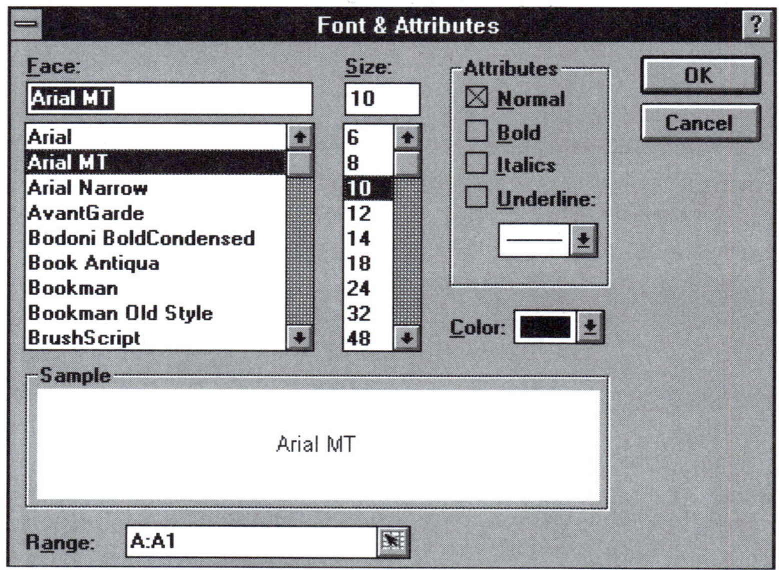

Figure 4.4 *Font & Attributes dialog box.*

This dialog box is split into six sections with different elements and options. Let's start at the bottom and work clockwise around the window. At the bottom of the dialog box is the Range Selector (seen in earlier chapters). Remember, you can either select a range of cells, and then go to the Font & Attributes dialog box, or first go to the dialog box, and then select a range.

Above the Range Selector is the Sample box. This space is used to show you how the font you have chosen will appear in your worksheet. Currently, it says Arial MT. This text changes as you change the font, its size, its attributes, or style and color.

Above the Sample box is the Font or Face Selector. This consists of a scrolling list of typefaces. The space above this list shows the currently selected font name. The typefaces displayed in this list will vary from computer to computer, depending on the fonts you have purchased and installed. Many software companies sell additional typefaces; you can purchase them if you feel the need to increase your font options. You can choose a font either by using the mouse to click on a font name, or by typing the name of a font in the space above the list.

To the right of the Font Selector is the Size Selector. This function lets you change the size of the font. Again, you can do this by clicking on a size with the mouse, or by typing a size into the space above the scrolling list.

Next to the Size Selector is the Attribute Selector. Here you can change the font style from normal to any combination of bold, italic, or underline. Notice that there is a pull-down list below the underline choice. If you click with the mouse on this arrow, 1-2-3 displays three types of underlining, as shown in Figure 4.5.

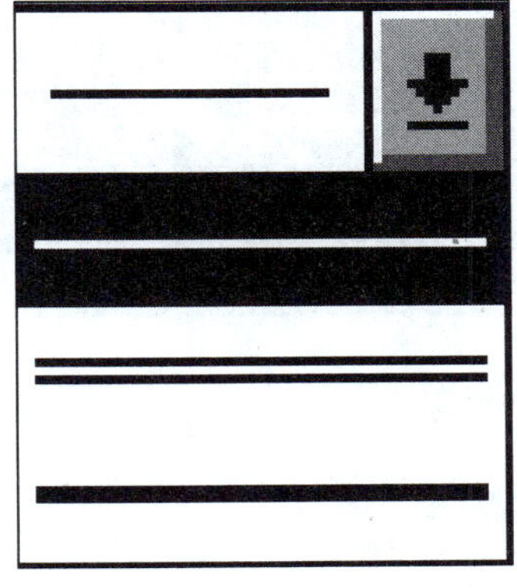

Figure 4.5 *Three types of underlining.*

You have the option to underline a word or other data entry with a single line, a thicker single line, or a double line.

The different options for cell borders are discussed later. The underlining function applies to the data in a cell, not to the cell border itself.

Finally, below the Attribute Selector is the Color Selector. Like the underline attribute, the Color Selector has an arrow that shows you a pull-down list. If you click on the arrow, you see the choices for colors (see Figure 4.6).

These color choices differ depending on your computer. Some computers and color monitors have the capability to display more colors than others. Once this palette of colors appears, you can use the mouse to click on any square to select that particular color. Some monochromatic computer systems display various shades of gray.

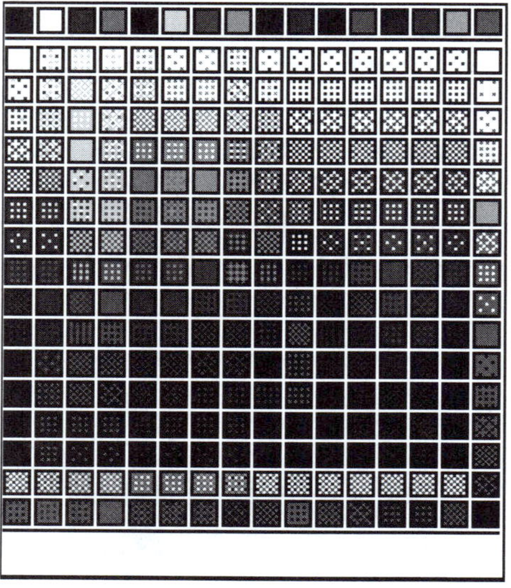

Figure 4.6 *Color choices.*

All of the options in the Font & Attribute dialog box are there to let you enhance your worksheet. Feel free to experiment with different fonts and styles to determine what you like best.

Now, return to your example worksheet to try out the different formatting techniques you just learned. Let's first change the font of the title, Caroline's Budget, in the Budget worksheet (worksheet A).

To change the font, complete the following steps:

1. Select cell **A:A1**.

2. From the Style menu, choose **Font & Attributes**.

   Remember that you can switch steps 1 and 2 if you would rather use the **Range Selector** in the Font dialog box.

   The Font dialog box appears.

3. Choose a serif font, using the mouse to highlight and click, or by typing its name.

   In the example, Times Roman has been chosen. If you don't have this font, look at the Sample box as you click with the mouse on different typefaces until you see a serif font.

4. Change the size to **24**.

5. Choose **Bold**.

6. Change the color to **Blue**.

7. Click **OK**.

Now the title on worksheet Budget has a different face, style, size, and color (see Figure 4.7).

	A	B	C	D	E	F	G	H
1	Caroline's budget							
2			Jan	Feb	Mar	Apr	May	Jun
3	Income							
4		Salary	1400	1400	1400	1400	1400	1400
5		Interest	20	20	20	20	20	20
6		Dividends	150	0	0	0	0	0
7								
8		Total Income						
9	Expenses							
10		Rent	550	550	550	550	550	550
11		Food	200	200	200	200	200	200
12		Automobile	320	100	100	100	100	100
13		Phone	100	100	100	100	100	100
14		Utilities	120	120	120	120	120	120
15		Entertainment	120	80	80	80	80	80
16		Loan Payment	60	60	60	60	60	60
17		Miscellaneous	100	50	50	50	50	50
18								
19		Total Expenses						

Figure 4.7 *Caroline's Budget font changes.*

An easy way to change the font face or font size is to click on these respective sections on the status bar (see Figure. 4.7 and 4.8). When you click on either of these sections, a pop-up list appears. By selecting from the list, you can quickly change the font or size for your selected cell or range. An easy way to select bold, italic, or a single underline is to click the appropriate SmartIcon.

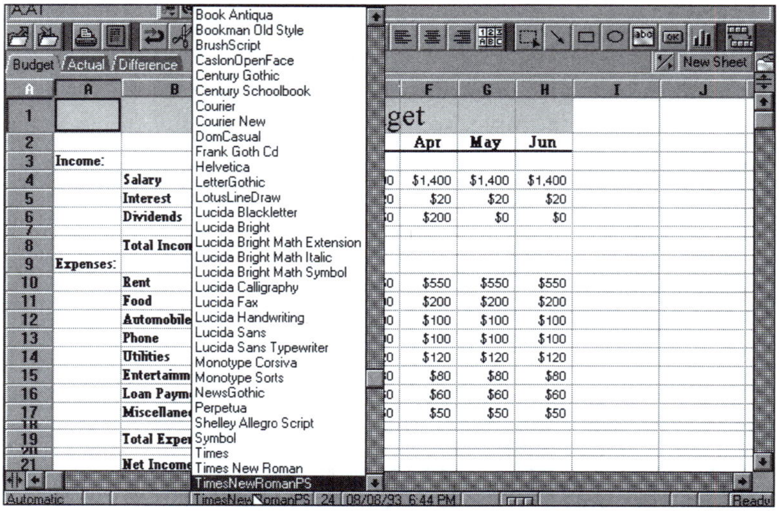

Figure 4.8 *Pop-up font list on the status bar.*

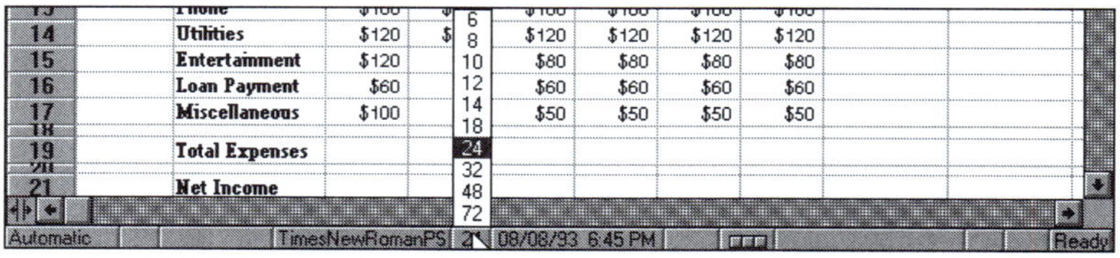

Figure 4.9 *Pop-up size list on the status bar.*

Group Mode

Now you have changed cell A1 on worksheet A, Budget. There are, however, two more worksheets that have not changed. The font changes you made affected only the first worksheet.

Suppose that you want to make changes that would affect all the worksheets. There are two ways to do this. First, you can manually go through each worksheet and make the same changes over and over again. If, however, you are working on a file with 80 worksheets, that process would become pretty tedious. Therefore, Lotus 1-2-3 Release 5 has created an easier way to perform these operations, called Group Mode.

The Group Mode command can be found in the Style menu in the Worksheet Defaults dialog box (see Figure 4.10).

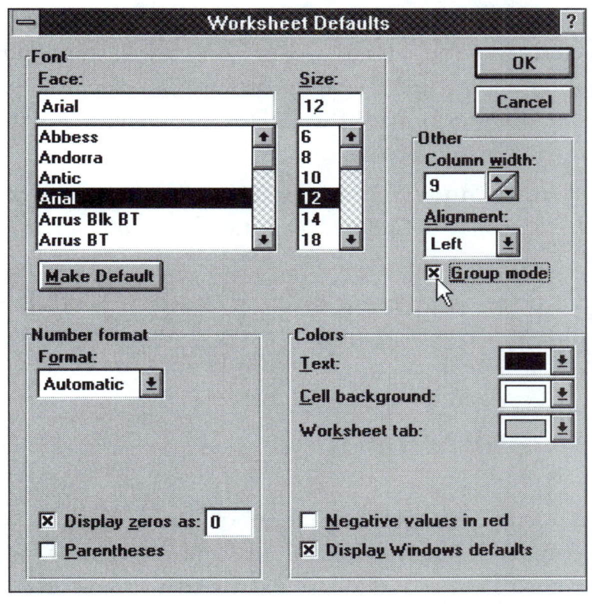

Figure 4.10 *Group mode on Worksheet Defaults dialog box.*

The other options in this dialog box are discussed in Appendix B, "Customizing Lotus 1-2-3."

After you select the **Group Mode** and click **OK**, 1-2-3 returns you to your file. Notice that the status bar at the bottom of your screen displays Group in the fourth box from the right (see Figure 4.11). Now, if you make a change to your worksheet, there is also a change in your other worksheets.

Figure 4.11 *Group mode list on the status bar.*

When you select **Group Mode**, all format changes that you make in one worksheet also appear on the other worksheets throughout your file. This means that if you delete rows, columns, or ranges of cells in one worksheet, they also are deleted in your other worksheets. Therefore, when using Group Mode, be careful when doing anything that can disrupt your other worksheets. Keep an eye on the status bar to determine whether Group Mode is selected.

Group Mode applies only to formatting. In other words, entering and editing data is not affected by Group Mode. Also, you can be working on any worksheet when making a formatting change in Group Mode. If, for example, you change some aspect of the format of the Actual worksheet, it will affect both the Budget and Difference worksheets.

Now, select **Group Mode** and follow the previous steps to change the Font and Attributes for Caroline's Budget. This time, the title changes on all three worksheets.

Once you are done with Group Mode, go back to Worksheet Defaults and deselect the **Group Mode** box.

Changing Number Formats

Suppose that you want to format your numbers. In Chapter 3, you learned that the default for Lotus 1-2-3 Release 5 automatically formats your numbers. That means, if you were to type **$100**, 1-2-3 knows that this is the number 100 formatted using the currency format. Similarly, if you type **5%**, the program knows that this is .05 formatted with the percent format.

Suppose, however, that you just typed plain numbers, as you did for your budget. Now you want to go back and format these numbers as currency or something else so their meaning would become apparent to the reader. To do this, you begin by opening the **Number Format** dialog box (see Figure 4.12).

This dialog box has three main sections. In the bottom left corner is the familiar Range Selector. Above this is the Format Selector. This is where you change the number format you want to apply. In the bottom right is the Sample box. Here, the contents of the active cell are displayed. As you change the format type, this box will display your cell's contents with that formatting. If you have selected a range of cells, the Sample box displays the first cell of the range. Table 4.1 shows a sample of some of the more common number formats available.

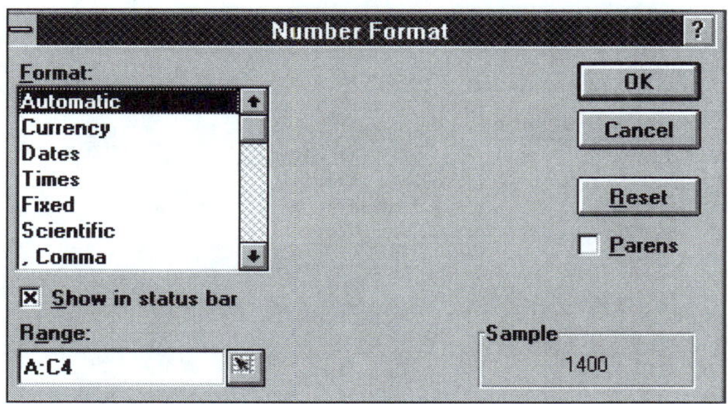

Figure 4.12 *Number Format dialog box.*

Table 4.1 *Number formats.*

Format	Sample
General	1400.00
Fixed (with two decimal places)	1400.00
Scientific (with two decimal places)	1.40E+03
Currency (with two decimal places)	$1400.00
Comma (with two decimal places)	1,400.00
Percent (with two decimal places)	140000.00%

Lotus 1-2-3 Release 5 also has some less common number formats, such as +/-. This format fills the cell with either +'s or -'s, depending on the value of the number in that cell.

You may notice in the table that some of the formats are followed by a parenthetical phrase that reveals the number of decimal places. In Figure 4.12, however, there was no visible option to change the number of decimal places. This is because Lotus 1-2-3 Release 5 displays this option only for the number formats that are capable of using it. Therefore, if you select **Currency Format** in the Number Format dialog box, another option appears that enables you to change the number of decimal places (see Figure 4.13), as well as the currency symbol you want to appear in the selected cells.

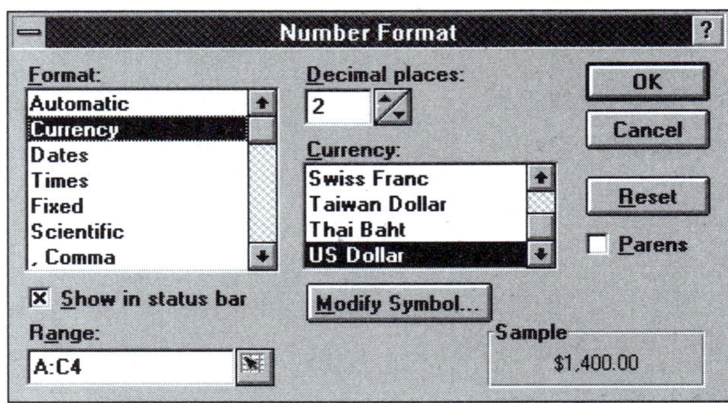

Figure 4.13 *Number of Decimal Places option.*

You can change the number of decimal places by clicking on the up or down arrows to increase or decrease the number, respectively. Alternatively, you can type the desired number of decimal places into the box.

Now let's format some numbers in your worksheet. Follow these steps:

1. Select the collection **A:C4..A:H6** and **A:C10..A:H17**.

   Remember that to select a collection of cells, click and drag the mouse to select **A:C4..A:H6**, hold down the **Ctrl** key and select **A:C10..A:H17**.

2. From the Style menu, choose **Number Format**.

3. Select **Currency Format** with **0** decimal places.

4. Click **OK**.

Now the number values in your worksheet are formatted with a dollar sign and a comma for the thousands separator.

Notice that the first item on the status bar, at the far left, shows the name of the format for the current cell.

N O T E

The Number Format command is also used to format dates. If your worksheet has a date in it, you can change the way 1-2-3 displays that date. For example:

1. Go to an empty cell and type **02/21/73**.
2. Open the **Number Format** dialog box.

   Notice that the Sample box shows 02/21/73.
3. Select different **Date** formats in the dialog box and watch how the date in the Sample box is affected.
4. When you have finished, clear the cell in which you entered the date.

You can do the same thing with times as well as dates if you want to change the way Lotus 1-2-3 Release 5 displays times in your worksheet.

Changing Cell Alignment

Another formatting feature that you may want to change on your worksheet is the cell alignment. This is the way Lotus 1-2-3 displays data in a cell. The contents of a cell can be flush left, flush right, centered, and so on. Changing the alignment of data often makes it easier to read. If, for example, you are trying to look down a column, you may find it easier to center items in the column so that your eye has a "line" to follow down the column. How you decide to format your cell alignment depends entirely on your personal preference. There is no right or wrong way.

Remember that when you enter text with label-prefix characters, Lotus 1-2-3 Release 5 aligns your data based on the prefix character you choose. This character can be changed using the following methods described.

Cell alignment is adjusted from the Alignment dialog box inside the Style menu (see Figure 4.14) or from the SmartIcons.

There are many options from which to choose in the Alignment dialog box. In the bottom left corner is the ubiquitous Range Selector. In the top left corner of the dialog box is the Horizontal Alignment Selector. This option enables you to choose whether you want the data in the cell to be aligned flush left, centered, flush right, or evenly spaced throughout the cell. Another option, General, is the default for Lotus 1-2-3 Release 5. If this alignment is selected, numeric values are aligned to the right of the cell and text labels are aligned to the left. To choose one of the horizontal alignment options, simply click it. (Remember that you can use the Alt key plus the underlined letter in the option to select it without having to use the mouse.)

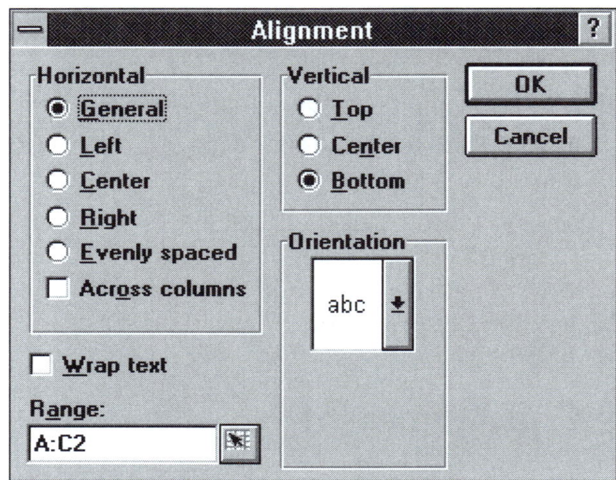

Figure 4.14 *Alignment dialog box.*

You can select left, center, or right alignment without opening the Alignment dialog box. Just click the appropriate SmartIcon.

Under the Evenly Spaced option is another option that displays across columns. This is used to align data horizontally across a specified range instead of in one cell. For example:

1. Select cell **A:A1**, your title cell.
2. From the Style menu, choose **Alignment**.
3. Choose the **Center Horizontal Alignment** option.
4. Click **OK**.

Notice how the title, Caroline's Budget, is not completely visible anymore. It is centered in a cell that is too small to fit the entire text (see Figure 4.15). To center data across a range, follow these steps:

1. Select the range **A:A1..A:H1**.
2. Open the **Alignment** dialog box from the Style menu.

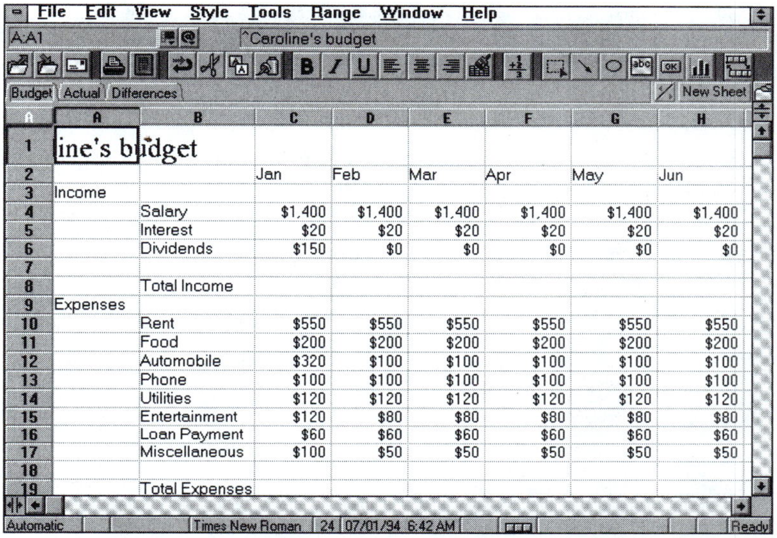

	A	B	C	D	E	F	G	H
1	ine's b	udget						
2			Jan	Feb	Mar	Apr	May	Jun
3	Income							
4		Salary	$1,400	$1,400	$1,400	$1,400	$1,400	$1,400
5		Interest	$20	$20	$20	$20	$20	$20
6		Dividends	$150	$0	$0	$0	$0	$0
7								
8		Total Income						
9	Expenses							
10		Rent	$550	$550	$550	$550	$550	$550
11		Food	$200	$200	$200	$200	$200	$200
12		Automobile	$320	$100	$100	$100	$100	$100
13		Phone	$100	$100	$100	$100	$100	$100
14		Utilities	$120	$120	$120	$120	$120	$120
15		Entertainment	$120	$80	$80	$80	$80	$80
16		Loan Payment	$60	$60	$60	$60	$60	$60
17		Miscellaneous	$100	$50	$50	$50	$50	$50
18								
19		Total Expenses						

Figure 4.15 *Center Horizontal Alignment of Caroline's Budget.*

3. Choose **Center** and **Across Columns**.
4. Click **OK**.

Now notice that the title, Caroline's Budget, is centered across columns A through H (see Figure 4.16). This function is especially useful when you want to center a title on your page.

Below the Horizontal Alignment Selector is the Wrap Text option. You use this option when data is too long to fit into a cell, but you don't want it to extend beyond the cell width. When you select Wrap Text, 1-2-3 displays as much text as will fit into the cell, and then it extends the row downward so that the rest of the text can fit below it. Although you will not be using this option now, Figure 4.17 shows an example of how text wrap would look. The column width was only wide enough to fit the word Caroline's, so Budget wrapped down below it.

To the right of the Horizontal Alignment Selector is the Vertical Alignment Selector. The options align data at the top, bottom, or center of the cell. Figure 4.18 demonstrates how vertical alignment would look. It shows three cells; one is aligned at the top, one is centered, and the last is aligned at the bottom.

Figure 4.16 *Caroline's Budget centered across columns.*

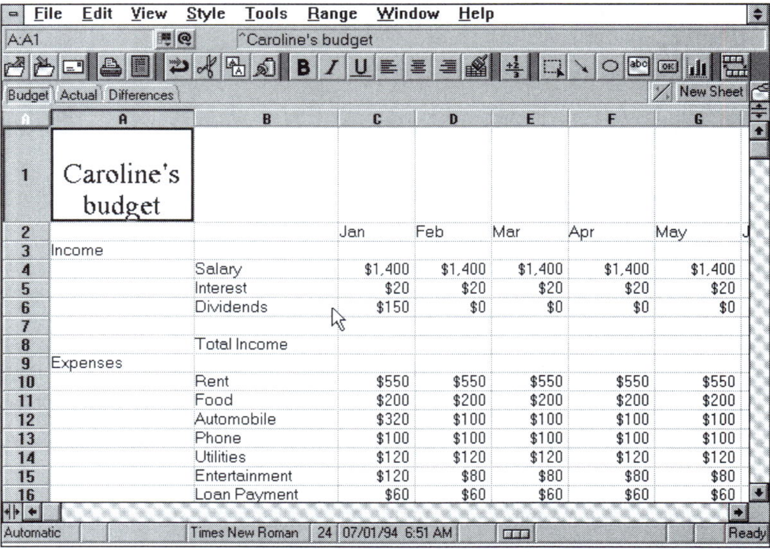

Figure 4.17 *An example of text wrap.*

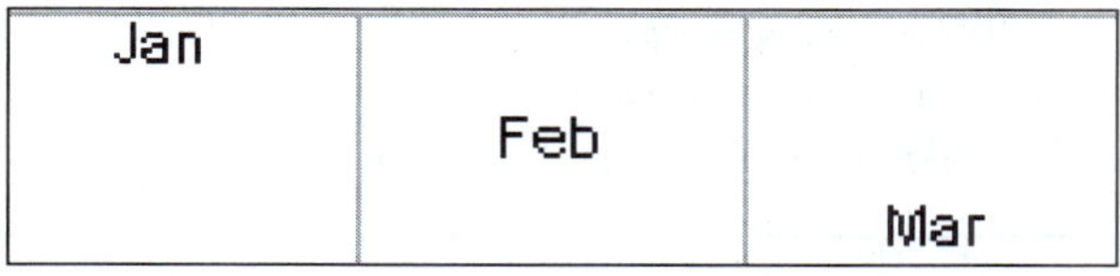

Figure 4.18 *An example of vertical alignment.*

Changing Column Width and Row Height

Sometimes a column is too narrow or a row too short for the data to fit. Or you may find that your rows and columns are bigger than you need. For this reason, Lotus 1-2-3 Release 5 enables you to adjust the column widths and row heights. There are two ways to do this.First, you can manually drag heading borders to resize the columns and rows. To change column width manually, follow these steps:

1. Move the cursor over the border of a column heading until the cursor changes shape (see Figure 4.19).

Figure 4.19 *Manually changing column widths.*

You resize a column by dragging its right border. Therefore, if you want to change the size of column C, you would move the cursor over the border between the letters C and D in the column heading.

2. Once the cursor changes shape, click and drag the mouse to the right to increase the size of the column or to the left to reduce its size.

    While you are dragging the column width, you will see a line that represents the new location for the right edge of the column (see Figure 4.20).

3. Release the mouse button when the column is the desired size.

The process for changing row height is similar. Instead of putting the mouse over the right edge of a column, however, you put it over the bottom edge of a row heading until it changes shape (see Figure 4.21).

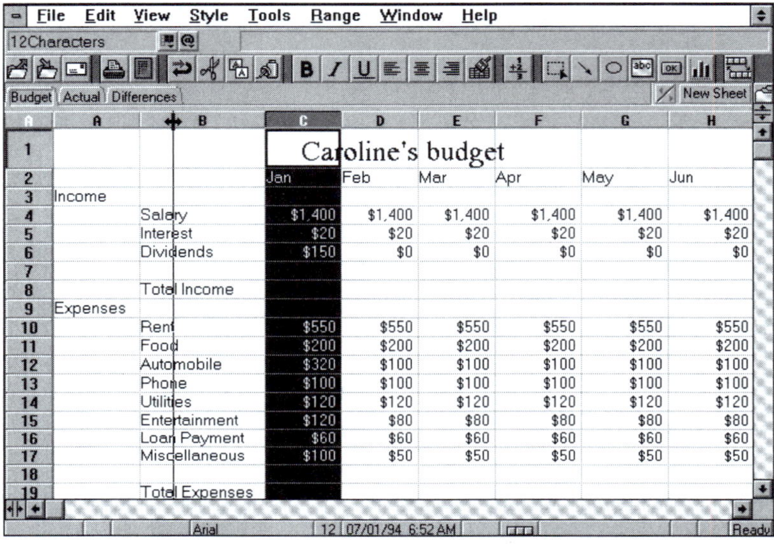

	A	B	C	D	E	F	G	H
1			Caroline's budget					
2			Jan	Feb	Mar	Apr	May	Jun
3	Income							
4		Salary	$1,400	$1,400	$1,400	$1,400	$1,400	$1,400
5		Interest	$20	$20	$20	$20	$20	$20
6		Dividends	$150	$0	$0	$0	$0	$0
7								
8		Total Income						
9	Expenses							
10		Rent	$550	$550	$550	$550	$550	$550
11		Food	$200	$200	$200	$200	$200	$200
12		Automobile	$320	$100	$100	$100	$100	$100
13		Phone	$100	$100	$100	$100	$100	$100
14		Utilities	$120	$120	$120	$120	$120	$120
15		Entertainment	$120	$80	$80	$80	$80	$80
16		Loan Payment	$60	$60	$60	$60	$60	$60
17		Miscellaneous	$100	$50	$50	$50	$50	$50
18								
19		Total Expenses						

Figure 4.20 *Manually widening column A.*

Figure 4.21 *Manually changing row height.*

Again, once the mouse changes shape, click and drag the mouse upward to shrink the row height, or downward to increase the row height.

Lotus 1-2-3 Release 5 also enables you to resize a column or row automatically. To automatically change a column width, follow these steps:

1.   Select the column you want to change.

2.   From the Style menu, choose **Column Width**.

The Column Width dialog box appears (see Figure 4.22).

This dialog box has three options. First, you can set the width to a particular number of characters. To do this, click on the up and down arrows or type the number into the box. Second, you can reset the column width to the default size. Third, you can have 1-2-3 automatically size the column so that it can fit the largest entry. You probably will want to use this option when you don't know the number of characters of the data that will be entered into your longest cell but you want to make sure that everything fits in the column width.

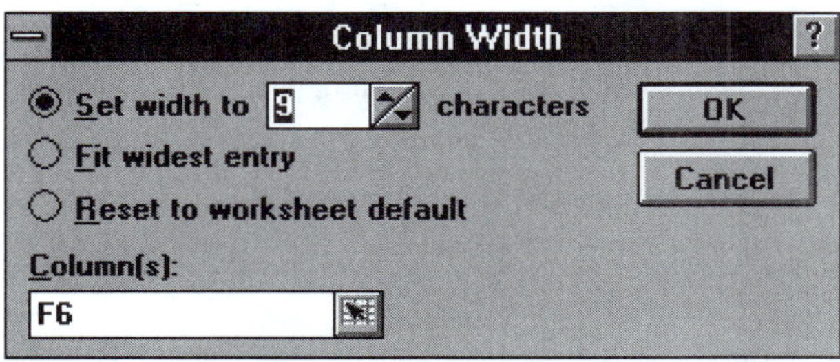

Figure 4.22 *Column Width dialog box.*

3. Select one of these options and click **OK**.

    If you double-click the right edge of a column heading, the column is automatically resized to fit the largest entry. If, for example, you click the border between columns C and D, column C is automatically resized to fit its largest entry.

Changing row height is very similar to changing column width. To change a row height, follow these steps:

1. Select the row you want to resize.

2. From the Style menu, choose **Row Height**.

    The Row Height dialog box appears (see Figure 4.23).

    When the Row Height dialog box is open, you have two options. You can tell 1-2-3 to size the row to a particular point size (which corresponds to font point sizes) or you can have 1-2-3 automatically size the row to fit the largest font in the row.

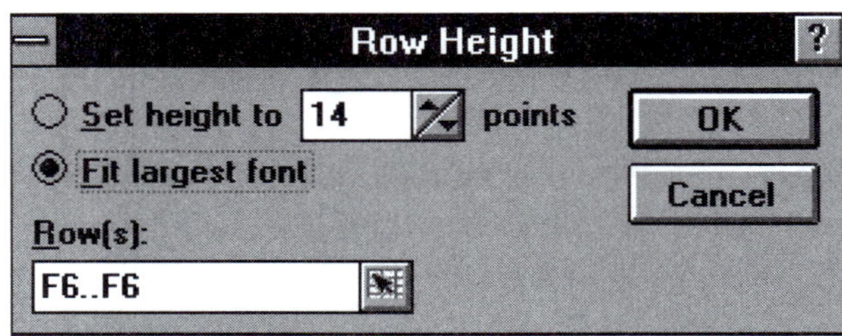

Figure 4.23 Row Height dialog box.

3. Select the option you want and click **OK**.

    As with column widths, if you double-click on the bottom edge of a row heading, 1-2-3 automatically resizes the row to fit the largest font size.

Adding Borders

Enhancing your worksheet with a border can make your data clearer. You may want to insert a border to separate certain columns or rows or to set apart a range from the rest of the worksheet. To add borders, go to the **Style** menu and open the **Lines & Color** dialog box (see Figure 4.24). Right now, we are concerned with the lower half of this dialog box (the top half, which is used to change colors, is discussed shortly).

When you add a border, you can add it to the bottom, top, left, or right of all selected cells. To show an example, let's put a bottom border under all the months in the budget. To insert a border, follow these steps:

1. Select the range **A:C2..A:H2**.

2. From the Style menu, choose **Lines & Colors**.

    The Lines & Colors dialog box appears.

3. Look at the area of the dialog box that displays Border. Here, you have the option to select the type of border you want. Choose on the type of border you want. In this example, **Bottom Border** was selected.

    Next, you can choose the line style and color of your border. As in other dialog boxes, you select these by clicking on the down arrow and choosing your option from a list.

4. Select the line style (a thick single line in this example).

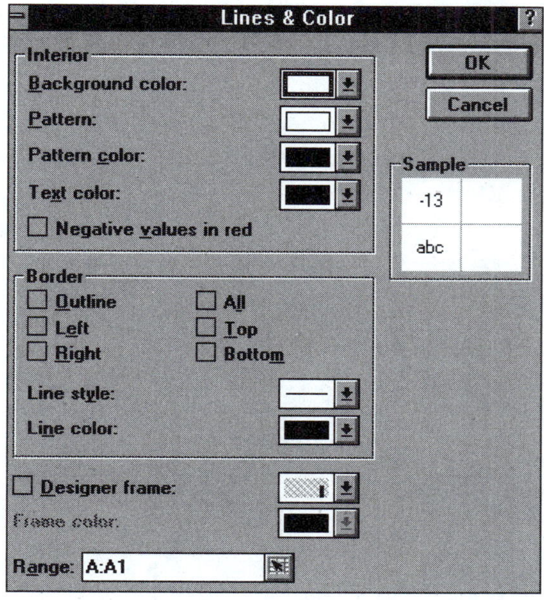

Figure 4.24 *Lines & Color dialog box.*

5. Select the line color (red in this example).

8. Click **OK**.

By looking at the Sample box you can see how the selection will look.

You can also have 1-2-3 create an outline box to separate a selected range of cells. To put an outline box around a range of cells, follow these steps:

1. Select the range **A:C2..A:H2**.

2. Go to the Style menu and open the **Lines & Colors** dialog box.

3. Choose **Outline** and select the line type and color you want.

4. Click **OK**.

Notice that by choosing **Outline**, 1-2-3 put a box around the selected range and set it apart from your other data.

If you had selected **All** for the range, the program would have put a left, right, top, and bottom border on every cell. In the example, by selecting

Outline, 1-2-3 equipped the left-most cell in the range with a top, left, and bottom border, put a top, right, and bottom border on the right-most cell, and put just top and bottom borders on the middle cells.

1-2-3 also has another feature called Designer Frames. These are pre-designed borders that are fancier than the standard choices. Figure 4.25 shows the different designer frame choices.

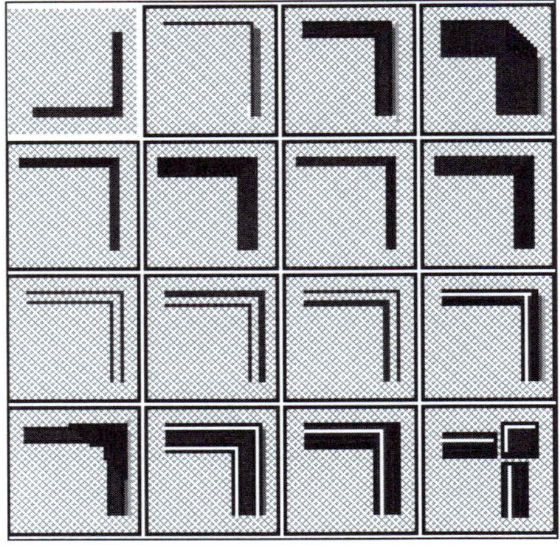

Figure 4.25 *Designer frames.*

Designer frames can be applied only as outlines. In other words, you cannot use a designer frame just for a bottom border.

To apply designer frames, follow these steps:

1. Select the range you want to frame.
2. Go to the Style menu and open the **Lines & Colors** dialog box.
3. Use the mouse to scroll down the list of possible **Designer Frames** and colors and choose the one you want.
4. Click **OK**.

Figure 4.26 shows an example of how a designer frame might look.

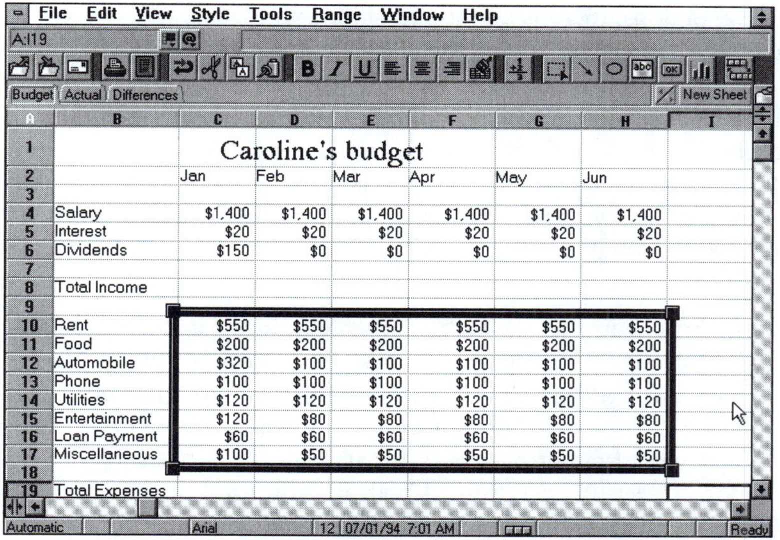

Figure 4.26 *Sample Designer Frame.*

Changing Colors

Now that you have taught yourself to alter the border of your cells, you can move on to enhancing the cells themselves. One feature of the Lines & Colors dialog box enables you to add color backgrounds and patterns to the inside of your cells. To apply a color background and pattern, follow these steps:

1. Select a range of cells.

2. Go to the Style menu and open the **Lines & Colors** dialog box.

3. Choose a background color from the list you activate by clicking with the mouse on the down arrow next to Background Color.

4. Use the same steps to select a pattern for the cell.

5. Choose a color for the pattern.

6. Choose a color for the text in that range of cells.

7. Click **OK**.

Within these options, there is an infinite number of combinations you can use to embellish your worksheet. You can select a color with no pattern, colored text with a plain background, or any number of possible changes. You may find a particular style you like best and continue to use it on all your worksheets, or you can change the colors and patterns frequently. In any case, it is best not to go wild with patterns and colors. The key is for your work to be readable. These features can enhance your worksheet, but if you use them all at once, a spreadsheet with professional data may end up looking very unprofessional. Use your judgment.

Another feature in the dialog box is called Negative Values in Red. If you want 1-2-3 to display any negative values in red, choose this feature, which is located right under the Text Color option. By choosing to represent negative values in red, you can see on your budget, quite literally, if you are "in the red." If, however, you would rather not have that unfortunate fact show so clearly, you can opt not to select this feature and both negative and positive values are displayed in the same color, whatever you designated.

The Right Mouse Button

1-2-3 enables you to use a shortcut to access the different formatting options. If you click the right mouse button, 1-2-3 displays a pop-up menu wherever your cursor is (see Figure 4.27).

This is helpful when you are selecting a range of cells and you don't want to go back up to the menu bar to access menu choices. In the pop-up box, 1-2-3 displays the most common features you would choose to perform on your selection. Most of these commands relate to formatting.

Using Named Styles

You may grow to like a particular formatting and use it over and over consistently on a particular file. In such a case, it is helpful to create a named style for that format. A named style is a collection of formatting options that you can name and call on at a later date by its name. This is similar to naming a range so that you can easily go back to it. The philosophy behind this kind of option is that if you use something often enough, whether it be a range or a formatting style, you should be able to name it and refer to it easily instead of having to select it manually each time it is needed.

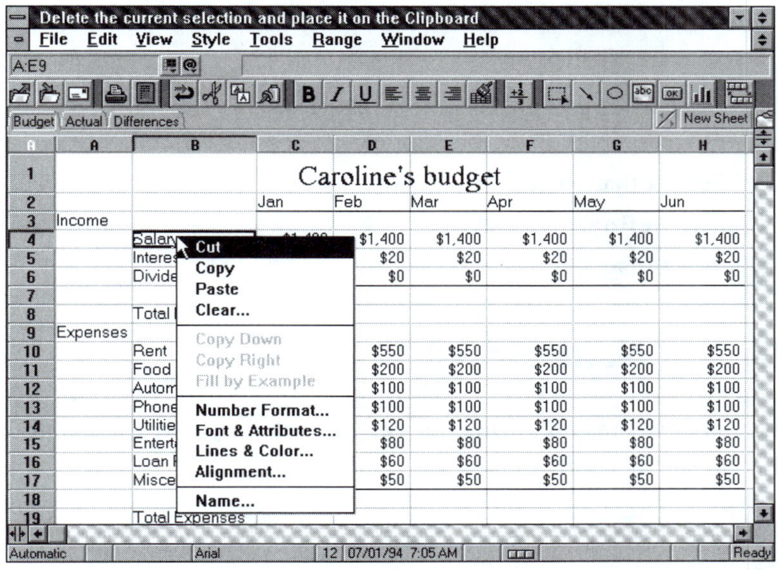

Figure 4.27 *Pop-up menu.*

You may, for example, frequently center your text and put a bottom border on the cell. If this were the case, you could create a named style featuring those options. By using a named style, you can just tell 1-2-3 to apply those features as a default to your selection instead of manually applying all of the attributes.

When you define certain cells with a named style, you can reformat quickly. You can change the definition of your named style and all the cells defined by it will change automatically. If, for example, you decide to change the text color from black to blue, you can redefine your named style to include this new characteristic and 1-2-3 will automatically change the text color of all the cells defined by that named style.

Creating a Named Style

To create a named style, you must first format a cell with the attributes you want. In this example, you format a cell with Times font, 12 point, bold, blue center horizontal alignment, and a bottom border.

To create a named style incorporating these characteristics, follow these steps:

1. Format a cell with the desired characteristics.
2. Select the formatted cell.
3. From the Style menu, select **Named Style**.

    The Named Style dialog box appears (see Figure 4.28).
4. In the box that displays Style Name, type in a name for the style.
5. Choose **Define**.
6. Choose **Close**.

Applying a Named Style

Now that you have created a named style, apply that style to a cell or to a range of cells:

1. Select the cell or range of cells to which you want to apply the named style.
2. From the Style menu, open the **Named Style** dialog box.
3. Select the named style you want from the list.
4. Click **OK**.

The selection you chose is now defined by the particular named style. If you change the named style at all, every cell that is defined by that named style will change automatically.

Using the Gallery

To make your life even easier, 1-2-3 has predefined styles that are stored in the Gallery. The contents of the Gallery dialog box, found in the Style menu, are shown in Figure 4.29.

On the left side of this dialog box is a scrolling list of templates that are pre-programmed and can be applied to your worksheet like named styles. When you click on the name of the template, 1-2-3 shows you a sample of this template in the box next to the name list. You can play around with the different gallery templates to see which ones you like and which ones are most suited to your worksheet's needs.

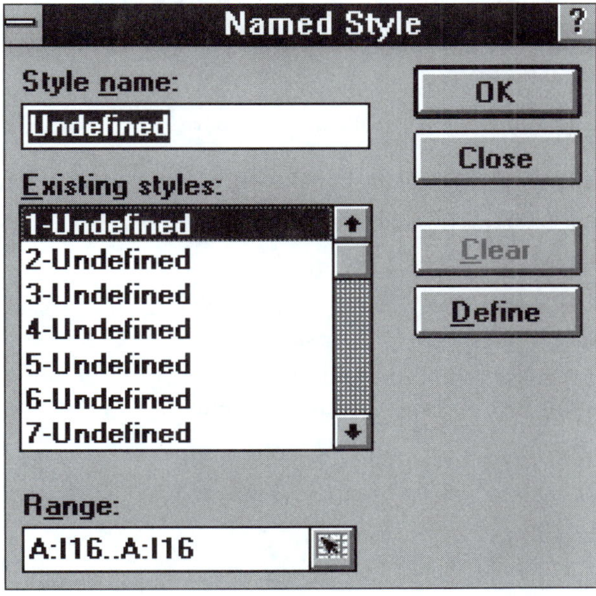

Figure 4.28 *Named Style dialog box.*

If you apply a gallery template and you don't like it, you can immediately select Undo from the Edit menu to remove the gallery template. However, selecting **Undo** must be the first thing you do after you install the gallery template.

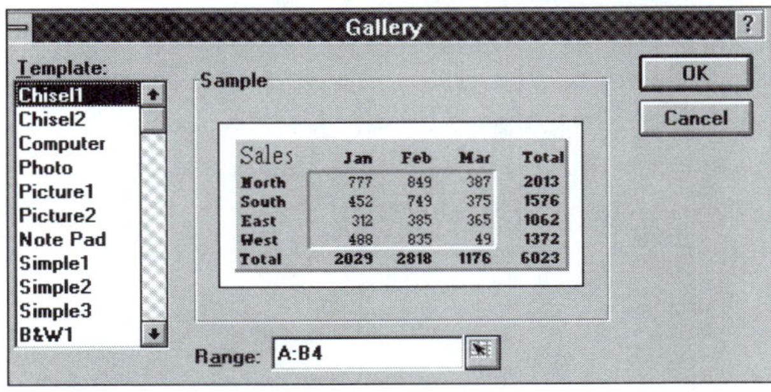

Figure 4.29 *Gallery dialog box.*

If you install a gallery template and later decide you don't like it, you can remove it later by activating the worksheet it is on and selecting **Clear Styles Only**. Your data will not be affected.

To apply a gallery template, follow these steps:

1. Select the range of cells to which you want to apply the template.
2. From the Style menu, choose **Gallery**.

   The Gallery dialog box appears.
3. Select the named template you want from the list. (Click each template and watch the sample box to see what it looks like. Notice that most of the templates assume that the top row and left column contain titles and the bottom row and right column contain totals or averages.)
4. Click **OK**.

Hiding Cells

At times you may find yourself working on a spreadsheet that contains cells you don't want to print, or you don't want other people to see. To accommodate your needs for privacy, 1-2-3 lets you hide particular columns or entire work-sheets. There are two ways to hide items. First, if you want to hide a column or row, you can drag the column width completely to the left, or a row height completely down so that the column or row disappears. To bring it back, just drag the mouse back to the right.

The other way to hide items is to open the **Hide** dialog box, located in the Style menu (see Figure 4.30). This dialog box gives you the option to hide either columns or sheets. Sometimes it is useful to hide one of your worksheets if it is only a temporary workspace that you don't want other people to see, but it may have important information that you cannot just discard. This option enables you to hide the worksheet until you are ready to access it later. To access it after it has been hidden, you can return to the Hide dialog box, select the range you hid, and select Show.

Practice

Now that you have explored the various formatting attributes, let's practice for-matting the rest of the worksheet. Figure 4.31 is an example of Caroline's Budget that has already been formatted. Using the skills you have learned, duplicate this format in each of your worksheets. Once you have completed the formatting of your file, you are ready to move on to Chapter 5 where you learn how to work with calculations and @Functions.

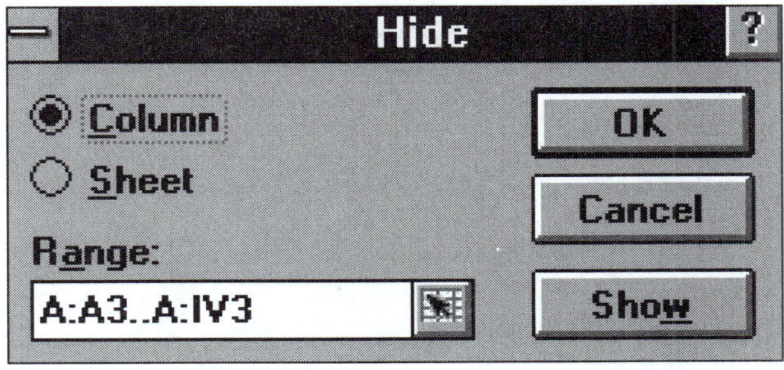

Figure 4.30 *Hide dialog box.*

To Sum Up

In this chapter, you learned the many ways you can improve the appearance of your worksheet. We discussed a number of the formatting features of 1-2-3, including changing fonts and attributes and using Group Mode to allow your formatting to apply to all the worksheets in your file. We went on to discuss ways of formatting numbers and aligning the data in your cells to suit your preference, and to make use of pop-up menus to facilitate your formatting tasks.

You learned how to personalize your worksheet by using named styles or pre-formatted Gallery Templates. You also learned how to hide parts of your file for privacy.

Now that you know more about formatting, you might want to take another look at some of the SmartMasters to see how the experts use these same formatting techniques to create smart, sophisticated-looking worksheets. Look particularly at how they use shading, borders, fonts, alignment, and spacing. You now have all these tools at your fingertips. All you have to do is apply them.

What You Learned

Change a font or its attributes:

1.   Select a cell.

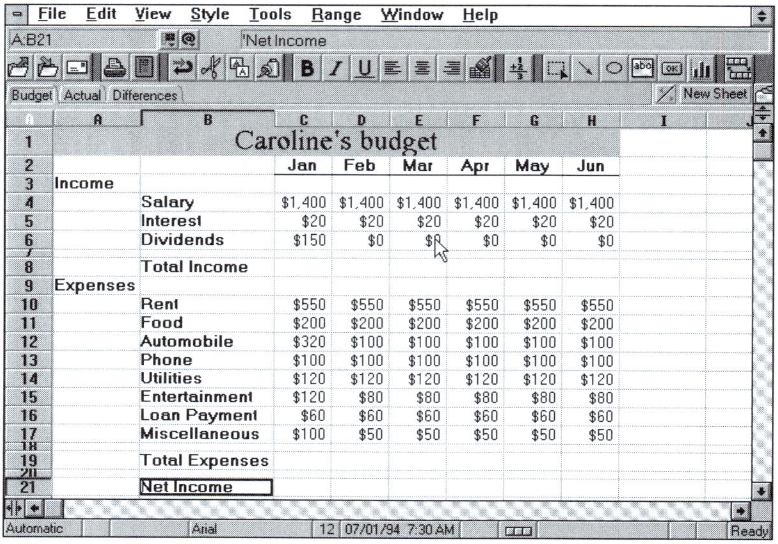

Figure 4.31 *Formatted Caroline's Budget.*

2. From the Style menu, choose **Font & Attributes**.

   Remember that you can switch steps 1 and 2 if you would rather use the **Range Selector** in the Font dialog box.

   The Font dialog box appears.

3. Choose a font, either by using the mouse to highlight and click, or by typing.

4. Change the size.

5. Choose a style, such as **Bold**.

6. Change the color.

7. Click **OK**.

Activate Group Mode to have your formatting apply to all worksheets on a file:

1. Go to the Style menu and select **Worksheet Defaults**.

   The Worksheet Defaults dialog box appears.

2. Select **Group Mode**.

3. Click **OK**.

Change number format:

1. Select the collection or range of cells you want to format.

    Remember, that to select a collection, you click and drag the mouse to select the cells, and then hold down the **Ctrl** key to select more cells.

2. From the Style menu, choose **Number Format**.

3. Select the number format you desire.

4. Click **OK**.

Change date format:

1. Go to an empty cell and type the date you want formatted.

2. Open the **Number Format** dialog box from the Style menu.

3. Choose different **Date** formats in the dialog box and watch how this affects the date in the Sample box.

4. Select a format and click **OK**.

Alter cell alignment:

1. Select the desired cell.

2. Click the appropriate SmartIcon or go to Style and choose **Alignment**.

3. Choose the appropriate alignment option.

4. Click **OK**.

Alter column width and row height manually:

1. Move the cursor over the border of a column heading until the cursor changes shape

2. Once the cursor changes shape, click and drag the mouse to the right to increase the size of the column or to the left to reduce its size.

    While you are dragging the column width, or row height, you will see a line that represents the new location for the right edge of the column, or bottom edge of the row.

3. Release the mouse button when the column is the desired size.

Alter column width automatically:

1. Select the column you want to change
2. From the Style menu, choose **Column Width**.
3. The Column Width dialog box appears.
4. Select the option you want and click **OK**.

Alter row height automatically:

1. Select the row you want to resize.
2. From the Style menu, choose **Row Height**.
    The Row Height dialog box appears.
3. Select the option you want and click **OK**.

Add borders to your cells:

1. Select the range of cells you want to have a border.
2. From the Style menu, choose **Lines & Color**.
    The Lines & Colors dialog box appears.
3. Look at the area of the dialog box that displays Border. In this area you have the option to select the type of border you want. Choose the type of border you want.

    You have the option to choose the line style and color of your border. As in other dialog boxes, you choose these by clicking on the down arrow and choosing your option from the list.
4. Select the line style.
5. Select the line color.
6. Click **OK**.

Add outlines to your cells:

1. Select the range of cells to which you want the outline to apply.
2. Go to the Style menu and open the **Lines & Color** dialog box.
3. Choose **Outline** and select the line type and color you want.
4. Click **OK**.

Add designer frames to your cells:

1. Select the range you want to frame.
2. Go to the Style menu and open the **Lines & Colors** dialog box.
3. Use the mouse to scroll down the list of possible designer frames and colors and choose the one you want.
4. Click **OK**.

Add a color background and pattern to your cells:

1. Select a range of cells.
2. Go to the Style menu and open the **Lines & Colors** dialog box.
3. Choose a background color from the list you activate by clicking with the mouse on the down arrow next to Background Color.
4. Use the same steps to select a pattern for the cell.
5. Choose a color for the pattern.
6. Choose a color for the text in that range of cells.
7. Click **OK**.

Create a named style:

1. Format a cell with the desired characteristics.
2. Select the formatted cell.
3. From the Style menu, select **Named Style**.

    You will see the Named Style dialog box.
4. In the Style Name box, type in a name for the style.
5. Choose **Define**.
6. Choose **Close**.

Apply a named style:

1. Select the cell or range of cells to which you want to apply the named style.
2. From the Style menu, open the **Named Style** dialog box.

3. Select the named style you want from the list.

4. Click **OK**.

Apply a template from the Gallery:

1. Select the range of cells to which you want to apply the template.

2. From the Style menu, choose **Gallery**.

    You will see the Gallery dialog box.

3. Select the named template you want from the list.

4. Click **OK**.

Hide cells:

1. Go to the Style menu and select **Hide**.

2. Select the column or worksheet you want to hide.

3. Click **OK**.

Show hidden cells:

1. Go to the Style menu and select **Hide**.

2. Type the hidden column or worksheet you want to see.

3. Click **OK**.

Chapter 5

Spreadsheet Calculations

You are now comfortable with many essential aspects of working with a spreadsheet program, from entering, editing, and manipulating data to making your worksheets look their professional best. Now you can move on to the task of making worksheet calculations that enable you to quickly figure out the answers to any number of questions that would take anyone hours to do by hand.

Throughout this chapter, there are many mathematical references. Don't be scared off. We have tried to explain what the important formulas are and how they work in simple terms. Always remember that the key in equations is to pay attention to detail.

In this chapter, you learn to:

- Understand the way formulas work.

- Recognize numerical, text and logical formulas.

- Follow guidelines to create and use formulas without error.

- Enter formulas so that the computer understands them.

- Use formulas that refer to cells that have moved.

We will then explore one particular type of calculation that is especially important, the @Function. You learn how to:

- Recognize the parts of an @Function and the way to set one up.
- Use the @Function Selector and @Function List to choose the equation you desire.
- Embed @Functions in long equations for complicated formulas.

Using Formulas

What is a formula and why do you need one? A *formula* is an equation that you create and that a spreadsheet program, such as Lotus 1-2-3 Release 5, can then apply to your data and solve for you. This is where you can find the real power of a spreadsheet. Computers are capable of solving equations more quickly and with greater accuracy than human beings. It may not seem like much when you use simple formulas. If, for example, you had a $10 bill, two $5 bills, and five $1 bills, you could quickly calculate that you have $25. An equation in a spreadsheet to perform this calculation may look as follows:

```
(1*10)+(2*5)+(5*1)
```

For this little problem, it may seem easier to add your bills in your head instead of programming a spreadsheet. Suppose, however, that you had 100 of these equations to solve. A spreadsheet like Lotus 1-2-3 can solve these in just about as much time as it would take you to solve one. Also, if you were to change a small part of your formula, Lotus 1-2-3 can instantaneously recalculate your problem. Similarly, when you start to use formulas that reference other cells in the worksheet, you will see the ease with which you can solve a problem using Lotus 1-2-3.

Types of Formulas

All of the formulas for which you could use Lotus 1-2-3 Release 5 can be broken down into three categories: numeric formulas, text formulas, and logical formulas. In this chapter, you learn about each of these three categories.

Numeric Formulas

A numeric formula simply calculates numbers or values. It is useful for mathematical equations and tasks involving large quantities of numbers, like those in the budget example. This is the type of formula with which everyone is most familiar. Numeric formulas use standard operators as symbols to stand for the mathematical functions, as shown in table 5.1.

Table 5.1 *Standard Operators in Numerical Formulas*

Symbol	Function
+	Addition
-	Subtraction
*	Multiplication
/	Division
^	Exponentiation, that is, to the x power

An example of a numeric formula would be the example of the dollar bills. To calculate the value of the money, you multiplied the number of bills you had by their relative dollar values (10*1, 5*2, and 5*1), and you then summed their products. The resulting numeric formula provided you with the correct value. As you learn later on, numeric formulas don't only involve numbers. They can (and will) include references to other cells in the worksheet.

When you use numeric formulas, 1-2-3 calculates the value to a precision of 18 or 19 total digits. It will, however, display only the number of digits required by the number format you set for that cell (as you did in Chapter 4). If you formatted your worksheet to show values to two decimal places, that is all that will be shown.

Text Formulas

Text formulas are used to manipulate text around the worksheet. You can use a text formula to combine the labels in two different cells. Suppose that you had one cell that contains *Total* and another cell that contains *Sales*. You could use the text formula to create a new cell displaying *Total Sales*.

Text formulas use the ampersand (&), to join text or cells that contain text. In the Total Sales example, the formula might look as follows: =Total & Sales. Although with this example it may seem easier to type Total Sales yourself, the text formulas often can help save you time by enabling you to combine the text of different cells instead of having to retype that text. The usefulness of text formulas in Lotus 1-2-3 Release 5 is due to the fact that instead of typing the actual text into the formula, you can define the text by its cell address. Imagine a worksheet that has cells containing large amounts of text. You could simply type **= A:D21 & A:T21** to save time and energy by eliminating the need to retype any of that data.

Logical Formulas

Logical formulas are statements that evaluate a condition and reply by answering true (1) or false (0). These types of formulas often are used to determine whether one item is greater than, equal to, or less than another item. This kind of formula is handy for all sorts of quick calculations, which, if done manually, would take hours to complete. Suppose, for example, that used your worksheet to calculate net sales for each month, and you wanted to determine, at a glance, which month's actual sales were greater than its budgeted sales. In long hand, this task could take quite a while. Alternatively, you could use a logical formula that asked whether each month's sales were greater than the budgeted sales. In response, 1-2-3 would answer by displaying 1s and 0s, indicating the results found. You could then quickly inspect all of the months marked by 1's; these would be the months that satisfied the requirement of sales greater than budget.

Table 5.2 lists the conditions that Lotus 1-2-3 Release 5 uses in logical formulas.

Table 5.2 *Logical Conditions*

Condition	Difinition
=	Equal to
>	Greater than
<	Less than
>=	Greater than or equal to
<=	Less than or equal to
<>	Not equal to

Lotus 1-2-3 Release 5 can also evaluate statements containing complex conditions. You might, for example, want to determine whether a month had both sales greater than budget and costs less than budget. Using simple conventions in its formulas, Lotus 1-2-3 Release 5 lets you figure out complicated situations that involve multiple variables. Table 5.3 lists the various connectors that you can use in 1-2-3 to create complex conditions.

Table 5.3 *Logical Formula Connectors*

Condition	Difinition
#AND#	Condition A and B must be true in order to get a 1.
#OR#	Condition A and B must be true in order to get a 1.
#NOT#	Condition A must not be true in order to get a 1.

Guidelines for Creating Formulas

One of the most important matters regarding formulas is keeping track of all the guidelines you must follow to ensure that your formula will work. Following are some guidelines for using Lotus 1-2-3 Release 5. If you follow these and understand their purposes, you will have no problems with these formulas.

Always begin your formula with an equal (=) sign.

The equal sign is like a prefix in which you are telling the computer that the rest of what you type will be a formula. It is your way of saying to the computer, "Get ready, a formula is coming up!" Although you don't always need to have an equal sign, it is good to develop the habit of using one whether or not you need it. This way, your equation will work whether the equal sign was necessary or not. Technically, a formula can begin with +, _, =, @, ., #, or $. However, instead of trying to remember when to use which symbol, you can always use the = sign to begin an equation and Lotus 1-2-3 Release 5 will know it is a formula. Think of it this way: Use = to begin an equation, because you are telling Lotus 1-2-3 Release 5 that this cell is equal to the following formula.

Use parentheses in numeric formulas.

Lotus 1-2-3 Release 5 follows the order of operations you learned back in grade school. Now, don't cringe at the memory of your seventh grade math teacher! It's really quite simple: When following order of operations if, for example, your formula is 2+3*5^2, Lotus 1-2-3 Release 5 will add 2+3, and then multiply that sum by 5 to the second power, or 25.

Now, if you wanted the program to multiply the 3 times 25 and then add 2, you would need to bypass the order of operation. To do this, you need parentheses. Your formula would have to be 2+(3*5^2) or 2+(3*(5^2)). The parentheses are like a sign indicating to do that part of the equation first. In the last example, you could read it as "2 plus the quantity of 5 to the second power times 3." By using the parentheses, the computer knows to first square 5, then multiply by 3, then add 2. As far as parentheses go, the philosophy is, when in doubt, use parentheses. It cannot hurt to use them, but if you don't, 1-2-3 may give the wrong result.

Don't forget to close your parentheses. This means, if you use a (, there must be a corresponding) to close that operation. This can be quite troublesome when you have very complex formulas, such as (2+(3*(4+(3^3)*(((4+5)/2)*19)))). If you don't close all your parentheses, Lotus 1-2-3 Release 5 will close them for you if it can clearly figure out where they should be closed. Otherwise, it will beep and refuse to accept the formula.

When you see formulas like this, try to remain calm and not develop a facial twitch. Remember, the beauty of this program is that the computer does this math for you! You just have to know how to enter the formula.

Don't put spaces in your formula.

Unless you are using a text formula that requires you to put spaces inside quotation marks, never use spaces in a formula. If you are adding 5 and 8, your formula should look like this: =5+8, not =5 + 8. This may feel strange at first but it will soon be natural.

A cell that you reference in a formula will receive a value of 0 if it is empty.

If your formula references another cell in your worksheet that is empty, Lotus 1-2-3 Release 5 assumes that this cell has a value of 0.

An error in a formula will return the result ERR.

If you enter a formula containing an error, one of two things may happen. First, you might try to enter a formula when you have forgotten a necessary item. You may, for example, have inserted a space or forgotten an operator or parenthesis. Lotus 1-2-3 Release 5 beeps and will not accept the formula. The erroneous formula you typed will remain in the edit line so that you can fix it.

If, however, your formula has an error that is not in the syntax, Lotus 1-2-3 Release 5 may accept it at first, but it will return ERR, to inform you that there is an error in your formula. If, for example, your formula tries to divide something by the number 0, 1-2-3 returns ERR because it is impossible to divide by zero.

If the result of the formula is too large to fit in the cell, 1-2-3 displays asterisks (*).

Sometimes your calculation will return a result that has too many digits to fit in your cell. When this happens, 1-2-3 fills the cell with asterisks. If this happens, you can do two things. First, you can make your column widths larger. Remember, if you double-click on the right cell edge in the column headings, 1-2-3 automatically resizes the columns to fit the largest entry. Alternatively, you can change the number format so that it displays fewer digits. You can, for example, remove the decimal places in Currency Format.

Entering a Formula

Now that you have covered the simple laundry list of items to remember when it comes to formulas, you are ready to actually enter a formula into the budget. As with data entry, you can enter a formula either into the cell directly or into the edit line. In either case, you enter the same things.

For the first formula, let's add the Salary Income, Interest Income, and Dividend Income for January into cell A:C8. To enter this formula, follow these steps:

1. Select cell **A:C8**.
2. Type **=A:C4+A:C5+A:C6** (see Figure 5.1).

   Instead of having to type the cells A:C4, A:C5, and A:C6, you could type

=, click with the mouse on A:C4, type **+**, click with the mouse on A:C5, type **+** and so on.

	A	B	C	D	E	F	G	H	I
1			Caroline's budget						
2			Jan	Feb	Mar	Apr	May	Jun	
3	Income								
4		Salary	$1,400	$1,400	$1,400	$1,400	$1,400	$1,400	5.4
5		Interest	$20	$20	$20	$20	$20	$20	
6		Dividends	$150	$0	$0	$0	$0	$0	
8		Total Income	=A:C4+A:C5+A:C6						
9	Expenses								
10		Rent	$550	$550	$550	$550	$550	$550	
11		Food	$200	$200	$200	$200	$200	$200	
12		Automobile	$320	$100	$100	$100	$100	$100	
13		Phone	$100	$100	$100	$100	$100	$100	
14		Utilities	$120	$120	$120	$120	$120	$120	
15		Entertainment	$120	$80	$80	$80	$80	$80	
16		Loan Payment	$60	$60	$60	$60	$60	$60	
17		Miscellaneous	$100	$50	$50	$50	$50	$50	
19		Total Expenses							
21		Net Income							

Figure 5.1 *Cell A:C4+A:C5+A:C6.*

3. Click the **Confirm** button or press **Enter**.

Now, cell A:C8 displays the Total Income for January, which is $1,570 (see Figure 5.2).

Notice that the edit line for cell A:C8 displays the formula for the cell; the cell itself shows the calculated value. This way, you can always remember the formula you used to get the answer that appears in the cell.

Although the formula was entered with an = sign at the beginning, 1-2-3 does not show it in the edit line, because the program does not technically need it. As mentioned earlier, however, it is best always to use the equal sign when entering a formula and let 1-2-3 remove it if it is not needed.

Your Total Income for January may or may not be displayed in currency format, depending on whether you had applied the currency number format to this cell earlier. If not, you can apply it now, or at some time in the future.

Now, let's enter another formula. This one will be the Net Income for January. Caroline's Net Income value is the difference between the Total Income and the Total Expenses (which you will calculate later). To calculate net income, follow these steps:

A	B	C	D	E	F	G	H	I
1		Caroline's budget						
2			Jan	Feb	Mar	Apr	May	Jun
3	Income							
4		Salary	$1,400	$1,400	$1,400	$1,400	$1,400	$1,400
5		Interest	$20	$20	$20	$20	$20	$20
6		Dividends	$150	$0	$0	$0	$0	$0
8		Total Income	$1,570					
9	Expenses							
10		Rent	$550	$550	$550	$550	$550	$550
11		Food	$200	$200	$200	$200	$200	$200
12		Automobile	$320	$100	$100	$100	$100	$100
13		Phone	$100	$100	$100	$100	$100	$100
14		Utilities	$120	$120	$120	$120	$120	$120
15		Entertainment	$120	$80	$80	$80	$80	$80
16		Loan Payment	$60	$60	$60	$60	$60	$60
17		Miscellaneous	$100	$50	$50	$50	$50	$50
19		Total Expenses						
21		Net Income						

Figure 5.2 *Total income for January.*

1. Select cell **A:C21**.

2. Type **=(A:C8-A:C19)**.

3. Click the **Confirm** button or press **Enter**.

Cell A:C21 is equal to the difference between A:C8 and A:C19 (see Figure 5.3). Again notice that the edit line displays the formula, and 1-2-3 has removed the = before the formula.

Because there is nothing in cell A:C19, 1-2-3 assumes that it has a value of 0. That accounts for why the total income equals the net income.

By using these formulas you have told the computer that cell A:C21 is a function of cell A:C8. In other words, the value of cell A:C21 relies on the value of cell A:C8. A:C8, in turn, relies on, or is a function of, cells A:C4..A:C6. If you changed any one of the income entries for January, it would automatically change the Total Income and the Net Income. For example, go to cell A:C4 and change the salary entry from 1,400 to 1,500. Notice that the Total Income increased by $100 as did the Net Income (see Figure 5.4).

Figure 5.3 *Net income.*

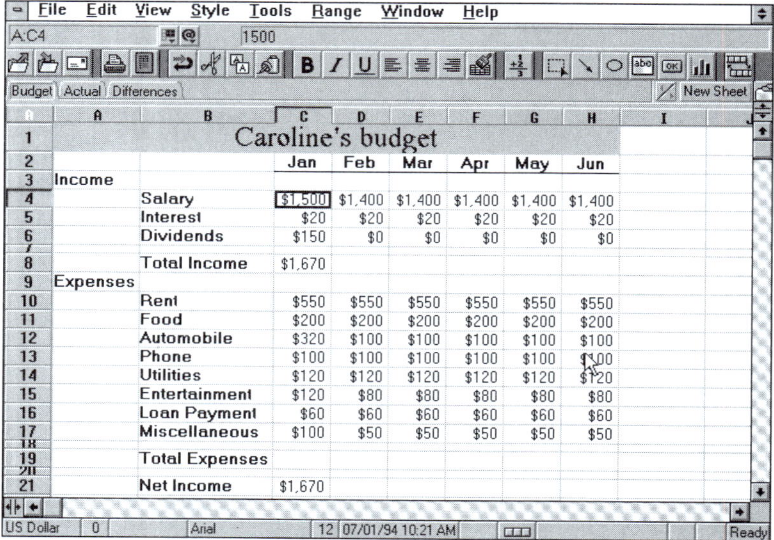

Figure 5.4 *Total income and net income increased by $100.*

So far, you have created formulas that contained references to other cells in the worksheet. You are not limited to this format. In 1-2-3, you also can use references to named ranges in your worksheet. For example, let's name cell A:C8 January Income:

1. Select **A:C8**.

2. From the Range menu, choose **Name**.

3. Name the range **JANUARY INCOME** (see Figure 5.5).

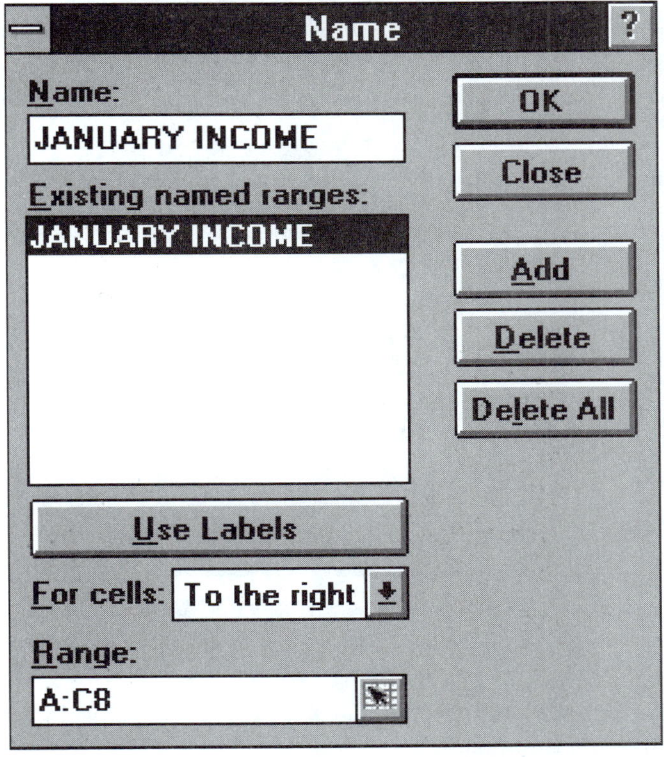

Figure 5.5 *Name range January income.*

4. Click **OK**.

Now, suppose that you want to make Entertainment Expense, cell A:C15, equal to 5 percent of Total Income. You could do this by making the formula for cell

A:C15=.05*A:C8. But sometimes it is easier to use the named range. To create a formula using a named range, follow these steps:

1. Select **A:C15**.

2. Type **=.05***.

3. Before you click the **Confirm** button, click the **Navigator** button on the edit line. A list drops down with the name ranges (see Figure 5.6).

Figure 5.6 *Navigator named range list.*

Because you named only one range, it is the only choice in the list.

4. Click **January Income**. 1-2-3 automatically enters this named range into the formula (see Figure 5.7).

Figure 5.7 *Named range was entered into the formula.*

Now January's Entertainment Expense is equal to 5 percent of January's Total Income. If Caroline's income increased in January, so would her entertainment expense, which would increase her total expense. Because Net Income is equal to Total Income less Total Expenses, a $100 increase in Total Income would now result in only a $95 increase in Net Income, because the Total Expenses would increase by $5.

You can also use 1-2-3 to refer to cells and ranges on other worksheets. You have, for example, one worksheet for the budget, one for the actual numbers, and one called difference. To see how close you are to the budget, you want to take the difference between the values in the Budget and Actual worksheets. To reference worksheets, follow these steps:

1. Go to worksheet C, Difference.
2. Select cell **C:C4**.
3. Type =.
4. Click the worksheet tab for worksheet Budget.
5. Select cell **BUDGET:C4** (see Figure 5.8).

		Jan	Feb	Mar	Apr	May	Jun
Income							
	Salary	$1,500	$1,400	$1,400	$1,400	$1,400	$1,400
	Interest	$20	$20	$20	$20	$20	$20
	Dividends	$150	$0	$0	$0	$0	$0
	Total Income	$1,670					
Expenses							
	Rent	$550	$550	$550	$550	$550	$550
	Food	$200	$200	$200	$200	$200	$200
	Automobile	$320	$100	$100	$100	$100	$100
	Phone	$100	$100	$100	$100	$100	$100
	Utilities	$120	$120	$120	$120	$120	$120
	Entertainment	$120	$80	$80	$80	$80	$80
	Loan Payment	$60	$60	$60	$60	$60	$60
	Miscellaneous	$100	$50	$50	$50	$50	$50
	Total Expenses						
	Net Income	$1,670					

Figure 5.8 *Select cell A:C4.*

6. 1-2-3 automatically jumps back to the Difference worksheet and the cursor appears in the edit line or cell C:C4. The formula entry now displays =A:C4.

7. Type '.

8. Click on the worksheet tab for Actual Worksheet and select cell **ACTUAL:C4**. (see Figure 5.9).

File	Edit	View	Style	Tools	Range	Window	Help

B:C4   =Budget:C4-Actual:C4

Budget | Actual | Differences   New Sheet

	A	B	C	D	E	F	G	H
1	Caroline's budget							
2			Jan	Feb	Mar	Apr	May	Jun
3	Income							
4		Salary	1438	1438	1438	1438	1438	1438
5		Interest		22	22	22	22	22
6		Dividends	150	0	0	0	0	0
7								
8		Total Income						
9	Expenses							
10		Rent	550	550	550	550	550	550
11		Food	200	195	207	202	198	200
12		Automobile	330	50	80	110	120	120
13		Phone	130	117	120	100	105	109
14		Utilities	125	100	97	90	110	122
15		Entertainment	100	98	90	80	80	100
16		Loan Payment	60	60	60	60	60	60
17		Miscellaneous	67	25	40	50	90	60
18								
19		Total Expenses						

Automatic   Arial   12 | 07/01/94 10:29 AM   Point

Figure 5.9 *Select cell B:C4.*

9. Click the **Confirm** button to accept the formula =BUDGET:C4-ACTUAL:C4 (see Figure 5.10).

In effect, what you are saying to worksheet C is, "I want C4 on this worksheet to equal the value of BUDGET:C4 minus ACTUAL:C4." When you think about it, it's all pretty simple. It's just that 1-2-3 can do the calculations faster than you can!

You can type in the entire entry if you don't want to jump back and forth between the worksheets with the mouse. Just remember to put the worksheet label before the cell address (A:C4, not just C4) and always double-check your formula before confirming.

The result you should get in cell DIFFERENCE:C4 is 62. Because this is a positive number, Caroline's budget figure was larger than the actual figure for her income. Go back to cell BUDGET:C4 and change Caroline's salary back to $1,400. Notice that cell DIFFERENCE:C4 displays -38, because the budget amount was more than the actual amount.

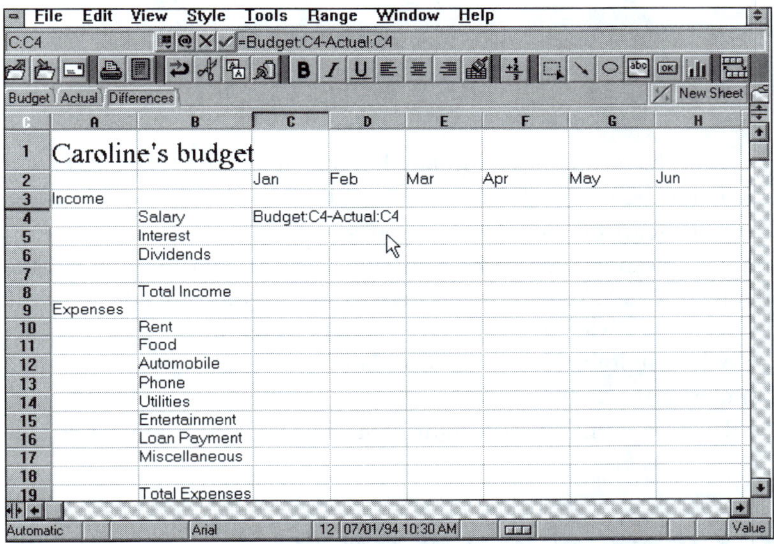

Figure 5.10 *Confirm your formula.*

Notice that the entertainment expense item on worksheet Budget also decreased, because the Total Income figure on which it is based decreased.

1-2-3 also can reference cells in different files. In a particular worksheet, you can have a formula that tells 1-2-3 to look at another file on your disk for a cell address. Suppose, for example, that instead of having three worksheets in the budget file, you had only the budget worksheet. In another file you had the actual values, and in a third file you had the differences. To calculate the differences, you would need to reference across two files. In a formula, 1-2-3 references another file by using the following format:

```
<<FILENAME>>range
```

The file name needs to be the entire name, including the three-character extension. For example, the entry might look like this:

```
=(<<Budget.wk4>>C4)-(<<Actual.wk4>>C4)
```

Because in this hypothetical you have only one worksheet per file, the cell addresses you are subtracting are both C4, but one is in the file BUDGET.WK4 and the other is in ACTUAL.WK4. Again, the parentheses are not necessary, but they make it easier to see what is being subtracted from what.

Relative versus Absolute References

So far you only have entered formulas for the month of January. Part of what makes a spreadsheet so useful is the capability to copy and paste formulas to other places. Instead of having to retype all of these formulas, you can copy these formulas to other cells. When you copy cells and paste them to other cells, 1-2-3 shifts the formula references relative to where you moved the formula. For example, copy cell A:C8 to A:D8. (Don't forget you can do this very simply by dragging it while holding down the **Ctrl** key.) You have copied and shifted the formula one column to the right. Now the cell references in the formula have also moved one column to the right. This is called a relative reference (see Figure 5.11).

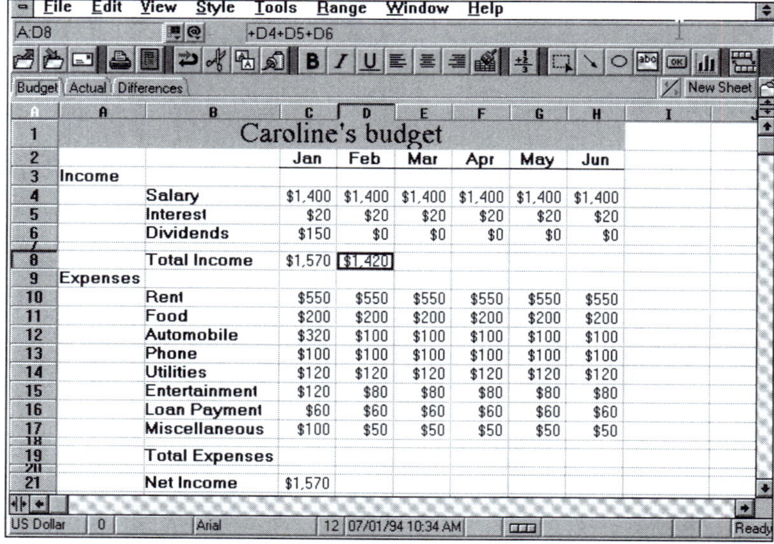

Figure 5.11 *Relative reference.*

What used to be (C4+C5+C6) is now (D4+D5+D6). Now you can copy the formula to the right for the rest of the months. To copy the formula with relative references to the right, follow these steps:

1. Select **A:D4..A:H4**.
2. From the Edit menu, choose **Copy Right**.
3. Repeat for the range **A:C21..A:H21**.

However, you will not always want 1-2-3 to adjust your formula references relatively because they may address a particular cell that is the same for every entry. In some cases you will want all cells to reference one stationary cell, even if the rest of your cells are copied to the right. For example, remember that cell A:C15 is .05*January Income. Suppose that, instead of .05, it referenced a particular cell that contained the percentage, such as A:I9. Cell A:C15 would then say =A:I9*January Income.

You would do this if you wanted to be able to change this percentage without having to retype all of the formulas. Because 1-2-3 is referencing this cell, you can change the value of the cell and it will automatically update the formula.

You want this percentage to apply to all months, but if you copy right, the next month will not reference A:I9. It will reference A:J9, and the next month A:K9, and so on. In this case, you need to create an absolute reference.

An absolute reference will not change when you copy it to another location. To create an absolute reference, put a dollar sign, $, before the entry. For example:

1. Go to cell A:I9 and type **5%**.
2. Go to cell A:C15 and edit the entry to read **A:I9*JANUARY INCOME**.
3. To make cell A:I9 an absolute reference, type a dollar sign, **$**, before the A, I, and 9.
4. Your entry should read $A:$I$9*JANUARY INCOME.

    You have to put the $ before all three parts of the cell reference because you want 1-2-3 to refer only to that cell on that worksheet without shifting. If you did not put the $ before each item, you would create a mixed reference. Table 5.4 lists the various combinations of mixed references and a brief description of the result if you were to copy this formula to another cell.

Table 5.4 *Mixed References*

Example	Result
A:19	Lotus 1-2-3 Release 4 will relatively shift the column, row, and worksheet
A:1$9	Lotus 1-2-3 Release 4 will hold the row absolute but it will shift across the columns and across worksheets.
A:$19	Lotus 1-2-3 Release 4 will hold the column absoltue but it will shift up and down the rows and across worksheets.
$A:19	Lotus 1-2-3 Release 4 will hold the work sheet constant but it will shift the rows and columns.
A$1$9	Lotus 1-2-3 Release 4 will hold the cell constant but it will shift the worksheet
$A:$19	Lotus 1-2-3 Release 4 will hold the work sheet and the column constant but it will shift up and down the rows.
$A:1$9	Lotus 1-2-3 Release 4 will hold the work sheet and the row constant but it will shift across the columns.

5. Now, if you select the range A:C15..A:H15 and copy the formula to the right, 1-2-3 holds the reference to cell A:I9 absolute (see Figure 5.12).

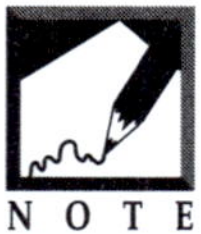

The reference to January Income is not marked as absolute, and Lotus 1-2-3 did adapt it for each of the columns it was copied to. Because the other columns don't have range names for the compara-ble cell, the cell address is used. Click cells **D15, E15,** and so on to see what formula Lotus 1-2-3 inserted into each cell.

Moving Formulas

We have been discussing the effects of copying formulas. But sometimes you also need to move a formula to a different place in your file. In this case, 1-2-3 produces different results, depending on what you do with the data to which the formula refers.

Figure 5.12 shows a spreadsheet titled "Caroline's budget":

	A	B	C	D	E	F	G	H	I
1			Caroline's budget						
2			Jan	Feb	Mar	Apr	May	Jun	
3	Income								
4		Salary	$1,400	$1,400	$1,400	$1,400	$1,400	$1,400	
5		Interest	$20	$20	$20	$20	$20	$20	
6		Dividends	$150	$0	$0	$0	$0	$0	
8		Total Income	$1,570	$1,420	$1,420	$1,420	$1,420	$1,420	
9	Expenses								5%
10		Rent	$550	$550	$550	$550	$550	$550	
11		Food	$200	$200	$200	$200	$200	$200	
12		Automobile	$320	$100	$100	$100	$100	$100	
13		Phone	$100	$100	$100	$100	$100	$100	
14		Utilities	$120	$120	$120	$120	$120	$120	
15		Entertainment	$79	$71	$71	$71	$71	$71	
16		Loan Payment	$60	$60	$60	$60	$60	$60	
17		Miscellaneous	$100	$50	$50	$50	$50	$50	
19		Total Expenses							
21		Net Income	$1,570	$1,420	$1,420	$1,420	$1,420	$1,420	

Figure 5.12 *Absolute reference.*

If you move the formula but not the data to which the formula refers, the references in the formula don't change. If, for example, you move the formula from A:C8 to A:C9 but it still is the sum of January's income, the formula would still sum A:C4..A:C6 (see Figure 5.13).

If you move the data to which a formula refers, the formula will change to reference the new address of the data. If, for example, you moved January's income values (A:C4..A:C6) to A:I4..A:I6, the formula for January Total Income would automatically change to (A:I4+A:I5+A:I6) (see Figure 5.14).

Using @ Functions

So far you have worked with formulas you created yourself. There is, however, an easier way to work with some formulas. These are called @Functions.

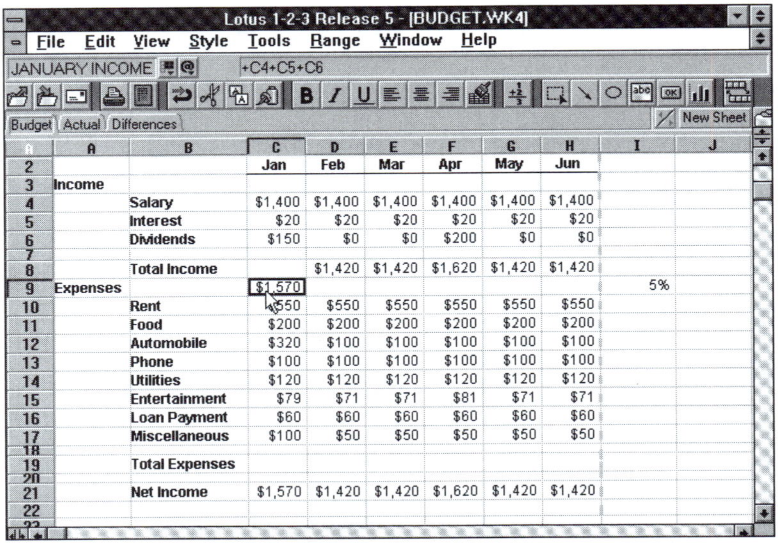

	A	B	C Jan	D Feb	E Mar	F Apr	G May	H Jun	I	J
3	Income									
4		Salary	$1,400	$1,400	$1,400	$1,400	$1,400	$1,400		
5		Interest	$20	$20	$20	$20	$20	$20		
6		Dividends	$150	$0	$0	$200	$0	$0		
7										
8		Total Income		$1,420	$1,420	$1,620	$1,420	$1,420		
9	Expenses		$1,570						5%	
10		Rent	$550	$550	$550	$550	$550	$550		
11		Food	$200	$200	$200	$200	$200	$200		
12		Automobile	$320	$100	$100	$100	$100	$100		
13		Phone	$100	$100	$100	$100	$100	$100		
14		Utilities	$120	$120	$120	$120	$120	$120		
15		Entertainment	$79	$71	$71	$81	$71	$71		
16		Loan Payment	$60	$60	$60	$60	$60	$60		
17		Miscellaneous	$100	$50	$50	$50	$50	$50		
18										
19		Total Expenses								
20										
21		Net Income	$1,570	$1,420	$1,420	$1,620	$1,420	$1,420		

Figure 5.13 *Moving a formula.*

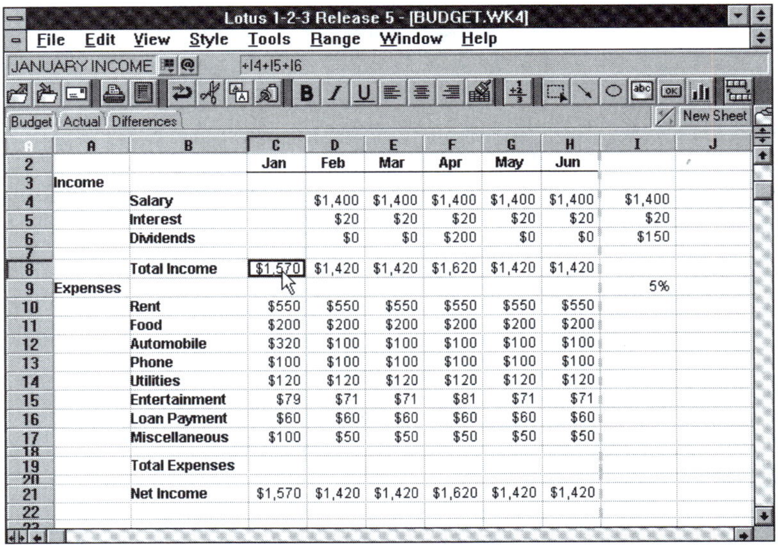

	A	B	C Jan	D Feb	E Mar	F Apr	G May	H Jun	I	J
3	Income									
4		Salary		$1,400	$1,400	$1,400	$1,400	$1,400	$1,400	
5		Interest		$20	$20	$20	$20	$20	$20	
6		Dividends		$0	$0	$200	$0	$0	$150	
7										
8		Total Income	$1,570	$1,420	$1,420	$1,620	$1,420	$1,420		
9	Expenses								5%	
10		Rent	$550	$550	$550	$550	$550	$550		
11		Food	$200	$200	$200	$200	$200	$200		
12		Automobile	$320	$100	$100	$100	$100	$100		
13		Phone	$100	$100	$100	$100	$100	$100		
14		Utilities	$120	$120	$120	$120	$120	$120		
15		Entertainment	$79	$71	$71	$81	$71	$71		
16		Loan Payment	$60	$60	$60	$60	$60	$60		
17		Miscellaneous	$100	$50	$50	$50	$50	$50		
18										
19		Total Expenses								
20										
21		Net Income	$1,570	$1,420	$1,420	$1,620	$1,420	$1,420		

Figure 5.14 *Moving data that is referenced by a formula.*

What Is an @Function?

An @Function is a predefined formula that comes with 1-2-3. The Release 5 version of Lotus 1-2-3 has more than 300 built-in formulas. Like the Gallery Templates and SmartMasters, @Functions are given to you by 1-2-3 as a list of options that you don't need to create yourself, but that the program thinks you might find helpful. Appendix D contains a list and brief explanation of the more common @Functions.

Unlike user-defined formulas that can begin with a variety of characters, although you suggest using =, @Functions get their name because they must begin with @. Following the @ is the name of the function.

Function Arguments

The name of the @Function is followed by parentheses that contain the arguments to be calculated. An argument is the data you provide for 1-2-3 to calculate. For example, the most common @Function is @SUM. This function sums a selected range of cells. If you wanted to calculate Total Income, instead of typing =A:C4+A:C5+A:C6, the @Function equivalent would be @SUM(A:C4..A:C6). The argument in this @Function is A:C4..A:C6.

@Function arguments can be a range of cells, a single value, or text, depending on the particular function you are using. There are two types of @Function arguments: required and optional.

Required arguments, as their name implies, are required for you to enter. Optional arguments, on the other hand, don't have to be used. They enable you to factor more variables into your calculation. If, however, you are going to use one of the optional arguments, you must use all optional arguments that precede it, although you don't have to use optional arguments that follow it. To demonstrate this, consider the @Function, @NORMAL. This statistical function calculates the normal distribution. It can equalize two different items so that you can compare them. If you wanted to calculate the normal distribution of x, you could type **@Normal(x)**. If you wanted to do so, you could provide other optional information, such as the mean, standard, type, or region. In this case, the arguments for this function would look as follows:

```
@NORMAL(x;[mean];[std];[type];[region])
```

The arguments in brackets, ([ ]), are options. To calculate the normal distribution of x, you need only to provide this @Function with the value x. Any other information is optional. If you decide to provide the mean, you don't need to provide anything else, because there are no optional arguments that precede it. If, however, you wanted to provide the standard deviation, std, you would first have to provide the mean because the standard deviation is based on the mean and thus follows it.

There are three ways to enter an @Function. First of all, you can do it manually. If you already know the @Function you need and you also know the arguments required, you can manually type the @Function name in the cell as you would enter any other data. For example, let's enter the @SUM function into cell A:C19 to sum January expenses:

1. Select cell **A:C19**.

2. Type **@SUM(A:C10..A:C17)**.

3. Click the **Confirm** button or press **Enter** (see Figure 5.15).

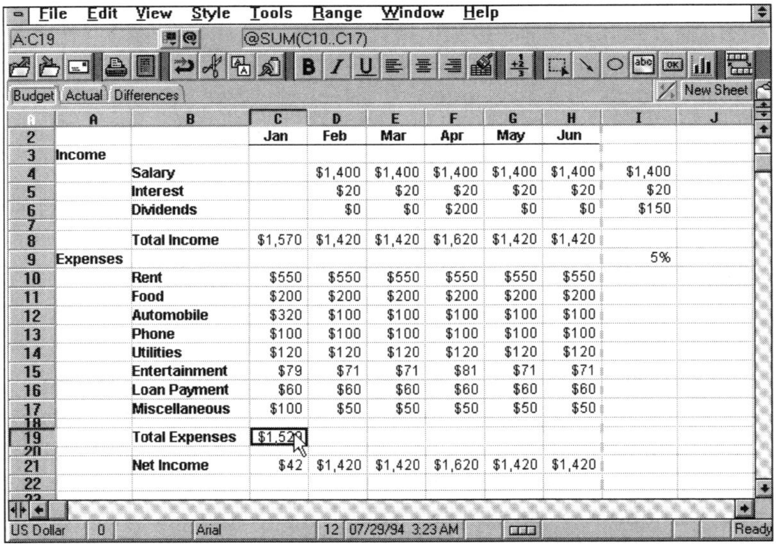

File   Edit   View   Style   Tools   Range   Window   Help

A:C19   @SUM(C10..C17)

Budget | Actual | Differences   New Sheet

	A	B	C	D	E	F	G	H	I	J
2			Jan	Feb	Mar	Apr	May	Jun		
3	Income									
4		Salary		$1,400	$1,400	$1,400	$1,400	$1,400	$1,400	
5		Interest		$20	$20	$20	$20	$20	$20	
6		Dividends		$0	$0	$200	$0	$0	$150	
7										
8		Total Income	$1,570	$1,420	$1,420	$1,620	$1,420	$1,420		
9	Expenses								5%	
10		Rent	$550	$550	$550	$550	$550	$550		
11		Food	$200	$200	$200	$200	$200	$200		
12		Automobile	$320	$100	$100	$100	$100	$100		
13		Phone	$100	$100	$100	$100	$100	$100		
14		Utilities	$120	$120	$120	$120	$120	$120		
15		Entertainment	$79	$71	$71	$81	$71	$71		
16		Loan Payment	$60	$60	$60	$60	$60	$60		
17		Miscellaneous	$100	$50	$50	$50	$50	$50		
18										
19		Total Expenses	$1,529							
20										
21		Net Income	$42	$1,420	$1,420	$1,620	$1,420	$1,420		
22										

US Dollar   0   Arial   12 | 07/29/94 3:23 AM   Ready

Figure 5.15 *@SUM(C10..C127).*

Notice how much easier it is to use this @Function instead of having to type in all of the cells that needed to be added together. This is why you waited to sum the expenses, because it would have taken too long to sum them manually. The difficulty with manual input of @Functions is that you need to know all about the @Function and how to set it up. If you are not so familiar, you can use other methods to employ @Functions.

@Function Selector

The second way to employ @Functions is by using a feature called the @Function Selector. This is a handy feature to use if you don't know what arguments are required for an @Function or if you simply prefer to use the mouse instead of the keyboard. The @Function Selector, located on the edit line, features some of the more common @Functions (see Figure 5.16).

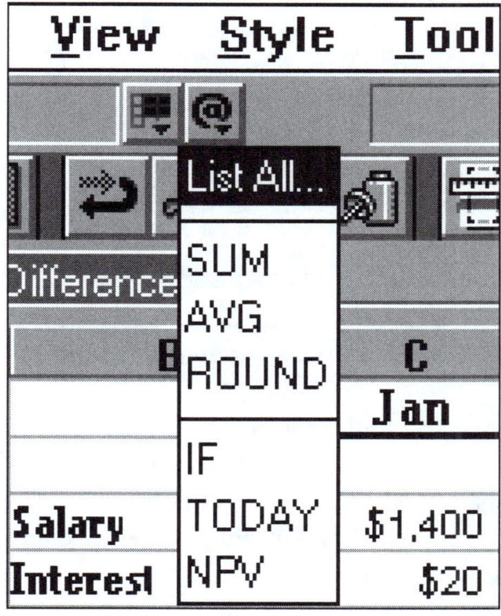

Figure 5.16 *@Function Selector.*

In this figure, you can see that this menu contains @Functions for summing a range (SUM), averaging a list of values (AVG), rounding a value to the nearest multiple of the power of 10 (ROUND), performing If-Then statements (IF), calculating the current date (TODAY), and calculating the net present value of a series of cash flows (NPV). Appendix A discusses customizing 1-2-3 when you want to change the @Functions that appear on this menu.

If you select an @Function from this menu, 1-2-3 enters @, the function name, parentheses, and the arguments, required and optional, to the edit line. Notice that the arguments are highlighted (see Figure 5.17).

File	Edit	View	Style	Tools	Range	Window	Help

A:C19 @SUM(list)

Budget | Actual | Differences   New Sheet

	A	B	C	D	E	F	G	H	I
1			Caroline's budget						
2			Jan	Feb	Mar	Apr	May	Jun	
3	Income								
4		Salary	$1,400	$1,400	$1,400	$1,400	$1,400	$1,400	
5		Interest	$20	$20	$20	$20	$20	$20	
6		Dividends	$150	$0	$0	$0	$0	$0	
8		Total Income	$1,570	$1,420	$1,420	$1,420	$1,420	$1,420	
9	Expenses								5%
10		Rent	$550	$550	$550	$550	$550	$550	
11		Food	$200	$200	$200	$200	$200	$200	
12		Automobile	$320	$100	$100	$100	$100	$100	
13		Phone	$100	$100	$100	$100	$100	$100	
14		Utilities	$120	$120	$120	$120	$120	$120	
15		Entertainment	$79	$71	$71	$71	$71	$71	
16		Loan Payment	$60	$60	$60	$60	$60	$60	
17		Miscellaneous	$100	$50	$50	$50	$50	$50	
19		Total Expenses	@SUM(list)						
21		Net Income	$42	$1,420	$1,420	$1,420	$1,420	$1,420	

US Dollar | 0 | Arial | 12 | 07/01/94 10:58 AM | Edit

Figure 5.17 *@Function arguments are pasted with the function.*

Because the arguments are highlighted, when you start typing, they will be erased. This is done so that you don't have to delete them first. If, however, you need to see what these arguments are, make sure that you do so before you erase them. You can get rid of the highlighting by clicking with the mouse somewhere else in the worksheet.

@Function List

Another way of applying @Functions is to use the @Function List. This feature shows every @Function available, so it is useful when the @Function you want is not showing in the @Function Selector or when you want to know what a particular @Function does. By using the @Function List, you can view a list of every @Function available. To access this list, select **List All** from the @Function

Selector (see Figure 5.16). When you do, 1-2-3 opens the @Function List dialog box (see Figure 5.18).

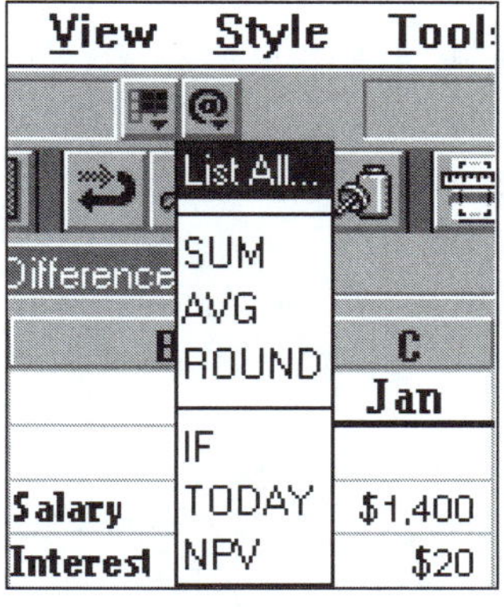

Figure 5.18 *@Function dialog box.*

We will discuss the three main areas of this dialog box (the fourth area is addressed in Appendix B).

At the top of the dialog box is a drop-down list that lets you select the category of @Function to display (see Figure 5.19)

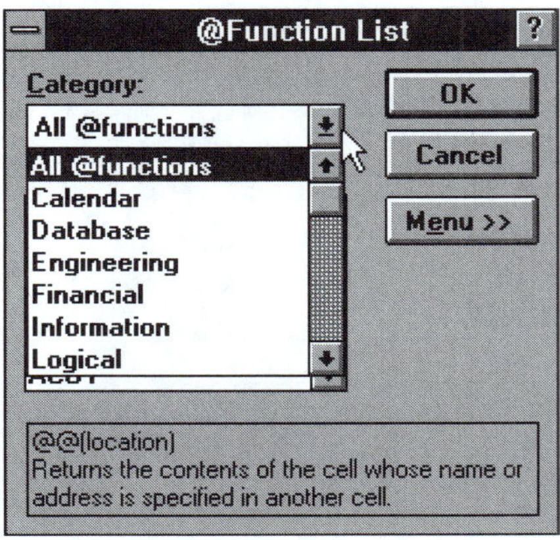

Figure 5.19 *@Function category list.*

The default setting displays All @Functions. If, however, you only want to look at Financial @Functions or Statistical @Functions, you can view the applicable functions by selecting the category you want from this list.

To change the category of @Functions shown, follow these steps:

1. Click the down arrow at the right of the category box.
2. Scroll through the list until you see the category you want.
3. Click that category.

Below the category selection list is the @Function list. This box displays all the @Functions that relate to the category you have selected. Again, the default setting is All categories.

Finally, at the bottom of the @Function dialog box is a description box. This section is like the Sample box you have seen earlier. It displays the selected @Function with its arguments as well as a brief description of the function's purpose. You can, for example, switch the category to Statistical and look for NORMAL (see Figure 5.20).

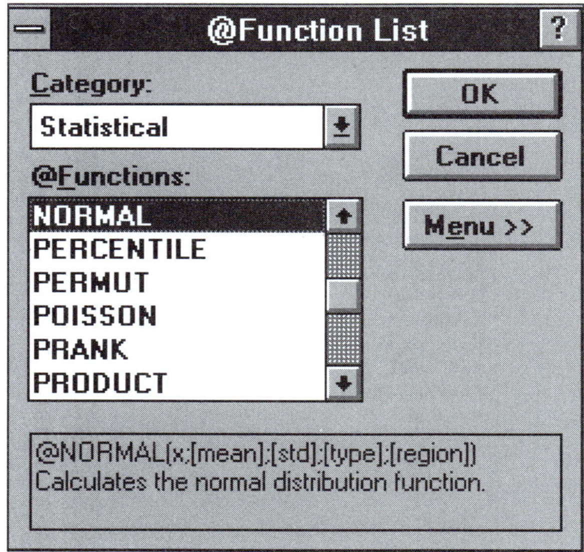

Figure 5.20 *@NORMAL function.*

We mentioned this function earlier. Notice that the description box displays the function with its arguments and the description "Calculates the normal distribution function." If you are confused as to which @Function to choose, you will find this dialog box very helpful.

Nested @Functions

It is worth noting that you can embed @Functions in other @Functions. Although you will not be using this in the budget, consider the following example. Suppose that you were using an If-Then statement in a worksheet. For example:

> If sales are greater than 100, then sum the values. If not, then average the values.

For this problem, your equation would look as follows:

```
@IF(Sales>100,@SUM(A:A1..A:A10),@AVG(A:A1..A:A10))
```

Notice the form of the equation. There is a specific way to write @IF equations. First you type **@IF**. Then, as in other @Functions, there are parentheses in which you insert the argument. In @If Functions, however, the first element of the argument is the condition. In this case the condition is "Sales greater than 100." After the condition is a comma, followed by directions for what to do if the condition is true. In this case, if the condition of sales is greater than 100 is true, 1-2-3 should sum the indicated range. Following the true clause is a comma, which is followed by directions for the computer to follow in case the condition is false. In this example, if sales are not greater than 100, Lotus 1-2-3 should average the indicated range. Thus, the format of an @IF function is as follows:

```
@IF(condition, true clause, false clause)
```

By using this equation, if the named range Sales is greater than 100, 1-2-3 will sum the range A:A1..A:A10. If sales are less than or equal to 100, the 1-2-3 will average this range.

This is called an embedded @Function or a nested @Function because you have one @Function as an argument for another @Function. It is important when you are using nested @Functions to watch your parentheses. You must close all open parentheses. Notice, for example, that the very end of the equation has a second parenthesis because it has to close the very first open parenthesis.

Practice

Now that you have learned how to use formulas in 1-2-3, go through Caroline's Budget and fill in the rest of your equations. Experiment using different approaches to creating the different formulas and using the @Functions. When you are done, your worksheets should look like Figures 5.21, 5.22, and 5.23.

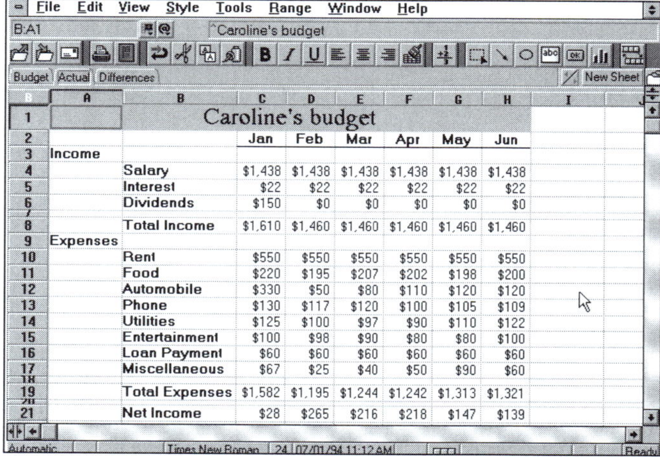

Figure 5.21 *Budget worksheet.*

Figure 5.22 *Actual worksheet.*

	Jan	Feb	Mar	Apr	May	Jun
Caroline's budget						
Income						
Salary	($38)	($38)	($38)	($38)	($38)	($38)
Interest	($2)	($2)	($2)	($2)	($2)	($2)
Dividends	$0	$0	$0	$0	$0	$0
Total Income	($40)	($40)	($40)	($40)	($40)	($40)
Expenses	$0	$0	$0	$0	$0	$0
Rent	$0	$0	$0	$0	$0	$0
Food	($20)	$5	($7)	($2)	$2	$0
Automobile	($10)	$50	$20	($10)	($20)	($20)
Phone	($30)	($17)	($20)	$0	($5)	($9)
Utilities	($5)	$20	$23	$30	$10	($2)
Entertainment	($22)	($27)	($19)	($9)	($9)	($29)
Loan Payment	$0	$0	$0	$0	$0	$0
Miscellaneous	$33	$25	$10	$0	($40)	($10)
Total Expenses	($54)	$56	$7	$9	($62)	($70)
Net Income	$14	($96)	($47)	($49)	$22	$30

Figure 5.23 *Difference worksheet.*

To Sum Up

In this chapter you learned about the different formulas you can use to perform spreadsheet calculations. We discussed the different types of formulas[md]numeric, text, and logical[md]and their respective accompanying symbols. We then listed several guidelines for using formulas, to help you enter them in a way the computer can understand.

After getting an idea about using formulas, we discussed the manner of entering formulas to calculate items on a worksheet, across multiple worksheets, and through different files, using the underlying format =(FORMULA). We discussed that your formulas will be maintained even if your cells move, and showed you how to create an absolute reference to perform a calculation referring to a cell that does not change relative to other factors.

We then discussed a major category of formula, the @Function, which is used to make many tasks, such as summing, quick and easy to do. You taught yourself to use the standard @Function name(argument) and to use the @Function Selector and @Function List to review the different @Functions and their uses. Finally, you even learned to decipher and use complicated equations featuring nested @Functions.

What You Learned

To enter a formula:

1. Select the cell into which you want the formula to apply.
2. Type the formula.
    Begin all formulas with = except for @Functions, which begin with @.
3. Click the **Confirm** button or press **Enter**.

To create a formula using a named range:

1. Name the **Range** you will need to refer to.
2. Select the cell into which you want the formula to apply.
3. Type the formula.
4. Click the **Navigator** button on the edit line.
5. Select the appropriate named **Range**.

To enter a formula that refers to other worksheets:

1. Go to the first worksheet you will refer to.
2. Select the cell you will refer to on that worksheet.
3. Type **=**.
4. Click the next worksheet tab you need.
5. Select the cell you need on that worksheet.
6. Type in the symbol you need for your formula, for example, **+**, **'**, and so on.
7. Click the worksheet tab you need to locate the next cell in the equation.
8. Click the **Confirm** button to accept the formula.

To enter formulas referencing other files:

1. Type **=(**.
2. Type **<<**.

3. Type the complete file name, including the three-character extension.

4. Type **>>**.

5. Type the appropriate cell or range in that file including the worksheet it is on.

6. Type **)**.

7. Type the formula symbol you want, such as **+**, **'**, and so on.

8. Type **(** followed by the complete file name in <<..>> and cell location of the rest of the formula.

To copy a formula to the right with relative references:

1. Select the **Range** you want to copy.

2. From the Edit menu, choose **Copy Right**.

3. Repeat for the next range.

To create an absolute reference cell:

Type a dollar sign, **$**, before each part of the cell address.

To enter an @Function:

1. Select the cell location for that function.

2. Type **@**.

3. Type the name of the @Function (for example, **SUM**).

4. Type **(**.

5. Type the argument for that function.

6. Type **)**.

7. Click the **Confirm** button or press **Enter**.

To change the category of @Function shown in the @Function Selector:

1. Select the **@Function Selector** from the edit line.

2. Select

    The List All dialog box opens.

3. Click the down arrow at the right of the category box.

4. Scroll through the list until you see the category you want.

5. Click that category.

Chapter 6

Printing

You have learned all the fundamentals of using Lotus 1-2-3 Release 5 and have done extensive work on your file BUDGET.WK4. Now you will learn how to print out your work so that you can hang your first Lotus 1-2-3 Release 5 project on the refrigerator door or frame it and place it on your desk.

Of course, there are many ways to print out your work. In this chapter, you teach yourself how to:

- Print quickly using the program's default settings.
- Print one worksheet only, all worksheets, or a selected range of cells.
- Use the Print Preview feature to examine what your worksheet will look like on paper.
- Insert Page Breaks after a selected column or row.

We will also talk about the three ways to open the handy Page Setup dialog box that lets you:

- Change the way your data is oriented on a page.
- Change margins on a page.

- Insert headers and footers on different parts of a page.
- Print row and column headings and gridlines.
- Scale your worksheet to a certain size.
- Print column and row titles.
- Save the settings you like to use when you print.

Quick Printing

Now that you have completed the basic work on Caroline's Budget, let's print your worksheets on paper and show off your new skills to all your friends! As with all the other functions we have covered, printing in Lotus 1-2-3 Release 5 allows for many different settings with which you can change the way your worksheet is printed. But before you get to these, you can quickly print your data using the program's default settings. This is the quickest way to print in Lotus 1-2-3 Release 5.

In order to print, your printer must be connected to your computer, and your computer should be set up to print. There is a Printer Setup command in the file menu that enables you to configure the system for printing Lotus 1-2-3 Release 5. This command is very similar to the general printer setup command in Windows. If you go to the File menu and select **Printer Setup**, you see the dialog box shown in Figure 6.1.

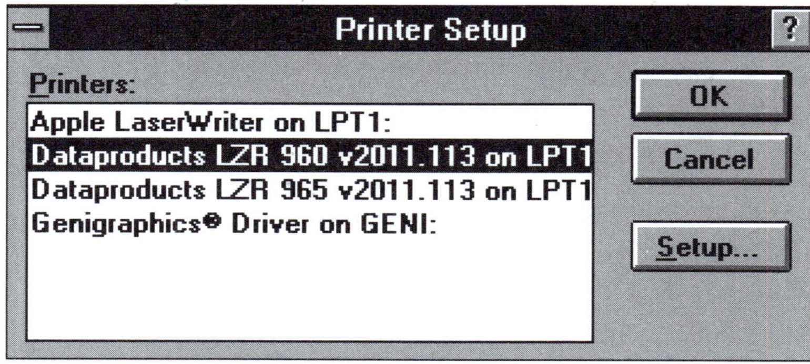

Figure 6.1 *Printer Setup dialog box.*

This command enables you to choose a printer for your data. By using this command, you can also change the settings associated with that printer. There are literally hundreds of different printers, so it is impracticable to discuss every setting. If you are having trouble setting up your printer, consult your printer manual or your Windows manual.

If you choose to quick print using the Lotus 1-2-3 Release 5 default settings, your output will be printed on whichever printer you selected in Windows. When you quick print, there are three items you can print: the current worksheet, all the worksheets, or a selected range of data on a worksheet. Any of these three options is easy to print using the default settings. We first demonstrate quick printing, and then go on to show you how you can exercise your personal preferences to print your worksheets.

Suppose that you want to print only the Budget worksheet. To do this you would activate that worksheet and tell 1-2-3 to print only the current worksheet. To print a current worksheet, follow these steps:

1. Click the worksheet tab to open the worksheet you want to print. This makes that worksheet the active worksheet. In the example, click on the Budget worksheet tab so that it is on top.

2. From the File menu, select **Print** or click the **Print** SmartIcon.

    The Print dialog box appears (see Figure 6.2).

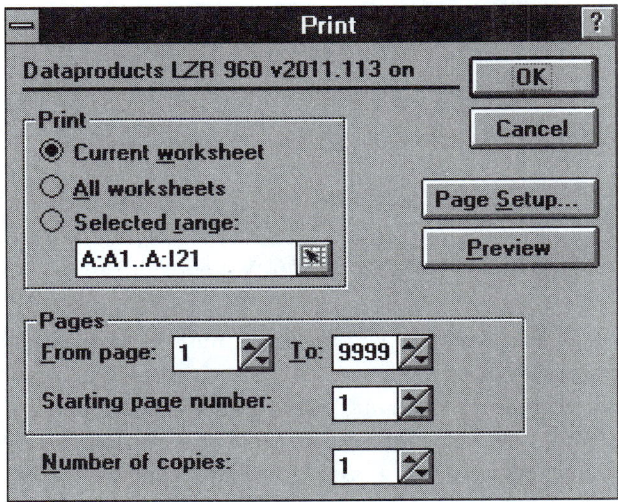

Figure 6.2 *Print dialog box.*

3. To print your work, 1-2-3 must know three things: which worksheet(s) to print, how many copies to make, and what pages to print. These are all questions you will find in the Print dialog box. At the top of the box is the Print Selector. In this area you can select the item to be printed: the current worksheet, all worksheets, or a selected range. We want to print only the current worksheet, so to follow the example, make sure that the radio button next to Current Worksheet is selected.

   At the bottom of the dialog box is a Number of Copies selector. Here, you tell 1-2-3 how many copies of the current worksheet to print.

   Finally, between these two selections is the Pages selector. Here is where you tell 1-2-3 what pages to print. This is useful when you know the exact page you want printed. Suppose, for example, that all you needed was another copy of page 2 of the current worksheet. You would enter **From Page 2 To 2** in this area (see Figure 6.3). Alternatively, you could choose to print the whole document (From Page 1 To 9999), or a smaller range of pages.

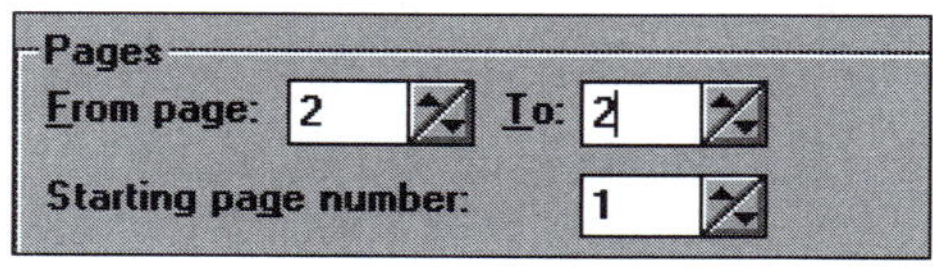

Figure 6.3 *To print only page 2.*

4. Click the radio button for **Current Worksheet**.
5. Set the number of copies.
6. Set the pages to be printed, or leave this at the default.
7. Click **OK**.

After you click OK, 1-2-3 routes your current worksheet to the printer. Your output should look similar to Figure 6.4.

When you use the quick print default settings, 1-2-3 prints all the cells in your worksheet that contain data as well as charts and graphics (which you learn how to create in later chapters). Notice that the printed output in Figure 6.4 even includes the cell value of 5% (that was the absolute reference example in Chapter 5), even though it is outside the main worksheet area. Because this worksheet is printed with default settings, it is printed in portrait mode and it does not have any header, footer, gridlines, or row and column headings. These specifics are options that you learn to use later in this chapter.

	Jan	**Feb**	**Mar**	**Apr**	**May**	**Jun**
Income:						
Salary	$1,400	$1,400	$1,400	$1,400	$1,400	$1,400
Interest	$20	$20	$20	$20	$20	$20
Dividends	$150	$0	$0	$200	$0	$0
Total Income	$1,570	$1,420	$1,420	$1,620	$1,420	$1,420
Expenses:						
Rent	$550	$550	$550	$550	$550	$550
Food	$200	$200	$200	$200	$200	$200
Automobile	$320	$100	$100	$100	$100	$100
Phone	$100	$100	$100	$100	$100	$100
Utilities	$120	$120	$120	$120	$120	$120
Entertainment	$79	$71	$71	$81	$71	$71
Loan Payment	$60	$60	$60	$60	$60	$60
Miscellaneous	$100	$50	$50	$50	$50	$50
Total Expenses	$1,529	$1,251	$1,251	$1,261	$1,251	$1,251
Net Income	$42	$169	$169	$359	$169	$169

Figure 6.4 *Printed output for current worksheet, Budget.*

Printing All Worksheets

Suppose that you wanted to print all the worksheets in a file. In the BUDGET.WK4 file that would mean you would print the Budget, Actual, and Difference worksheets. To print all worksheets, follow these steps:

1. From the File menu, select **Print** or click the **Print** SmartIcon.

   The Print dialog box appears (see Figure 6.5).

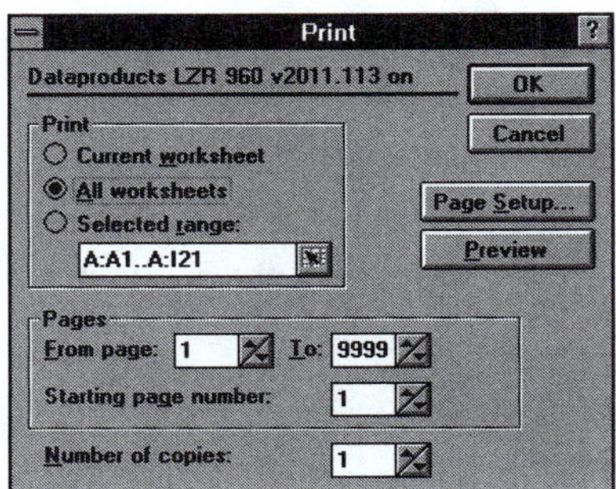

Figure 6.5 *Print dialog box.*

This is the same dialog box that appears when you print only the current worksheet. However, this time select **All Worksheets**.

3. Click the radio button for **All Worksheets**.
4. Set the number of copies.
5. Set which pages should be printed, or leave this at the default.
6. Click **OK**.

After you click OK, 1-2-3 routes all your worksheets to the printer. Your output should look similar to Figure 6.6.

Here again you used the quick print default settings to print all your worksheets. 1-2-3 printed all the cells that contained data in all the worksheets. If you had any charts and graphics, they would have been printed as well. Notice that in the printed output shown in Figure 6.6, each worksheet is printed immediately after the prior one. When you line up these three worksheets one after another, their total length is longer than one printed page. Therefore, when they are printed, the result is two printed pages of data. In this case, the page break occurs after Rent Expense on the Difference worksheet. As noted when you quick printed the worksheet only, the worksheets are printed without a header, footer, gridlines, or row and column headings, and they are printed in the portrait mode. Again, these details are discussed later in the chapter.

Printing a Selected Range

Suppose that you want to print only a selected portion of your worksheet. For example, you want to print the Budget worksheet without including the 5% cell you inserted in Chapter 5. To print a selected range, follow these steps:

1. Select the range you want to be printed. In the example, this is range **A:A1..A:H21**.

   As you know, you can use the Range Selector within the Print dialog box to select the range if you do not select it before you do step 2.

2. From the File menu, select **Print** or click the **Print** SmartIcon.

   The Print dialog box appears (see Figure 6.7).

   This is the same dialog box that appears when you print only the current worksheet or all worksheets. However, this time you want to choose **Selected Range**.

Caroline's Budget

	Jan	Feb	Mar	Apr	May	Jun
Income:						
Salary	$1,400	$1,400	$1,400	$1,400	$1,400	$1,400
Interest	$20	$20	$20	$20	$20	$20
Dividends	$150	$0	$0	$200	$0	$0
Total Income	$1,570	$1,420	$1,420	$1,620	$1,420	$1,420
Expenses:						
Rent	$550	$550	$550	$550	$550	$550
Food	$200	$200	$200	$200	$200	$200
Automobile	$320	$100	$100	$100	$100	$100
Phone	$100	$100	$100	$100	$100	$100
Utilities	$120	$120	$120	$120	$120	$120
Entertainment	$79	$71	$71	$81	$71	$71
Loan Payment	$60	$60	$60	$60	$60	$60
Miscellaneous	$100	$50	$50	$50	$50	$50
Total Expenses	$1,529	$1,251	$1,251	$1,261	$1,251	$1,251
Net Income	$42	$169	$169	$359	$169	$169

Caroline's Budget

	Jan	Feb	Mar	Apr	May	Jun
Income:						
Salary	$1,438	$1,438	$1,438	$1,438	$1,438	$1,438
Interest	$22	$22	$22	$22	$22	$22
Dividends	$150	$0	$0	$200	$0	$0
Total Income	$1,610	$1,460	$1,460	$1,660	$1,460	$1,460
Expenses:						
Rent	$550	$550	$550	$550	$550	$550
Food	$220	$195	$207	$202	$198	$200
Automobile	$330	$50	$80	$110	$120	$120
Phone	$130	$117	$120	$100	$105	$109
Utilities	$125	$100	$97	$90	$110	$122
Entertainment	$100	$98	$90	$80	$80	$100
Loan Payment	$60	$60	$60	$60	$60	$60
Miscellaneous	$67	$25	$40	$50	$90	$60
Total Expenses	$1,582	$1,1956	$1,244	$1,242	$1,313	$1,321
Net Income	$28	$265	$216	$418	$147	$139

Caroline's Budget

	Jan	Feb	Mar	Apr	May	Jun
Income:						
Salary	($38)	($38)	($38)	($38)	($38)	($38)
Interest	($2)	($2)	($2)	($2)	($2)	($2)
Dividends	$0	$0	$0	$0	$0	$0
Total Income	($40)	($40)	($40)	($40)	($40)	($40)
Expenses:						
Rent	$0	$0	$0	$0	$0	$0
Food	($20)	$5	($7)	($2)	$2	$0
Automobile	($10)	$50	$20	($10)	($20)	($20)
Phone	($30)	($17)	($20)	$0	($5)	($9)
Utilities	($5)	$20	$23	$30	$10	($2)
Entertainment	($22)	($27)	($19)	$1	($9)	($29)
Loan Payment	$0	$0	$0	$0	$0	$0
Miscellaneous	$33	$25	$10	$0	($40)	($10)
Total Expenses	($54)	$56	$7	$19	($62)	($70)
Net Income	$14	($96)	($47)	($59)	$22	$30

Figure 6.6 *Printed output for All Worksheets.*

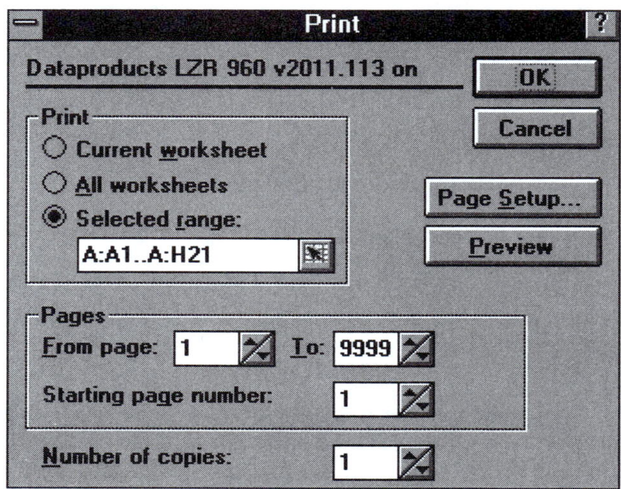

Figure 6.7 *Print dialog box.*

3. Click the radio button for **Selected Range**.

4. Verify that the selected range box contains the range you want printed. If not, use the **Range Selector** to change this range.

5. Set the number of copies.

6. Set which pages should be printed, or leave this at the default.

7. Click **OK**.

After you click **OK**, 1-2-3 routes the range selected to the printer. Your output should look similar to Figure 6.8.

When you use the quick print default settings to print only a selected range, 1-2-3 prints all the cells in the range you select (as well as any charts and graphics that fall in this range). Notice that the printed output in Figure 6.8 has the Budget worksheet printed without the 5% cell, because that was not selected as part of the range to print. This selected range is printed without any headers or footers, without gridlines or row and column headings, and it is printed in portrait mode.

	Jan	**Feb**	**Mar**	**Apr**	**May**	**Jun**
Income:						
Salary	$1,400	$1,400	$1,400	$1,400	$1,400	$1,400
Interest	$20	$20	$20	$20	$20	$20
Dividends	$150	$0	$0	$200	$0	$0
Total Income	$1,570	$1,420	$1,420	$1,620	$1,420	$1,420
Expenses:						
Rent	$550	$550	$550	$550	$550	$550
Food	$200	$200	$200	$200	$200	$200
Automobile	$320	$100	$100	$100	$100	$100
Phone	$100	$100	$100	$100	$100	$100
Utilities	$120	$120	$120	$120	$120	$120
Entertainment	$79	$71	$71	$81	$71	$71
Loan Payment	$60	$60	$60	$60	$60	$60
Miscellaneous	$100	$50	$50	$50	$50	$50
Total Expenses	$1,529	$1,251	$1,251	$1,261	$1,251	$1,251
Net Income	$42	$169	$169	$359	$169	$169

Figure 6.8 *Printed output for selected range only.*

Print Preview

Before your worksheet was actually printed, you were unaware of how your printed page would appear. To give you an idea of what your finished product will look like, 1-2-3 gives you the option to preview your printing before you send it to the printer. There are two ways to preview your work:

1. From the File menu, select **Print Preview** or click the **Print Preview** SmartIcon.

    The Print Preview dialog box appears (see Figure 6.9).

3. This dialog box looks very much like the Print dialog box. Here, you tell 1-2-3 whether you want to preview the current worksheet, all worksheets, or just a selected range. In addition, you tell 1-2-3 what pages to preview. For now, let's leave it on the default setting for Current Worksheet.

4. Click **OK**.

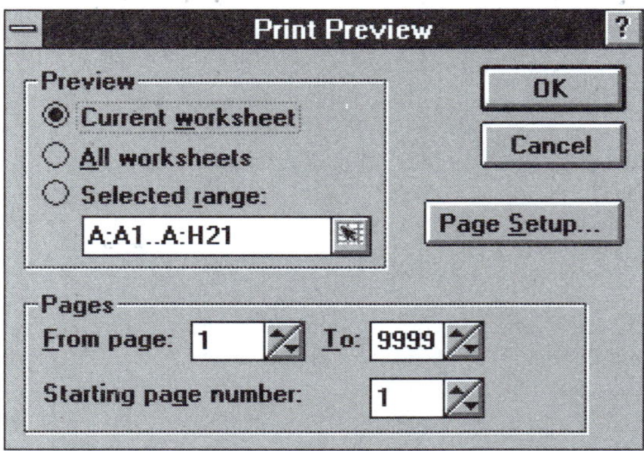

Figure 6.9 *Print Preview dialog box.*

When you click **OK**, 1-2-3 opens the Print Preview window shown in Figure 6.10.

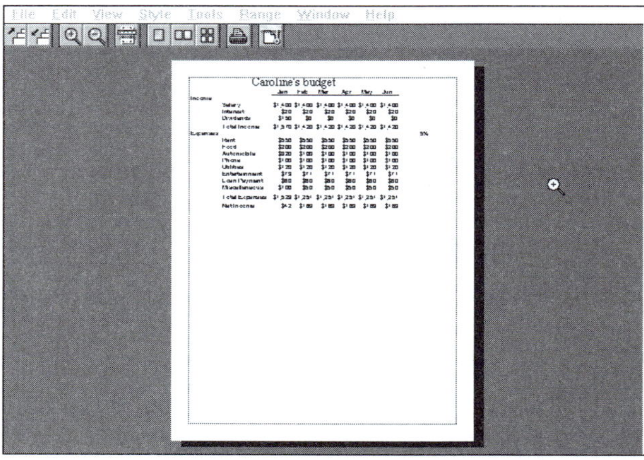

Figure 6.10 *Print Preview window.*

This is a preview of what your page will look like when it is printed. 1-2-3 zooms out so that you can view the entire page at once. At the top of the Print Preview window are buttons that enable you to maneuver through the print preview (see Figure 6.11).

The button farthest to the left is used to advance to the next printed page. In the example, because you are viewing only one worksheet, there is only one printed page, so you will not use this button.

Figure 6.11 *Print preview buttons.*

The next button lets you return to a previous printed page. If you were on page 5 of a document, this button would return you to page 4, and then to page 3, and so on. Again, in the case, you have only one page, so you will not be using this button.

Suppose that you want to zoom in to see the items in your document. The next button enables you to zoom in. Accordingly, it looks like a magnifying glass with a + sign. If you click this button, 1-2-3 magnifies the worksheet for you (see Figure 6.12). Print preview offers three levels of magnification: the two shown in Figures 6.10 and 6.12, and a third, even closer, view. The zoom + button stops working when you reach the closest level. After you have zoomed in for a closer look, you can scroll the view to see details as needed.

Figure 6.12 Magnified preview of a worksheet.

When you are finished working on the details and want to see the entire page again, you can use the mouse to click the button to the right, which is a magnifying glass with a ^{X} sign, and zoom out.

You don't really need to use the zoom buttons to zoom in and out. There's an even easier way. The mouse is automatically a zoom tool. The pointer looks just like the zoom in button, as you can see in Figures 6.10 and 6.12. Click it once to zoom closer. Click directly on the area that you want to see, because Print Preview will focus on the area you click. Click it again to zoom to the closest level. The + in the pointer changes to a - at this time. One more click returns you to the full page view.

The next button is the Page Setup button. If you click here, 1-2-3 opens the Page Setup dialog box. This dialog box lets you change the print default settings and print according to your own special needs. We discuss the Page Setup dialog box in depth later in this chapter.

The next three buttons determine how many pages you can see at once. The default is a single page, represented by the first button. Next comes the two-page button, so that you can view two pages side-by-side. Finally, the multiple page button lets you see four pages, or, by clicking it twice, nine pages. Of course, the pages are so small on your monitor that you probably won't be able to read any data, but you can see roughly what's on each page, and that can tell you if you need to set some page breaks, which is explained next. You can click any page to zoom in on it for details, and then zoom back out to see the multiple pages view again.

The next to last button is the Print button. Clicking on this button opens the Print dialog box, which you saw earlier. You can follow the directions in the Print dialog box and go on to print your data.

The last button is the Escape button. This lets you leave the Print Preview window and return to your worksheet.

It is always useful to look at Print Preview before you print. This reduces both the amount of wasted paper and the frustration that inevitably arises when you print a worksheet with mistakes or bad page breaks in it.

Page Breaks

In general, 1-2-3 will prepare your work for a print job and automatically divide the data into separate pages. In a large worksheet, however, you may want to control where pages end and new pages begin. You can manually tell 1-2-3 where to insert a page break[md]to the left of a column, above a row, or both[md]by using the Page Break command.

To insert a page break along a column, follow these steps:

1. Determine the column that you want to be the first column on the next page, such as column I.

2. Click the mouse on any cell in column I.

3. From the Style menu, select **Page Break**.

    The Page Break dialog box appears (see Figure 6.13).

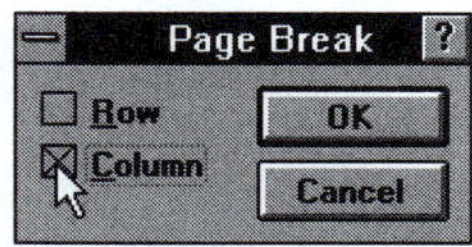

Figure 6.13 *Page Break dialog box.*

4. Click the box next to Column.

5. Click **OK**.

When you insert a page break, 1-2-3 puts dotted lines where the break will be (see Figure 6.14).

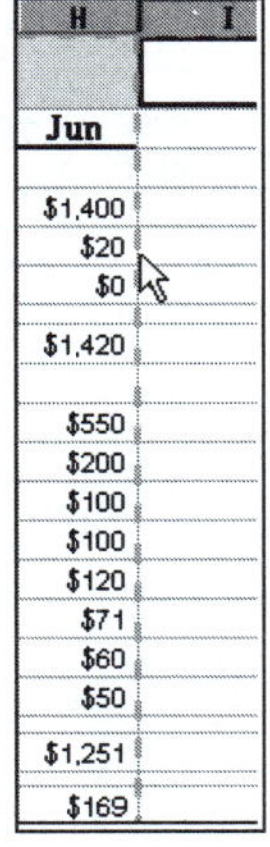

Figure 6.14 *Dotted lines signify a page break.*

In this example, 1-2-3 put dotted lines in between columns H and I because you put a column page break between these columns.

To insert a page break along a row, follow these steps:

1. Determine the row you want to begin the next page. In the example, that is row 22.

2. Click any cell in row 22.

3. From the Style menu, select **Page Break**.

The Page Break dialog box appears (see Figure 6.15).

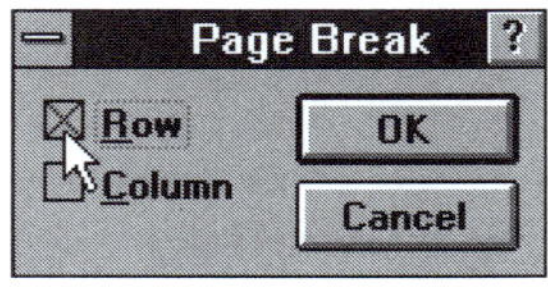

Figure 6.15 *Page Break dialog box.*

4. Click the box next to Row.

6. Click **OK**.

This time, 1-2-3 puts dotted lines between rows 21 and 22 (see Figure 6.16).

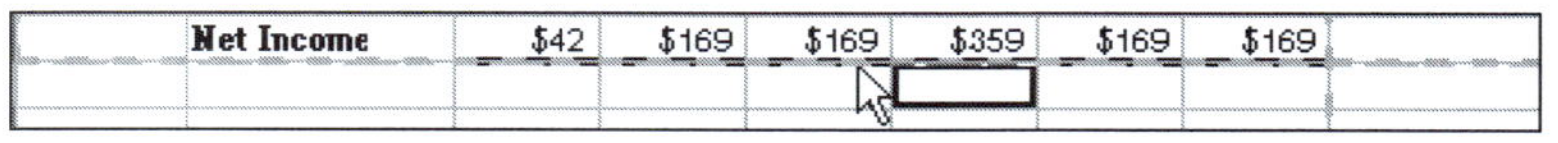

Figure 6.16 *Dotted lines signify a page break.*

If you want to remove page breaks, you can do this by activating a cell in the row or column where you put a page break, opening the Page Break dialog box, and deselecting the row and column boxes.

Page Setup

Previously, we mentioned a command called Page Setup. By opening this dialog box, you can stop 1-2-3 from printing your worksheet with the default settings and change the settings to your own needs. The Page Setup dialog box is shown in Figure 6.17.

All the remaining printing options can be found in the Page Setup dialog box.

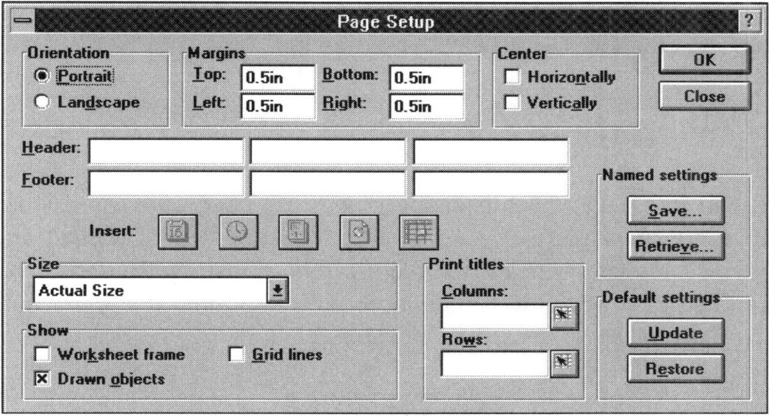

Figure 6.17 *Page Setup dialog box.*

There are three different ways to access this dialog box.

- From the File menu, select **Page Setup**.
- From the File menu, select **Print**, and in the Print dialog box, click on the **Page Setup** button (see Figure 6.18).

Figure 6.18 *Page Setup button in Print dialog box.*

- From the File menu, select **Print Preview**, and in the Print Preview window, click with the mouse on the **Page Setup** button.

The reason 1-2-3 provides three ways to access the Page Setup dialog box is that there are many different ways you will want to use it. If, for example, you go to Print but forget to change something in Page Setup, you can access it from in the Print dialog box. Similarly, you may preview a page and wonder how it will look if you change the Page Setup. Therefore, you have access to page setup from in the Print Preview window. No matter how you happen to open the Page Setup dialog box, you will see the same dialog box.

In the rest of the chapter, you learn about the different options available when you open the Page Setup dialog box.

Print Orientation

The first item in the Page Setup dialog box is the page orientation (see Figure 6.19). There are two options for a printed page's orientation: portrait and landscape. Portrait orientation means the page will be printed with more information down the page than across it. Generally, it will be printed down a standard 8.5 by 11-inch piece of paper, as shown in Figure 6.20.

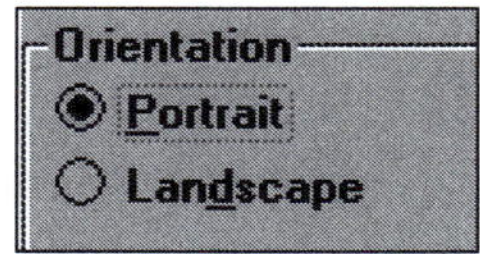

Figure 6.19 *Orientation Selector in Page Setup dialog box.*

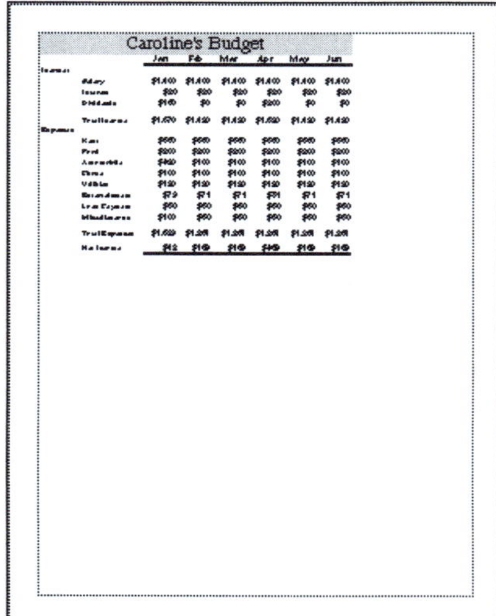

Portrait orientation.

Landscape, on the other hand, is left to right orientation, like a wide picture of a landscape. There will be more information printed horizontally across the page than down it. Generally, this is a standard page rotated to 11 by 8.5 inches (see Figure 6.21).

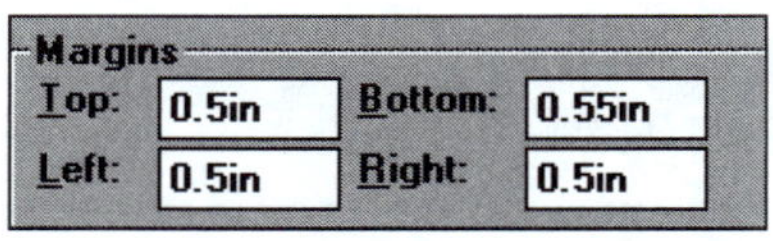

Figure 6.21 *Landscape orientation.*

To change the orientation of a document, follow these steps:

1. Open the **Page Setup** dialog box.
2. Click the radio button next to **Portrait** or **Landscape**.

The default setting is portrait orientation. However, you often will find yourself switching to landscape if you use wide spreadsheets. If your spreadsheet does not fit on the printed page, try switching the orientation to landscape.

Margins

The next option in the Page Setup dialog box lets you alter the page margins (see Figure 6.22).

Figure 6.22 *Page margin setting.*

Margins are the blank space that 1-2-3 leaves around the edge of your printed page.

Sometime you may want to decrease the page margins to allow more data to fit on a page. Other times, you may want to increase the page margins to move your worksheet toward the center of the page. For example, in Figure 6.22, Caroline's Budget prints in the upper left corner of the page. However, it is also possible to shift this worksheet over to the right and lower it so that it will appear more centered on the page. To change the page margins, follow these steps:

1. Open the **Page Setup** dialog box.
2. Type new margins into the **Top**, **Bottom**, **Left**, and **Right** boxes. In the example, change the Top and Left margins to **2.0** inches instead of .5 inches.

N O T E

Most laser and inkjet printers cannot print too closely to the margins of the page. If you make the margins too small, your printer might not be able to print all the data. In many cases, your printer driver knows the limitations of your printer and refuses to set impossible margins. It won't beep, but if you look at the Page Setup dialog box again, you'll see that the margins have been set to your printer's minimum instead of your choices.

When you change these margins, the printed page will appear as shown in Figure 6.23.

		Jan	Feb	Mar	Apr	May	Jun
Caroline's budget							
Income							
	Salary	$1,400	$1,400	$1,400	$1,400	$1,400	$1,400
	Interest	$20	$20	$20	$20	$20	$20
	Dividends	$150	$0	$0	$0	$0	$0
	Total Income	$1,570	$1,420	$1,420	$1,420	$1,420	$1,420
Expenses							
	Rent	$550	$550	$550	$550	$550	$550
	Food	$200	$200	$200	$200	$200	$200
	Automobile	$320	$100	$100	$100	$100	$100
	Phone	$100	$100	$100	$100	$100	$100
	Utilities	$120	$120	$120	$120	$120	$120
	Entertainment	$79	$71	$71	$71	$71	$71
	Loan Payment	$60	$60	$60	$60	$60	$60
	Miscellaneous	$100	$50	$50	$50	$50	$50
	Total Expenses	$1,529	$1,251	$1,251	$1,251	$1,251	$1,251
	Net Income	$42	$169	$169	$169	$169	$169

Figure 6.23 *Caroline's Budget with large page margins.*

When changing the margins before you print, it will be especially helpful for you to refer to Print Preview (discussed earlier in this chapter), to see how narrow or wide margins will look and where on the page your data will be placed.

1-2-3 offers an even easier way to center the data on the printed page. Just choose Horizontally or Vertically in the Center area of the Page Setup dialog box. You can choose both options to center the printed matter in both directions on the page.

Headers and Footers

The next item in the Page Setup dialog box is an option for Headers and Footers (see Figure 6.24).

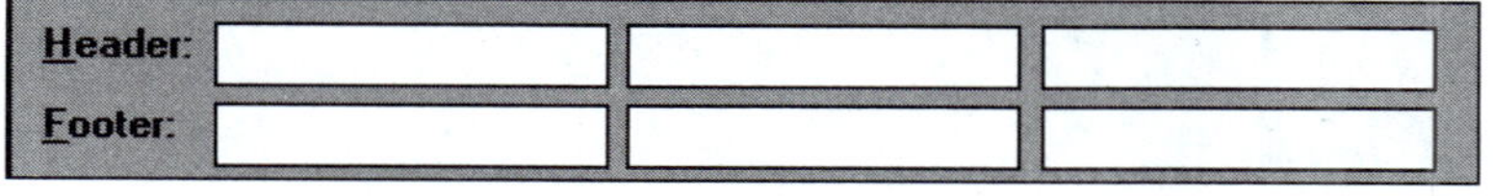

Figure 6.24 *Headers and footers.*

A header is a line of text that appears at the top of every printed page. A footer is a line of text that appears at the bottom of every printed page. Headers and footers can either be centered on the page or aligned with the right side or the left side of the page. Accordingly, 1-2-3 provides three boxes for you to enter your selections regarding headers and footers. If your text is entered into the middle box for Header, it will appear centered at the top of the page. Similarly, if you enter text into the box at the far right for Footer, 1-2-3 will place that text at the bottom right of every page.

Headers and footers are usually used to place titles on worksheets or page numbers, dates or times of printing, file names, or even general information as to the contents of a cell. Although you can simply type text into the header and footer boxes in the Page Setup dialog box, 1-2-3 provides some shortcuts to enter certain commonly used information. Below the Header and Footer boxes are a line of buttons labeled Insert (see Figure 6.25).

Table 6.1 contains a list of the buttons together with their function and their keyboard equivalents, should you want to type the entry instead of using the mouse to click the insert button.

Figure 6.25 *Insert buttons.*

Table 6.1 *Insert Buttons*

Button	Function	Keyboard Equivalent
	Date of Printing	å
	Time of Printing	+
	Page Number	#
	File Name	^
	Contents of a Cell	\ (followed by a cell address)

Because the keyboard equivalents (@, +, #, ^, and \) have special meaning in a header or footer, you cannot use them for their usual meaning unless you mark them in some way. To print any one of these characters in a header or footer, you must precede that character by typing an apostrophe ('). If, for example, you want to enter the page number in a footer, preceded by the number sign (#1, #2, and so forth), you would type:

'##

The apostrophe before the first # tells 1-2-3 that the first # should be printed as is. The second # tells the program to print the page number. (You can always check out the result in Print Preview before printing to make sure that you're getting what you want.)

To enter a header or footer, follow these steps:

1. Open the **Page Setup** dialog box.

2. Click the box that relates to the type of text (header or footer) and its desired placement, centered or aligned left or right on the page.

3. Enter the text or click the **Insert** button that corresponds to the entry you want.

4. Click **OK**.

Hiding Row and Column Headings and Gridlines

The next item in the Page Setup dialog box gives you the option to hide or show the row and column headings and the gridlines (see Figure 6.26).

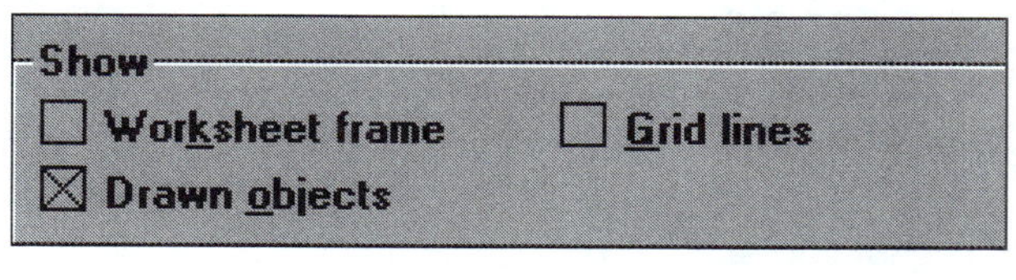

Figure 6.26 *Row and column headings and gridlines.*

When 1-2-3 uses its default settings while printing, it does not print the row and column headings of the worksheet; nor does it print the cell gridlines. You may sometimes, however, find it useful to have those items appear on your worksheet. If, for example, you are working with a large spreadsheet, you probably will find it easier to follow the rows and columns of data if you can see the gridlines. Similarly, you may want to see the column and row headings to help you find your place on a large worksheet. If you want 1-2-3 to show either the row and column headings or the cell gridlines, follow these steps:

1. Open the **Page Setup** dialog box.
2. Click the box next to **Gridlines** to make them visible.
3. Click the box next to Worksheet Frame to show the row and column headings.
4. Click **OK**.

Scaling

Another option in the Page Setup dialog box enables you to scale or size your worksheet (see Figure 6.28).

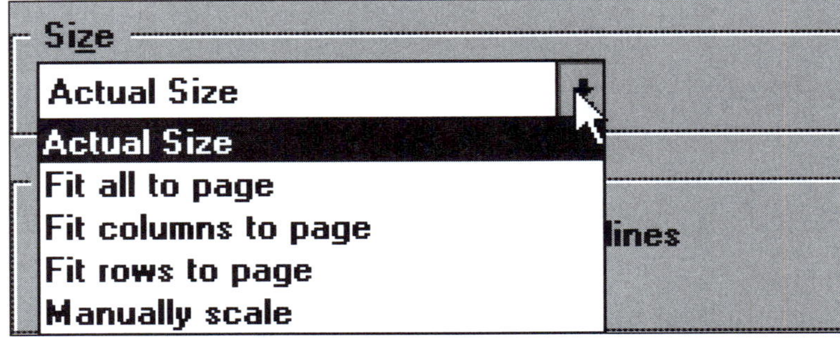

Figure 6.27 *Scaling option in the Page Setup dialog box.*

The default setting for the size of your worksheet is Actual Size. However, you may also choose to print out your work in a different size. Table 6.2 lists the choices available to you and a brief description of their purpose.

The scaling option is one of the most useful features of 1-2-3. For instance, earlier in the budget example you printed all three worksheets at once. As you may recall, they required one and a half pages to print. If you wanted to conserve your paper and improve your convenience by printing all three worksheets on one page, you could have done so by changing the page setup so that the documents fit on one page (see Figure 6.28).

Note if you choose manual scaling, a little box appears, asking you for a percentage to scale the document (see Figure 6.29). The document will be scaled proportionally by the percentage you select. That means that both the width and height are adjusted by that percentage. To use this option effectively, you must be able to imagine what a differently scaled worksheet would look like. Because this may be difficult, you might want to refer to Print Preview to double-check the way your worksheet will look when it is scaled to a different percentage.

Table 6.2 *Size Options*

Option	Function
Actual Size	Worksheet is printed in its actual size.
Fit All to Page	Worksheet is automatically scaled so that it prints on one page.
Fit Columns to Page	Worksheet is automatically scaled so that its width prints on one page.
Fit Rows to Page	Worksheet is automatically scaled so that its length prints on one page
Manually Scale	Lotus 1-2-3 Release 5 prompts you to provide a percentage by which to scale thw worksheet.

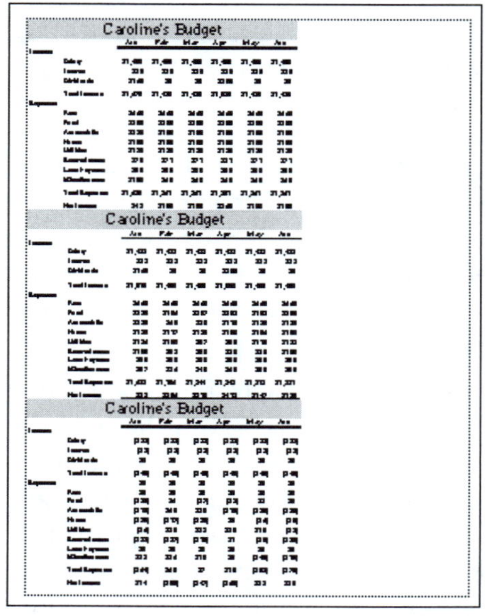

Figure 6.28 *All worksheets scaled to fit on one page.*

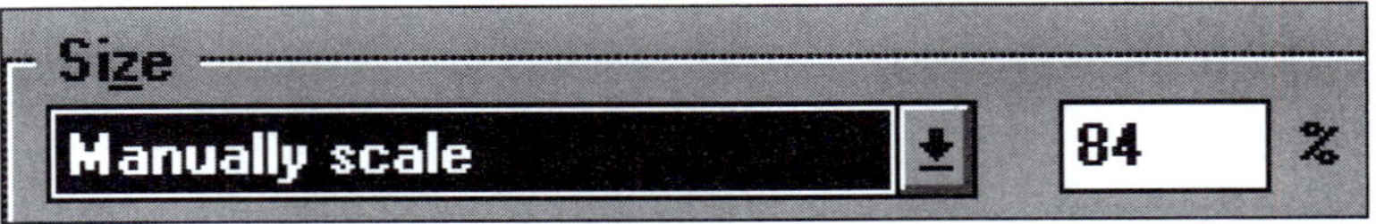

Figure 6.29 Manual scaling.

Print Titles

The Page Setup dialog box also provides you with an option to Print Titles (see Figure 6.30).

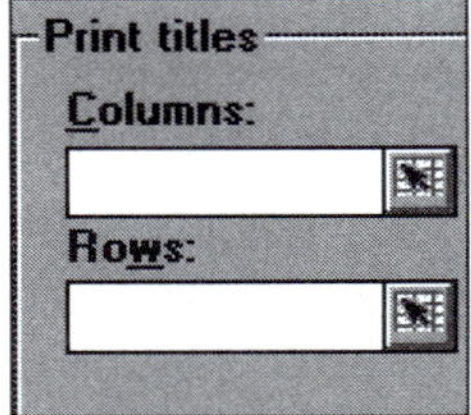

Figure 6.30 Print Titles option in the Page Setup dialog box.

Suppose that you are working with a large spreadsheet whose length or width spans multiple pages. Without the Printed Titles option, only the first page would show the titles of your rows and columns, such as Salary (on the left) and January (at the top). It could be very difficult to interpret the data on the second and subsequent pages. Columns that did not fit on page one would not have the expense item names that refer to the data. Similarly, rows that did not fit on page one would lack month names.

One solution to this problem might be to use the scaling option to print Caroline's Budget on one page. If, however, the worksheet is a large one, the printed result may be too small to read. This is the time to use the print titles option, which enables you to identify the rows and columns that contain the titles for your data. You simply select the range that contains all the month names and designate them to be column titles. Similarly, you could designate the range with the expense names to be the row titles. By doing so, every printed page would have the respective months and expense names, making it easier to understand your data.

To assign row and column titles, follow these steps:

1. Open the **Page Setup** dialog box.
2. Type the range for the column and row titles into the respective boxes, or use the Range Selector to select the range from the worksheets.
3. Click **OK**.

Remember that column titles are found all in one row and row titles are found all in one column. This can be a little confusing at times, but if you get them backwards the first time, the result will be a spreadsheet that is so memorably peculiar that you will have no difficulty keeping these options straight from then on. You can also take the guesswork out of this option by using Print Preview.

Saving and Retrieving Settings

The final option in the Page Setup dialog box is to name your settings (see Figure 6.31).

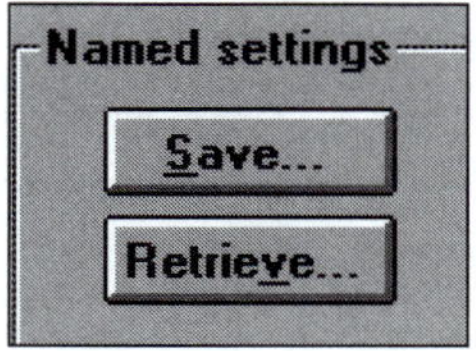

Figure 6.31 *Named Settings option in the Page Setup dialog box.*

If you use the same print settings often, you may find it helpful to give those settings a name so that you can retrieve them later. This is similar to creating a named style or range so that you can conveniently refer to it at a later time. To save a named setting:

1. Open the **Page Setup** dialog box.
2. Alter the print settings to reflect exactly what you want.
3. Click the **Save** button.
4. The Save As dialog box appears. Give the settings a file name and location for 1-2-3 to save it.

5. Click OK.

To retrieve a named setting:

1. Open the **Page Setup** dialog box.
2. Click the **Retrieve** button.
3. The Open dialog box appears. Locate the **Named Setting** file you want to use and select it.
4. Click **OK**.
5. After you retrieve the Named Settings file, click **OK** to exit the Page Setup dialog box.

If you want to reset 1-2-3 to its default Page Setup settings, click the **Restore** button in the Page Setup dialog box (see Figure 6.32).

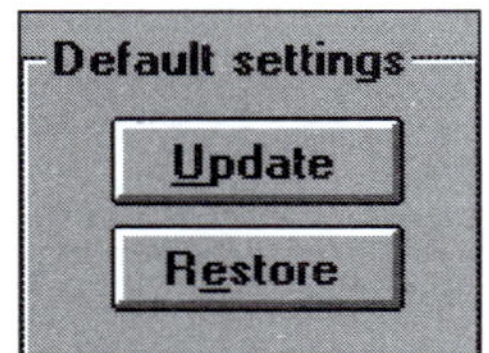

Figure 6.32 *Restore Page Setup settings to default.*

In Appendix B, you learn about customizing the default page setup settings.

To Sum Up

You finally have solid evidence that you can use 1-2-3 Release 5 printed copies of your worksheets. In this chapter you learned the commands to print quickly using default settings, printing one worksheet, a whole file of worksheets, or merely a selected range of cells. You also learned to use Print Preview in order to see in advance, the way your file will appear on paper and, if you want, to insert Page Breaks where desired. You also discovered how to use the powerful Page Setup dialog box that enables you to alter the orientation, margins, and scaling of your worksheet and to insert headers, footers, row and column headings, gridlines, and titles. Finally, you learned how to save and retrieve your favorite print settings.

What You Learned

Print the current worksheet:

1. Open the worksheet you want to print.
2. From the File menu, select **Print**.

    The Print dialog box appears.
3. Click the radio button for **Current Worksheet**.
4. Set the number of copies.
5. Set the pages to be printed.
6. Click **OK**.

Print all worksheets:

1. From the File menu, select **Print**.

    The Print dialog box appears.
2. Click the radio button for **All Worksheets**.
3. Set the number of copies.
4. Set the pages to be printed.
5. Click **OK**.

Print a selected page:

1. Select the range you want to be printed.
2. From the File menu, select **Print**.

    The Print dialog box appears.
3. Click the radio button for **Selected Range**.
4. Verify that the Selected Range box contains the range you want printed.
5. Set the number of copies.
6. Set the pages to be printed.
7. Click **OK**.

Open the Print Preview function:

1. From the File menu, select **Print Preview**.

    The Print Preview dialog box appears.

2. Choose whether you want to preview the current worksheet, all work-sheets, or just a selected range.

3. Choose which pages to preview.

4. Click **OK**.

Insert a page break after a specified column:

1. Determine the column you want to begin the next page.

2. Click any cell in that column.

3. From the Style menu, select **Page Break**.

    The Page Break dialog box appears.

4. Click the box next to **Column**.

5. Click **OK**.

Insert a page break after a specified row:

1. Determine the row you want to begin the next page.

2. Click any cell in that row.

3. From the Style menu, select **Page Break**.

    The Page Break dialog box appears.

4. Click in the box next to **Row**.

5. Click **OK**.

Open the Page Setup dialog box in three different ways:

1. From the File menu, select **Page Setup**.

2. From the File menu, select **Print**, at the Print dialog box, click the **Page Setup** button.

3. From the File menu, select **Print Preview**, and in the Print Preview window, click on the **Page Setup** button.

Change orientation:

1. Open the **Page Setup** dialog box.
2. Select either **Portrait** or **Landscape** by clicking the appropriate radio button.
3. Click **OK**.

Change margins:

1. Open the **Page Setup** dialog box.
2. Type in the selected margins.
3. Click **OK**.

Insert headers and footers:

1. Open the **Page Setup** dialog box.
2. Click the box for the type of header or footer desired and place it to the left, center, or right.
3. Enter the text, or click the **Insert** button corresponding to the entry you want.
4. Click **OK**.

Insert row or column headings or gridlines:

1. Open the **Page Setup** dialog box.
2. Click the box next to **Gridlines** to make them visible, or click the box next to **Worksheet Frame** to show row and column headings.
3. Click **OK**.

Alter the scaling of a worksheet:

1. Open the **Page Setup** dialog box.
2. Select a size from Table 6.1 or choose to scale manually.

   If you choose to scale manually, type in the percentage you want to scale to.

3. Click **OK**.

Print titles:

1. Open the **Page Setup** dialog box.
2. Type the range for column and row titles into the respective boxes.
3. Click **OK**.

Save the print settings you like:

1. Open the **Page Setup** dialog box.
2. Alter the print settings to the ones you like.
3. Click the **Save** button.
4. The Save As dialog box appears.
5. Give the file a name and location to save to.
6. Click **OK**.

Retrieve a named setting:

1. Open the **Page Setup** dialog box.
2. Click the **Retrieve** button.

   The Open dialog box appears.
3. Locate the **Named Setting** file you want and select it.
4. Click **OK**.
5. After you retrieve the named settings file, click **OK** to exit the Page Setup dialog box.

Chapter 7

Charts

So far, the work you have done and the data you have entered have gone onto worksheets in straight textual or numerical form. Sometimes, however, it may be helpful to portray your data as a chart or a graph, so that the information is more clearly understandable by the reader. To help you, Lotus 1-2-3 Release 5 provides the capability to convert numerical data into a pictorial format, or chart. As you will see in this chapter, these charts are easy to create and are automatically updated by 1-2-3 as you edit data in the cells of your worksheet.

In this chapter, you learn all the fundamentals you need to know when you are working with charts, as you teach yourself to:

- Identify different chart types and parts of charts.
- Decide which type of chart suits your needs.
- Create a chart using the 1-2-3 Quick Chart default settings.
- Name your chart and find a named chart.
- Change a chart's type, orientation, and placement in a chart box.
- Change and move chart headings and notes.

- Enhance and move your chart's legend.

- Change labels and units on the axes.

- Change the scale of a chart.

- Explode pieces of a pie chart.

- Alter lines and color to format a chart the way you like.

- Print a chart.

- Manually create a chart, formatting it with the options you like.

What Is a Chart?

Charts are graphical representations of your worksheet data. They convey information in pictorial form, enabling it to be easily understood. There are many types of charts, each with its own purpose. As you become familiar with the several chart alternatives that 1-2-3 provides, you will find that certain kinds of data are well expressed in one type of chart whereas other kinds of data are better represented in another chart. But, no matter which kind of chart you decide to use, most charts have a few features in common, as shown in Figure 7.1.

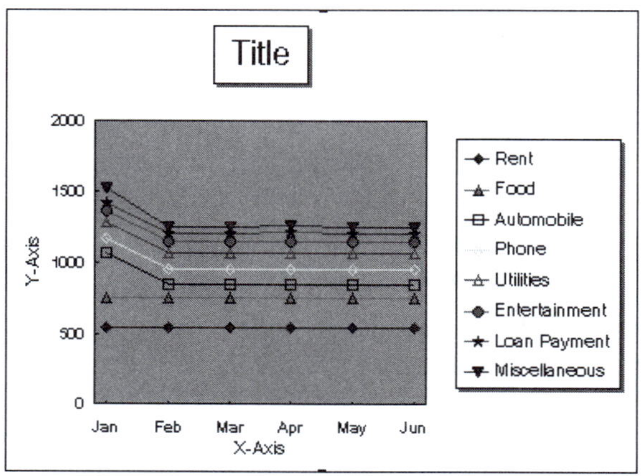

Figure 7.1 *Most charts have common features.*

Most charts have two axes: the X axis and the Y axis (sometimes called the horizontal and vertical axes, respectively). The X, or horizontal, axis is usually the "category" axis, because the data categories are represented on this axis. The X axis might, for example, represent months of the year and that each point along the axis is one month. The Y, or vertical, axis usually reflects "values" of the data pertaining to the categories on the X axis. The types of data plotted are called the *series*. In the example above, there are separate lines for the various budget expense items, such as Rent and Food. These expenses are the series in this particular graph.

There are always exceptions. For example, pie charts do not have X and Y axes.

Most charts also have a title, labels for the axes, and a legend. The title gives a brief description of the data represented in the chart. The labels on the axes identify the categories and values. A *legend* is the box that labels the different data series, because those cannot be labeled on either axis.

Chart Types

There are many different types of charts. You can create 12 types of charts in 1-2-3. Some charts have different options to differentiate them even further. Table 7.1 lists some of the more common types of charts that you can use in 1-2-3.

Table 7.1 *The More Common Types of Charts*

Picture	Type
	Line Chart
	Area Chart
	Bar Chart
	Stacked Bar Chart

Table 7.1 *Continued*

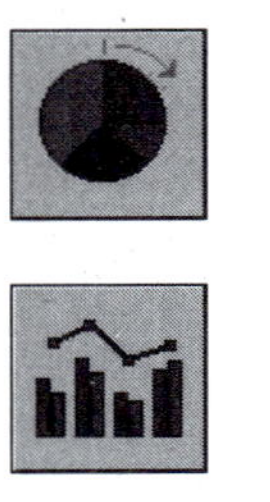 Pie Chart

 Mixed Chart

 3D Line Chart

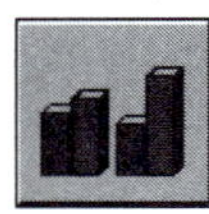 3D Area chart

 3D Bar Chart

 3D Pie Chart

XY Chart

Before you begin to create charts, take a moment to consider which type will best represent your data. Line charts, for example, are particularly useful to show changes or trends in data over a period of time. In a line chart, 1-2-3 plots the Y values for the different X categories (which usually represents time intervals, such as months), and then fits a line to these data points. Because you can see the progression of this line over time (from left to right), it is easy to see trends or changes that have occurred. You could, for example, use a line chart to plot the change in total expenses over the months in the budget, as shown in

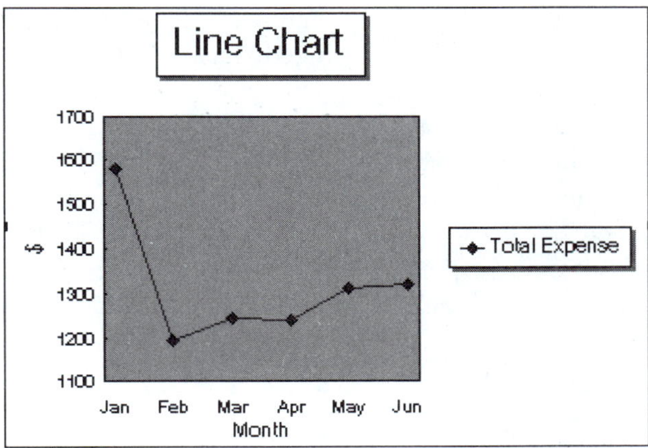

Figure 7.2 *Line chart of total expenses.*

Area charts are similar to line charts. Instead of just fitting a line to the data series, however, 1-2-3 shades in the area under the line. This creates an area that graphically represents the data point. This type of chart emphasizes the magnitude of changes over time, because you can see the area under the curve grow and shrink. You could, for example, plot the same graph as the line chart but this time use a chart that fills in the area under the line, as shown in Figure 7.3. This would be particularly helpful to show how great or small the expenses are.

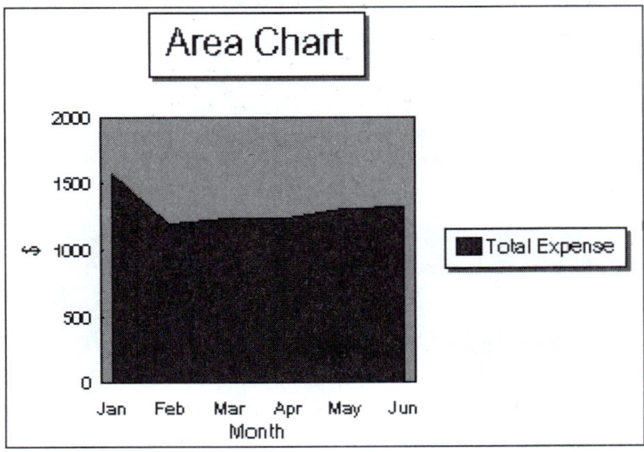

Figure 7.3 *Area chart of total expenses.*

Bar charts are a bit different than line and area charts. Although you can use them to see changes over time, bar charts emphasize individual data values. For this reason, bar charts are well-suited for comparing the different data values for each category. 1-2-3 plots the data points as it does with line charts, but instead of fitting a line to these data points, it creates bars that represent each data point. You could, for example, plot Total Expenses for each month to see how they compare to each other. Instead of seeing whether the expenses have increased or decreased over time, this type of chart lets you effectively demonstrate that January's expenses are higher than February, and so forth (see Figure 7.4).

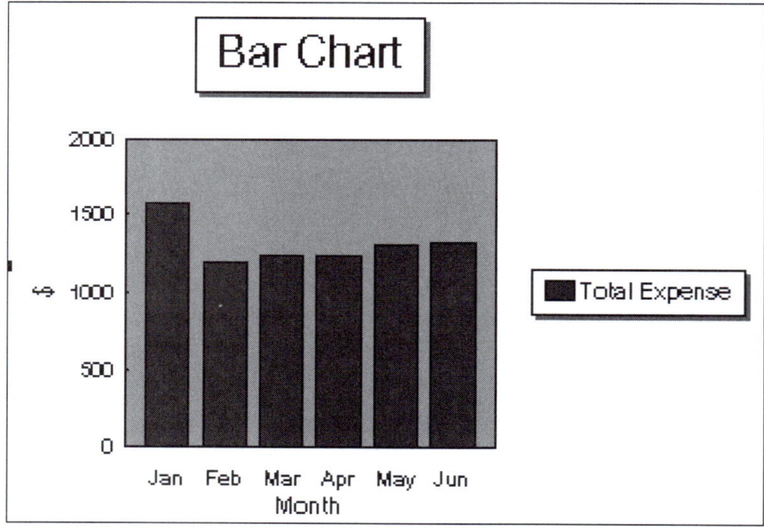

Figure 7.4 *Bar chart of total expenses.*

Stacked bar charts are similar to bar charts, but instead of clustering bars next to each other, the data series for each category is stacked one on top of the other. This type of chart is especially useful when you need to compare the individual values in a category against the total for that category. If, for example, you were to plot all the expense items in a stacked bar chart, you would be able to see, for each month, how the individual expense items compared to the total expense for the month, as shown in Figure 7.5, and you will still be able to see the progression of the totals from month to month.

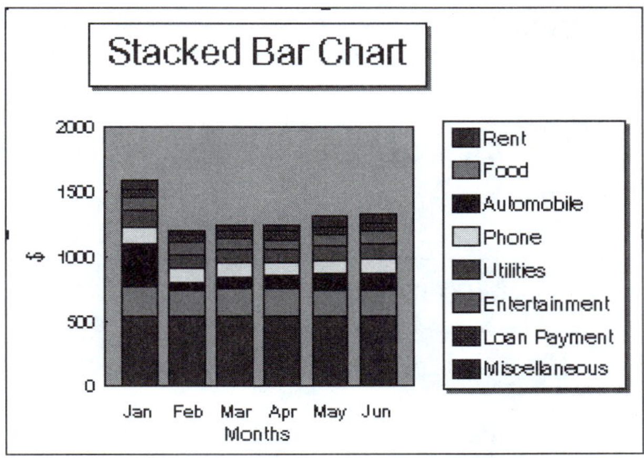

Figure 7.5 *Stacked bar chart of different expense items.*

Pie charts are similar to stacked bar charts in that they represent data values in relation to a total. Stacked bar charts show the actual values in relation to the total value. In contrast, pie charts represent the values as percentages of a total pie. Each piece of the pie is a different data point as a percent of the total of all data points. As seen in Figure 7.6, you could use the pie chart to represent graphically each expense item as a percent of January's total expenses.

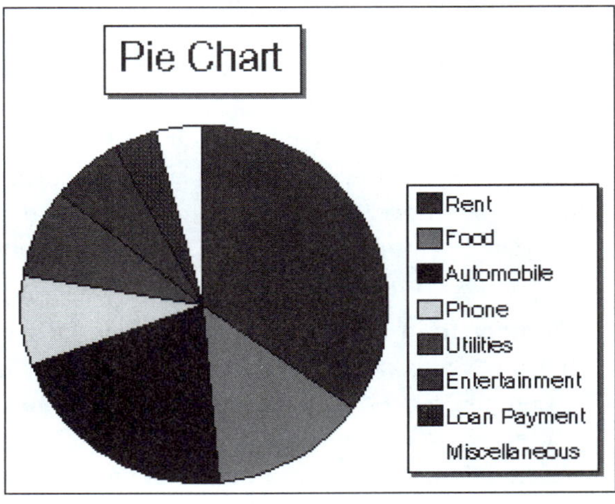

Pie chart of January's expenses.

1-2-3 also can combine different chart types in one chart. Instead of showing two data series as line charts or bar charts, for example, you could show one as a line and the other as a bar. With 1-2-3, you can combine parts of line, area, and bar charts into one chart. You could, for example, plot Caroline's total expenses as a bar chart, and then plot the net income for the months as a line chart to show how it changes over time, as shown in Figure 7.7.

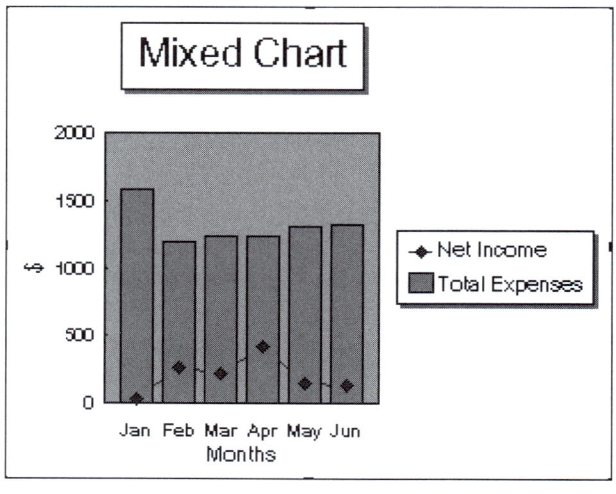

***Figure* 7.7** *Mixed chart of total expenses and net income.*

With 1-2-3 Release 5, you also can create three-dimensional line, area, bar, and pie charts. These are similar to and have the same uses as the charts already discussed, but they have a three-dimensional appearance. Despite their fancy, professional look, however, they are often more difficult to read, particularly the Y axis values. You should use discretion when creating a three-dimensional chart. Remember that the underlying purpose of charts is to show data clearly. Try to choose a chart that simplifies, rather than complicates matters.

XY charts are different from all other charts. Instead of having categories, such as months, along the X axis, XY charts plot data values against a numeric X axis. XY charts are often just plotted as data points with no lines, bars, or areas. These are called scatter plots or scatter charts. This type of chart is a good choice when you are examining statistics to determine whether there is a correlation or relationship between X and Y values. If the data points tend to fall along a line, there is a correlation between the two items. An example of an XY chart is a graph that plots the amount of gas you use to heat your house against the average temperature for that month. By using this type of chart, you would probably find a correlation between these two values, because on colder days you use more heat and on warmer days you use less heat. You would find a negative correlation, meaning that as the X value (temperature) increases, the Y value (amount of gas) decreases.

Creating a Chart

Now that you have discussed the main types of charts and their uses, let's create one. There are two main ways to create a chart in 1-2-3 Release 5. First, 1-2-3 can create a chart quickly from a selected range of cells. If you use this method, 1-2-3 uses its default settings to create a chart based on a range of cells you select.

When you use 1-2-3 to create a chart, you need to decide whether the worksheet rows represent categories and the columns represent the series, or vice versa. In the example worksheet, because the expense items represent the series and the months are the categories, the columns are the series and the rows are the categories. 1-2-3 uses the following assumptions:

1. If the selected range has more rows than columns of data, then 1-2-3 assumes the data series is by columns, as shown in Figure 7.8.

$550	$550
$220	$195
$330	$50
$130	$117
$125	$100
$100	$98
$60	$60
$67	$25

Figure 7.8 *More rows than columns, so series by columns.*

2. If the selected range has more columns than rows of data, then 1-2-3 assumes the data series is by rows, as shown in Figure 7.9.

$550	$550	$550	$550	$550
$220	$195	$207	$202	$198
$330	$50	$80	$110	$120
$130	$117	$120	$100	$105
$125	$100	$97	$90	$110

Figure 7.9 *More columns than rows, so data by rows.*

3. 1-2-3 ignores blank rows and columns in a selected range.

If you choose to use the Quick Chart method, there is something else you should know. If you have your series formatted by column, as in Figure 7.10, or formatted by row, as in Figure 7.11, then 1-2-3 automatically selects your chart title, legend entries, and X axis labels from the selected range.

	A	B	C
1	Title		
2	Subtitle		
3			
4		Legend Label	Legend Label
5	X Axis Labels	1st Column Data Series	2nd Column Data Series
6			
7			
8			
9			
10			
11			
12			
13			

Figure 7.10 *Formatted series by column.*

	A	B	C	D	E
1	Title				
2	Subtitle				
3					
4		X Axis Labels			
5	Legend Label	1st Row Data Series			
6	Legend Label	2nd Row Data Series			
7					

Figure 7.11 *Formatted series by row.*

If, however, the range you select contains only numerical data, 1-2-3 creates a default title, axis label, and legend entry for you.

In any event, anything that is automatically created by 1-2-3 can be changed at a later time, so it does not really matter whether everything is formatted perfectly the first time around.

Let's begin creating a chart by plotting a range. To use Quick Chart, you must select the range first, and then select **Chart** from the Tools menu or click the **Chart** SmartIcon. The mouse pointer turns into a chart tool, as shown in Figure 7.12.

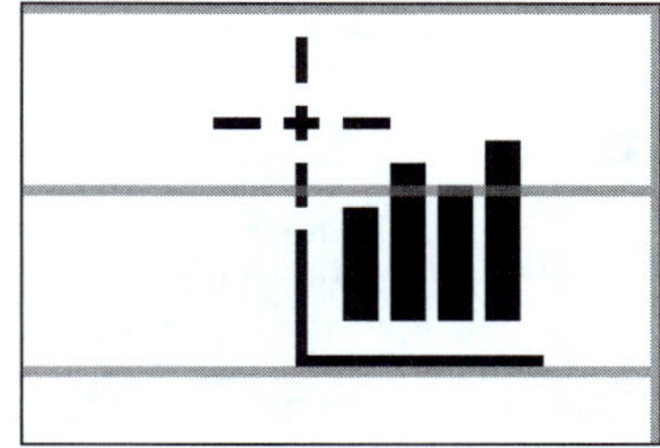

Figure 7.12 *Chart tool.*

With this cursor, you create a box in which 1-2-3 creates your chart, as seen in Figure 7.13. You create this box by clicking and dragging the mouse until it creates a box the size you want your chart to be. You create the chart right in your 1-2-3 worksheet, so it looks like it is lying on top of the worksheet.

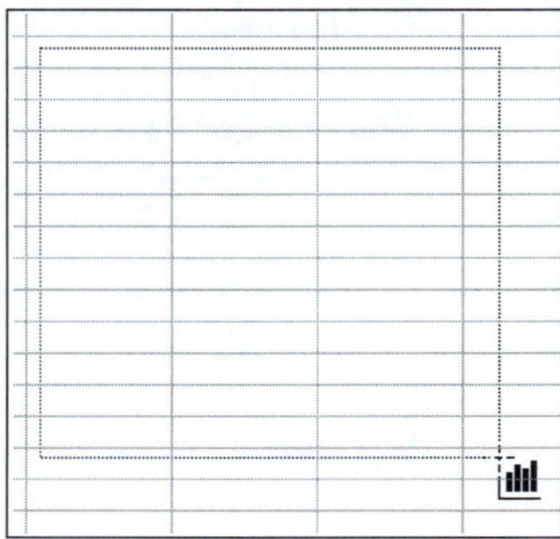

Figure 7.13 *Use the chart tool to create a box*

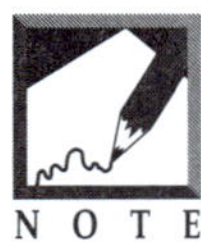

If you merely click the chart tool in a cell, Lotus 1-2-3 will decide the size of the chart, positioning the upper left corner in the location that you clicked.

It does not really matter where in the worksheet you create this box, because the chart can always be dragged to a new location.

Using Quick Chart

Let's use the **Quick Chart** feature in an example.

1. Select Range **B:A1..B:H6**, as shown in Figure 7.14.

B	A	B	C	D	E	F	G	H
1			Caroline's Budget					
2			Jan	Feb	Mar	Apr	May	Jun
3	Income:							
4		Salary	$1,438	$1,438	$1,438	$1,438	$1,438	$1,438
5		Interest	$22	$22	$22	$22	$22	$22
6		Dividends	$150	$0	$0	$200	$0	$0

Figure 7.14 *Select range B:A1..B:H6.*

2. From the Tools menu, choose **Chart** or click the **Chart** SmartIcon.

3. Click and drag a box anywhere you want in the actual worksheet to create the chart.

    1-2-3 automatically creates the bar chart, as shown in Figure 7.15.

Notice that 1-2-3 automatically placed the title, Caroline's Budget, on this chart, created a legend with the labels for the data series, and created X axis categories for the months.

Now see how it would look if you selected only numerical data:

1. Select Range **B:C4..B:H6** (see Figure 7.16).

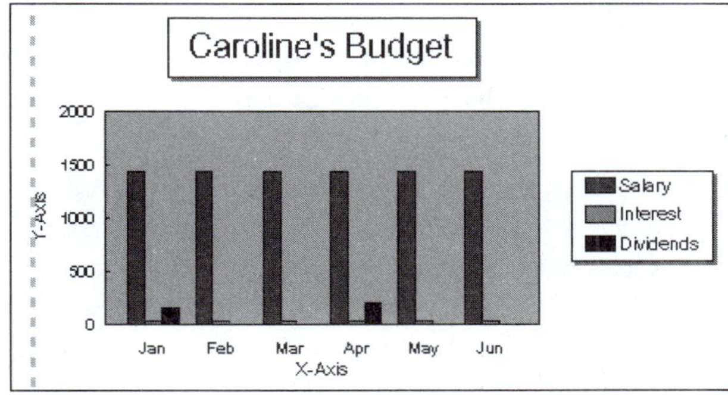

Figure 7.15 *1-2-3 automatically creates this chart.*

2. From the Tools menu, choose **Chart** or click the **Chart** SmartIcon.

3. Click and drag a box anywhere you want in the actual worksheet to create the chart.

    1-2-3 automatically creates the bar chart, as shown in Figure 7.17.

B	A	B	C	D	E	F	G	H
1			Caroline's Budget					
2			Jan	Feb	Mar	Apr	May	Jun
3	Income:							
4		Salary	$1,438	$1,438	$1,438	$1,438	$1,438	$1,438
5		Interest	$22	$22	$22	$22	$22	$22
6		Dividends	$150	$0	$0	$200	$0	$0

Figure 7.16 *Select range B:C4..B:H6.*

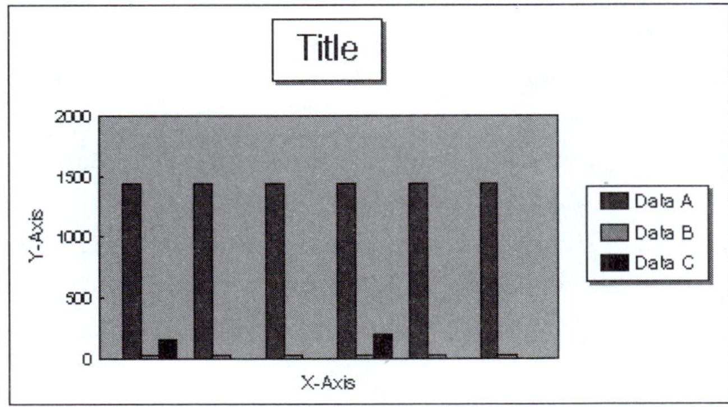

Figure 7.17 *1-2-3 automatically creates this chart.*

This time, because there were no data available for 1-2-3 to use to make a title, legend labels, or X axis categories, it created a generic title and generic legend labels. But, as mentioned earlier, this is not a problem. You can always change any of this information, as you learn shortly.

After you create a chart, 1-2-3 changes the Range menu to a Chart menu. Anytime you select a chart in your document, this menu item changes. Also, the SmartIcon bar changes to include several charting SmartIcons (you can see them in Figures 7.15 and 7.17). When you select some other part of your worksheet, such as a cell or a range, the Chart menu disappears, the Range menu returns, and the SmartIcon bar returns to its usual condition.

Creating a Chart Manually

The other way to create a chart in 1-2-3 is to start from scratch and create it manually. This approach is often preferred because many times your worksheet is not laid out in a way that allows you to use the Quick Chart method. In these cases, instead of using Quick Chart to create a chart, and then changing all or many of its aspects, you may find it quicker and less frustrating to create a chart manually, step by step. The rest of this chapter is devoted to teaching you how to change the different elements of a chart and how to create the chart you desire, manually.

Naming Charts

After you have created charts, you may discover that it is difficult to locate a chart you need promptly, particularly if your worksheet is a large one. Or, having hidden a chart for privacy, you may not be able to find it right away. To alleviate these problems and expedite the chart-finding process, you can (and should) name your charts.

1-2-3 automatically assigns a default name to every chart you create. By default, they are named CHART1, CHART2, and so on.

To rename charts, use the **Name** command from the Chart menu. When you select this item, you see the Chart Name dialog box (see Figure 7.18).

To name a chart:

1. Select a chart in your worksheet by clicking on it with the mouse.

   When a chart is selected, you see placeholders around the chart box.

Placeholders are little black squares that can be used to make a chart box larger or smaller, as shown in Figure 7.19.

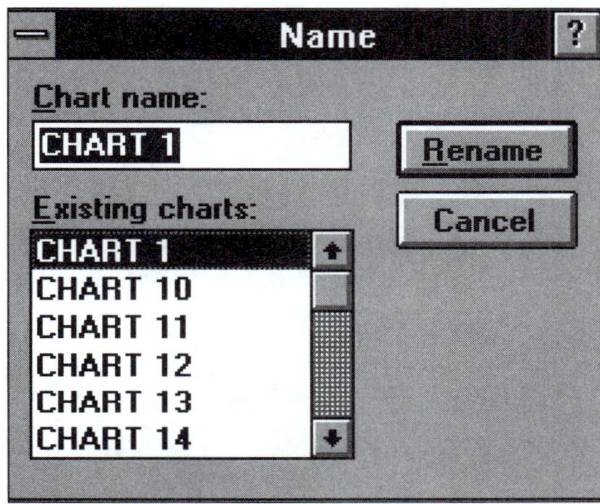

Figure 7.18 *Chart Name dialog box.*

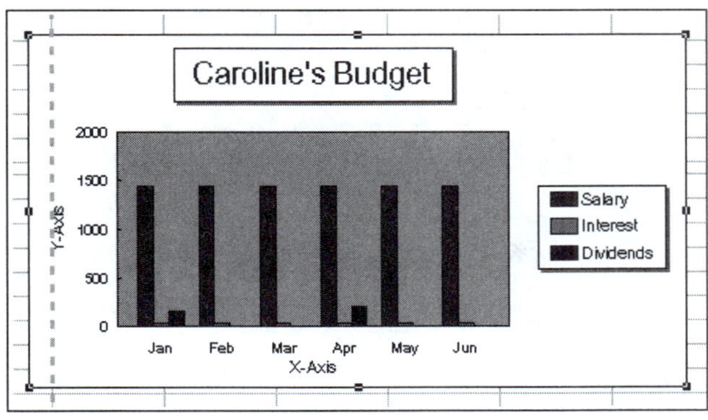

Figure 7.19 *Placeholders around a chart box.*

2. From the Chart menu, select **Name**.

3. Type a name into the Chart Name box.

4. Click **Rename**.

You cannot use the same name for more than one chart.

Finding Chart By Name

Now that you have named your chart, you can select it by using the GoTo command. To find a named chart:

1. From the Edit menu, select **GoTo**.

    The GoTo dialog box appears.

2. Make sure that the Type of Item selector says *Chart*, as shown in Figure 7.20. (If not, click the down arrow to drop down the list and select **Chart**.)

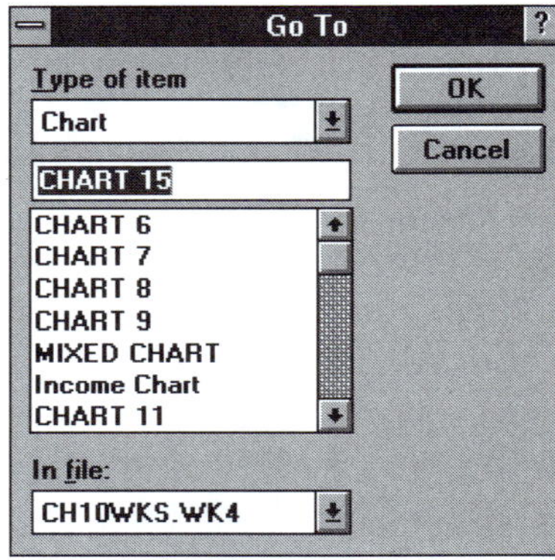

Figure 7.20 *GoTo dialog box.*

3. Select the named chart you want from the list.
4. Click **OK**.

1-2-3 displays the named chart you have selected from the name you chose on the GoTo list.

Changing Chart Type

After you have created a chart, you may want to change its type. This is especially true if you used Quick Chart which, by default, creates a bar chart.

Suppose that you wanted to change the first bar chart you made earlier into a line chart or a stacked bar chart. To change a chart type, use the **Type** command from the Chart menu or click the SmartIcon for the type of chart you want to use. When you select the **Type** command, 1-2-3 displays the Chart Type dialog box, as shown in Figure 7.21.

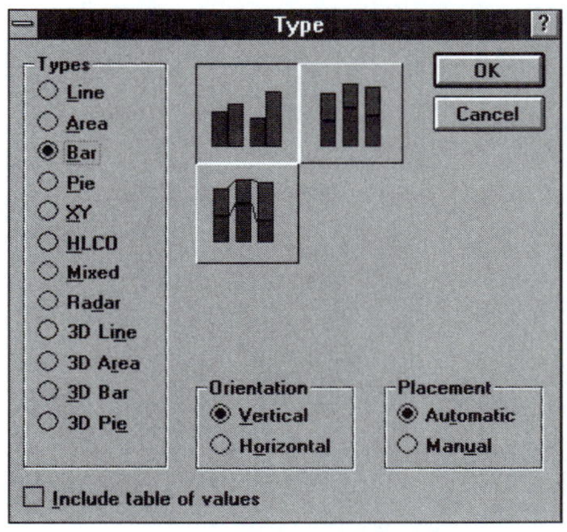

Figure 7.21 *Chart Type dialog box.*

If you double-click with the mouse in the chart box, it automatically opens the Chart Type dialog box. Be sure to click an empty area in the chart; if you click on the title or some other data, you may get a different result.

In this dialog box you can select from any of the 12 types of charts 1-2-3 can create. To select a chart, click with the mouse on the radio button for the type of chart you want. When you select a chart type, various square buttons appear to the right of that type of chart. These are the different styles of charts in each type. In Figure 7.21, for example, the bar chart type shows three styles. The first one is a standard bar chart. The one to the right is a stacked bar chart. The one below the standard bar chart is a stacked bar chart with comparison lines.

After you have selected a type of chart, you need to choose a style of that type by clicking on its square. When you click on a style, the square appears to be pushed in. In Figure 7.21, for example, you can see that the standard bar chart has been selected because it is the square that is pushed in.

There are three other settings in this dialog box. First, you can alter a chart's orientation, as shown in Figure 7.22.

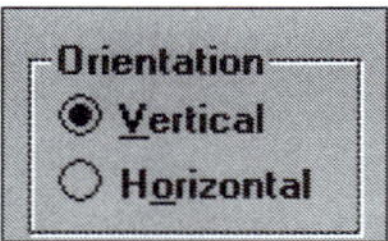

Figure 7.22 *Orientation selector.*

In this box, you can tell 1-2-3 to display the chart in the standard vertical orientation or rotate it to a horizontal orientation. If a chart is horizontal, the X and Y axes are switched and the squares that display the styles of each type of chart change to reflect this new orientation.

The second setting in this dialog box is placement, as shown in Figure 7.23.

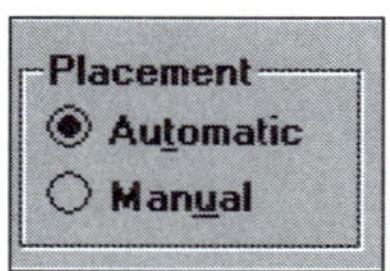

Figure 7.23 *Placement selector.*

Here you can tell 1-2-3 where to place the graph in the chart box. The default setting for 1-2-3 automatically positions the chart in its own box. Sometimes, however, you may want to move the chart manually to a different location in the chart box. To do this, click on **Manual**, and then click and drag the chart in its box.

The final setting in this dialog box is the table of values. 1-2-3 has the capability to include in the chart box a table of the values that make up the chart. After you click with the mouse on the **Include Table of Values** box, your chart should look like the one shown in Figure 7.24).

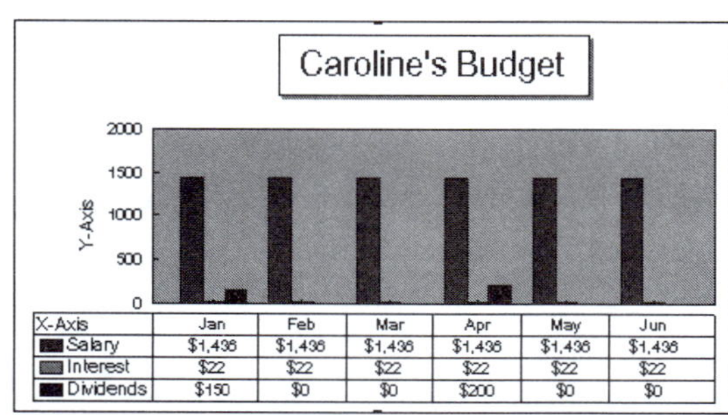

X-Axis	Jan	Feb	Mar	Apr	May	Jun
Salary	$1,436	$1,436	$1,436	$1,436	$1,436	$1,436
Interest	$22	$22	$22	$22	$22	$22
Dividends	$150	$0	$0	$200	$0	$0

Figure 7.24 *Table of values included in chart.*

When you select this option, 1-2-3 moves the legend so that it becomes part of the table of values. This is often a good way to present your charts because a reader will know what the values are for a graph without having to read the numbers from the scale. This makes your chart easier to analyze.

If you click the right mouse button in the chart, the pop-up menu that appears lists common charting commands. When you were formatting text, this pop-up menu listed commands for text formatting. But now that you have selected a chart, this list changes to contain charting commands. Which commands appear on the menu depend on where you click the right mouse button. If, for example, you click the right button somewhere on the X axis, the commands that appear pertain to the X axis.

Formatting Chart Appearance

As you proceed in creating your chart manually, you may want to enhance its appearance and personalize it. 1-2-3 enables you to alter and adjust many of the details of a chart through formatting.

Chart Headings

If you need to change your chart heading or if you did not initially put one on your chart, you can easily add one by using the **Headings** command from the Chart menu. When you select this command, the Heading dialog box appears (see Figure 7.25).

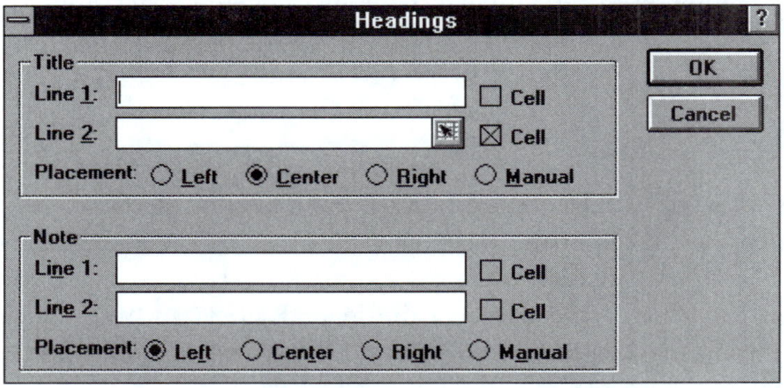

Figure 7.25 *Headings dialog box.*

You also can access the Headings dialog box by double-clicking on the chart heading or by clicking the right mouse button on the heading and choosing **Headings** from the pop-up menu.

In this box you select what you want to enter for the heading (Line 1) and subheading (Line 2). There are two ways to enter a heading:

1. Type the heading into the Line 1 and Line 2 boxes.
2. Click in the Cell box next to Line 1 or Line 2. When you do this, a Range Selector button appears. (In Figure 7.25, the Cell box is selected for Line 2 but not for Line 1). You can either use the Range Selector or type the address of a cell that contains the text you want for a heading.

Moving Chart Headings

Now that you have created your heading, you can choose where to place it by clicking on the left, right, or center radio buttons. You could also place the heading on the chart manually. By selecting the **Manual** radio button, you can click and drag the heading to wherever you want it in the chart box.

Chart Notes

Another option in the Headings dialog box lets you create notes. Notes are like headings except that they appear at the bottom of the chart box in a smaller typeface. Creating a note is just like creating a heading. Accordingly, you can create or move a note in the same way you would a heading.

Legend

Your chart's legend is the little box on the right side of the chart. It serves as a reference for the names of the different data series in the chart. In a bar chart, the legend informs a reader what color or pattern bars belong to which data series. You can change the name of the legend labels and the location of the legend by using the **Legend** command under the Chart menu. The Legend dialog box that appears looks as shown in Figure 7.26.

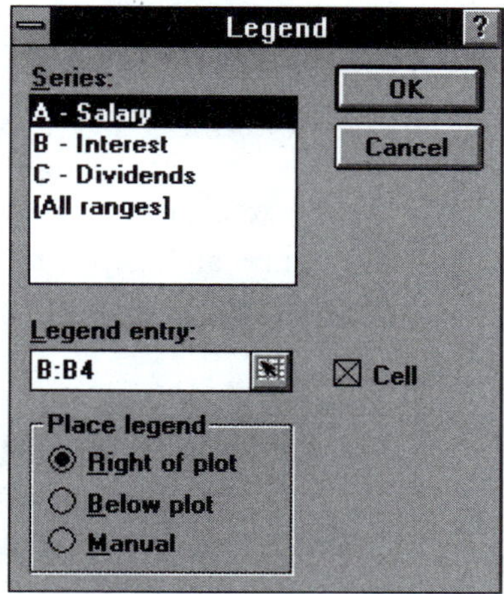

Figure 7.26 *Legend dialog box.*

You also can access the Legend dialog box by double-clicking with the mouse on the legend in the chart or by clicking the right mouse button on the legend and choosing from the pop-up menu.

1-2-3 labels the different data series with a letter of the alphabet (A, B, C, and so on.). After this label is a name. When no name is provided, 1-2-3 uses the default names Data A, Data B, Data C, and so on. Of course you can change this name to anything you want. Again, there are two ways to name a legend label:

1. Type a name into the label entry line.
2. Click on the **Cell** box. A Range Selector button appears. You can use this to select a cell that contains the text for the legend label, or you can type the address for that cell directly into the box.

Legend Placement

As with headings and notes, the Legend box can be placed automatically or you can do it manually. 1-2-3 can automatically place a legend to the right of a plot or directly below the plot. However, you can click on manual, and then use the mouse to click and drag the legend box wherever in the plot you want it to be.

Axes

1-2-3 enables you to change the labels for the X and Y axes. By default, the program calls the chart axes X Axis and Y Axis. To change the axis labels, use the **Axis** command from the Chart menu. When you choose the **Axis** command, a hierarchical menu extends to the right, enabling you to change names of the X axis and Y axis separately. Whichever one you choose, 1-2-3 displays the Axis dialog box, shown in Figure 7.27.

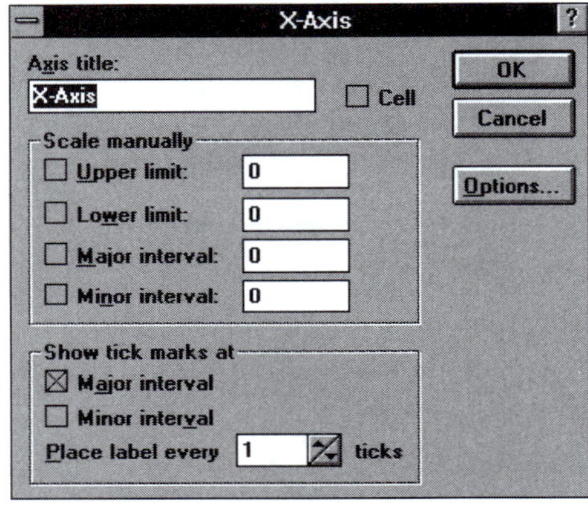

Figure 7.27 *X Axis dialog box.*

As with the other chart labels, there are two ways to change the name of the axis label:

1. Type a name into the Axis Title box.
2. Click on the **Cell** box. A Range Selector appears. Select a range that contains the text for the axis title, or directly type the address of a cell that contains the text.

You also can open the Axis dialog box by double-clicking the X or Y axis or by clicking the right mouse button on an axis and choosing **X-Axis** or **Y-Axis** from the pop-up menu.

SHORTCUT

Changing Axis Units

1-2-3 also enables you to change the units on the axes and the labels for these units. If you click on the **Options** button in the Axis dialog box, 1-2-3 displays the Axis Options dialog box, shown in Figure 7.28.

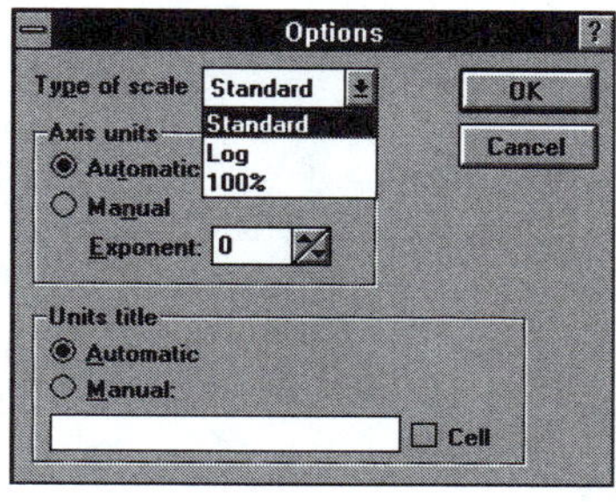

Figure 7.28 *Axis Options dialog box.*

At the center of this dialog box is the Axis Units selector. The default setting in 1-2-3 automatically assigns values corresponding to the data values on your chart. Sometimes, however, you may want to change this. In the chart you created earlier, for example, the Y axis units were expressed as dollars, ranging from 0 to 2,000. This same scale could be represented as 0 x 1E+02 to 20 x 1E+02. If you wanted to change the units on your axes in this way to an exponential unit, you could change the automatic axis units setting to **Manual** and set the exponent value to 2. After you clicked **OK**, the scale would be changed accordingly. In addition, 1-2-3 automatically changes the title for the units (see Figure 7.29).

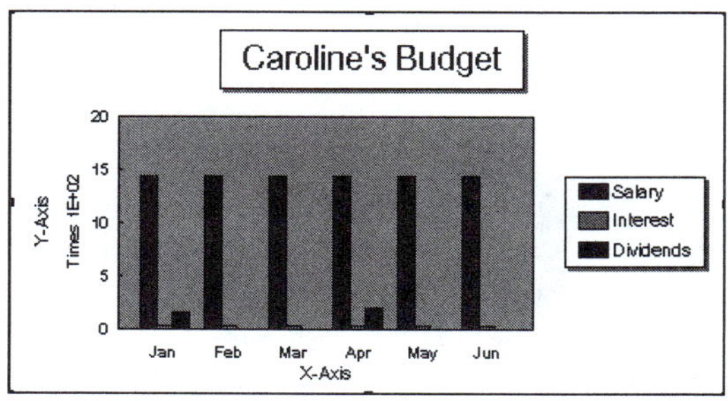

Figure 7.29 *Exponential units and Unit Title.*

Now the chart says *Times 1E+02*, and the units range from 0 to 20. You also can change the unit label manually from the Axis Options dialog box, under Units Title. You can enter any title you want into this box. Again, you can use the Range Selector to select a cell that contains the text you want for the label.

Scale

You also can use the Axis dialog boxes to change the scale of your chart in two ways. First, you can manually change the upper limit, the lower limit, and the major and minor intervals of the axes by using the Axis dialog box. This is useful if you want to compress or expand your chart. By increasing the difference between the upper and lower limits, you compress the size of your chart and allow for a greater range of values in the same chart size. By contrast, if you decrease this difference, you expand your chart.

The other way you can change the scale of the chart is to go to the Axis Options dialog box and change the **Type of Scale**. You can, for example, change the scale from standard to logarithmic. When you have a particular need for a chart, it is helpful to experiment a bit with the different scaling options to see which scales will best fit that need.

Fun with Pie Charts

If you are working with pie charts, 1-2-3 lets you explode the pieces of the pie. An *exploded* pie piece is one that has moved away from the rest of the pie. This is quite useful to highlight a particular piece of data, as shown in Figure 7.30.

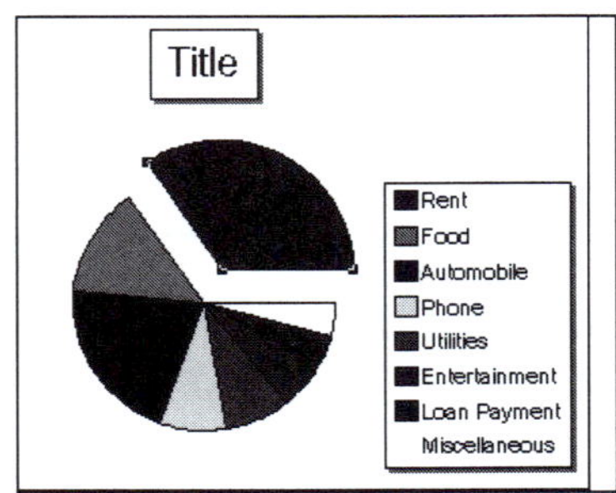

Figure 7.30 *Exploded pie piece.*

It is easy to explode pie pieces. Follow these steps:

1.   Click the piece in the pie chart.

2.   Drag the piece away from the center of the pie.

3.   Release the mouse button when you are done.

There is another way to explode a pie chart. While the pie chart is selected, from the Chart menu select **Data Labels**, and the Pie Data Labels dialog box appears, as shown in Figure 7.31.

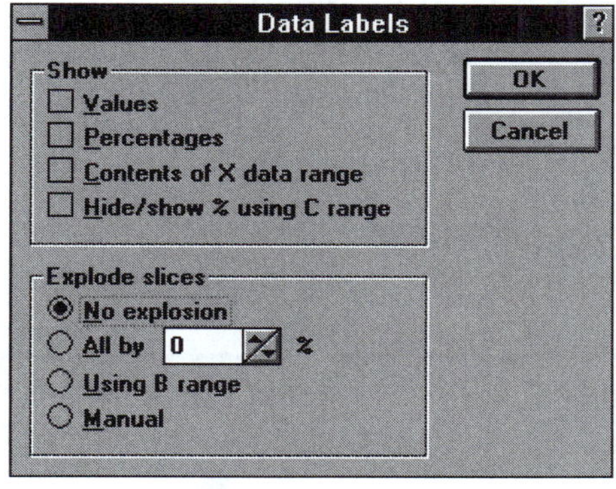

Pie Data Labels dialog box.

At the bottom of this dialog box you can set the program so that no slices explode, or all slices explode by a certain percentage, or only certain specified individual slices explode.

You also can open the Data Labels dialog box by double-clicking any data label in the pie chart or by clicking the right mouse button on a data label and choosing Data Labels from the pop-up menu.

SHORTCUT

The Pie Chart Data Labels dialog box has other features that enable you to enhance your pie charts even further. At the top of the dialog box you can set 1-2-3 to show the values for the pie slices, the percentages represented by the slices, or the text labels that correspond to each particular slice. You can try various settings to see how they look by clicking on the check box next to the item.

Lines and Colors

The Lines & Colors formatting that you did in Chapter 4 also can be applied to charts. If you don't like the color that 1-2-3 chose by default for the data series in your chart, you can change it by opening the Lines & Colors dialog box and changing the settings, as shown in Figure 7.32.

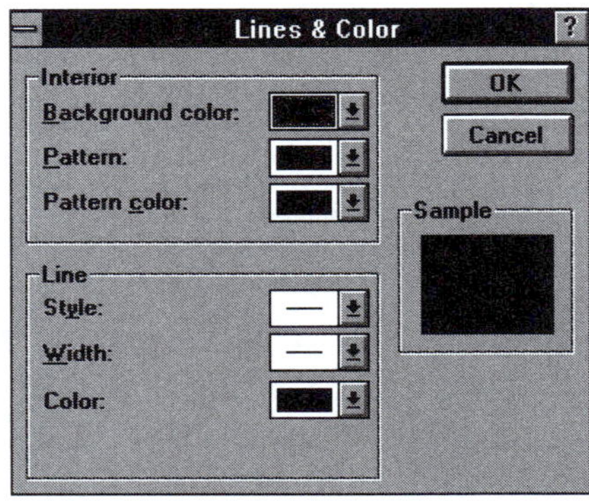

Figure 7.32 *Modified Lines & Colors dialog box.*

To change the color of a data series:

1. Click on the data series in the chart to select it.

2. From the Style menu, choose **Lines & Colors**, or click the **Lines and Colors** SmartIcon.

3. A modified **Lines and Colors** dialog box appears. It has fewer options because this formatting is only for the data series in the chart.

4. Change the formatting to the way you want.

5. Click **OK**.

Frames

You also have the ability in 1-2-3 to create a frame around your chart box. You might, for example, want to use a designer frame around the chart to make it stand out against your worksheet. To create a frame:

1. Click on the chart box to select it (remember, you should see placeholders at the corners of the box).

2. From the Style menu, choose **Lines & Colors**, or click the **Lines & Colors** SmartIcon.

   The full Lines and Colors dialog box appears, as shown in Figure 7.33.

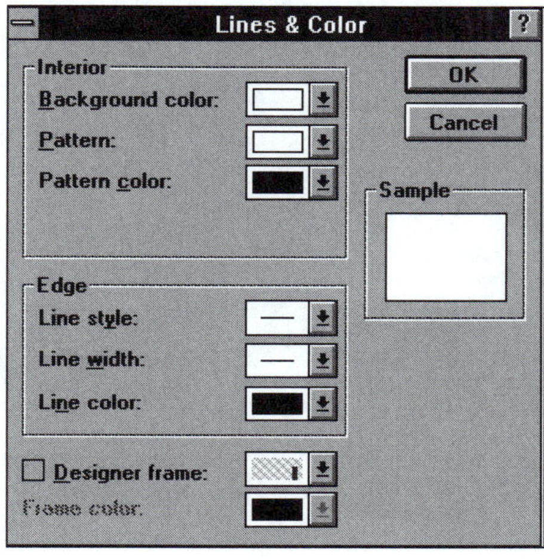

Figure 7.33 *Full Lines & Colors dialog box.*

5. Create any border or designer frame you want.

6. Click **OK**.

Printing Charts

There are three guidelines for printing charts:

1. If you print the entire worksheet or all worksheets, your chart will print together with the worksheet.

2. If you print a selected range, the chart prints only if it is visible in that selected range.

3. If you want to print only the chart, first select the chart, and then from the Print menu, choose **Selected Chart**.

When you have selected a chart, the Selected Range changes to say *Selected Chart*. If you have selected only one chart, 1-2-3 displays the name of that chart in the Selected Chart box. On the other hand, if you have selected multiple charts, the label says *Selected Drawn Object* and the box is labeled *Collection*, as shown in Figure 7.34.

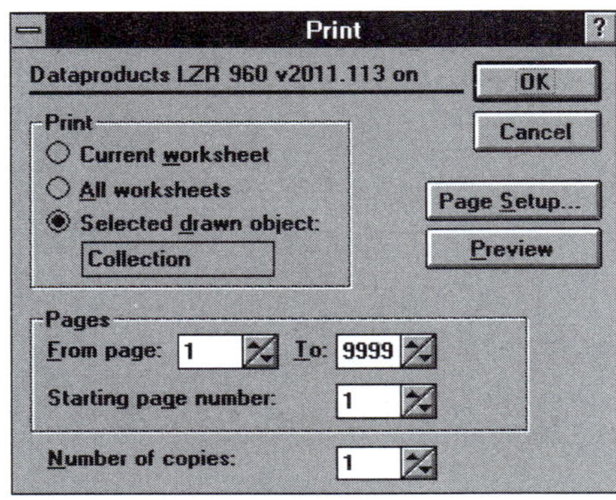

Figure 7.34 *To print selected collection of drawn objects.*

Practice

Now would be a good time to practice your skills by creating different charts with Caroline's Budget. Don't limit your experimentation to formatting. Instead, try using different charts and types that would result in useful and clear graphical representations of your numerical data. Remember, practice makes perfect. There is nothing like actually sitting down at the computer and trying out all the functions to get yourself acquainted with them. You will find that your practice is well rewarded, because charts add a professional touch to any worksheet. When you print them, you will be proud to show off your work to your friends.

To Sum Up

In this chapter, you taught yourself how to display your data pictorially, by using charts. We discussed a variety of the charting options that 1-2-3 provides, such as choosing the type of chart that is best suited to your data, creating your chart easily and quickly with the program's Quick Chart default settings, naming your chart so that you can readily find it, and changing and moving the location of your chart's headings, notes, legends, axes, and scale. You learned how to explode pieces of pie charts and personalize the lines and colors of your chart so that it could better fulfill your needs and reflect your tastes. Because all of these lessons would be of little value if you didn't print your work, we also covered how to print a chart.

What You Learned

Create a chart with Quick Chart:

1.   Select a **Range**.
2.   From the Tools menu, choose **Chart**, or click the **Chart** SmartIcon.
3.   Click or drag a box anywhere on your worksheet.

     If the range selected includes a title, legend, and axis, they automatically become part of the chart. If the range selected omits this information, then a generic title, legend, and axis are supplied.

Name a chart:

1.   Select a chart by clicking on it.
2.   From the Chart menu, select **Name**.

     The Name dialog box appears.
3.   Type a name into the Chart Name Box.
4.   Click **Rename**.

     You cannot use the same name for more than one chart.

Find a named chart:

1.   From the Edit menu, choose **GoTo**.

     The GoTo dialog box appears. Make sure that the Type of Item selector says *Chart*.
2.   Select the named chart from the list.

3. Click **OK**.

Change a chart type:

1. Click the appropriate SmartIcon, or from the Chart menu choose **Type**, or double-click in a blank area in the chart box.

   The Chart Type dialog box appears.

2. Click on the radio button for the chart type you wish.

3. Click on the applicable square button to select orientation, placement and table of values.

   You can alter the placement by clicking on the **Manual** button, and then clicking and dragging the chart elsewhere in the chart box.

   When the table of values is selected for inclusion in the chart, the legend automatically moves to become part of the table of values.

Change a chart heading or note:

1. From the Chart menu, choose **Headings**, or double-click on the chart heading.

   The Chart Heading dialog box appears.

2. Type the heading and subheading into the Line 1 or Line 2 boxes, or click in the Cell box next to Line 1 or Line 2 to access a Range Selector button to use for the address of a cell that contains the heading text.

   The same procedure is applicable for changing notes.

Move a chart heading or note:

1. From the Chart menu, choose **Headings**, or double-click on the chart heading.

   The Chart Heading dialog box appears.

2. Move the heading by clicking on the right, left, or center radio buttons, or select the **Manual** button and click and drag the heading to a new location.

   The same procedure is applicable to moving notes.

Change a legend:

1. From the Chart menu, choose **Legend**, or double-click on the legend.

   The Legend dialog box appears.

2. Type a name into the Label Entry line.

3. Click on the Cell box and a Range Selector appears; use it to select a cell in the text of the legend label or type the address of that cell into the Cell box.

Place a legend:

1. Open the **Legend** dialog box as described in step 1 of the preceding set of instructions.

2. Select **Right** or **Below** for placement to the right of or directly below the plot, or select **Manual**, and then click and drag the legend box to a new location.

Change labels of axes:

1. Open the **Axis** dialog box.

2. Select **Options**.

   The Axis Options dialog box appears.

3. Select the **Axis Units** selector or **Manual** to change labels.

Change the scale:

1. Open the **Axis** dialog box.

2. Change upper or lower limits or major or minor intervals.

   To change the scale from standard to logarithmic, go to the Axis Options dialog box and change the **Type of Scale**.

Explode pieces of a pie chart:

1. Click on a piece of a pie chart.

2. Drag the piece away from the pie's center.

3. Release the mouse button.

Or

1. From the Chart menu, select **Data Labels**.

    The Pie Chart Data Labels dialog box appears.

2. Set the desired percentage of explosion.

    The Pie Chart Data Labels dialog box also enables for showing values of pie slices, percentages of total pie represented by slices, and text labels for each slice.

Change colors:

1. Click on data series to select it.

2. From the Style menu, choose **Lines & Colors**, or click on the **Lines & Colors** SmartIcon.

    The Lines & Colors dialog box appears.

    Because the dialog box was selected for formatting a data series, it has fewer positions than it would if it were selected for formatting a worksheet.

3. Change the colors.

4. Click **OK**.

Add frames:

1. Click on chart box to select it.

2. From the Style menu, choose **Lines & Colors**, or click on the **Lines & Colors** SmartIcon to open the Lines & Colors dialog box.

3. Create the desired frame or border.

4. Click **OK**.

Print charts:

The rules for printing worksheets discussed in Chapter 6 apply, but these three guidelines should be borne in mind:

1. When an entire worksheet (or several worksheets) are printed, the charts contained in that worksheet(s) also are printed.

2. When only a selected range of one or more worksheets is printed, a chart is printed only if it is visible in that range.

3. To print only a chart, click on the **Chart** box to select it. From the Print menu, choose **Selected Drawn Objects**.

# Chapter 8

Graphics

Once your data is entered and formatted to your satisfaction, you may want to enhance your worksheet by using Lotus 1-2-3 Release 5 Graphics functions. This program lets you clarify data on your worksheet with lines, arrows, boxes, and so on, and even lets you add graphics you draw yourself with the mouse. In this chapter, you learn all about the different 1-2-3 graphics capabilities as you teach yourself to:

- Create objects such as:
    - lines.
    - arrows.
    - arcs.
- Create closed drawn objects such as:
    - rectangles.
    - ellipses.
    - circles.

- Create polylines and polygons.
- Draw freehand graphics.
- Create, edit and format text block.
- Import pictures from other graphics programs.
- Work with objects to:
    - select them.
    - resize them.
    - copy them.
    - move them.
    - arrange them.
    - fasten them to a range of cells.
    - group them together.
    - lock them to an area of your worksheet.
    - delete them.

Once you have created drawn objects, you will teach yourself to adjust them as you see fit by:

- Changing lines and arrows.
- Adding frames.
- Changing colors and patterns.
- Flipping objects.
- Rotating an object's orientation.

What Is a Drawn Object?

When you use graphics in Lotus 1-2-3 Release 5, you can create drawn objects. They are called objects because each is an individual item that can be selected, moved, copied, resized, and manipulated in a variety of ways. Graphics are similar to charts in that they are individual items that become part of the worksheet in which you create them. If you print the worksheet, these images print as well. Also, you can select one or more drawn objects and print them separately.

You will practice working with drawn objects in Lotus 1-2-3 Release 5 by creating a fourth worksheet in the BUDGET.WK4 file. This new worksheet appears after the Difference worksheet. Name this worksheet Graphics. This enables you to practice on a clean sheet without having to maneuver around the data and charts you entered in previous chapters. Of course, you can create graphics in your current worksheets, but for the purposes of learning fundamentals, it is easiest to practice on a clean canvas.

To create a Graphics worksheet, select the **Difference** worksheet and click the **New Sheet** button on the Worksheet Tab Bar. A new worksheet is created after the Difference worksheet. The new worksheet is called "D." Double click on the **"D"** and type the name **Graphics**. For more information on creating worksheets, refer to Chapter 2.

Creating Drawn Objects

There are many different types of drawn objects that you can create in Lotus 1-2-3 Release 5. The following sections explain these different types of objects and how to create them.

Lines

The most basic graphic object you can create is a line, as shown in Figure 8.1.

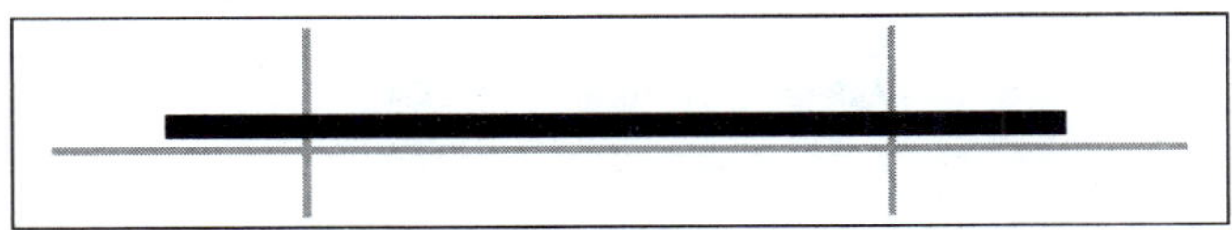

Figure 8.1 *A line.*

Lines are particularly useful for "attaching" text to an item in your worksheet. If, for example, you wanted to create your own label for a piece of a pie chart, you could use a line to connect text that you added (see Figure 8.2). Creating a text block is discussed later in this chapter.

To create a line:

1. From the Tools menu, select **Draw** and choose **Line**.

    The Draw command is a hierarchical menu item on the Tools menu.

Therefore, if you select **Draw**, another menu appears to the right of Draw from which you can select the graphics commands.

2. The cursor changes to a + sign, as shown in Figure 8.3.

3. Click and drag the mouse to create a line.

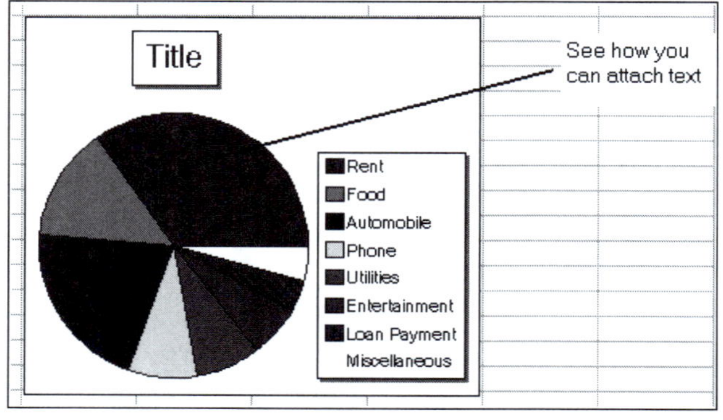

Figure 8.2 *Lines are good for connecting items in your worksheet.*

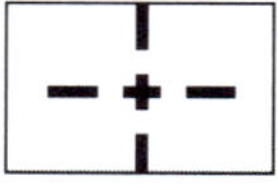

Figure 8.3 *The line tool cursor.*

To draw a perfectly horizontal, vertical, or 45-degree angle line, hold down **Shift** while you drag the mouse.

N O T E

4. When the line is at the desired length and angle, release the mouse button.

As with other Lotus 1-2-3 Release 5 functions, you can modify the size and angle of your line later, should you want to do so.

After you release the mouse button, 1-2-3 displays a line on your worksheet with a square dot at each end of the line. These dots are the placeholders that enable you to change the line later if need be. They indicate that the line is now the selected object. They are not part of the line and will disappear when you select something else.

Arrows

Arrows can be created as quickly as lines. In fact, graphically speaking, arrows are just lines with arrow heads at one or both ends. Arrows are useful when you want to link several objects in your worksheet visually. When inserting arrows, be aware of what they might imply to a reader. Whereas lines simply link two items together, arrows may connote a causal relationship between the two items, depending on where they are and how many arrow heads you use. Always take care to review what data you are communicating to a reader and bear in mind that small subtleties often can make important differences (see Figure 8.4).

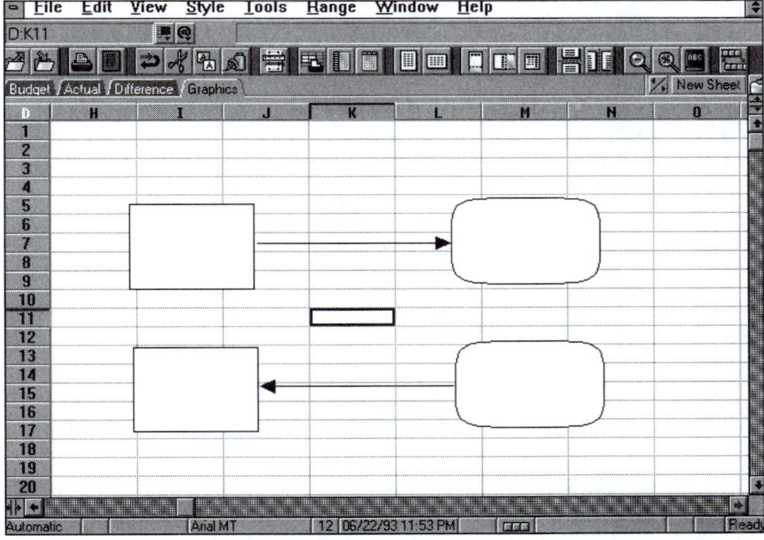

Figure 8.4 *Boxes connected by arrows.*

In this figure, a right arrow connects the top set of rectangles and a left arrow connects the bottom set of rectangles. When you look at the top set of rectangles, the natural assumption is that the square-edged rectangle precedes the round-edged rectangle, because the arrow originates at the left and terminates at the arrow head at the right. In contrast, when you look at the bottom set of rectangles, the assumption is that the rounded rectangle leads to the square rectangle because the arrow originates on the right and goes to the left.

On your worksheet, you also can create arrows that have arrow heads at both ends of the line. When you do this, the implication may be that there is a reciprocal or equivalent relationship between the two items, as shown in Figure 8.5.

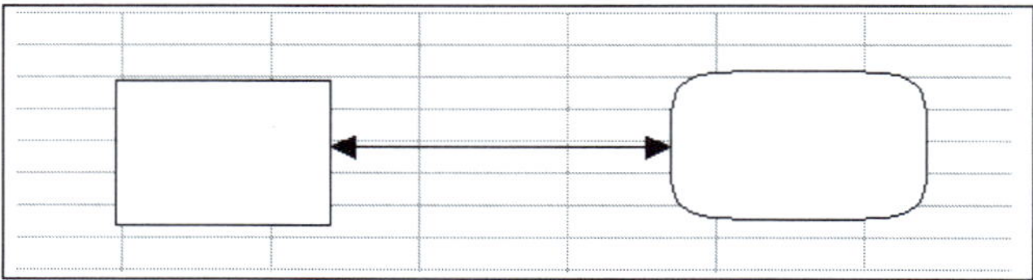

Figure 8.5 *Double-headed arrow.*

By default, Lotus 1-2-3 creates a one-sided arrow. It puts the arrow head at the end where you terminated the line. If, for example, you clicked the mouse and dragged to the right, the arrow head would be put on the right end of the line. In contrast, if you clicked the mouse and dragged to the left, the arrow head would be put on the left end, where you terminated the line.

To create an arrow:

1. From the Tools menu, select **Draw** and choose **Arrow**, or click the **Draw Arrow** SmartIcon.

   The mouse pointer becomes a cross, as before.

2. Click and hold the mouse button where you want to originate the arrow and drag the mouse to create an arrow.

   When you start dragging, the mouse pointer becomes a faint arrow, so that you can see exactly where it begins and ends.

To draw a perfectly horizontal, vertical, or 45-degree angle arrow, hold down **Shift** while you drag the mouse.

N O T E

3. Release the mouse button where you want the arrow to end.

Lotus 1-2-3 Release 5 automatically puts an arrow head at the end of the line.

Arcs

Arcs, as their name implies, are lines that curve to form an arc (see Figure 8.6).

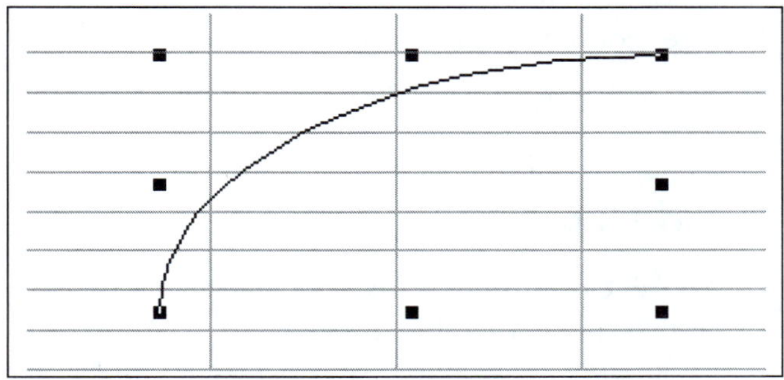

Figure 8.6 *An arc.*

Arcs are particularly useful when you need to insert a curved edge on your worksheet but don't want to create an entire circle or ellipse. You can create a half circle by creating two arcs and joining them, as shown in Figure 8.7.

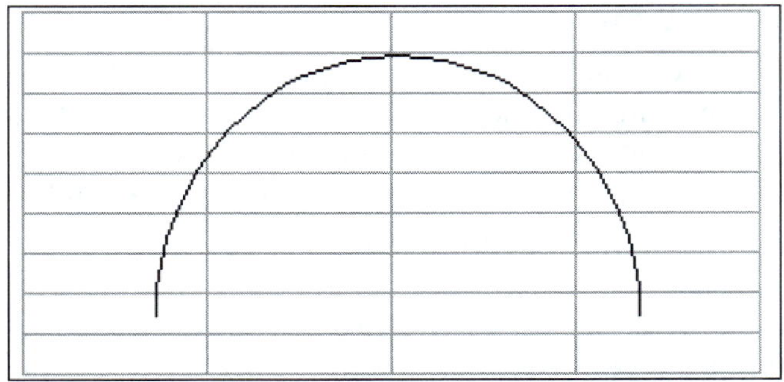

Figure 8.7 *A half circle formed by joining two arcs.*

These graphic images are stored as single objects so that you cannot erase a piece of the image. You cannot, for example, draw a circle and erase half of it to create a half circle. Instead, you must construct a half circle from two arcs (which are two objects and can be erased separately). You learn how to create drawn objects made up of arcs later in this chapter. For now, you begin with arcs.

To create an arc:

1. From the Tools menu, select **Draw** and choose **Arc**.

2. Click and hold the mouse button where you want the arc to originate and drag the mouse to create an arc.

3. Release the mouse button when the arc is the shape and length you want it to be.

Rectangles and Ellipses

You also can create enclosed drawn objects, such as rectangles and ellipses. They are similar in that they are both useful for outlining a particular section of your worksheet. You can, for example, put a box around a section of your worksheet to make it stand out. You might want to highlight a particular piece of data, such as net income, by containing it within a closed drawn object. There are three types of these closed drawn objects, or boxes, that you can create with Lotus 1-2-3 Release 5: rectangles, rounded rectangles, and ellipses, as shown in Figure 8.8.

An ellipse is similar to a circle, except that an ellipse can appear as a circle or an oval. By using an ellipse, you can create a perfect circle or an oval depending on your needs.

In all cases, when you create a rectangle, a rounded rectangle, or an ellipse, 1-2-3 begins by showing the object in one corner. (You don't start in the center and work your way out to make the object bigger.) You start to create the object in one corner and drag the mouse out and down to create the full object.

To create a rectangle, a rounded rectangle, or an ellipse:

1. From the Tools menu, select **Draw** and choose **Rectangle**, **Rounded Rectangle**, or **Ellipse**. (For an ellipse, you also can click the **Draw Ellipse** SmartIcon.)

2. Click and hold the mouse where you want the corner of the object to begin.

3. Drag the mouse out and up (or down) to create the object.

4. When the object is the correct size and shape, release the mouse button.

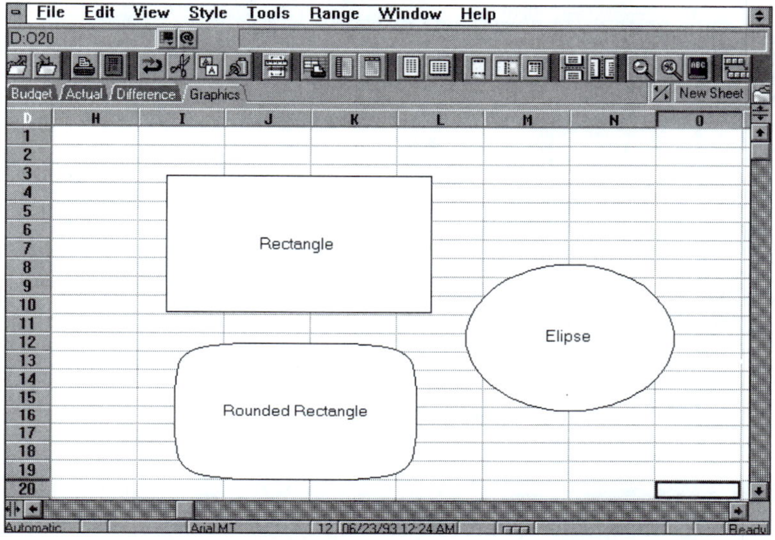

Figure 8.8 *Rectangles, rounded rectangles, and ellipses.*

To create a perfect square or circle, hold down the **Shift** key while you drag the mouse.

5. When the object is the correct shape, release the mouse button.

A perfect circle might look like an oval on your monitor, but it will be perfectly round when printed.

N O T E

Polylines and Polygons

Sometimes you may need to create a drawn object that consists of a sequence of lines that are all touching. Or you may want to draw a closed drawn object that is not a standard rectangle or circle. To create these images, 1-2-3 provides you with graphic tools that it calls polyline and polygon.

Polylines are a collection of lines that are linked together in sequence, as shown in Figure 8.9.

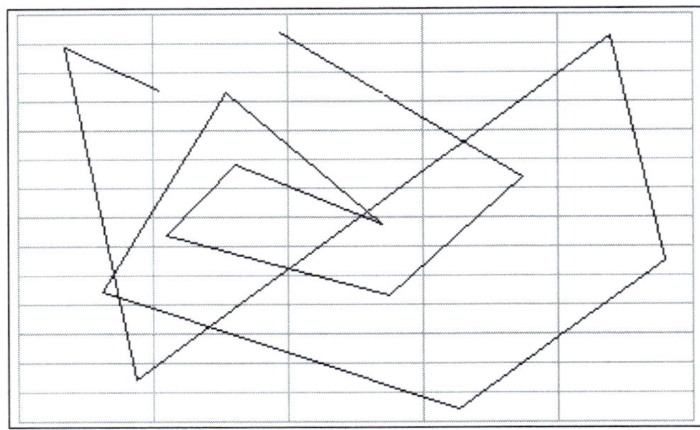

Figure 8.9 *Polylines.*

Polygons are similar to polylines, in that they have a collection of lines that are linked together in sequence, but polygons are closed objects. When you create a polygon, Lotus 1-2-3 Release 5 automatically connects a line between the beginning and end of your collection of lines, as shown in Figure 8.10.

Both polygons and polylines are useful when you want to create an object that has straight edges. Were you to accomplish this task by using the simple line graphic, you would need to create many lines and then join them to form the object. The main feature of polygons and polylines, however, is that they start each new line at the point that the preceding line ends, so that all of your lines are always connected, automatically. To create a polyline:

1. From the Tools menu, select **Draw** and choose **Polylines**.

2. Click and hold the mouse button where you want the polyline object to begin.

3. Drag the mouse to the location you have chosen as the end of the first edge.

NOTE

To draw the edge at a perfect horizontal, vertical, or 45 degree angle, hold down the **Shift** key while you drag the mouse. To draw a freehand line segment (which does not have to be straight), hold down the **Ctrl** key while you drag the mouse.

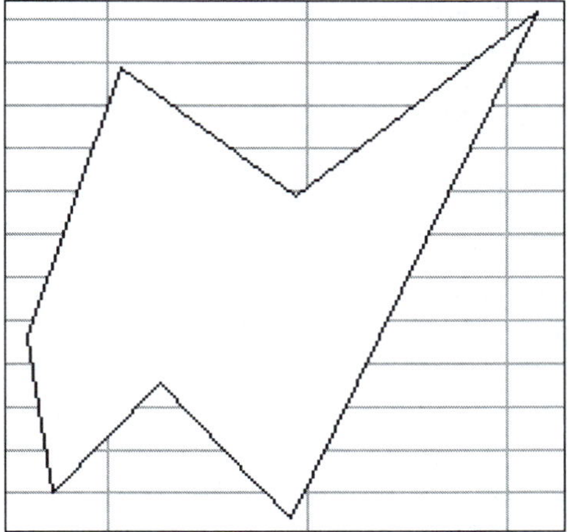

Figure 8.10 *Polygon.*

4. Click the mouse button. Notice that Lotus 1-2-3 Release 5 now begins the next line in the sequence.

5. Drag the mouse to the location you have chosen as the end of the second edge.

6. Continue this click and drag process for as many edges as you want in your polyline object.

7. Double-click the mouse button to end the polyline.

To create a polygon:

1. From the Tools menu, select **Draw** and choose **Polygon**.

2. Click and hold the mouse button where you want the polygon object to begin.

3. Drag the mouse to the location you have chosen as the end of the first edge.

To draw the edge at a perfect horizontal, vertical, or 45 degree angle, hold down the **Shift** key while you drag the mouse. To draw a freehand line segment (which does not have to be straight), hold down the **Ctrl** key while you drag the mouse.

4. Click the mouse button. Notice that Lotus 1-2-3 Release 5 now begins the next line in the sequence.

5. Drag the mouse to the location you have chosen as the end of the second edge.

6. Continue this click and drag process for as many edges as you want in your polygon.

7. You can either create the final connecting line (between the beginning point of your first line and the end point of the last of your collection of lines) simply by double-clicking the mouse, in which case Lotus 1-2-3 Release 5 automatically creates a segment to connect the beginning and end points, or by using the steps already described to create the final connecting line.

Freehand Drawing

At times you may want to create an object that is not a standard line, rectangle, or ellipse and does not have straight edges like polylines or polygons. To help you with this task, Lotus 1-2-3 Release 5 provides a Freehand Drawing tool. With this tool you can draw any freehand shape, and then store it as an object, as shown in Figure 8.11.

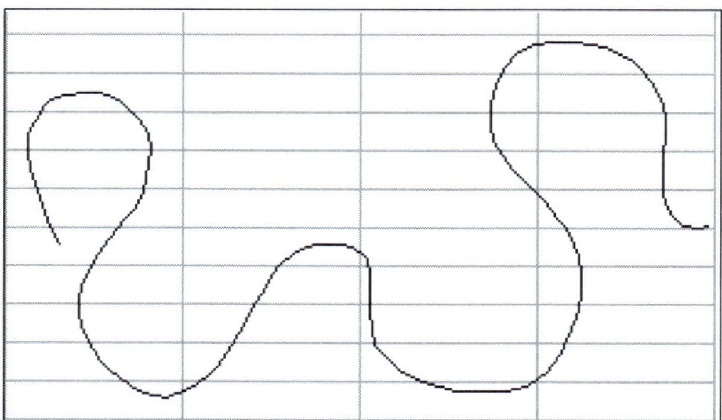

Figure 8.11 *Freehand object.*

This tool takes a bit of practice to get used to. It is very much like sketching, except that you use your mouse as your pencil. When you click and hold the mouse button, it is as though the pencil is touching the paper. When you release the mouse button, it is as if you are lifting the pencil. Do not get discouraged if at first you have trouble; this tool requires the most practice of all of the drawing tools. Even if you are not a budding Picasso, however, you will be able to create attractive graphics once you get used to the process.

To create a freehand object:

1. From the Tools menu, select **Draw** and choose **Freehand**.

2. Click and hold the mouse button at the location you have chosen to begin the freehand object.

    The cursor changes to look like a pencil when you click and hold down the mouse button (see Figure 8.12).

Figure 8.12 *Freehand cursor.*

3. Move the mouse as if it were really a pencil to draw the object.

4. Release the mouse button when you are done.

Text Blocks

Text blocks are one of the most useful tools available in Lotus 1-2-3 Release 5. Text blocks are objects similar to closed drawn objects, but you can enter text into them, as shown in Figure 8.13.

They are particularly useful because instead of being limited to the location and size of a cell, text blocks are movable and their size is variable.

Remember that when you enter text into a cell, that data continues to the right until it encounters a cell that already contains data, unless you choose the Wrap Text option (in the Alignment dialog box) for the cell. When you employ text boxes, however, the text you enter automatically wraps downward so that it fits in the box, as shown in Figure 8.14.

To enhance your text boxes or to make them look special, you can use designer frames, colors, and the other formatting features discussed in Chapter 4. With a little practice, you can create text blocks that look like attractive notes in your worksheet. The flexibility you have with text blocks makes them a useful tool for personalizing a worksheet or giving it a professional look.

Figure 8.13 *Text block.*

Creating Text Blocks

To create a text block:

1. From the Tools menu, select **Draw** and choose **Text**, or choose the **Text Box** SmartIcon.

2. The cursor changes to a +, as it did when you created a line.

3. Click the mouse button where you want the text block to begin.

4. Drag the mouse to create a box.

Hold down **Shift** while you drag the mouse to create a perfectly square text box.

NOTE

5. When your box is the desired size, release the mouse button.

6. You will see a vertical line insertion point (|) in the text block.

7. Begin typing the text for the box.

8. Click with the mouse anywhere outside the text block when you are finished.

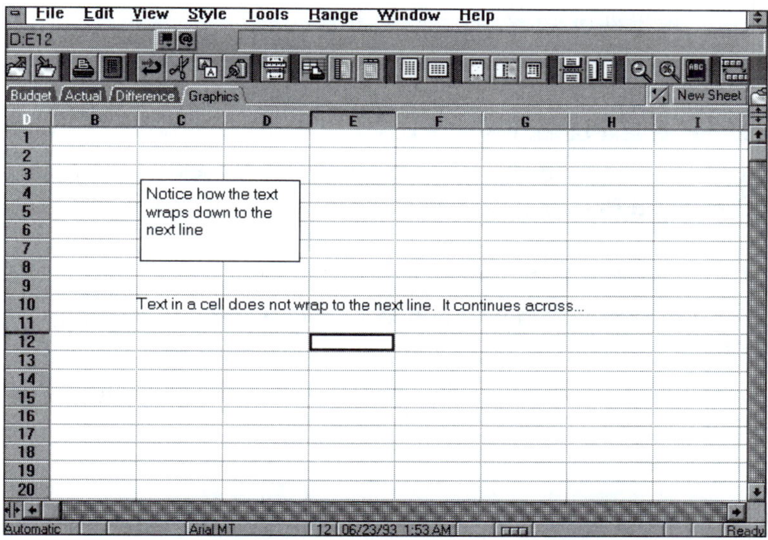

Figure 8.14 *Text in a text block wraps to the next line.*

Editing Text Blocks

After you have entered text into a text block, you may want to edit it. To edit the text in a text block, follow these steps:

1. Double-click the mouse on the text block.
2. The vertical insertion point (|) appears.
3. Edit your text.
4. Click with the mouse anywhere outside the text block when you are finished.

Formatting Text Blocks

Text that is entered into a text block can be formatted the same way that you format the text in your worksheet.

Unlike the rest of your worksheet, text blocks can be formatted with only one font, style, attribute, color, and so forth. That is, you cannot change just certain words in your text block. The whole text block must be treated as a single unit.

To format the text of a text block:

1. Select the text block by clicking on it with the mouse.

   When the text block is selected, you will see placeholders around it.

2. From the Style menu, choose **Font & Attributes**, **Lines & Colors**, or **Alignment** to format the text block the way you would like.

Review Chapter 4 for help on formatting text.

You can use the right mouse button to access the quick pop-up menu for formatting text.

You also can resize a text block or create a designer frame around it, as you will see shortly.

Importing Pictures

Suppose that you create a picture, such as your corporate logo, in a program outside of Lotus 1-2-3 Release 5 and you want to place that picture into your 1-2-3 worksheet. You can import the picture using the Windows clipboard. As you mentioned in Chapter 2, the clipboard is a temporary storage place for items that you cut or copy from one document and later paste into another document.

To import a picture from another program onto your worksheet:

1. Select the picture in the other program.
2. Choose **Copy** from that program's Edit menu.
3. Change to your Lotus 1-2-3 Release 5 worksheet.
4. From the Edit menu, select **Paste** (or press **Ctrl+V**), or click the **Paste** SmartIcon.
5. Lotus 1-2-3 Release 5 will paste the picture into a picture box that can be moved, resized, or formatted later.

Working with Objects

After you have created an object in Lotus 1-2-3 Release 5, there are many ways to work with it. Objects can be resized, copied, moved, joined, and even locked.

The following sections provide a brief overview of different options available as you work with objects.

Selecting Objects

To begin working on an object, you must first select it in your worksheet. The object you want to select may be superimposed on top of your cells. Nevertheless, you will still be able to select the cells behind an object, as shown in Figure 8.15.

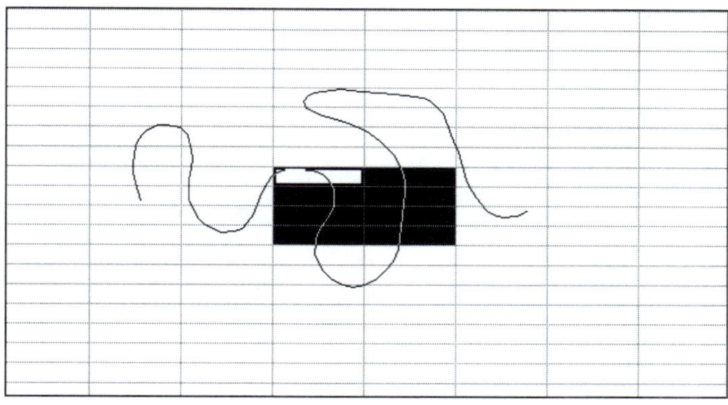

Figure 8.15 *Selecting a range which is behind an object.*

As long as you can see the cells, you can use the arrow cursor to select a range.

You need to be able to see the cells to select them with the cursor. If the object is a solid one (such as a rectangle) which totally blocks the underlying cells, you must move the object before you can select the hidden cells.

If you choose to select an object, the cursor must be placed over the object itself. When you use the mouse to move the cursor this way, the cursor changes and a small square appears after the arrow, as shown in Figure 8.16.

Figure 8.16 *Cursor for selecting objects.*

After the cursor changes, you can click on the object to select it. When you do, placeholders appears around the object as shown in Figure 8.17.

These placeholders enable you to resize the objects.

Resizing Objects

Sometimes you may find that an object you created is not the size you need it to be. You might, for example, create a text block, and then discover that the words you entered don't fit on the line you thought they would. To remedy this situation, you can resize the text block so that it fits the text. Another example involves a drawn object, such as a rectangle. You might create a rectangle to outline an area of your chart, only to find it too big or too small. You can resolve the problem simply by resizing the object.

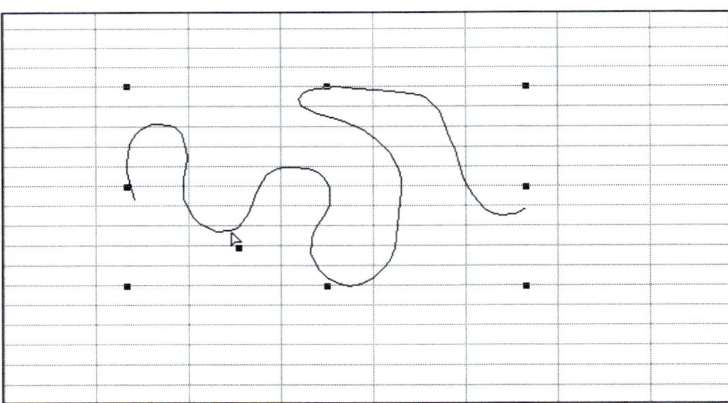

Figure 8.17 *Selected object with placeholders.*

It does not matter which type of object you are dealing with. In all cases, the procedure for resizing is the same. To resize an object:

1. Select the object. Placeholders appear around the object.
2. Click and hold the mouse button on a placeholder for the object.
3. Drag the mouse until it changes the shape and size of the object.
4. Release the mouse button when you are finished.

If you want to resize an object proportionally, hold the Shift key down while you click and drag the mouse.

When you resize an object, Lotus 1-2-3 Release 5 automatically scales the image to reflect the new size. If, for example, you resized the object using the placeholder at the middle of the top or bottom edge of the object, the new size would be either shorter or taller than the original size. Therefore, Lotus 1-2-3 Release 5 scales the image so that it is either taller or shorter than the original. Similarly, if you used the placeholders on the right or left edges of the object, the new size would be narrower or wider than the original. Therefore, 1-2-3 scales the image so that it is narrower or wider than the original, as shown in Figure 8.18.

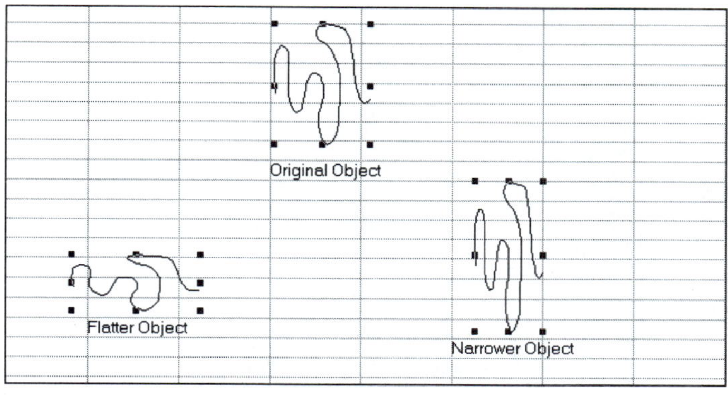

Figure 8.18 *Resized objects.*

Copying Objects

Sometimes you may want to copy an object to duplicate it. For example, when you made a half-circle earlier, you could have made one arc and copied it instead of making two separate arcs.

To copy an object:

1. Select the object.

2. Copy it just as you would a cell or a range. (You can drag it or use the clipboard.)

Moving Objects

Sometimes an object you created is not where you need it to be. To move an object, follow these steps:

1. Select the object.

2. Click and hold the mouse button while you drag the object.

    The cursor changes to a hand and you will see an outline of the object move along with the hand, as shown in Figure 8.19.

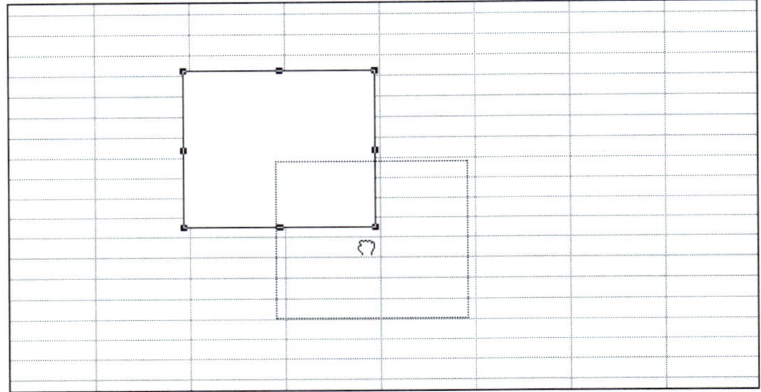

Figure 8.19 *Moving an object.*

When you want to move an object, do not click and drag on a placeholder. This resizes the object. Click somewhere on the object other than the placeholders to move it.

Arranging Objects

Often you will create multiple objects that lie on top of each other on your worksheet. In this situation, you may find it difficult to select and work with the one particular object in which you are interested. To help select the objects you intend, Lotus 1-2-3 Release 5 has Send To Back/Bring To Front commands that help to arrange objects.

Notice that in Figure 8.20, the ellipse is on top of the rectangle. Suppose that you want to move the rectangle to the front and the ellipse to the back, as shown in Figure 8.21.

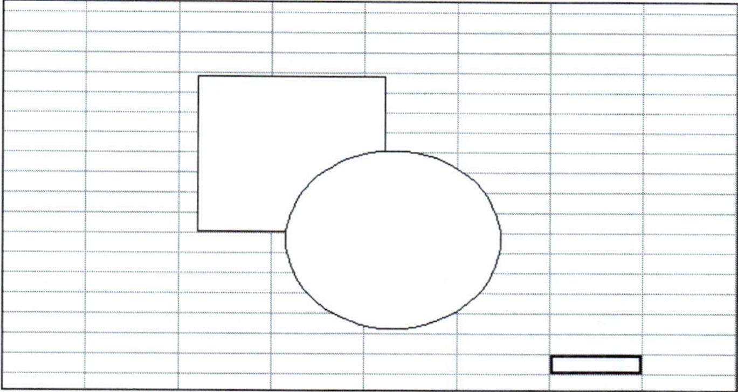

Figure 8.20 *Ellipse is on top of the rectangle.*

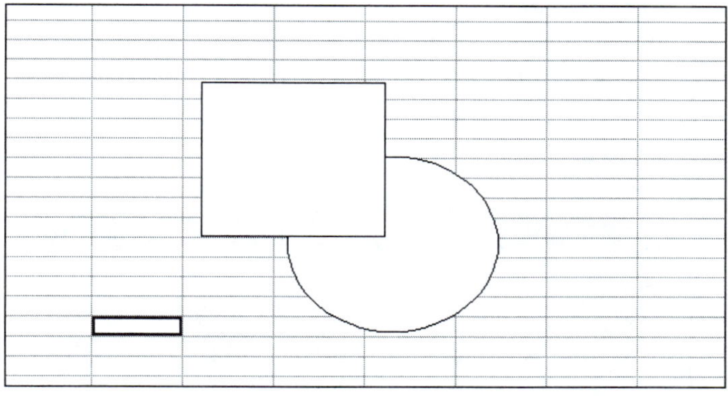

Figure 8.21 *Ellipse is behind the rectangle.*

You can accomplish your goal in two ways. One is to send the ellipse to the back, which brings the rectangle to the front. The other way is to bring the rectangle to the front, sending the ellipse to the back. To arrange objects:

1. Select one object you want to move.

2. From the Edit menu, choose **Arrange** and select **Bring To Front** or **Send To Back**, depending on what you want to do with your object.

When you choose any graphic object, the SmartIcon bar changes to provide several graphics functions, including Bring to Front and Send to Back SmartIcons. You can use these SmartIcons rather than going through the Edit menu.

In this case, involving only two objects, either of the Arrange functions would produce the same result. If, however, you were dealing with several objects on top of one another, sending the top one to the back would not bring the bottom one to the front. The Arrange functions let you shuffle through the pile of objects, either from top to bottom or bottom to top.

Fastening Objects

Lotus 1-2-3 Release 5 has a special feature that enables you to fasten an object to a particular range of cells. When an object is fastened, you can change the width or height of the cells or insert or delete cells to the range, and the object will move accordingly. You also can fasten an object to a range so that the object's size changes with any changes you make to the range.

The commands that let you fasten an object are in the Fasten to Cells dialog box, as shown in Figure 8.22.

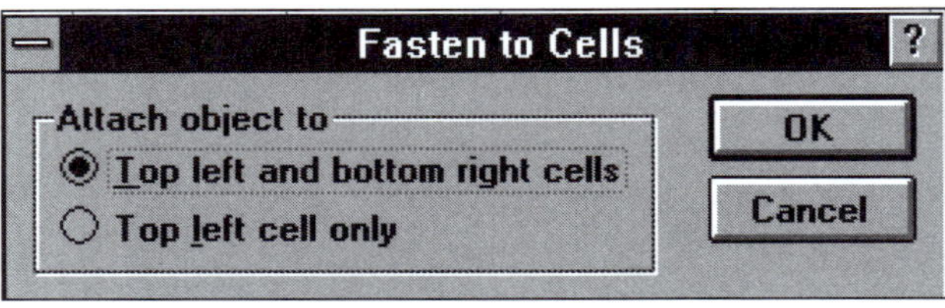

Figure 8.22 *Fasten to Cells dialog box.*

One option in the dialog box lets you attach the object to Top Left Cell Only. If you choose to do this, the fastened object will move as you move the top left cell that it touches. On the other hand, if you select the **Top Left** and **Bottom Right Cells** option, 1-2-3 performs two functions: it moves the object with the top left cell that it touches, and it resizes that object when you move or resize the cells behind it.

Figure 8.23, for example, shows a rectangle attached to the Top Left and Bottom Right Cells.

Now, suppose that you were to widen column J and make row 9 taller. This would also make the rectangle taller and wider, as shown in Figure 8.24.

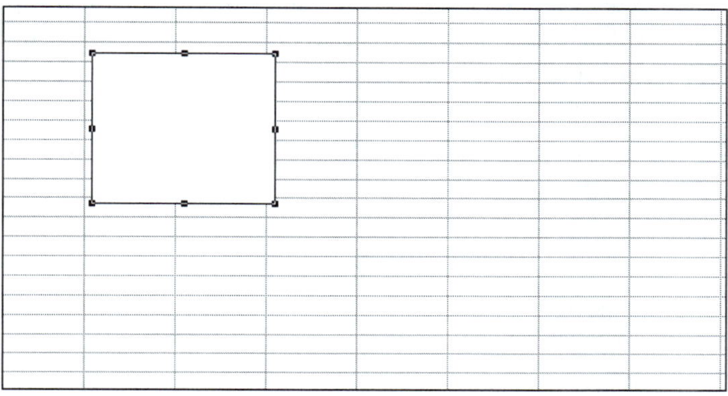

Figure 8.23 *Rectangle attached to top left and bottom right cells.*

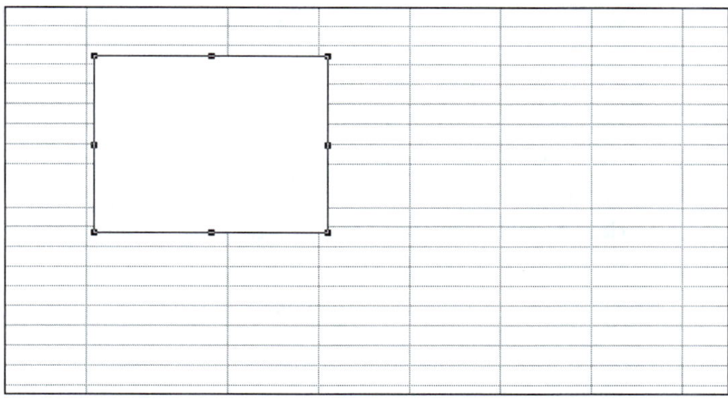

Figure 8.24 *The rectangle is wider and taller.*

To fasten a drawn object:

1. Select the object.
2. From the Edit menu, choose **Arrange** and select **Fasten To Cells**.
3. Choose the appropriate setting from the Fasten to Cells dialog box.
4. Click **OK**.

Grouping Objects

When you use Lotus 1-2-3 Release 5, you have the ability to group individual drawn objects so that they behave as one object. This way, you can resize, move, or copy a group of objects all at once.

In Figure 8.25, for example, you see a rectangle and an ellipse.

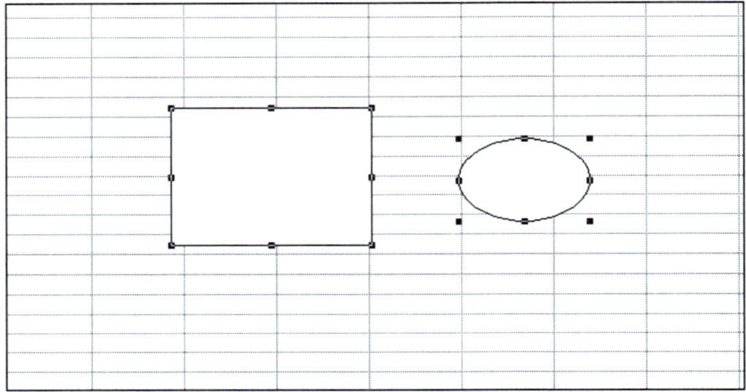

Figure 8.25 *Separate drawn objects.*

You can recognize these as two separate objects because each has its own placeholders. Were you to group these items, however, they would have only one set of placeholders, indicating that they are treated as one object, as shown in Figure 8.26.

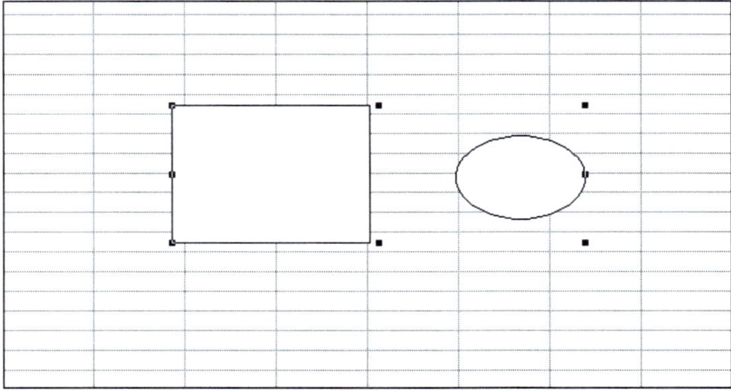

Figure 8.26 *Grouped drawn objects.*

To group a set of objects:

1. Select the group of objects.

    To select more than one object, hold the **Shift** key while clicking with the mouse.

2. From the Edit menu, choose **Arrange** and select **Group**, or click the **Group** or **Ungroup** SmartIcon.

Once objects are grouped, if you want to work with them separately, you have to ungroup them. To ungroup objects:

1. Select the grouped objects.
2. From the Edit menu, choose **Arrange** and select **Ungroup**, or click the **Group** or **Ungroup** SmartIcon.

The Group command changes to Ungroup when you have selected grouped objects.

Locking Objects

Sometimes you may want to lock drawn objects so that they cannot be moved or changed. This is a useful function when you know that you will need to keep your object in a certain place even though you may need to move the underlying cells around. To lock drawn objects:

1. Select the objects you want to lock.
2. From the Edit menu, choose **Arrange** and select **Lock**, or click the **Lock** or **Unlock** SmartIcon.

After an object (or object group) is locked, it cannot be moved, resized, or otherwise changed. If you need to unlock a locked object:

1. Select the locked object.
2. From the Edit menu, choose **Arrange** and select **Unlock**, or click the **Lock** or **Unlock** SmartIcon.

The Lock command changes to Unlock when you have selected locked objects.

Deleting Objects

If you want to delete a drawn object:

1. Select the object you want to delete.

2. Press the **Delete** key, or choose **Clear** from the Edit menu.

Be careful! When you delete an object, it will be lost forever unless you immediately choose **Undo** from the Edit menu after you delete the object.

Changing Objects

There are other ways to change your objects that enable you to customize or personalize them.

Changing Lines and Arrows

You can, for example, change the style of lines and arrows that you have created. You can even convert your lines into arrows by adding arrowheads. To change your lines and arrows, you need to open the **Lines & Colors** dialog box, as shown in Figure 8.27.

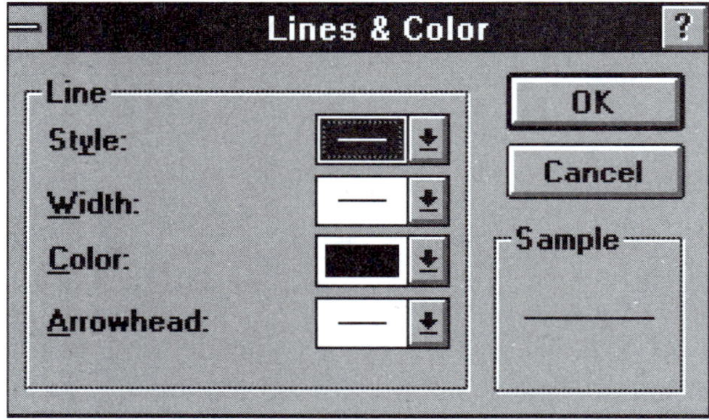

Figure 8.27 *Lines & Colors dialog box.*

When a line or arrow is selected, the Lines & Colors dialog box contains fewer choices than usual. Because you cannot add a designer frame or border to a line, 1-2-3 removes these options from the dialog box.

There are four remaining options. You can select from among various types of lines. There are solid lines, as well as several styles of dotted lines. You can adjust the line's width. You also can set the color of the line. Finally, you can choose to place arrowheads on the line, in which case, your choices are an arrowhead on the right end of the line, on the left end, on both ends, or on neither end.

To change a line or arrow:

1. Select the line or arrow.

2. From the Style menu, choose **Lines & Colors**, or click the **Lines & Colors** SmartIcon.

   The Lines & Colors dialog box appears.

3. Choose the settings you want.

4. Click OK.

Adding Frames

Another formatting function you may want to perform is to add borders and designer frames to your drawn objects. This function of Lotus 1-2-3 Release 5 is particularly useful for text blocks. The default setting is to put a thin border around a text block. You may, however, want to use a fancier designer frame to spruce up your work or to highlight a particular text box. This is shown in Figure 8.28.

Notice how the addition of a designer frame makes this text block stand out. It looks like a picture frame. To apply a designer frame to a text block or a rectangle:

1. Select the drawn object.

2. From the Style menu, choose **Lines & Colors**, or click the **Lines & Colors** SmartIcon.

   The Lines & Colors dialog box appears, as shown in Figure 8.29.

3. Choose the **Designer Frame** or regular border that you want.

4. Click **OK**.

If you apply a designer frame to a rectangle, the rectangle itself takes on the shape of the designer frame.

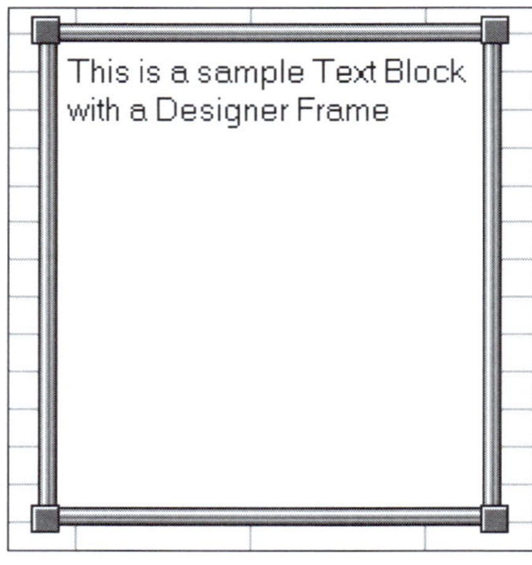

Figure 8.28 *Text block with designer frame.*

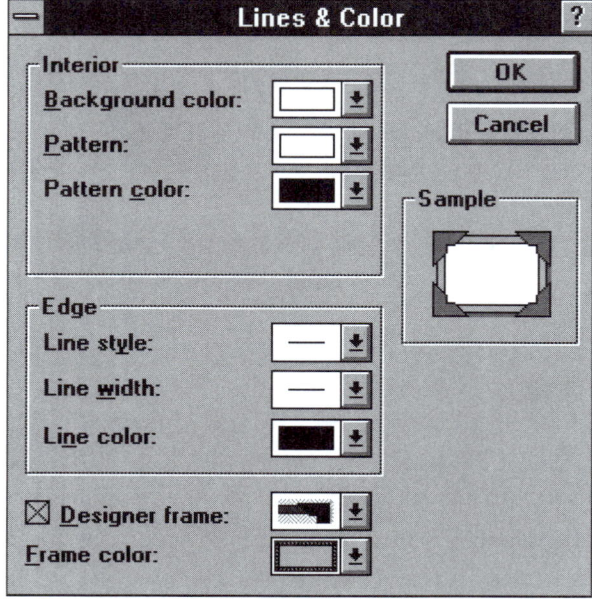

Figure 8.29 *Line & Colors dialog box.*

Changing Colors and Patterns

Lotus 1-2-3 Release 5 allows you to change the background color of a drawn object and fill in the background space. To change the color or pattern of a drawn object:

1. Select the object.

2. From the Style menu, choose **Lines & Colors**, or click the **Lines & Colors** SmartIcon.

   The Lines & Colors dialog box appears, as shown in Figure 8.29.

3. Choose the background color, the pattern, and the color for the pattern itself.

4. Click **OK**.

Flipping Objects

Another feature of Lotus 1-2-3 Release 5 is the capability to flip drawn objects. This is useful when you want to create symmetrical objects. Figure 8.30 shows a copied arc, for example. Figure 8.31 shows the flipped the copy so that the arcs are facing each other.When you want to flip an object, you can choose to flip it from left to right or from top to bottom. If you flip an object left to right, you are flipping it along an imaginary vertical line. That is, if a vertical line ran alongside one edge of the object, after flipping, the object would appear as a mirror image of it on the other side of that line. In contrast, if you flip an object top to bottom, you are flipping it along an imaginary horizontal line. In the half-circle example, the arc has been flipped left to right, so that it faces the other arc.

   To flip an object:

1. Select the object.

2. From the Edit menu, choose **Arrange** and select **Flip Left-Right** or **Flip Top-Bottom**, or click the appropriate **Flip** SmartIcon.

Rotating Objects

Another option available with Lotus 1-2-3 Release 5 is to rotate a drawn object. This is particularly useful if you want to rotate a block of text to show it at a different angle. When you rotate a drawn object, 1-2-3 changes the cursor to a + and displays a rotation handle that you move with the mouse to position the object. It also provides an outline of the figure as you rotate it so that you can see the degree of rotation you are applying (see Figure 8.32).

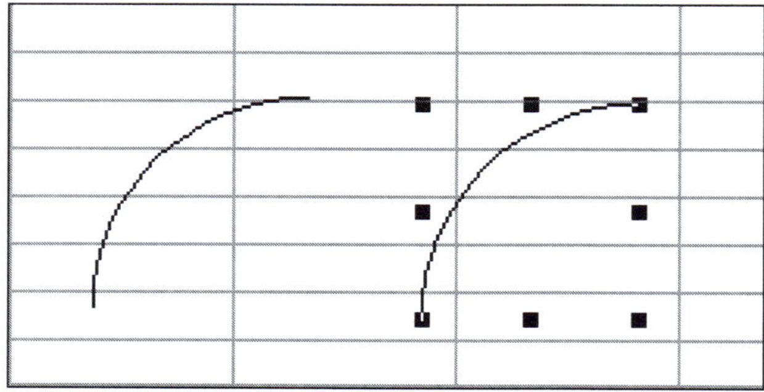

Figure 8.30 *Copied arc.*

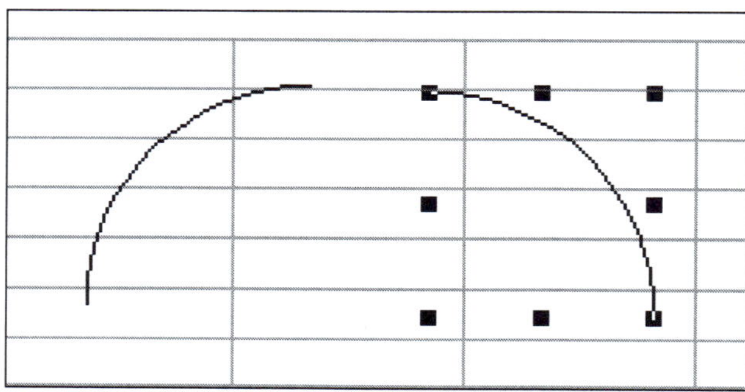

Figure 8.31 *Flipped arc left-right.*

To rotate an object:

1. Select the object.

2. From the Edit menu, choose **Arrange** and select **Rotate**, or click the **Rotate** SmartIcon.

3. Rotate the object by holding the mouse button while you move the mouse, using the figure outline as a guide.

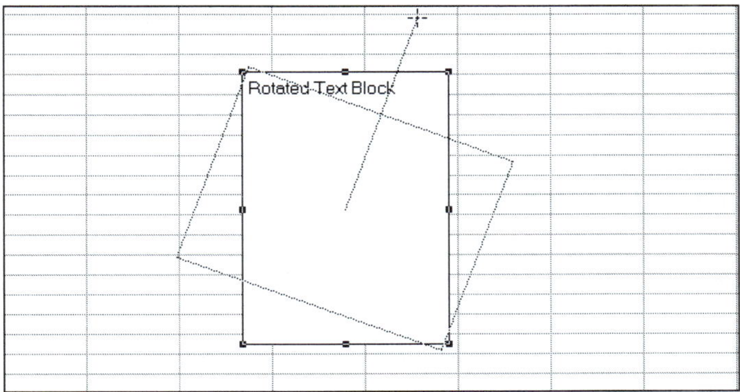

Figure 8.32 *Rotating a drawn object.*

4. Release the mouse button when the object is rotated the way you want.

    If you want to rotate the object in 45 degree increments, hold the **Shift** key while you rotate the image.

Practice

Use an empty worksheet to practice using the different drawn object tools. With a little practice you will feel comfortable using these tools which will help to enhance your worksheet.

To Sum Up

You are now familiar with the essential steps involved in creating and working with graphics on Lotus 1-2-3 Release 5. You can create drawn objects, closed drawn objects, and objects involving many different lines. You can work with a text block and format it as you want. You can draw freehand with the mouse, or import a graphic image you like from another program and place it into your worksheet.

After objects are created, you can work with them as you resize, copy, move, arrange, or delete them. You can make objects easy to locate by fastening them to a particular range of cells, grouping them together for formatting purposes, or locking them in an area of your worksheet.

When you have completed this work on your objects, you are free to change them by adding frames, colors, or patterns, or by flipping or rotating their orientation.

What You Learned

Create a line:

1. From the Tools menu, select **Draw** and choose **Line**.

   The cursor changes to a +.
2. Click and drag the mouse to create a line.
3. Release the mouse button when the desired length and angle is reached.

Create arrows:

1. From the Tools menu, select **Draw** and choose **Arrow**, or click the **Arrow** SmartIcon.
2. Click and hold the mouse button where you want the arrow to originate and drag the mouse to create the arrow.
3. Release the mouse button to place an arrow head at the end of the line.

Create an arc:

1. From the Tools menu, select **Draw** and choose **Arc**.
2. Click and hold the mouse button where you want the arc to originate and drag the mouse to create an arc.
3. Release the mouse button when the desired length of the arc is reached.

Create a rectangle, a rounded rectangle, or an ellipse:

1. From the Tools menu, select **Draw** and choose **Rectangle**, **Rounded Rectangle**, or **Ellipse**, or (for an ellipse) click the **Ellipse** SmartIcon.
2. Click and hold the mouse where you want the drawn object to originate and drag the mouse out and up (or down) to create the object.
3. Release the mouse button when the desired shape and size is reached.

To create a perfectly proportioned rectangle (that is, a square) or a perfectly proportioned ellipse (that is, a circle), press and hold the **Shift** key while you click and drag the mouse.

Create a polyline:

1. From the Tools menu, select **Draw** and choose **Polylines**.
2. Click and hold the mouse button where you want the polyline to originate and drag the mouse to the end of the first line.
3. Click and hold the mouse button to begin the next line and drag the mouse to the end of the second line.
4. Continue the click and drag process for as many lines as you want in your polyline object.
5. Double-click the mouse button to end the polyline.

Create a polygon:

1. From the Tools menu, select **Draw** and choose **Polygon**.
2. Click and hold the mouse button where you want the polygon to originate and drag the mouse to the end of the first line.
3. Click and hold the mouse button to begin the next line and drag the mouse to the end of the second line.
4. Continue the click and drag process for as many lines as you want in your polygon object.
5. Double-click the mouse button to automatically create the final line that connects the beginning point of the first line with the end point of the last line.

Create freehand objects:

1. From the Tools menu, select **Draw** and choose **Freehand**.
2. Click and hold the mouse button where you want to originate your freehand object.

   The cursor changes to a pencil.
3. Drag the mouse as you would a pencil.
4. Release the mouse button when you have finished.

Create text blocks:

1. From the Tools menu, select **Draw** and choose **Text**, or click the **Text Box** SmartIcon.

   The cursor changes to a +.

2. Click the mouse button where you want the text block to originate and drag the mouse to create a box.

3. Release the mouse button when the box is completed and a vertical insertion point (|) appears in the box.

4. Type the desired text block.

5. Click anywhere outside the text block when you are finished.

Edit text blocks:

1. Double-click with the mouse on the text block and a vertical insertion point (|) appears.

2. Edit the text.

3. Click anywhere outside the text block when you are finished.

Format text blocks:

1. Select the text box by clicking on it with the mouse.

   When the text block is selected you will see placeholders around it.

2. From the Style menu, choose **Fonts & Attributes**, **Lines & Colors**, or **Alignment** to format the text block.

   You can click with the right mouse button to access the pull-down menu for formatting text.

Import pictures from other software programs:

1. Select the picture in the other program.

2. From the Edit menu, select **Copy**.

3. Go to your worksheet.

4. From the Edit menu, select **Paste** or click the **Paste** SmartIcon.

   The picture will be pasted into the picture box.

Select an object:

    1. Click with the mouse when the cursor is over the object.

        After you click, a small square appears after the cursor arrow and place-holders appear on each of the lines of the box that encloses the object.

Resize an object:

    1. Select the object.

    2. Click and hold the mouse button on a placeholder for the object and drag the mouse until the size and shape of the box is changed.

        Use the placeholders on the top and bottom lines of the box to elongate or flatten the object; use the placeholders on the right and left lines of the box to widen or narrow the object.

    3. Release the mouse button when the desired shape and size is reached.

        To resize an object proportionally, press and hold the **Shift** key while you click and drag the mouse.

Copy an object:

    1. Select the object.

    2. Copy it just as you do a cell or range.

Move an object:

    1. Select an object.

    2. Click and hold the mouse button and drag to a new location.

        The cursor changes to a hand and an outline of the object will move with the hand.

        To move an object, click somewhere other than the placeholder. Clicking and dragging on a placeholder resizes an object; it doesn't move it.

Arrange an object:

    1. Select an object.

2. From the Edit menu, choose **Arrange** and select either **Bring To Front** or **Send To Back**, or click the appropriate SmartIcon.

Fasten objects to cells:

1. Select an object.

2. From the Edit menu, choose **Arrange** and choose **Fasten To Cells**.

    The Fasten To Cells dialog box appears.

3. Choose either **Top Left Cell Only** or **Top Left and Bottom Right Cells**.

    If you choose to fasten the object at only one point, use the **Top Left Cell Only** option and the object will move as you move the top left cell. On the other hand, if you choose to fasten the object at two points, use the **Top Left and Bottom Right Cells** option, in which case, not only will the object move with the attached cells, but it will resize as you resize the cells to which it is fastened.

5. Click **OK**.

Group and Ungroup a set of objects:

1. Select a set of objects.

    To select more than one object, press the **Shift** key while clicking with the mouse.

2. From the Edit menu, select **Arrange** and choose **Group**, or click the **Group or Ungroup** SmartIcon.

    To Ungroup a set of grouped objects, follow the same procedure. If in step 1 you selected a grouped object, the Group command in the Arrange menu changes to Ungroup.

Lock and Unlock an object:

1. Select the object.

2. From the Edit menu, select **Arrange** and choose **Lock**, or click the **Lock** or **Unlock** SmartIcon.

    To Unlock a locked object, follow the same procedure. If in step 1 you selected a locked object, the Lock command in the Arrange menu changes to Unlock.

Delete an object:

1. Select an object.

2. From the Edit menu, choose **Clear**, or press the **Delete** key.

   When you delete an object, it will be lost forever unless you immediately choose **Undo** from the Edit menu.

Change the style of an object that is a line (or an arrow):

1. Select the line (or arrow).

2. From the Style menu, choose **Lines & Colors**, or click the **Lines & Colors** SmartIcon.

   The Lines & Colors dialog box appears.

3. Choose the type of line (solid, dotted, and so on), the width of line, color of line, and arrowhead on either end, both ends or neither end.

4. Click **OK**.

Add a designer frame to an object:

1. Select the object.

2. From the Style menu, choose **Lines & Colors**, or click the **Lines & Colors** SmartIcon.

   The Lines & Colors dialog box appears.

3. Choose the designer frame or regular border you desire.

4. Click **OK**.

Change colors and patterns of an object:

1. Select the object.

2. From the Style menu, choose **Lines & Colors**, or click the **Lines & Colors** SmartIcon.

   The Lines & Colors dialog box appears.

3. Choose the background color, pattern, and color of the pattern you desire.

4. Click **OK**.

Flip an object:

1. Select an object.

2. From the Edit menu, select **Arrange** and choose **Flip Left-Right** or **Flip Top-Bottom**, or click the appropriate Flip SmartIcon.

Rotate an object:

1. Select the object.

2. From the Edit menu, select **Arrange** and choose **Rotate**, or click the **Rotate** SmartIcon.

3. Click and hold the mouse button and drag the object to rotate it.

   The cursor changes to a +, a rotation handle appears, and an outline of the object will rotate as you drag the handle with the mouse.

4. Release the mouse button when the object is rotated to the location you desire.

   To rotate an object in 45 degree increments, press and hold the **Shift** key while you click and drag the mouse.

Chapter 9

Analyzing Data

Until now, the skills you have learned have been intended to assist you in the presentation of your worksheets. These skills are commonly employed by spreadsheet users. For example, people enjoy using a spreadsheet to create an informative table of data or to create an attractive chart. Another important feature of a spreadsheet program, however, is its capability to let you analyze data.

What does it mean to analyze data? With Lotus 1-2-3 Release 5 you can create different versions of the same spreadsheet and compare them to each other. You can also answer "what-if" questions, such as "what if I change the interest rate?" This enables you to think about your data more creatively, refine your decision making and improve your work.

Version Manager

The Version Manager enables you to analyze different versions of your worksheet to see the effect that changes in certain data would have on other aspects of your spreadsheet. Suppose, for example, that you wanted to see how the net income of Caroline's Budget would vary with different sales and expense levels. With the Version Manager, you can create different potential versions of Caroline's Budget, such as High Sales, Low Sales, High Expenses, Low Expenses, and so on. Then you can use the Version Manager to compare these different scenarios.

For this example, you will be using Caroline's Budget again. Figure 9.1 shows what this spreadsheet should look like.

	A	B	Jan	Feb	Mar	Apr	May	Jun	I	J
			Caroline's Budget							
2			Jan	Feb	Mar	Apr	May	Jun		
3	Income:									
4		Salary	$1,400	$1,400	$1,400	$1,400	$1,400	$1,400		
5		Interest	$20	$20	$20	$20	$20	$20		
6		Dividends	$150	$0	$0	$200	$0	$0		
8		Total Income	$1,570	$1,420	$1,420	$1,620	$1,420	$1,420		
9	Expenses:								5%	
10		Rent	$550	$550	$550	$550	$550	$550		
11		Food	$200	$200	$200	$200	$200	$200		
12		Automobile	$320	$100	$100	$100	$100	$100		
13		Phone	$100	$100	$100	$100	$100	$100		
14		Utilities	$120	$120	$120	$120	$120	$120		
15		Entertainment	$79	$71	$71	$81	$71	$71		
16		Loan Payment	$60	$60	$60	$60	$60	$60		
17		Miscellaneous	$100	$50	$50	$50	$50	$50		
19		Total Expenses	$1,529	$1,251	$1,251	$1,261	$1,251	$1,251		
21		Net Income	$42	$169	$169	$359	$169	$169		

Figure 9.1 *Caroline's Budget.*

The Version Manager is also useful when several people are working on the same spreadsheet. If, for example, you and a partner are each working on the same spreadsheet but have differing ideas as to what the data values should be, you can use the Version Manager to compare both versions.

When you create a version of your worksheet, Lotus 1-2-3 Release 5 gives it a name, date, and time, indicating when it was created. Lotus 1-2-3 Release 5 also identifies the name of the person who created the version as well as optional comments.

To make use of this important feature, you must open the Version Manager. To open the Version Manager, select **Version** from the Range menu. 1-2-3 displays the Version Manager dialog box, shown in Figure 9.2.

Figure 9.2 *Version Manager dialog box.*

The Version Manager dialog box contains various items. At the top of the dialog box, the name of the range you have selected and any versions associated with that range are displayed. If you have more than one item in either of these two boxes, you should click on the down arrow to the right of the box. Clicking this arrow displays a drop-down list from which you can choose the version with which you want to work. Because you have not yet created a version, nothing appears in these boxes.

Below these two boxes is a line of squares, or buttons. You can click on each of these to perform a different task. Some of these buttons are gray, indicating that they are not in use because they aren't relevant at this particular time. For example, because you have not created any versions yet, the Delete button is gray. You must create a version before you can delete one.

The first button, as shown in Figure 9.3, is the Create button.

Figure 9.3 *Create button.*

This button is used to create new versions in your spreadsheet. The next button, as shown in Figure 9.4, is the Update button.

Figure 9.4 *Update button.*

If you make changes in your worksheet and those changes are part of an exist-ing version, you can either create a new version with these data values or update your existing version. To update the version, click on the **Update** button.

The next button, as shown in Figure 9.5, is the Info button.

Figure 9.5 *Info button.*

Once you create a version, you can view information about this version. This information includes the names of the version and its creator, the date and time of the version, and so on. The Info button also enables you to add comments to the version. A comment may be especially useful if you are working with some-one else and want to make explanatory remarks about the version.

The next button, as shown in Figure 9.6, is the Delete button.

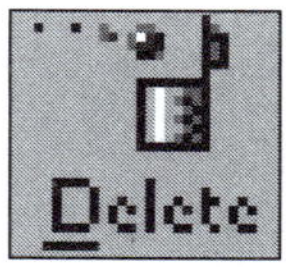

Figure 9.6 *Delete button.*

After you have created a version, you may decide to delete it from the work-sheet. To delete a version, select the version from the version list and click on the **Delete** button.

The next button, as shown in Figure 9.7, is the Close button. This button closes the Version Manager when you have finished using it.

Figure 9.7 *Close button.*

The last button, as shown in Figure 9.8, is the To Index button.

Figure 9.8 *To Index button.*

The Index is another way to work with versions. Whereas the Version Manager enables you to work with one version at a time, the Version Index enables you to work with multiple versions at the same time. The Version Index also enables you to create scenarios. You learn about scenarios later in this chapter. To switch to the Version Index, click on the **To Index** button. The Version Manager dialog box changes into the Version Manager Index dialog box, as shown in Figure 9.9. You use the Version Index later in this chapter.

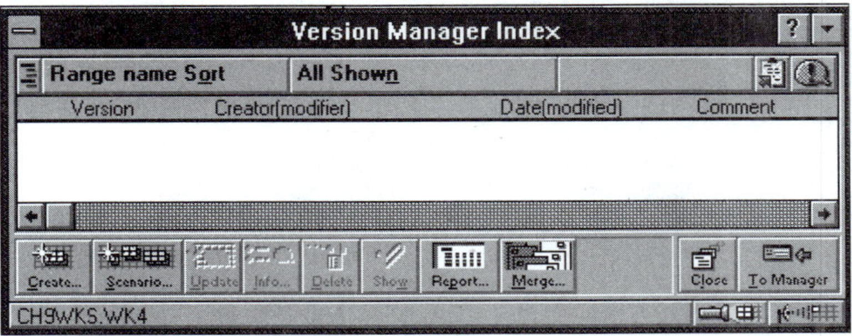

Figure 9.9 *Version Manager Index dialog box.*

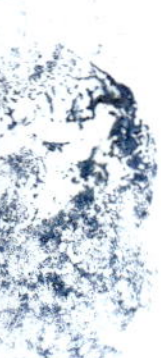

At the bottom of the Version Manager dialog box are two other buttons. The one on the left is the Highlight button; the one on the right is the Tracking button. The Highlight button outlines the ranges in your worksheet that contain named versions. The Tracking button selects a range in the worksheet when you select the version or the range in the Version Manager. You will not be using these buttons in the chapter examples, but they are helpful when finding versions and ranges in large worksheets.

Create a Version

Now let's create a version. In your example, you are going to create different versions of Caroline's Budget. Before you can create new versions of the worksheet, however, you must create a version for the current data values.

Name your first version *Medium Income*. This version will consist of the range that contains the Income, Dividend, and Interest values. You first need to select the range **A:C4..A:H6**, as shown in Figure 9.10.

	A	B	C	D	E	F	G	H	I	J
				Caroline's Budget						
2			Jan	Feb	Mar	Apr	May	Jun		
3	Income:									
4		Salary	$1,400	$1,400	$1,400	$1,400	$1,400	$1,400		
5		Interest	$20	$20	$20	$20	$20	$20		
6		Dividends	$150	$0	$0	$200	$0	$0		
8		Total Income	$1,570	$1,420	$1,420	$1,620	$1,420	$1,420		
9	Expenses:								5%	
10		Rent	$550	$550	$550	$550	$550	$550		
11		Food	$200	$200	$200	$200	$200	$200		
12		Automobile	$320	$100	$100	$100	$100	$100		
13		Phone	$100	$100	$100	$100	$100	$100		
14		Utilities	$120	$120	$120	$120	$120	$120		
15		Entertainment	$79	$71	$71	$81	$71	$71		
16		Loan Payment	$60	$60	$60	$60	$60	$60		
17		Miscellaneous	$100	$50	$50	$50	$50	$50		
19		Total Expenses	$1,529	$1,251	$1,251	$1,261	$1,251	$1,251		
21		Net Income	$42	$169	$169	$359	$169	$169		

Figure 9.10 *Select range A:C4..A:H6.*

Once you select this range, you can tell 1-2-3 to name the data values in this range Medium Income. To name a version, follow these steps:

1. Select the correct range.

2. From the Range menu, choose **Version**.

   The Version Manager dialog box appears.

3. Click on the **Create** button.

   The Create Version dialog box appears, as shown in Figure 9.11.

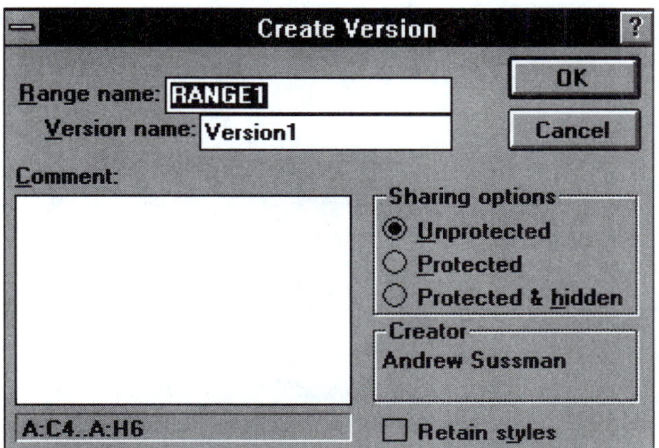

Figure 9.11 *Create Version dialog box.*

4. Type **Income** in the Range Name box.

   This names the range A:C4..A:H6 as Income.

5. Type **Medium Income** into the Version Name box.

   This is how Lotus 1-2-3 Release 5 knows that these data values make up the version that you have named Medium Income.

6. If you would like to add a comment regarding this version, click the Comment box and enter your remarks. For this example, leave it blank.

   The comment option is useful if your version name is a general one and more explanatory information is needed.

7. If you were working on this version with more than one person, you could use the Sharing Options feature, which lets you protect the version from changes, or hide it in your worksheet so that other people cannot see it. In this example, however, leave the setting Unprotected, because you don't want to protect this version.

   The Version Manager tells you the name of the creator of this version. If you are sharing your data file on a network, each computer will have its own name. If you are sharing your computer with other people, they will have to change the name in the User Setup dialog box.

8. When you are finished, click on the **OK** button.

After you create a version, Lotus 1-2-3 Release 5 returns you to the Version

Manager dialog box. Your version should now appear in the dialog box, as shown in Figure 9.12.

Figure 9.12 *Version Manager dialog box with your named version.*

If you have more than one named range or version for each range, you can change between them by clicking on the down arrow. A drop-down list appears that contains all your ranges or versions.

Suppose that you did not enter a comment when you created the version and now want to do so. Or perhaps you want to change either a comment or the name of the range associated with the version. These and other options can be effected by clicking on the **Info** button in the Version Manager. When you click on this button, 1-2-3 opens the Version Info dialog box, shown in Figure 9.13.

Notice that this dialog box is similar to the Create Version dialog box, with a few important differences. First, you cannot change the name of the version; Lotus 1-2-3 Release 5 enables you to change the name of the range only. Second, above the box that displays the name of the creator of the version, it now says Modified instead of Created. You are modifying an existing version rather than creating a new one.

Now suppose that you decide to delete a version. To do so, use the **Delete** button. When you click on this button, Lotus 1-2-3 Release 5 asks you to verify that you want to delete the version, as shown in Figure 9.14.

If you click **OK** or press **Enter**, Lotus 1-2-3 Release 5 erases your version. This does not delete the data values, only your entry in the Version Manager.

For this example, don't delete your version, so click **Cancel**.

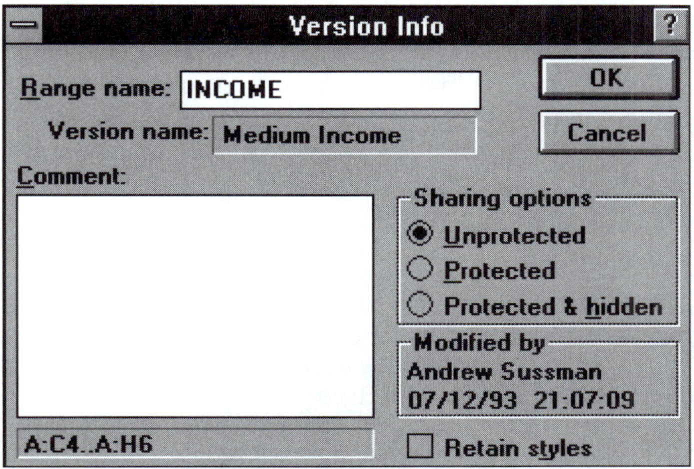

Figure 9.13 *Version Info dialog box.*

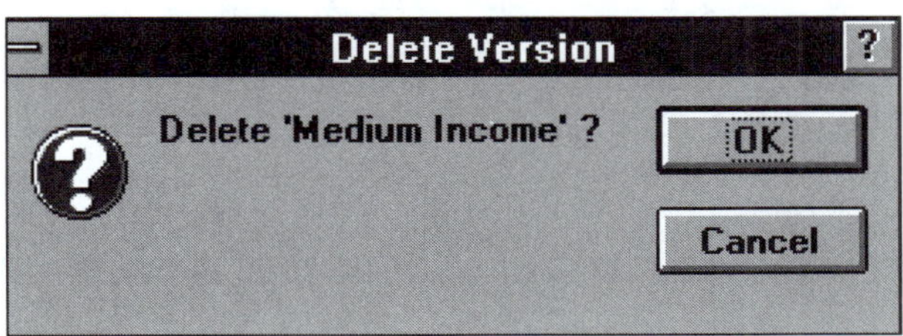

Figure 9.14 *Lotus 1-2-3 Release 5 warns you that you are deleting a version.*

Working with Multiple Versions

You now have one version for your Income range. Suppose that you want to change the values of your income data and create a new version for this income. If, for example, you thought your income might be higher than your first budgeted amount, you could create a new version called High Income.

To create a new version:

1. Change the data to whatever new values you want.

    The first version "memorized" the data values for your income entries. It is fine to change the data values, because you can always retrieve the original ones. However, this only applies to cells in the range you originally assigned to this version (in your example, the Income range). Therefore, if you change one of the expense values, it will overwrite your original data. In that case, the data cannot be retrieved, only retyped.

For this example, change your data so that it matches the values shown in Figure 9.15.

		Jan	Feb	Mar	Apr	May	Jun		
Caroline's Budget									
Income:									
	Salary	$1,600	$1,600	$1,600	$1,600	$1,600	$1,600		
	Interest	$25	$25	$25	$25	$25	$25		
	Dividends	$200	$0	$0	$300	$0	$0		
	Total Income	$1,825	$1,625	$1,625	$1,925	$1,625	$1,625		
Expenses:								5%	
	Rent	$550	$550	$550	$550	$550	$550		
	Food	$200	$200	$200	$200	$200	$200		
	Automobile	$320	$100	$100	$100	$100	$100		
	Phone	$100	$100	$100	$100	$100	$100		
	Utilities	$120	$120	$120	$120	$120	$120		
	Entertainment	$91	$81	$81	$96	$81	$81		
	Loan Payment	$60	$60	$60	$60	$60	$60		
	Miscellaneous	$100	$50	$50	$50	$50	$50		
	Total Expenses	$1,541	$1,261	$1,261	$1,276	$1,261	$1,261		
	Net Income	$284	$364	$364	$649	$364	$364		

Figure 9.15 *Change your data to match these income levels.*

Remember that the Total Income row contains an equation, so you don't need to change these cells manually. You only need to change the cells highlighted in Figure 9.15.

2. Select the range A:C4..A:H6.

3. From the Range menu, choose **Version**.

   The Version Manager dialog box appears, as shown in Figure 9.16.

   Notice that the Version Name box shows the name Medium Income. This is because you have selected the same range as Middle Income. However, this time the check mark to the left of the version name has a slash through it. This is because the version Medium Income has been changed.

Figure 9.16 *Version Manager dialog box.*

Notice also that the Update button is now available in the Version Manager. If you clicked this button, Lotus 1-2-3 Release 5 would change the memorized version to the current values.

Clicking on the **Update** button erases the values you previously named as this version. When you do this, you cannot switch back to your previous version.

Instead of updating the version Medium Income, create a new version for High Income.

4. Click on the **Create** button.

   The Create Version dialog box appears, as shown in Figure 9.17.

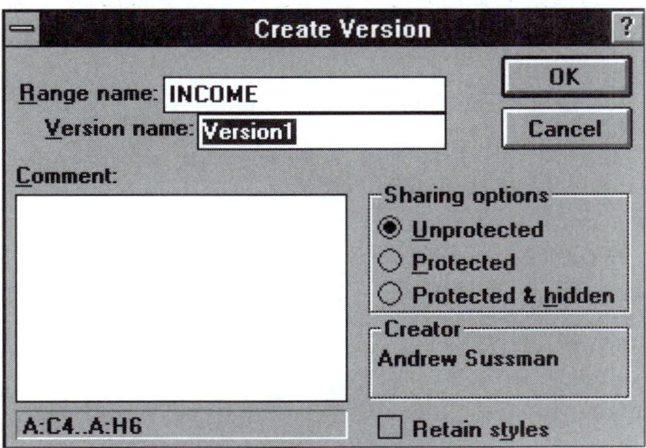

Figure 9.17 *Create Version dialog box.*

5.   Type **Income** into the Range Name box.

Because you named this range for the previous version, 1-2-3 already knows that this range is called Income.

6.   Type **High Income** into the Version Name box.

7.   Click **OK**.

Now you have created two versions for the same range. If you click on the down arrow next to the named version High Income, a drop-down list appears, as shown in Figure 9.18.

Figure 9.18 *Drop-down list of multiple versions.*

Notice that there is a check mark to the left of High Income. This tells you that Lotus 1-2-3 Release 5 is displaying the High Income version in the worksheet. If you select Medium Income, 1-2-3 displays the previous data values you assigned to the version Medium Income, as shown in Figure 9.19.

Now click on the High Income version. Lotus 1-2-3 Release 5 displays the new data values once again, as shown in Figure 9.20.

Let's make a third version called Low Income. Follow the same instructions as outlined previously, but change the data values so that they match those shown in Figure 9.21.

Now that you have three different versions of the same worksheet, the usefulness of the Version Manager becomes obvious. You don't need to create separate worksheets or files for the different hypothetical situations you may want to create.

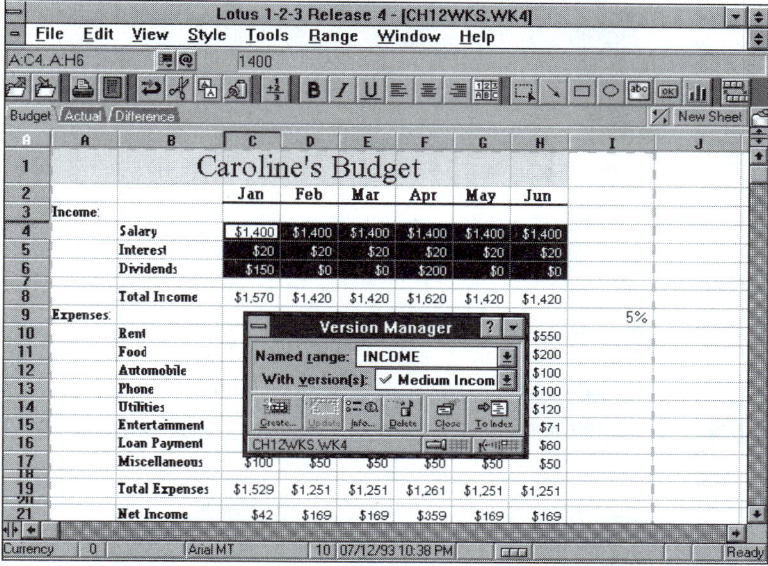

Figure 9.19 *Medium Income version.*

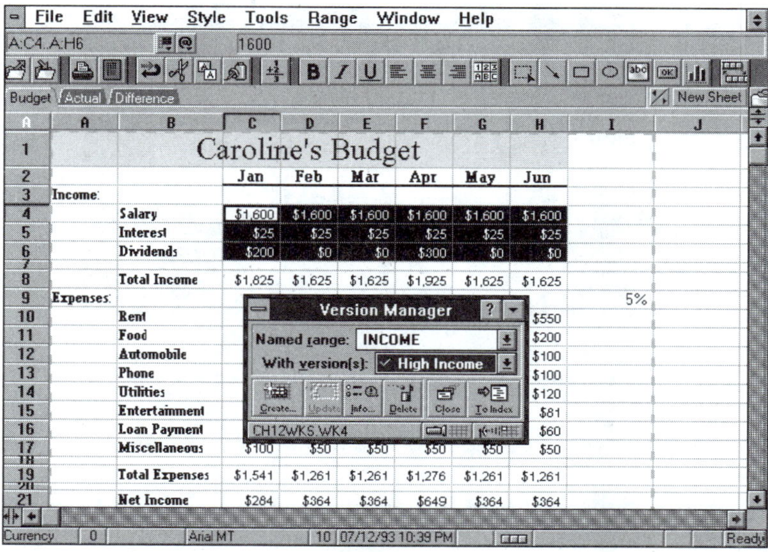

Figure 9.20 *High Income version.*

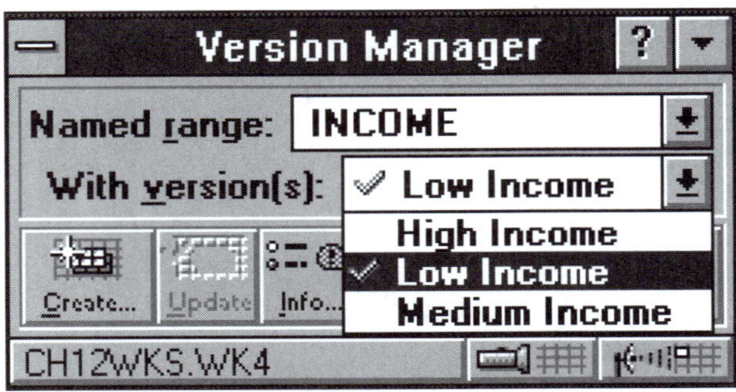

Figure 9.21 *Low Income Data values.*

When you have finished, you should have three different versions in your Version Manager. If you click on the down arrow to the right of the version box, a drop-down list appears with all three versions, as shown in Figure 9.22.

Figure 9.22 *Drop-down list with three versions.*

You are not limited to such simplistic versions as those dealt with in this example. Just because you call a version High Income does not mean that all cells in that range must be higher. You can include some that are higher and others that are lower. You can create any kind of version that contains variables of any data values you want. 1-2-3 will memorize these values so that you can alter your spreadsheet accordingly.

Now, let's create three more versions based on different expenses. First, you need to select the range **A:C10..A:H17** and create a version for Medium Expense, as shown in Figure 9.23.

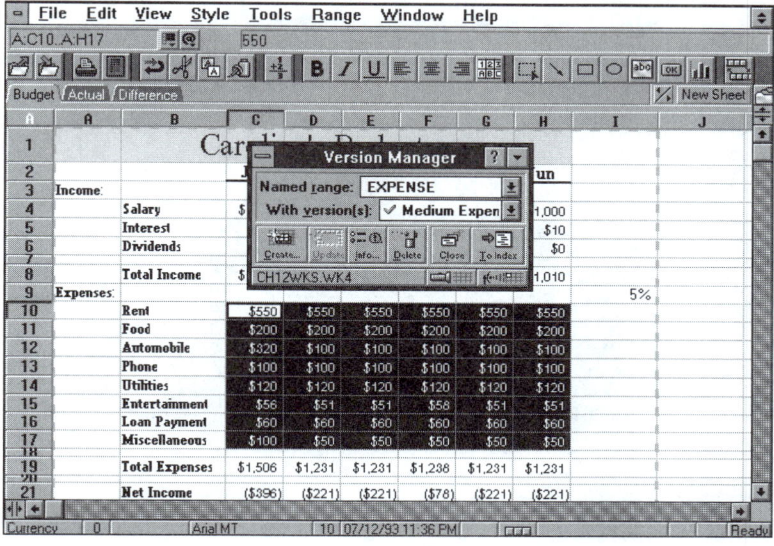

Figure 9.23 *Medium Expense version.*

When you create this version, name the range of cells Expense and the version Medium Expense. Remember, you need to create a version for your original data values in order for Lotus 1-2-3 Release 5 to memorize the data.

Next, create a version called High Expense. The data values should appear as shown in Figure 9.24.

Finally, create a version called Low Expense. Adjust your data to match the values shown in Figure 9.25.

Notice that in the Named Range box in the Version Manager, the name Expense is displayed. This is because you are looking at versions in the Expense range of the worksheet. If you click on the down arrow to the right of the version names, you will see the drop-down list of versions that are applied to that range (see Figure 9.26).

Suppose that you want to change the version of the Income range. Click on the down arrow to the right of the Named Range box. 1-2-3 displays a drop-down list that contains all the named ranges, as shown in Figure 9.27.

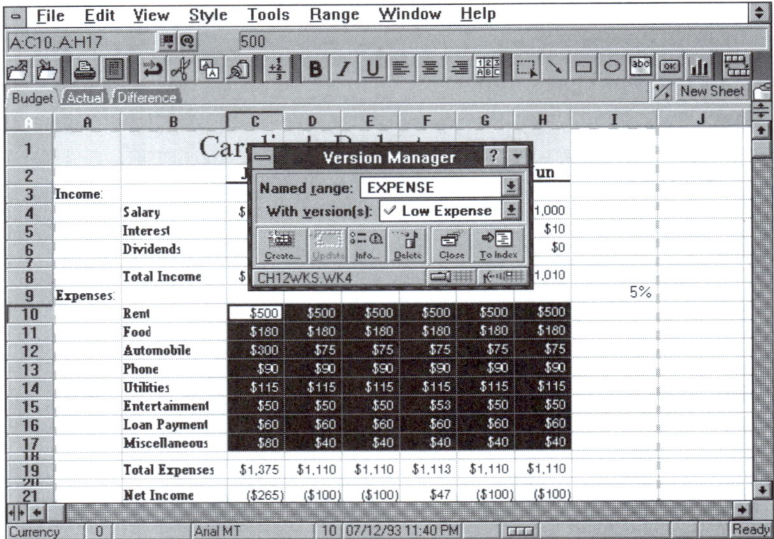

Figure 9.24 *High Expense version.*

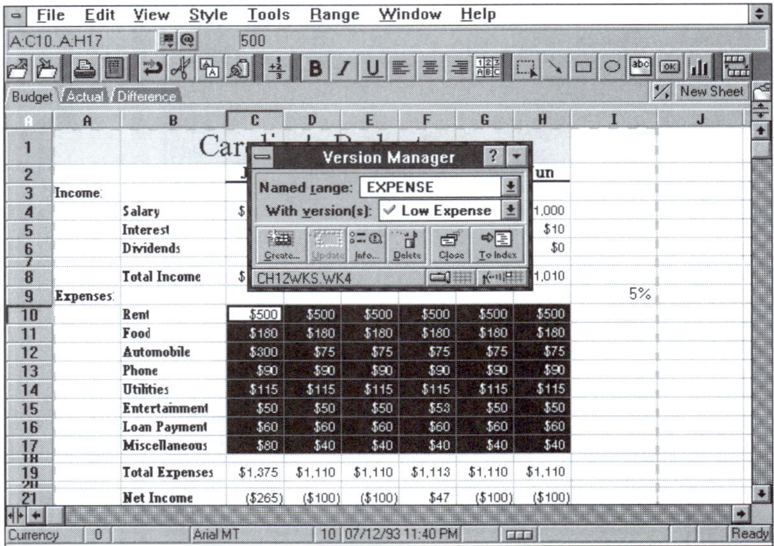

Figure 9.25 *Low Expense version.*

Figure 9.26 *Drop-down list of versions for Expense.*

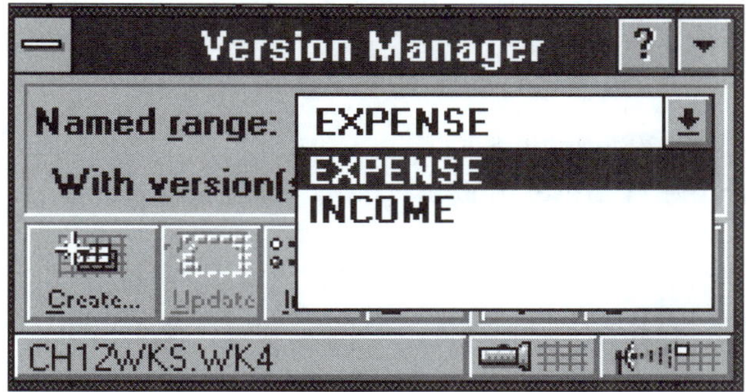

Figure 9.27 *Drop-down list of named ranges.*

In this case, 1-2-3 displays Income and Expense. If you select **Income** instead of **Expense**, 1-2-3 changes the list of versions that are applied to that range. Now the drop-down list displays High Income, Medium Income, and Low Income, as shown in Figure 9.28.

You have finished creating six versions. Three apply to the Income range, and three apply to the Expense range.

Version Manager Index

Earlier we made mention of the Version Manager Index. Unlike the Version Manager, which only enables you to work on one version at a time, the Version

Manager Index lists all your versions at once so that you can see and work with more than one version at a time. To open the Version Manager Index:

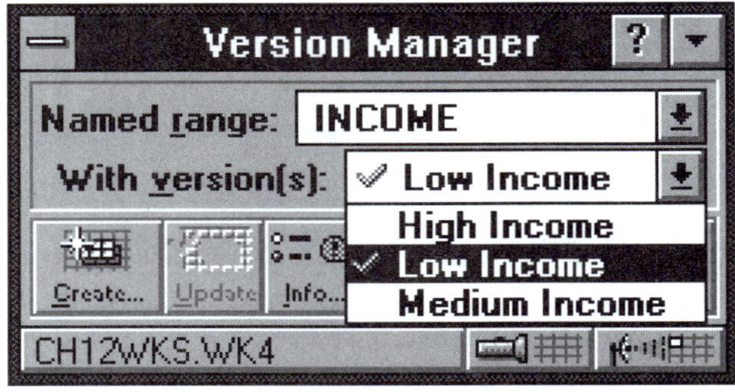

Figure 9.28 *Drop-down list of versions for Income.*

1. From the Range menu, select **Version**.
3. Click on the **To Index** button.

When you open the Version Manager Index, the Version Manager dialog box changes to the Version Manager Index dialog box, as shown in Figure 9.29.

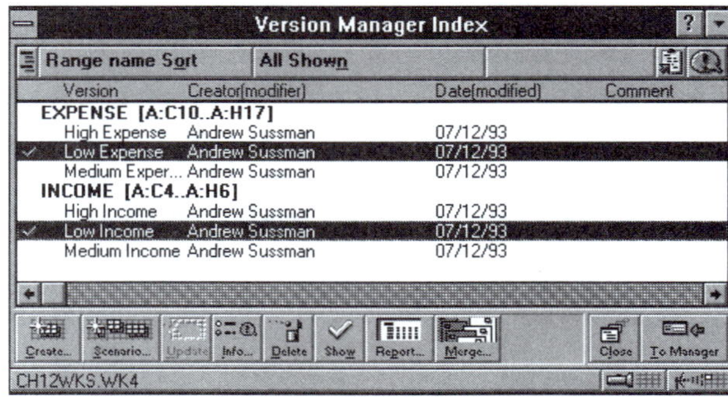

Figure 9.29 *Version Manager Index.*

If your dialog box is not large enough to display all the versions, as in Figure 9.29, you can enlarge the window. If you are working with a large number of versions, it may not be practical to enlarge the Version Manager Index to view all the versions at once. Because you have only six versions, however, it is helpful, for this exercise, to view them all at once.

Notice that the Version Manager Index is like the Version Manager's "big brother." Anything you can do in the Version Manager you also can do in the Index. There are, however, some additional features of the Index that cannot be duplicated in the Version Manager. Accordingly, because of its increased capabilities, it is often useful to work in the Version Manager Index mode.

To return to the Version Manager and leave the Index, click on the **To Manager** button at the bottom right of the Index dialog box.

The Version Manager Index has buttons for creating versions, changing version information, deleting versions, and so on. In addition to these, there are buttons that enable you to show versions, create scenarios, create reports, merge versions, and merge scenarios.

You will not be using the Merge button in this book. For your reference, however, this button enables you to take versions and scenarios from one file and merge them with or export them to another file.

Showing Versions in the Version Manager Index

The Show button is used in the Version Manager Index to display the data values for a particular version in your worksheet. To show a version:

1. Select a version from the Index list.

    When you select the version, it should be highlighted.

2. Click on the **Show** button.

Now your worksheet should display the data values for the version you selected.

Selecting more than One Version at the Same Time

1-2-3 does not limit you to selecting only one version at a time. Suppose, for example, that your worksheet displays the High Expense and High Income versions, and you want to change this to Medium Expense and Medium Income. In the Version Manager, you would have to do this by changing High Expense to Medium Expense, and then repeating that procedure for Income. With the Version Manager Index, however, you can select both Medium Expense and

Medium Income from the Index list and use the Show button to display both versions. This can save time, especially if you are working with multiple named ranges, as you are in this example.

To select more than one version to be shown:

1. Click on one version (for example, Medium Expense).

2. Hold down the **Ctrl** key and click on the second version (for example, Medium Income).

    The Version Manager Index should have selected and highlighted both Medium Expense and Medium Income versions, as shown in Figure 9.30.

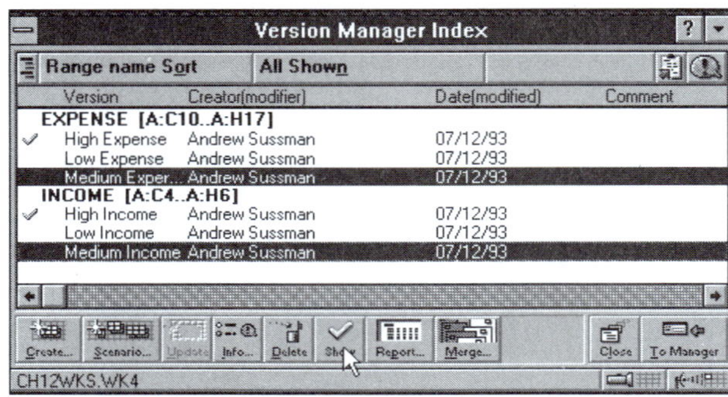

Figure 9.30 *Medium Expense and Medium Income are both selected.*

3. Click on the **Show** button.

If you now look at the Version Manager Index, the check marks to the left of High Expense and High Income have moved to Medium Expense and Medium Income, because they are now the visible versions, as shown in Figure 9.31.
You cannot select more than one version for the same named range and have 1-2-3 show them both at the same time. Accordingly, if you select High Expense and Medium Expense and click on the Show button, 1-2-3 displays only one of the versions.

Sorting versions

When you use 1-2-3, you can sort the versions in the Version Manager Index in five ways: by range name, version, scenario, date, or creator, as shown in Figure 9.32.

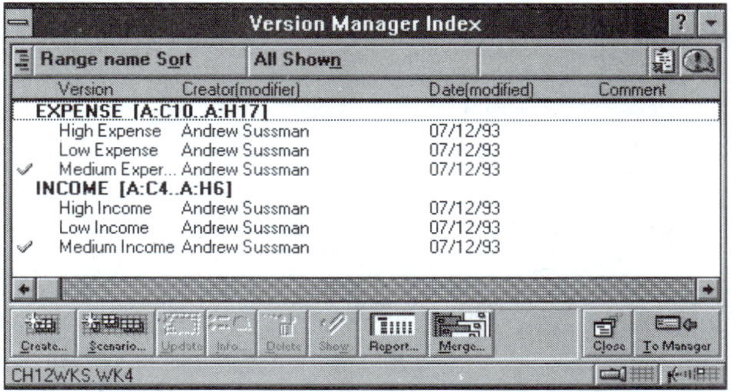

Figure 9.31 *Medium Expense and Medium Income are now visible versions.*

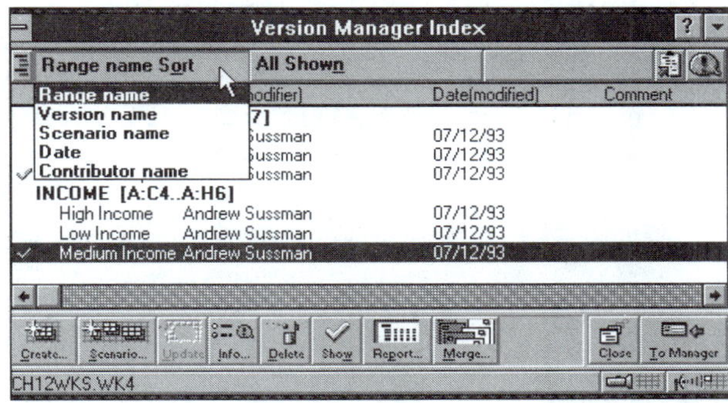

Figure 9.32 *You can sort versions in five ways.*

To change among the different sorting options:

1. Click on the button that tells you how the Index is currently being sorted, as shown in Figure 9.32.

2. Select the method of sorting you want from the drop-down list.

Currently, 1-2-3 is set to sort the Version Manager Index by range name, as shown in Figure 9.33.

When the Version Manager is set this way, different range names (in this case, Expense and Income) are sorted, and then in each range name, different versions of that range are sorted (High Expense, Low Expense, Medium Expense, and so on).

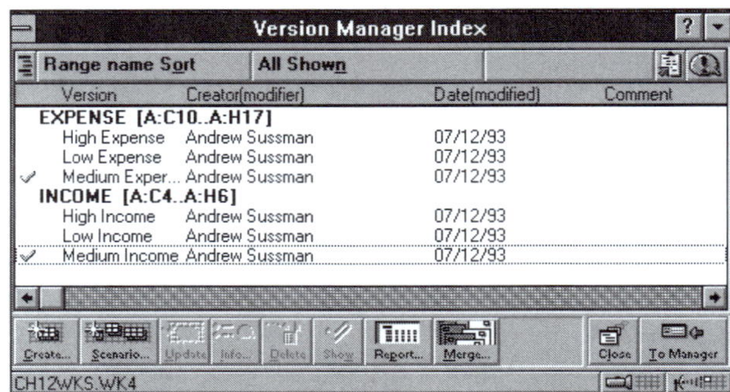

Another common way to sort the Version Manager Index is by version, as shown in Figure 9.34.

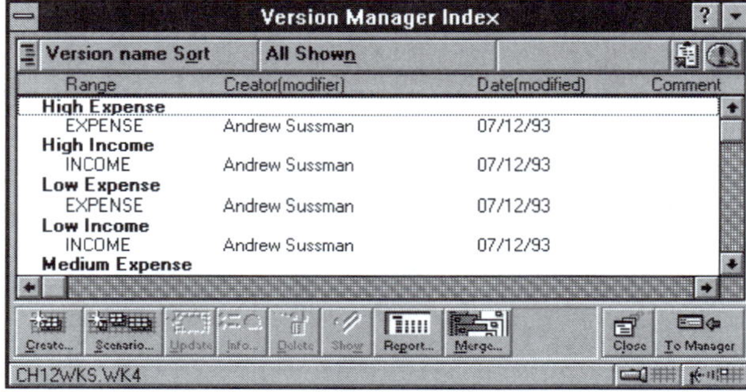

Figure 9.34 *Version Manager Index sorted by version.*

If you select this sorting option, 1-2-3 sorts the Index list by the different version names (High Expense, High Income, Low Expense, Low Income, and so on). Underneath each of these versions, 1-2-3 displays the name of the range to which that particular version applies.

The other sorting options are less common but often useful. If you select to sort by date, 1-2-3 displays the list in the chronological order in which the versions were created. First, the versions are grouped by date, and then, in each date, they are sorted by reference to the time they were created. If you sort by creator, 1-2-3 groups the versions by the person who created (or modified) the version. This is useful when you are sharing your worksheet with others and you want to know who created each version. Finally, sorting by scenario will group the versions by the scenarios that you create. (Because you have not yet created scenarios, however, 1-2-3 displays nothing.) You will get to scenarios in a few moments.

Version Reports

When you use the Version Manager Index, you can create version reports. Earlier we mentioned that you cannot view different versions of the same named range at the same time. By using the Report command, however, 1-2-3 will create a file that contains information about different versions in your worksheet. This report can give you two types of information: audit information and version data. Audit information includes information about the dates and creators of the versions, the person(s) who modified the versions, and the date(s) they were modified. Version data contains the cell address and the different versions of the data for those cell addresses. In addition, the report can include information about the effect of the different versions on a particular formula. You can, for example, create a report that shows the different Income versions you created and the effect on Net Income of each of these versions.

To create a version report:

1. Click on the **Report** button in the Version Manager Index.

   The Version Report dialog box appears, as shown in Figure 9.35. In this dialog box, you select the items you want to include in the report.

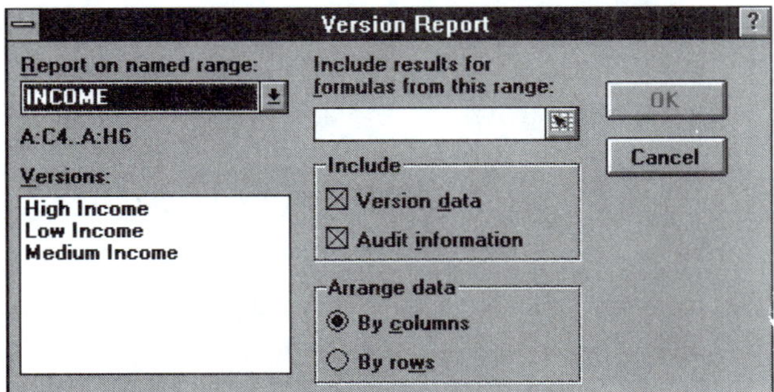

Figure 9.35 *Version Report dialog box.*

First you must select the named range on which the report will be made. Reports can be made on only one named range at a time. That is, you cannot create one report that contains the versions for Income and Expense. For this information you would need to create separate reports.

2. For this example, select **Income** from the drop-down list of named ranges.

   Next, you must choose which versions of the named range you want to include in the report. For example, you may only want to compare High Income versus Low Income, excluding Medium Income from the report. In this example, however, select all the versions.

3. To choose the versions, click on the version name in the box. This will highlight the version. Then, click on the next version. Continue this procedure until all the versions are highlighted in the window.

4. The next item you select determines whether you want 1-2-3 to report the results of the versions on particular formulas in the worksheet. In this example, you want to see the effect of the different income levels on the Net Income. Therefore, use the Range Selector to select **A:C21..A:H21**.

5. Now you must choose which information to include in the report: version data or audit information. By default, 1-2-3 includes both these items. For this example, make sure that there is an X in the boxes next to each of these items.

6. Finally, you must tell 1-2-3 whether to create this report by arranging data in rows or in columns. If you create a report in rows, all the information will extend across many columns in the Report worksheet. By contrast, if you choose to create a report in columns, the information will go down many rows of the Report worksheet. For this report, choose the By Columns option.

   After you are finished, the dialog box should appear as shown in Figure 9.36.

7. Click **OK** to create the report. After you click OK, 1-2-3 creates a new file that contains your report (see Figure 9.37).

This file is called REPORT01.WK4. If you create another report, it will named REPORT02.WK4, and so on. You can always change this file name by using the Save As command from the File menu.

The report starts with the name of the file from which the versions came. The report then tells you what named range the versions refer to. Next are the names of the versions being reported. Below this heading information, 1-2-3 reports the audit information (creator, date created, modifier, and date modified). The versions were never modified, so the last two items in the audit information are blank.

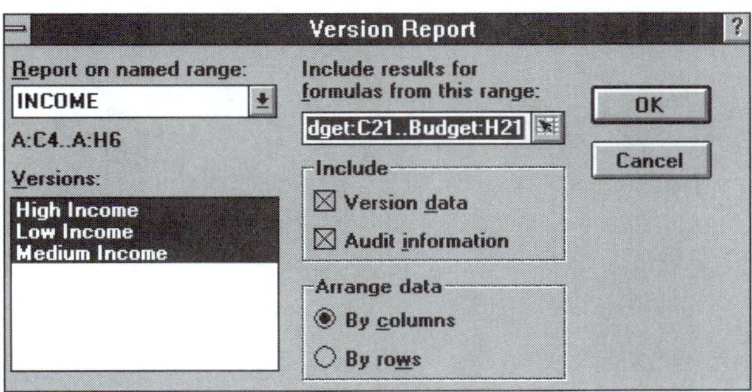

Figure 9.36 *Version Report dialog box.*

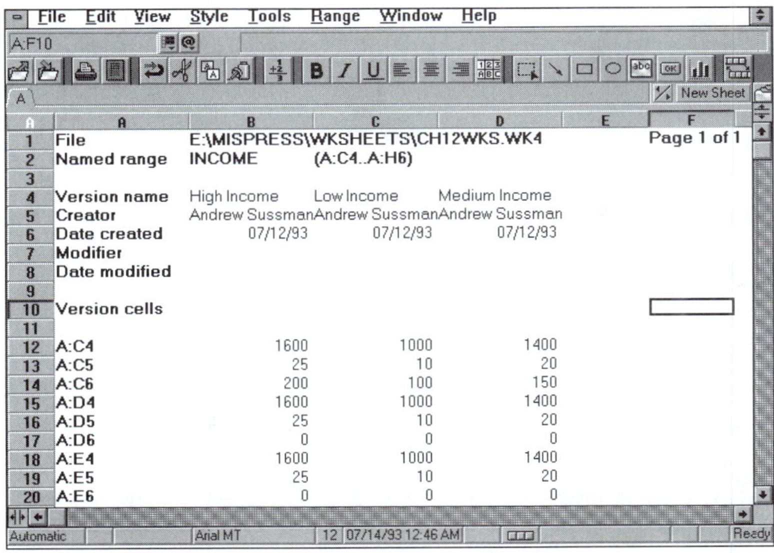

Figure 9.37 *Version report arranged by columns.*

The version data begins below the audit information. The first column lists the cell address for the data value. To the right of this address are the data values for the different versions, in their respective columns.

At the end of the report are the formula results for each version, as shown in Figure 9.38.

	A	B	C	D	E	F
22	A:F5	25	10	20		
23	A:F6	300	150	200		
24	A:G4	1600	1000	1400		
25	A:G5	25	10	20		
26	A:G6	0	0	0		
27	A:H4	1600	1000	1400		
28	A:H5	25	10	20		
29	A:H6	0	0	0		
30						
31	Formula results					
32						
33	A:C21	$284	($396)	$42		
34	A:D21	$364	($221)	$169		
35	A:E21	$364	($221)	$169		
36	A:F21	$649	($78)	$359		
37	A:G21	$364	($221)	$169		
38	A:H21	$364	($221)	$169		
39						
40						
41						

Figure 9.38 *Formula results.*

These results show the effect of the different Income levels on Net Income. It may, however, be a bit confusing to read this information because of the way it is arranged. Because you chose to create a report by columns, the Net Income values that are arranged in rows in your worksheet are now arranged by columns. The first entry (A:C21) is January Net Income. Across this row are the results of each version of January's Net Income. The next row down is February Net Income (A:D21). Below this is March Net Income (A:E21), and so on.

Because this may be difficult to analyze, it may be more helpful to create this report by arranging the data by rows. If you create the same report by rows, it will look as shown in Figure 9.39.

The file name for this new report is REPORT02.WK4, because it is the second report you have created. If you look at the far right end of the report, you will see the formula results, as shown in Figure 9.40.

If you look at the formula results now, they are easier to follow because they are arranged in the same order as they appear in the worksheet. The first column contains the formula results for January's Net Income (A:C21). Below this cell address are the results for each of the three versions. The next column is February's Net Income (A:D21), and so forth.

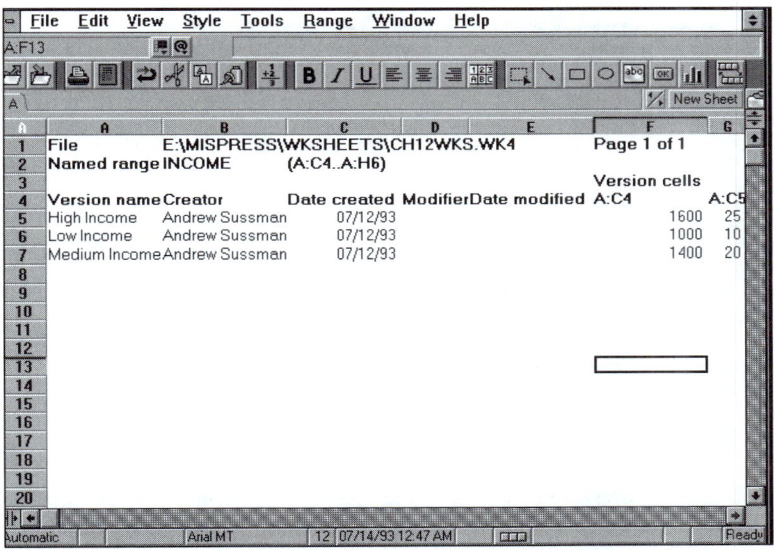

Figure 9.39 *Version report arranged by rows.*

These reports can now be printed, saved, manipulated, and so on. Because they are separate files from your original worksheet, they must be saved to your hard drive or floppy disk if you want to keep them. They will not be saved as part of your original worksheet.

Scenarios

Earlier we explained that you can select more than one version in the Version Manager Index and show several versions at once. However, you can only do this temporarily. That is, if at a later time you want to show the versions High Income and High Expense again, you must redo the same steps.

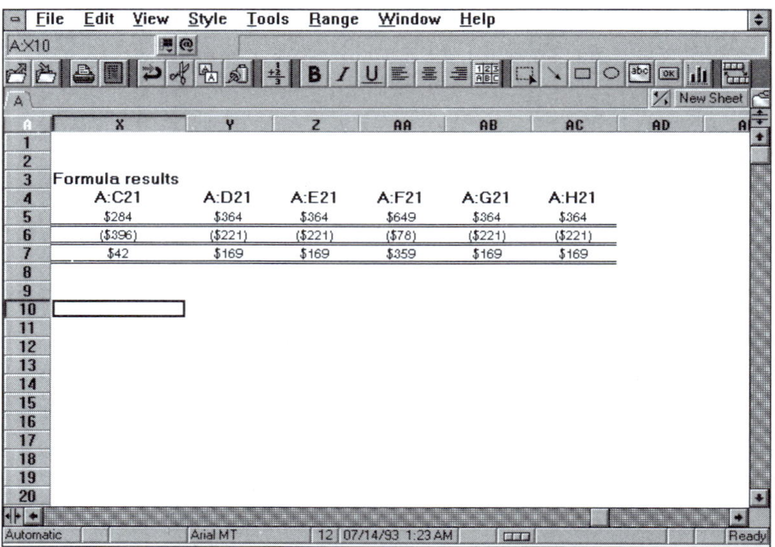

Figure 9.40 *Formula results arranged by rows.*

1-2-3, however, has a feature called Scenarios that enables you to create permanent groupings of versions. You can, for example, create a scenario called High, which consists of the versions High Income and High Expense. Or, you can create a scenario called Worst Case, which consists of Low Income and High Expense. This feature of the program enables you to combine different versions of named ranges to create different scenarios that might occur.

To create a scenario, click on the **Scenario** button in the Version Manager Index to open the Create Scenario dialog box, as shown in Figure 9.41.

This dialog box is similar to the Create Version dialog box, except that instead of selecting a range of cells, you must choose which versions you want to include in your scenario. At the bottom of the window are two boxes. The one on the left is called Selected Versions, the one on the right is Available Versions. You must select versions from the Available Versions list and move them to the Selected Versions list. To accomplish this, follow these steps:

1.   Select the version from the Available Versions list.

     The button between the two lists will become an arrow facing to the left (in the direction of the Selected Versions list) as shown in Figure 9.42.

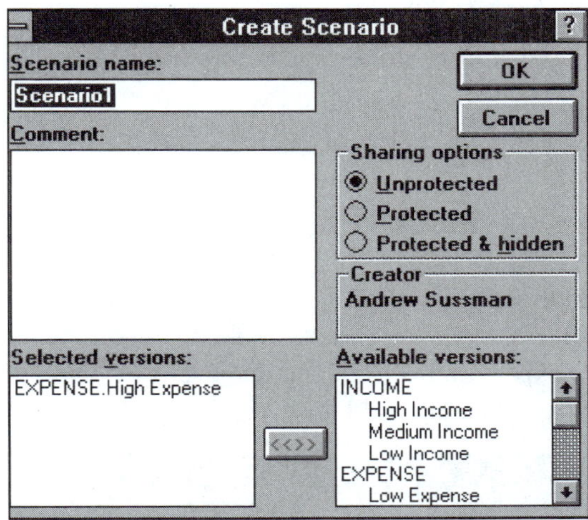

Figure 9.41 *Create Scenario dialog box.*

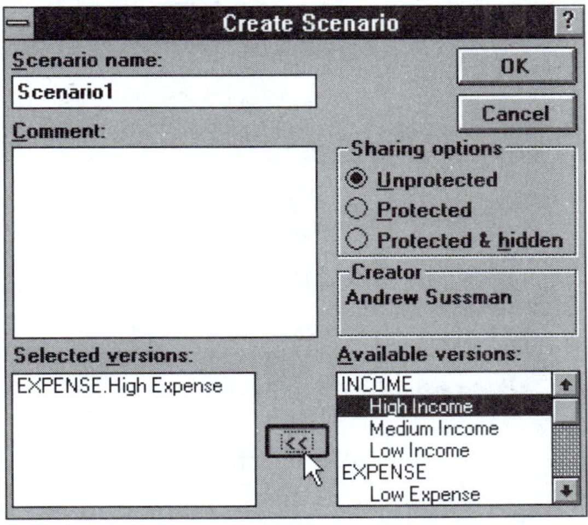

Figure 9.42 *To move available versions to the Selected Versions box.*

2. Click on the arrow.

   1-2-3 adds the version to the Selected Versions list and removes it from the Available Versions list.

If you want to remove a version from the Selected Versions list, select it and click on the arrow which now should be facing in the opposite direction. After it is removed, the version will be added to the Available Versions list.

Make sure that you have selected High Income and High Expense for your selected versions.

After you select the versions to include in your scenario, you must give the scenario a name. In this example, you call the scenario High. Because this name is general, it would be helpful to add a comment to this scenario so that when it appears in the Version Manager Index, you can remember what this scenario covers. Enter High Expense and High Income into the Comment box. When you have finished, the dialog box should look as shown in Figure 9.43.

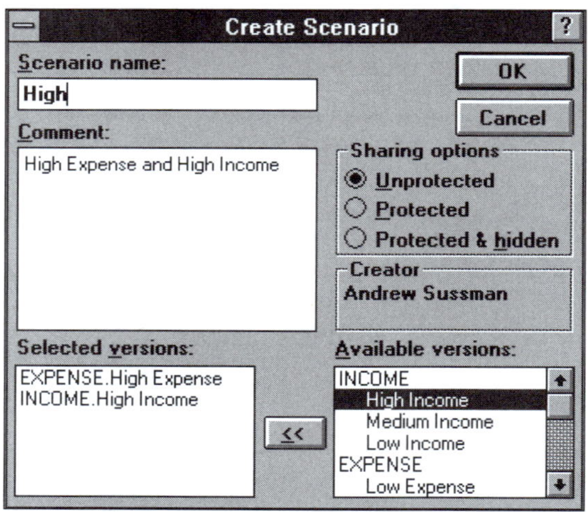

Figure 9.43 *Create Scenario dialog box.*

Click **OK** when you are finished. Now, create another scenario called Worst Case, which consists of Low Income and High Expense. When you have finished, the scenario should look as shown in Figure 9.44.

If you want to see the list of your scenarios, you must change the **Sort** option in the Version Manager Index to **Scenario Name Sort**. Once you have done this, 1-2-3 displays both scenarios that you created, together with a list of the versions used for each scenario, as shown in Figure 9.45.

If you want to return to the list of versions, change the **Sort** option back to Range Name.

Now that you have created scenarios, you can display the data values for the respective versions automatically. To display a scenario, follow these steps:

1. Select the scenario name from the Version Manager Index list.

2. Click on the **Show** button.

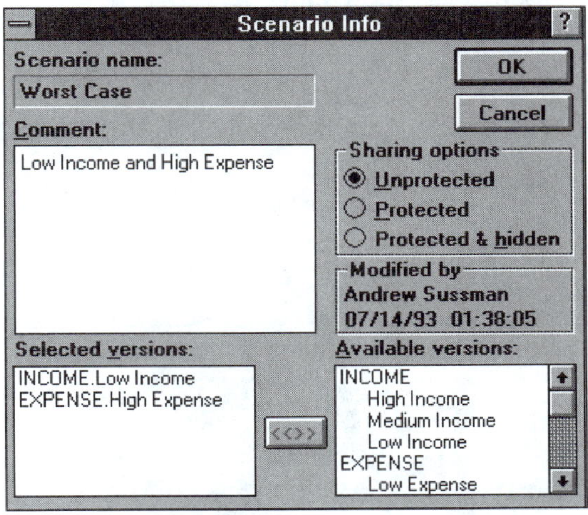

Figure 9.44 *Scenario Worst Case.*

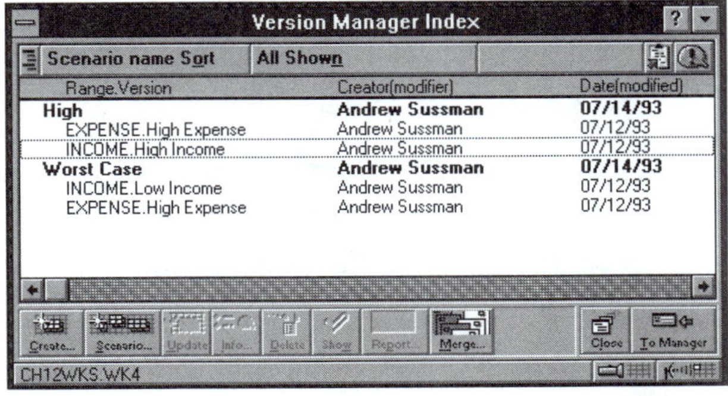

Figure 9.45 *Scenario Name Sort in the Version Manager Index.*

If, for example, you chose the scenario **Worst Case** and clicked on the **Show** button, 1-2-3 would change the data values in the worksheet to Low Income and High Expense values, as shown in Figure 9.46.

If you double-click on the name of a scenario in the Version Manager Index list, 1-2-3 displays that scenario automatically. If, for example, you double-click the scenario **Worst Case**, 1-2-3 changes the data values in the worksheet to Low Income values and High Expense values. If you select the scenario High, and click on the Show button, 1-2-3 automatically changes the values to High Income and High Expenses, as shown in Figure 9.47.

	Caroline's Budget	Jan	Feb	Mar	Apr	May	Jun		
Income:									
	Salary	$1,000	$1,000	$1,000	$1,000	$1,000	$1,000		
	Interest	$10	$10	$10	$10	$10	$10		
	Dividends	$100	$0	$0	$150	$0	$0		
	Total Income	$1,110	$1,010	$1,010	$1,160	$1,010	$1,010		
Expenses:									5%
	Rent	$600	$600	$600	$600	$600	$600		
	Food	$300	$300	$300	$300	$300	$300		
	Automobile	$350	$110	$110	$110	$110	$110		
	Phone	$150	$150	$150	$150	$150	$150		
	Utilities	$125	$125	$125	$125	$125	$125		
	Entertainment	$75	$70	$70	$80	$70	$70		
	Loan Payment	$60	$60	$60	$60	$60	$60		
	Miscellaneous	$105	$75	$75	$60	$60	$60		
	Total Expenses	$1,765	$1,490	$1,490	$1,485	$1,475	$1,475		
	Net Income	($655)	($480)	($480)	($325)	($465)	($465)		

Figure 9.46 *Worst Case scenario values.*

You easily can see the difference between situations in which your expenses are high and your income is low versus situations in which your expenses and income both are high. With scenarios, you can create any combination of versions and automatically display their respective data values.

What-If's

What is a what-if? Many times you may wonder what would happen if you changed some numbers and recalculated them to achieve a different answer. If you must do the work manually, this can be time-consuming and frustrating. If you use a spreadsheet program but don't take full advantage of its calculating powers, you may waste precious time. What-if's are 1-2-3's way of simplifying your life by enabling you to work backward to get the answer you are looking for, or by enabling you to ask questions, such as "what if I change variable X?"

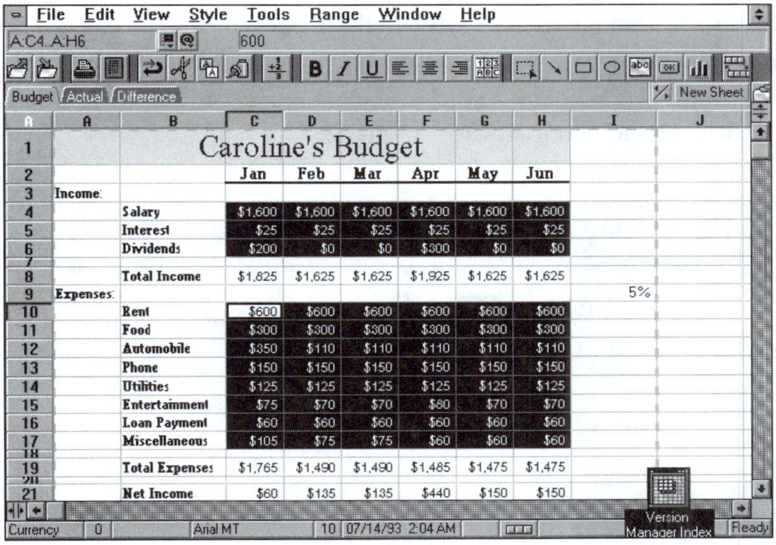

	A	B	C	D	E	F	G	H
			Caroline's Budget					
2			Jan	Feb	Mar	Apr	May	Jun
3	Income:							
4		Salary	$1,600	$1,600	$1,600	$1,600	$1,600	$1,600
5		Interest	$25	$25	$25	$25	$25	$25
6		Dividends	$200	$0	$0	$300	$0	$0
8		Total Income	$1,825	$1,625	$1,625	$1,925	$1,625	$1,625
9	Expenses:							
10		Rent	$600	$600	$600	$600	$600	$600
11		Food	$300	$300	$300	$300	$300	$300
12		Automobile	$350	$110	$110	$110	$110	$110
13		Phone	$150	$150	$150	$150	$150	$150
14		Utilities	$125	$125	$125	$125	$125	$125
15		Entertainment	$75	$70	$70	$80	$70	$70
16		Loan Payment	$60	$60	$60	$60	$60	$60
17		Miscellaneous	$105	$75	$75	$60	$60	$60
19		Total Expenses	$1,765	$1,490	$1,490	$1,485	$1,475	$1,475
21		Net Income	$60	$135	$135	$440	$150	$150

Figure 9.47 *High scenario values.*

For the following exercises, create two new worksheets in your file called Backsolver and What If's. This will make it easier to work with, because you will not have to worry about erasing any of Caroline's Budget.

One common use of what-if analysis is to calculate mortgages or other types of loans. When you are calculating your monthly mortgage payments, there are three variables that affect your answer: the principal or loan amount, the interest rate, and the term or number of time periods of the loan. In 1-2-3, the @PMT function automatically calculates your loan payment amount. The arguments for @PMT are as follows:

```
@PMT(principal;interest;term)
```

Suppose that you want to obtain a loan for $100,000 at an interest rate of 10 percent for 30 years. To calculate the monthly payment for this loan, your @Function would look as follows:

```
@PMT(100000;.1/12;30*12)
```

Because this is a monthly payment and the interest rate is given in yearly terms, you must divide the 10 percent interest rate by 12. Similarly, you must change the term of the loan from 30 years to 360 months, so you multiply the term by 12.

Rather than using actual numbers for the arguments, it is better to reference other cells in the worksheet for your formula. Figure 9.48 shows you one way to lay out your worksheet to calculate a mortgage.

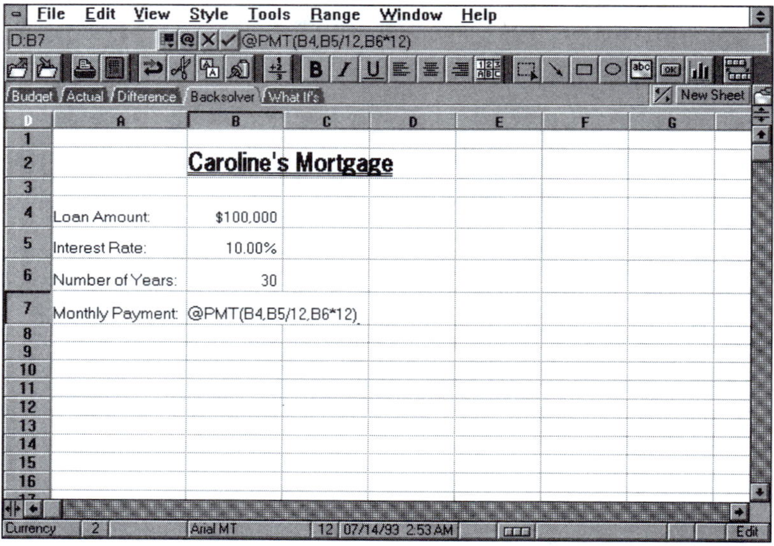

Figure 9.48 *Monthly mortgage loan payment worksheet.*

Notice that in the formula for the monthly payment, instead of using $100,000 as the argument for principal, this worksheet references cell B4. This way you can change the loan amount in cell B4 and 1-2-3 will automatically recalculate your loan payment. Similarly, instead of using 10 percent for the interest argument, this worksheet references cell B5, and for the term argument, it references cell B6. You still must divide the interest rate by 12 and multiply the term by 12 to convert the calculation from years to months.

After you enter all the data and the formula, 1-2-3 calculates that the monthly payment on a $100,000 loan at 10 percent for 30 years will be $877.57.

Backsolver

Suppose that you wanted to spend $750, rather than $877.57 per month on your mortgage. To do this, you would either have to reduce the size of the loan, reduce the interest rate, or increase the term of the loan. However, the calculations necessary to change these to achieve the desired results could be time-consuming. Backsolver is 1-2-3's way of working backward from the answer you are looking for to find the values of one or more variables in your formula. That is, with Backsolver, you can tell 1-2-3 that you want the formula @PMT to equal $750 by changing the principal, interest, or term.

To use Backsolver to change the loan amount to make the payment equal to $750, follow these steps:

1. From the Range menu, select **Analyze**.

2. Choose **Backsolver** from the hierarchical menu.

    Make sure that you choose **Backsolver** and not **Solver**, which is a different feature of 1-2-3.

3. The Backsolver dialog box appears, as shown in Figure 9.49.

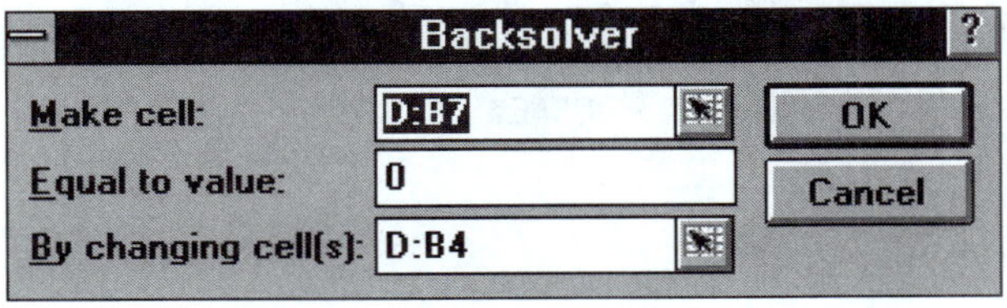

Figure 9.49 Backsolver dialog box.

In the Backsolver dialog box you must tell 1-2-3 which cell contains the answer to the formula, what you want the answer to be, and which cell to change to get this result.

4. In the box for **Make Cell**, use the Range Selector to select cell **D:B7**.

5. In the box for **Equal To Value**, enter **750**.

6. In the **By Changing Cell(s)** box, use the Range Selector to select cell **D:B4**.

    The dialog box should look as shown in Figure 9.50. You have told 1-2-

3 to make cell D:B7 equal to value 750 by changing cell D:B4. The dialog box may say D:B4 or Backsolver:B4. Both mean the same thing. One is just the generic way of addressing the worksheet D, the other uses the name given to the worksheet by the worksheet (Backsolver).

7. When you click **OK**, 1-2-3 returns you to the worksheet. The worksheet will show the value of your loan at $85,463, with the monthly payment reduced to $750 as desired (see Figure 9.51).

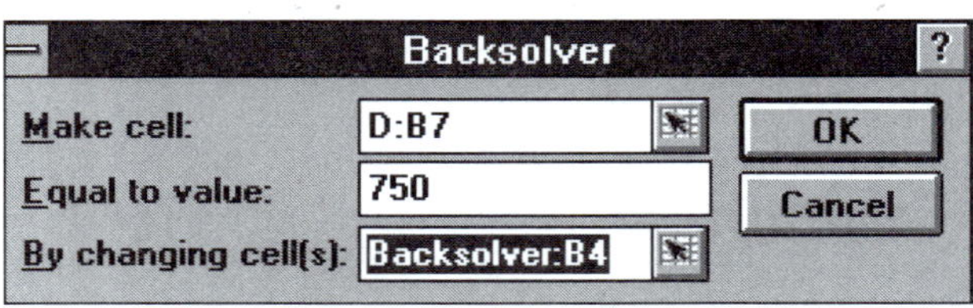

Figure 9.50 *Backsolver dialog box.*

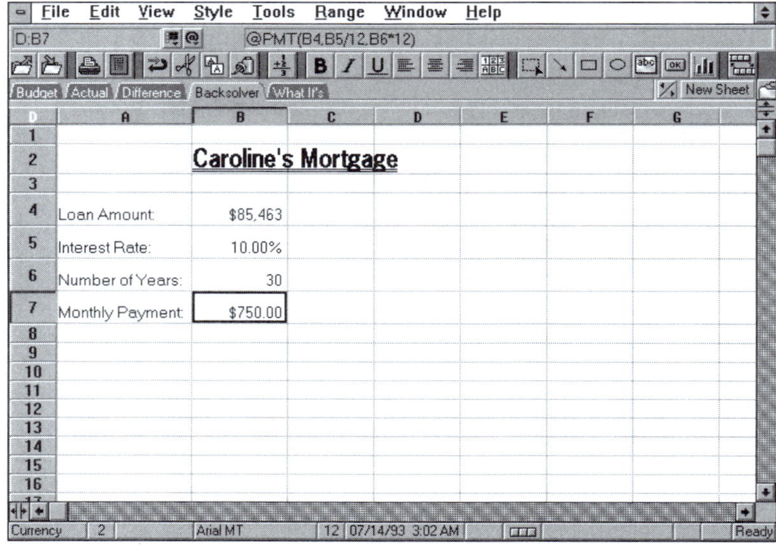

Figure 9.51 *Loan principal has been reduced and payment is now $750.*

You could just as easily have recalculated the interest rate or the term of the loan to achieve the result of $750 per month. 1-2-3 would have decreased the interest rate or increased the term of the loan accordingly.

Now, go back to cell D:B4 and enter $100,000 again. Your worksheet figures should return to the original values. Suppose that you want to reduce the payment to $750 but also want to change more than one variable. 1-2-3 enables you to change multiple variables with Backsolver. Instead of selecting one cell in the By Changing Cell box, you must select a range of cells. When you select multiple variables, 1-2-3 changes them proportionally. For example, consider a range of cells that are summed in another cell. If you use Backsolver to make the sum equal to a particular value by changing the entire range of cells, 1-2-3 will change each variable in the range by the same amount. 1-2-3 treats all the variables as equals and reduces or inflates the values by the same percentage.

If you use the Backsolver to make cell D:B7 equal to $750 by changing D:B4..D:B6, 1-2-3 returns the answer shown in Figure 9.52.

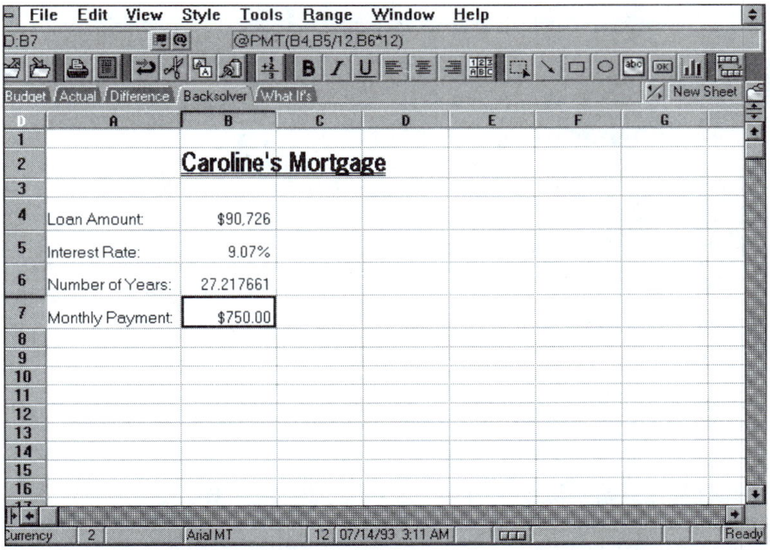

Figure 9.52 *Using the Backsolver to change multiple variables.*

What-If Tables

Suppose that instead of working backward to reach a desired answer, you want to see what would happen to your monthly payments at different loan amounts, or different interest rates, at different terms, or at some combination of these three. 1-2-3 contains a feature called what-if tables. What-if tables enter values into a formula to return different answers at each input value. These answers are placed into a table in your worksheet.

Four elements comprise a what-if table: a formula, an input cell, input values, and a table range. 1-2-3 plugs the input values into the formula. The *input* cell is a temporary place where 1-2-3 stores the different input values when it calculates the formula. With the @PMT function, for example, you must tell 1-2-3 where to find the interest rate. You use an input cell for a reference, and 1-2-3 plugs the different interest rates into this cell to perform the calculations. The *input values* are the different values used to calculate the table. The *table range* is where 1-2-3 looks for the input values and places the answers that it calculates for the table.

To use the What-If Table command, follow these steps:

1. From the Range menu, select **Analyze**.
2. Choose **What-If Table**.

   The What-If Table dialog box appears, as shown in Figure 9.53. In this dialog box, you must tell 1-2-3 how many variables you will be using (1, 2, or 3), the table range, and the input cell for each variable.

One-Variable Table

To start, let's try a one-variable table, as shown in Figure 9.54.

Figure 9.54 shows an example of how to set up your worksheet for a what-if table. In this worksheet, you have three variables on the left-hand side (principal, interest, and term). Next, is a range of cells that are your input values. For this example, you create a what-if table that substitutes different principal amounts into the @PMT function to calculate different monthly payments. Just above and to the right of this range is your formula for @PMT. Notice that this formula references the cells in column B. It is important that this formula be above and to the right of the input values. When you tell 1-2-3 the location of the table range, anything to the right of the input values will be overwritten by the table results. Accordingly, the formula must be just above the first input value row or else it may be overwritten.

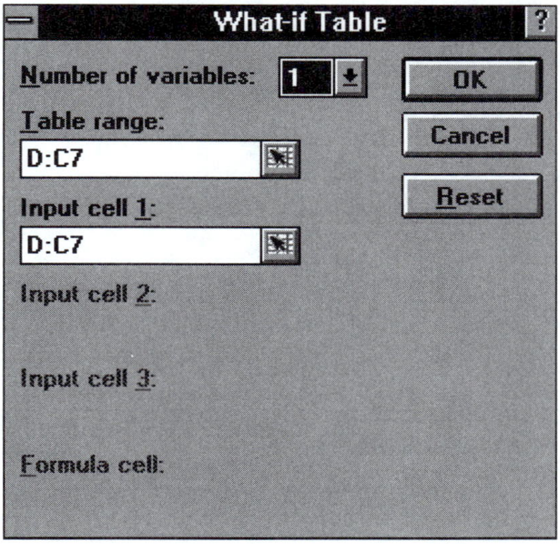

Figure 9.53 *What-if table dialog box.*

It does not matter what values you enter for the initial arguments. You are using these cells only as temporary input cells, so 1-2-3 ignores the cell's contents. 1-2-3 takes the values in the range E:D4..E:D8, temporarily places them in cell E:B2 (the input cell for principal), solves the formula in E:E3 using these values, and returns the results in range E:E4..E:E8.

To do this, follow these steps:

1. Open the **What-If** dialog box.

2. Select **1** as the number of variables.

3. Use the Range Selector to select **E:E3..E:D8** for the table range.

4. Use the Range Selector to select **E:B2** for Input Cell 1.

   Your dialog box should appear as shown in Figure 9.55.

   It is important that your table range include the cell that contains your formula. As long as there is a blank cell to the left of the formula, 1-2-3 will not overwrite the formula.

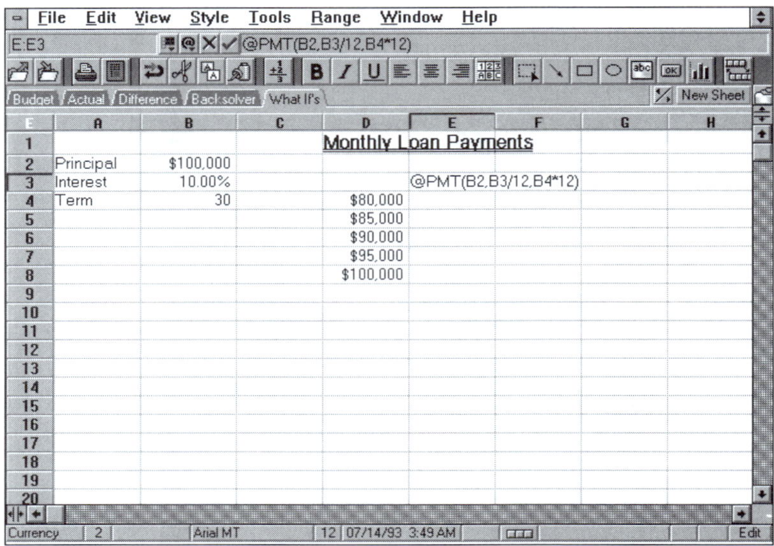

Figure 9.54 *One-variable what-if table.*

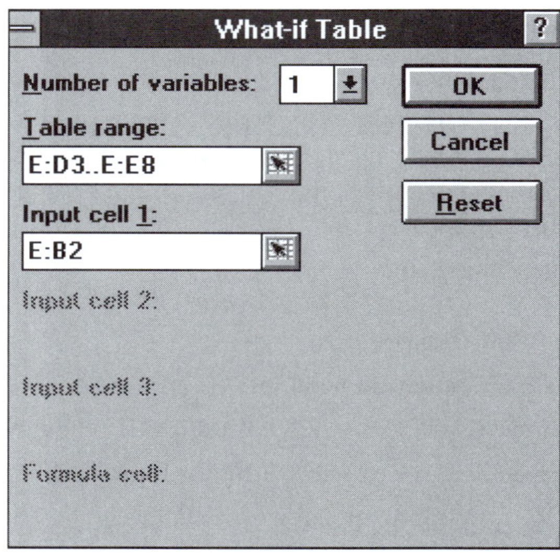

Figure 9.55 *Your What-If Table dialog box.*

5.   Click **OK** when you are finished.

After you click **OK**, 1-2-3 calculates your what-if table and fills in the answers in the range that you specified for the input table (see Figure 9.56).

	A	B	C	D	E	F	G	H
1				Monthly Loan Payments				
2	Principal	$100,000						
3	Interest	10.00%			$877.57			
4	Term	30		$80,000	$702.06			
5				$85,000	$745.94			
6				$90,000	$789.81			
7				$95,000	$833.69			
8				$100,000	$877.57			

Figure 9.56 *One-variable what-if table results.*

Two-Variable Table

Two-variable what-if tables are similar to one-variable tables. You still have input values, a formula, and a table range. In this case, however, there are two input cells and your formula must be placed in a different location.

For this example, let's change the variables Principal and Interest. To set up the two-variable what-if table, you must place one variable down the side of the table (as you did with one-variable tables) and a second variable across the top. In the cell where the two variables meet, you must put your formula. Figure 9.57 shows what your worksheet should look like. Notice that cell E:D3 contains the formula for the what-if table.

To create the what-if table, complete the following steps:

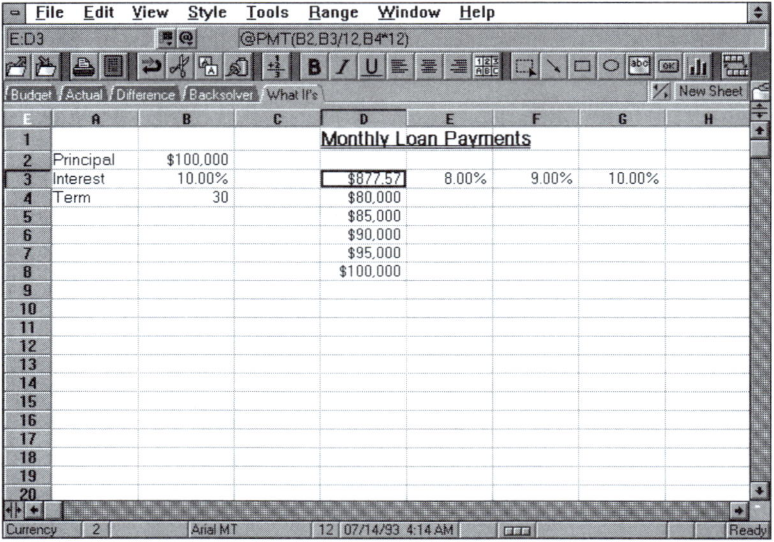

Figure 9.57 *Two-variable what-if table.*

1. Open the **What-If** Table dialog box.

2. Select **2** as the number of variables.

3. Use the Range Selector to select **E:D3..E:G8** for the table range.

    This table range must include the formula and all the input values.

4. Use the Range Selector to select **E:B2** for Input Cell 1.

    Input Cell 1 always refers to the input values that are down the left column.

5. Use the Range Selector to select **E:B3** for Input Cell 2.

    Input Cell 2 always refers to the input values that are across the top row.

    Your What-If Table dialog box should appear as shown in Figure 9.58.

6. When you are finished, click **OK**.

After you click OK, 1-2-3 calculates your formula using both sets of input values and creates a table that contains the results of these calculations. The table should appear as shown in Figure 9.59.

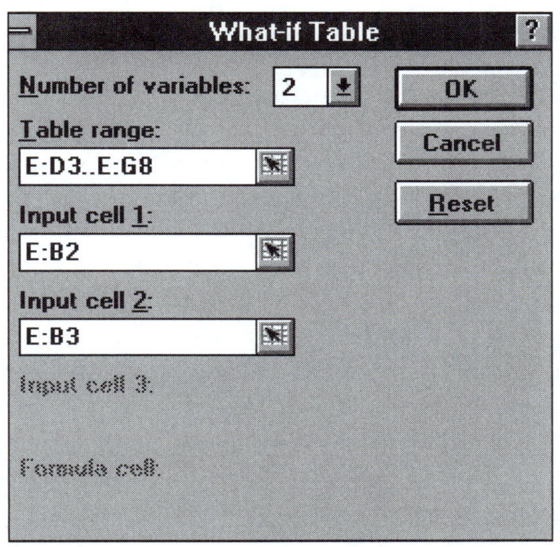

Figure 9.58 *Your What-If dialog box.*

Figure 9.59 *Two-variable what-if table results.*

Three-Variable Table

A three-variable table follows the same principles, but the layout of your table is somewhat different. Because you are adding a third variable to your table, you must add a third dimension to your worksheet. In the example, the loan principal goes down the left side of the table, and the interest rate goes across the top of the table. To create the third dimension, the same setup is used across multiple worksheets, each worksheet representing a different loan term. You place the loan term in the cell in which you placed the formula with two-variable what-if tables. Because your formula is no longer part of the table range, 1-2-3 adds an additional selector in the What-If dialog box for the formula. Figure 9.60 shows what your worksheets would look like.

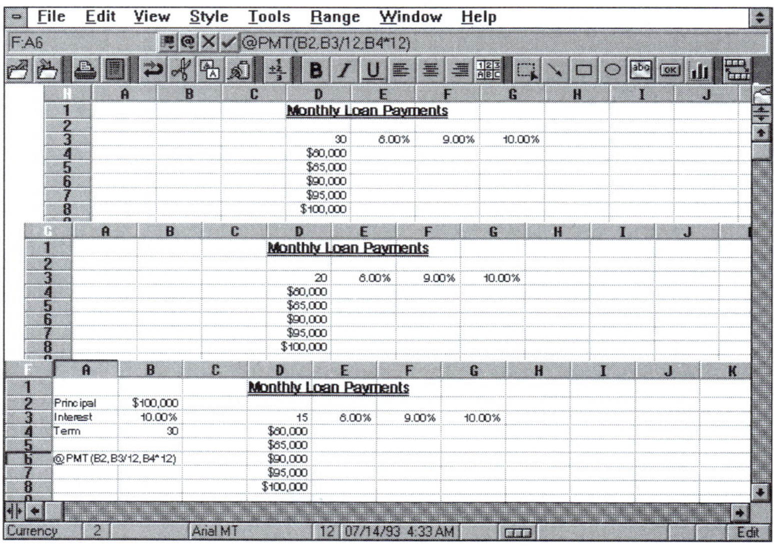

Figure 9.60 *Three-variable what-if table.*

You must create three new worksheets for this example (F, G, and H). Your table ranges must be in the same location on all three worksheets.

To create the three-variable what-if table, follow these steps:

1. Open the **What-If Table** dialog box.

2. Enter the range **F:D3.`H:G8** for the table range.

This is a 3D range because it extends across multiple worksheets.

3. Enter the cell **F:B2** for Input Cell 1.

   Input Cell 1 is always the input values in the left column of the table range.

4. Enter the cell **F:B3** for Input Cell 2.

   Input Cell 2 is always the input values in the top row of the table range.

5. Enter the cell **F:B4** for Input Cell 3.

   Input Cell 3 is always the input values in the top left corner of the table range.

6. Enter the cell **F:A6** for the formula cell.

   Your What-If Table dialog box should appear as shown in Figure 9.61.

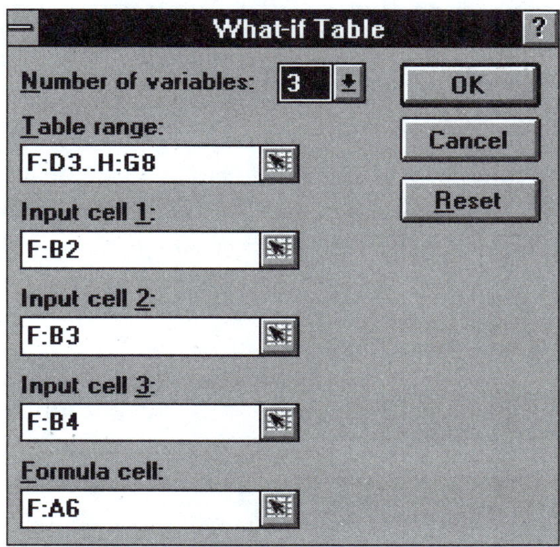

Figure 9.61 *Your What-If Table dialog box.*

7. Click **OK** when you are finished.

When you click OK, 1-2-3 automatically fills in the what-if table across the three worksheets. Your results should appear as shown in Figure 9.62.

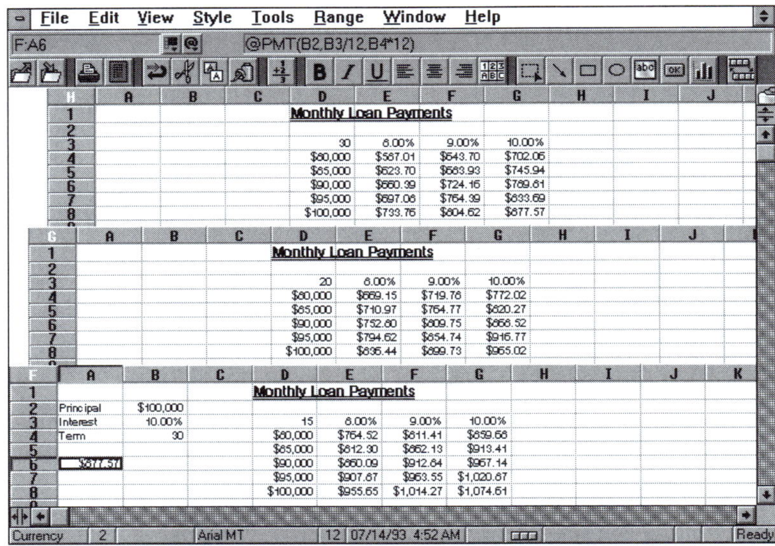

Figure 9.62 *Three-variable what-if table results.*

Now that you have completed your what-if tables, you can format them, print them, save them, or even graph the results. By using 1-2-3's what-if features you can save a great deal of effort and time figuring out answers to difficult problems.

To Sum Up

In this chapter you taught yourself to use 1-2-3 for the purpose of analyzing your data. Up to this point you focused on entering, organizing, and manipulating data. Now you are familiar with functions that enable you to see data in terms of its potential. Using the Version Manager, you can create different versions of a given spreadsheet. You also can add comments or change these versions. You also can use the Version Manager Index to work with many versions at once and sort them as you see fit. Moreover, the Version Report dialog box enables you to show different versions of the same named range. You also can create and display scenarios that permanently store information about different created versions. Finally, you can calculate the different potentials of your spreadsheet by using what-if functions. The Backsolver helps you figure out which variables to change to achieve a certain end result. On the other hand, the what-if tables enable you to figure out future results of one or more changed variables.

What You Learned

Open Version Manager:

From the Range menu, select **Version**.

Create a Version:

1. Select the desired range.
2. From the Range menu, choose **Version**.

   The Version Manager dialog box appears.
3. Click on the **Create** button.

   The Create Version dialog box appears.
4. Type the name of the range into the Range Name box.
5. Type a name into the Version Name box.

   To add a comment regarding this version, click in the box called Comment and enter your remarks.

   Make use of the Sharing Options feature to protect your version from changes or to hide it from others who may see your worksheet.
6. Click **OK**.

Create a new version:

1. Change your data values.
2. Select the desired range.
3. From the Range menu, choose **Version**.

   The Version Manager dialog box appears

   The Version Name box shows the same name as your first version. However, the check mark to the left of the version name has a slash through it.

   The Update button is now available so that memorized data from the first created version can be updated to reflect new data values. If you click this button, your original data values are erased.
4. Click on the **Create** button.

5. Type the name of the range used previously into the Range Name box.

   Because you named a range in a previous version, the program knows the name of the range automatically.

6. Type a new name into the Version Name box.

7. Click **OK**.

   A second version has been created using the changed data values.

   If you click on the down arrow to the right of the version box, a drop-down list appears with all the versions you have created.

Work with several versions at a time with the Version Manager Index:

1. Click on one version.

2. Hold down the **Ctrl** key and click on the second version.

   The Version Manager Index will select and highlight both versions.

3. Click on the **Show** button.

   You cannot select more than one version per named range.

Sort versions:

1. Click on the button that tells you how the Index is currently being sorted.

2. Select the method of sorting desired from the drop-down list.

   You can sort by range name, version, scenario, date, or creator.

Create version reports:

1. Click on the **Report** button in the Version Manager Index.

   The Version Report dialog box appears.

2. Select the named range on which the report will be made.

   Reports can be made only on one named range at a time.

3. Choose which versions of the named range you want to include in the report by clicking on the version names.

4. Use the Range Selector to select desired versions.

5. Choose which information to include: versions data and/or audit information.

By default, 1-2-3 includes both these items.

6. Choose whether to create the report in rows or columns.

7. Click **OK**.

Create scenarios:

1. Click on the **Scenario** button.

   The Create Scenario dialog box appears.

2. Select the version from the Available Versions list.

   The button between the two lists becomes an arrow facing to the left.

3. Click on the arrow; the version moves from the Available Versions list to the Selected Versions list.

   If you want to remove a version from the Selected Versions list, select it and click on the arrow, which now faces the opposite direction.

4. Name the scenario and make appropriate entries to the Comment box.

5. Click **OK**.

Display scenarios:

1. Select the scenario name from the Version Manager Index list.

2. Click on the **Show** button.

   If you double-click on the name of a scenario in the Version Manager Index list, that scenario is displayed automatically.

Use Backsolver:

1. From the Range menu, select **Analyze**.

2. Choose **Backsolver**.

   Make sure that you choose **Backsolver**, and not **Solver**, which is a different feature.

   The Backsolver dialog box appears.

3. In the **Make Cell** box, use the Range Selector to select the desired cell.

4. In the **Equal To Value** box, enter the desired result.

5. In the **By Changing Cell(s)** box, use the Range Selector to select the cell you want to change.

6. Click **OK**.

Use the What-If Table command to change one variable:

1. From the Range menu, select **Analyze**.
2. Choose **What-If Table**.

    The What-If Table dialog box appears.
3. Set the number of variables to **1**.
4. Use the Range Selector to select the table range.

    It is important that your table range include the cell that contains your formula.
5. Use the Range Selector to select the **Input Cell 1**.
6. Click **OK**.

Use the What-If Table command to change multiple variables:

1. Open the **What-If Table** dialog box.
2. Set the **Number of Variables** to the desired amount.
3. Use the Range Selector to select the table range.

    This table range must include the formula and all input values.

    With three variables, the range is a 3D range because it extends across multiple worksheets.
4. Use the Range Selector to select **Input Cells 1**, **2** and, if appropriate, **3**.
5. If you are changing three variables, enter the formula cell.
6. Click **OK**.

Chapter 10

Lotus 1-2-3 Database Fundamentals

You may be wondering why we included a chapter on databases when Lotus 1-2-3 Release 5 is a spreadsheet program. The fact is, the row/column format of a spreadsheet makes it well suited to accomplish basic database work. In addition to the usual spreadsheet functions, such as calculations, you also can use 1-2-3 as a database program.

In this chapter, you teach yourself the basics of the Lotus 1-2-3 Release 5 database functions such as:

- Identifying different parts of a database.
- Creating a database table.
- Naming database fields.
- Using queries to isolate certain data.
- Setting criteria to find the specific data you want.

- Creating queries with multiple criteria.

- Sorting your data in ascending or descending order.

What Is a Database?

A database is a collection of data, consisting of different categories of information, called *fields*, stored in records that can be easily retrieved and sorted in response to different search requests or queries. You could, for example, store all your friends' names, hair colors, and lists of idiosyncratic habits in cells. Then, you could call up the information sorted by name, hair color, or idiosyncrasy. A database is an exceptionally useful tool because it enables you to find information quickly. Imagine a list of 296 friends in your database. It would be quite tedious to inspect the list manually to find all the ones with brown hair who snored. But with a database, you could find this information instantly.

The data stored in a 1-2-3 database is stored in a database table. This table consists of multiple records (rows) that contain different fields (columns), as shown in Figure 10.1.

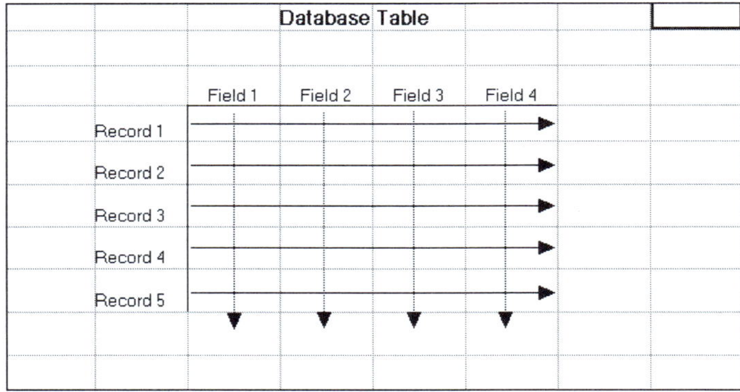

Figure 10.1 *Database table.*

In this chapter, we define database terms, such as record, field, and so on, by working with an example of a database. Figure 10.2 shows a database containing people's names and phone numbers. The next few sections describe database terms by reference to this example.

LastName	FirstName	AreaCode	PhoneNumber	Code	
Stoner	Ronnie & Jeff	407	555-1130	Family	
Smith	Bruce & Amy	607	555-0428	Friend	
Young	Marianne	808	555-1208	Family	
Brotman	Kenn	516	555-0611	Friend	
Sussman	Neil & Leslie	516	555-0126	Family	
Cohen	Rebecca	718	555-0626	Family	
Zivyak	Irene & Jeff	516	555-1208	Family	
Zivyak	Michael & Jenn	516	555-0427	Family	
Macharola	Heather & Joe	814	555-0930	Friend	
Xiao	Jack	412	555-1016	Friend	
Misciagna	Caroline	412	555-0416	Family	
Stone	Jen	716	555-0513	Friend	
Emens	Shelly	315	555-0309	Friend	
Magera	George	412	555-1019	Friend	
Fishman	Michael	412	555-1202	Friend	

Figure 10.2 *Phone list database table.*

Records

The records in the phone list are the different people on the list. Each person is stored as a different record and listed in a different row. Because the records start in row 2 and continue until row 16, there are 15 records in this list. Of course, database tables can contain many more records than this.

If you want to follow along with this example, enter the data into a new worksheet so that it looks like Figure 10.2. When you enter the phone numbers, make sure that you begin each data entry with an apostrophe ('); if you don't, 1-2-3 will think that the entry, for example 555-1130, calls for 1130 to be subtracted from 555. By putting the apostrophe before the entry, you are letting 1-2-3 know that this is a text entry rather than number or equation. See Chapter 6 to refresh your recollection of this rule.

Fields

The phone list in the example has five fields for each record. These fields are the columns across the database table. They are LastName, FirstName, AreaCode, PhoneNumber, and Code. Each field contains a separate category of data. Again, 1-2-3 can accommodate more fields than this, but for the sake of simplicity, this example is limited to five fields. Above the fields in the database table are the field names. They have been entered in bold letters and a border has been added to the cell. Although it is necessary to have field names, the formatting shown here is not necessary to make a database table. However, this formatting is helpful to improve reader comprehension by separating the field names from the data entries.

A database table, which can contain up to 256 fields and 8,191 records, must fit in a single worksheet.

Queries

After you create a database table, you can manipulate the data by performing queries. A *query* is a search request that is based on certain criteria. In other words, a query is a question that you ask the database. Your query of the phone list, for example, might be a request for all phone numbers corresponding to people who are classified in the Code field as Friends. Your data might originally be saved alphabetically by last name. By performing a query, you can sort by any variable. Queries are used to find and manipulate records in query tables.

If your database table consists of fields of numerical data, you can use formulas as part of your queries. If, for example, your database involves a field for Sales, you can create a query that searches for Sales greater than $10,000.

Creating A Database Table

Creating a database table is easy. As mentioned earlier, your database table must be able to fit in one worksheet, so it cannot have more than 256 fields (columns) or 8,191 records (rows). To create your database table you need to determine the structure of your file. To do this, you must determine the records you want in your database and the fields each record will contain. In the phone list, you already know that the records are going to the people and the fields for each record are going to be LastName, FirstName, AreaCode, PhoneNumber, and Code.

Creating Field Names

The next step in creating a database table is creating your field names. When creating field names, there are a few general guidelines you should follow:

- Use text labels, not numbers, for field names. 1-2-3 sometimes has trouble understanding numbers as field names. This may produce unexpected results. Therefore, stick to text labels.

- If you do choose to use numbers for field names, be sure to precede the entry with a label prefix character, such as an apostrophe for left-justified text.

- Use each field name only once in any particular database table.

- Table 10.1 lists characters that you should not use in your field names.

Table 10.1 *Characters Not To Use In Field Names*

Name	Character
Colon	:
Comma	,
Dash	– –
Exclamation Point	!
Hyphen	–
Mathematical Operators	= < > <>
Number Sign	#
Period	.
Space	n/a
Tilde	~

- Refrain from using field names that resemble cell addresses, for example, a letter/number combination, such as B12.

Keeping all these guidelines in mind, create your field names by entering the labels that are used in the sample phone list database table, shown previously in Figure 10.2.

Enter the Data

The next stage in developing a database table is to enter the data. Before you do this, remember: Don't put a blank row between your field names and the data.

In the phone list, for example, row 2 cannot be blank. It must contain the entries for the first record, or it will be misinterpreted by the program.

Enter the data values for the phone list in the example. It is worth noting that you can use any formatting you want for your database table. You can change the font, its style, borders, alignment, number formats, and so forth. To do so, simply follow the directions in Chapter 4 that discuss how to format your data.

Name the Database Table

After you have entered all the data into your database table, you might want to name the database table as a range. From the Range menu, select **Name**. In the Named Range dialog box, enter a name for this range, as shown in Figure 10.3.

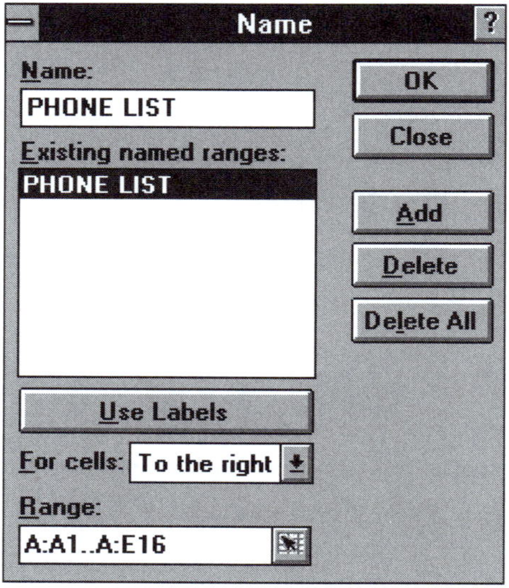

Figure 10.3 *Named Range dialog box.*

Two items are important to keep in mind before you name a database table:

- The field names must be the first row of the selected range. To comply with this, the sample database range is A1..E16.
- Do not use a field name as the name of any range.

After you enter a name for this database table, such as Phone List, click **OK**. Naming a database table makes it easier and quicker to find and use when you need to reference @Functions and database tools.

Using Queries

Any query you use will be based on certain criteria. As mentioned earlier, these criteria tell 1-2-3 the nature of the data you want to work with. If, for example, you wanted to work only with friends' phone numbers, the query would satisfy the criteria Code equal to Friend.

Creating Queries

To create a query, use the New Query command, which opens the New Query dialog box, shown in Figure 10.4. To access this dialog box, from the Tools menu, choose **Database** and select **New Query** from the hierarchical menu. In this dialog box 1-2-3 requests that you answer three questions. First, you must select the database table in which you will perform the query. Next, you need to select the fields and records in that database for 1-2-3 to search. Finally, you must select a range where 1-2-3 will display the new query table that is the result of your query.

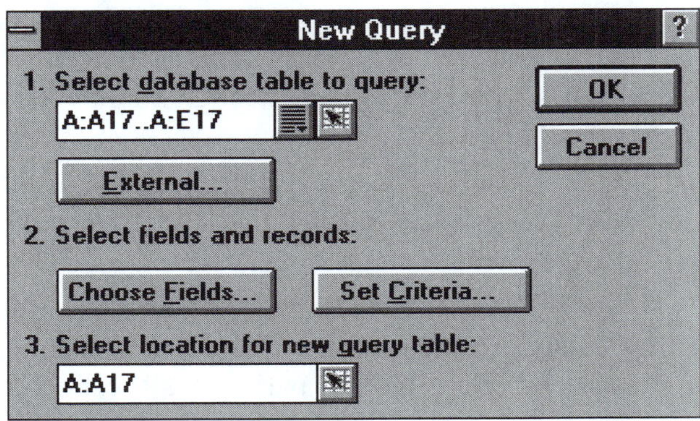

Figure 10.4 *New Query dialog box.*

Select a Database Table

1-2-3 offers three ways to select a database table:

- Type in a range name that contains the database table (in the example, A:A1..A:E16).

- Use the **Range Selector** to select the range that contains the database table (A:A1..A:E16).

- Use the **Navigator** to select the named range **Phone List**.

To enter the range manually, all you have to do is type the range that you want in the box provided. To use the Range Selector, you must click with the mouse on the **Range Selector** button, and then use the mouse to select the range. Finally, to use the Navigator to enter the range, click with the mouse on the **Navigator** button, as shown in Figure 10.5.

Figure 10.5 *Navigator button.*

You can use the Navigator to select the range only if you have previously named it. Because you have named the range of the database table Phone List, for example, you can find that range by clicking with the mouse on the **Navigator** button. When you do this, a drop-down list appears, indicating the named range, Phone List. If you select a named range from the drop-down list, it appears in the database table box.

The External button is used to access database files from other programs. For example, 1-2-3 can access database files from database programs, such as dBASE. Because most beginning and intermediate users of 1-2-3 will not deal with this level of complexity, we will not discuss this feature.

To work with a database table, you must select the entire table, including the field names. If you don't select the field names, 1-2-3 will not know what the fields are called when you select them.

Selecting Fields and Records

Having selected your database table, the next step is to select the fields and records that 1-2-3 will search.

Selecting the Location for a New Query Table

The final step is to select the location at which 1-2-3 will display the result of the search query that it has performed; your new query table. There are two ways to select a location for your new query table.

- Select the top left cell where you want the new query table to begin.
- Select a specific range of cells for the new query table to be displayed.

If you choose to select just the top left cell for the new query table, 1-2-3 displays as much of the query table as will fit in the boundaries of your worksheet. If you select a specific range of cells, 1-2-3 displays only as much of the new query table as will fit in that range. In the sample database, for example, if you select a range that is only two columns wide, the newly created query table will display only the LastName and the FirstName, the first two columns in the database table. Had you selected a range that was three columns wide, then the Area Code would also be displayed in the new query table.

In placing the new query table in the range you have selected, 1-2-3 will overwrite any data in that range. Be careful! It is advisable to select a location far from your other data so there is no chance of overwriting and deleting any of the data in your worksheet. For the same reason it is also advisable to select a specific range, rather than only the top left cell, in case the new query table turns out to be larger than you anticipate and, thus, unexpectedly deletes a portion of your data.

To select the location for the new query table, you can either enter it manually into the box or use the Range Selector. For the example, because the database table is a small one, you can safely select the top left cell of the new query table so that 1-2-3 can display as many rows and columns as it needs. To avoid deleting any data, select the cell A20 on the Phone List worksheet. This way, 1-2-3 can display the new query table below the database table without deleting any text.

Choosing Fields

As mentioned earlier, the second step in creating a database query is to select the fields and records. To select fields, click on the **Choose Fields** button in the New Query dialog box, shown in Figure 10.6. When you click on this button, 1-2-3 displays the Choose Fields dialog box, shown in Figure 10.7.

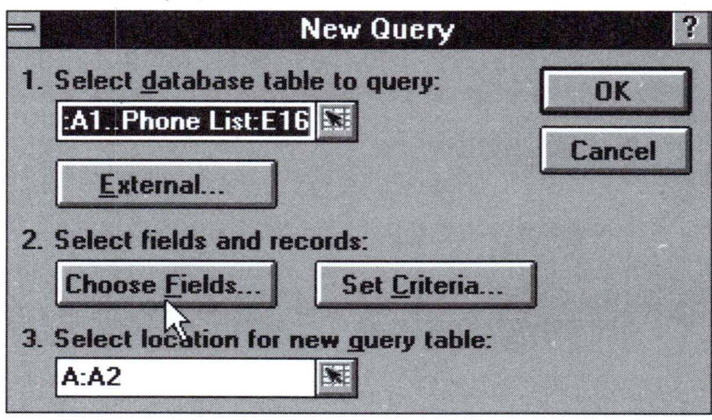

Figure 10.6 *Choose Fields button.*

In this dialog box, you choose which fields you want to be included in the query. If you don't include fields in a query, they will not be displayed in your new query table. Suppose, for example, that you want to search the phone list for all friends, but you only want to see their names, not phone numbers. You could accomplish this by selecting only the fields LastName and FirstName.

If you have already selected the database table range, when you open the Choose Fields dialog box, 1-2-3 will, by default, list all the fields in the Select Fields box, as shown in Figure 10.7. Because all the fields are displayed and there are no additional fields to select, the Add button is not available.

Suppose that you want only the LastName and FirstName fields to be displayed. There are two options. First, you could use the Clear button to delete individual fields from the list. Or you could use the Clear All button to delete all entries, and then use the Add button to add the fields you want to the list.

For this exercise, let's use the latter method and Clear All so that you can Add fields to the list. After you click **Clear All**, the Selected Fields box will be empty. When you click on the **Add** button, 1-2-3 displays the Add Fields dialog box, shown in Figure 10.8.

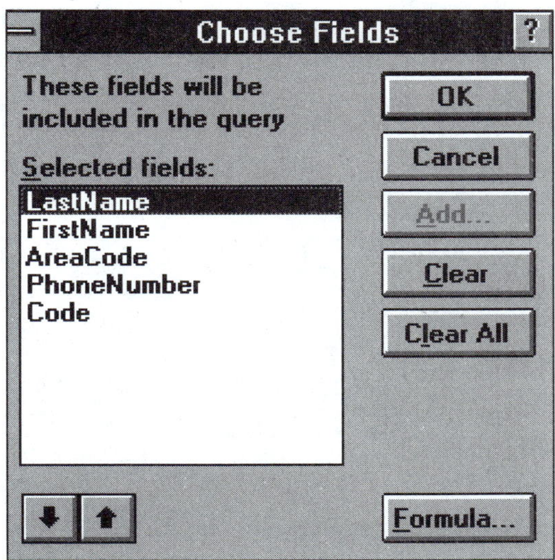

Figure 10.7 *Choose Fields dialog box.*

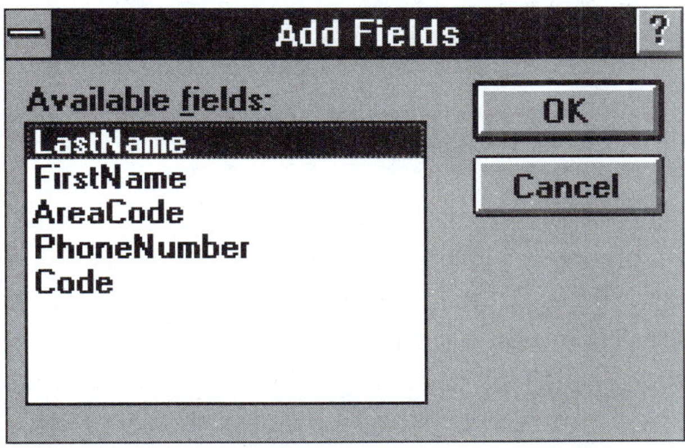

Figure 10.8 *Add Fields dialog box.*

The Add Fields dialog box displays all available fields that can be included in the query. For the example, you want to select only the fields LastName and FirstName. First select **FirstName**. Click with the mouse on the field **FirstName** in the list and click **OK**. 1-2-3 returns you to the Choose Fields dialog box, but now the field FirstName is listed in the Selected Fields box. Click **Add** again so that you can add LastName. Notice that the Available Fields box no longer shows FirstName. You have already added it, so it is no longer available. Click with the mouse on **LastName** and click **OK**. Notice that the Selected Fields box now lists LastName and FirstName, as shown in Figure 10.9.

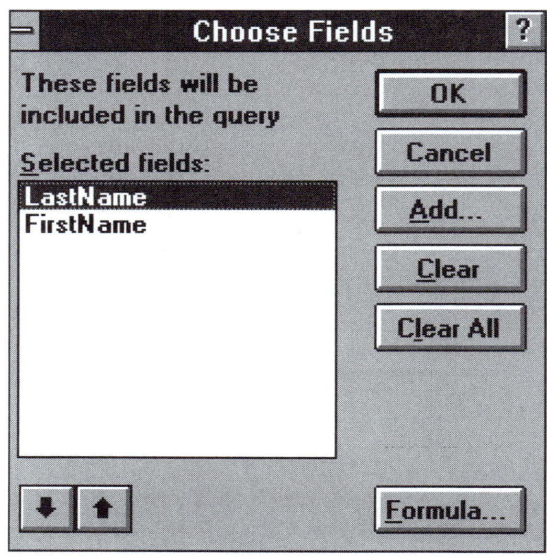

Figure 10.9 *Selected Fields LastName and FirstName.*

The order in which the fields are displayed in the list is the order in which they will be displayed in the new query table.

Suppose that you want the field FirstName to appear before LastName. As things now stand, they are listed in the opposite order. 1-2-3 enables you to change the order of the Selected Fields list, by using the up and down arrows at the bottom of the dialog box, as shown in Figure 10.10.

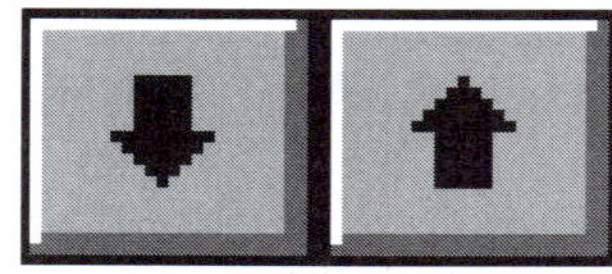

Figure 10.10 *Up and down arrows in the Choose Fields dialog box.*

These arrows enable you to move a field either up or down in the list by clicking on the corresponding arrow. Suppose, for example, that you want the query to list the FirstName, and then LastName. To do this, you need to move either the LastName down or the FirstName up. Let's move the LastName down. Click on **LastName** in the list, and then click the down arrow. Notice that the highlighted LastName field has shifted below the FirstName field, as shown in Figure 10.11.

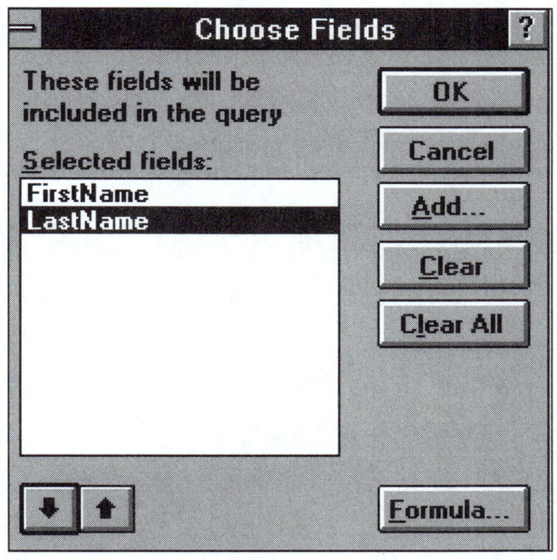

Figure 10.11 *LastName has shifted below FirstName.*

If there were multiple fields in this list, you could click the up or down arrow multiple times to shift the field more than one position.

Now that you have selected the fields FirstName and LastName and have arranged them in the correct order, you are ready to select records. Click OK to close the Choose Fields dialog box.

The Formula button in the Choose Fields dialog box enables you to use a formula to include a calculation in your query. If, for example, you want 1-2-3 to include a column in the new query table that represented 50 percent of another column's information in the database, you could create a new field (column) and include a formula that would calculate this new field's values for you. In the example, you will not be using this feature.

Setting Criteria

One of the most important features of a database query is the capability to automatically select certain records contained in a database. You tell 1-2-3 which records to select by providing a set of criteria. 1-2-3 selects only those records that satisfy the criteria. Suppose, for example, that you want to select all records that have a 516 area code. If you tell 1-2-3 to select all records that have the field AreaCode equal to 516, the program automatically goes through the list of records and pulls out only those that satisfy your request.

To set the criteria by which 1-2-3 selects records, click on the **Set Criteria** button in the New Query dialog box, as shown in Figure 10.12. When you click this button, the Set Criteria dialog box opens, as shown in Figure 10.13.

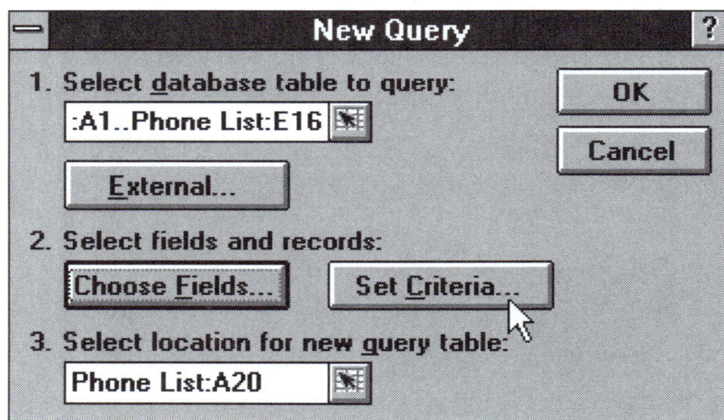

Figure 10.12 *Set Criteria button in the New Query dialog box.*

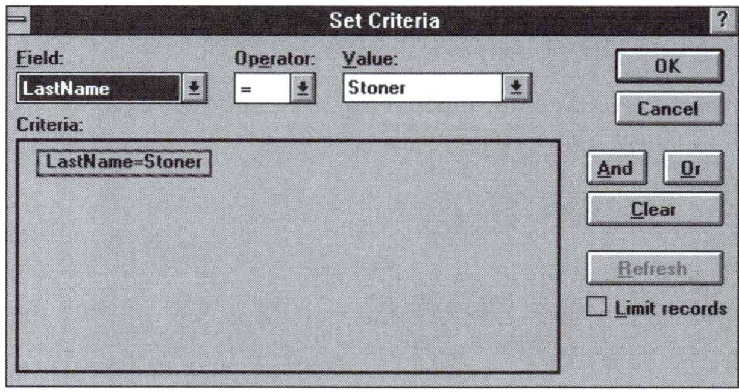

Figure 10.13 *Set Criteria dialog box.*

By default, when you open the Set Criteria dialog box, 1-2-3 creates a criteria based on the first field name and the first entry in that field. In Figure 10.13, for example, 1-2-3 created a criteria for LastName=Stoner, because LastName is the first field name and Stoner is the first entry in that field.

If you were to dissect a criteria, you would find three parts: a field, an operator, and a value. The field tells 1-2-3 which column to look in. The value tells 1-2-3 what to compare the field against. The operator is the part of the criteria that tells 1-2-3 when to select the record. Therefore, in the default criteria 1-2-3 created, the program would look in the field LastName for the value Stoner and if the record equals this value, it would be selected.

To create a criteria for the example, you must first delete the default criteria that was created by 1-2-3, by clicking with the mouse on the **Clear** button in the Set Criteria dialog box, as shown in Figure 10.14.

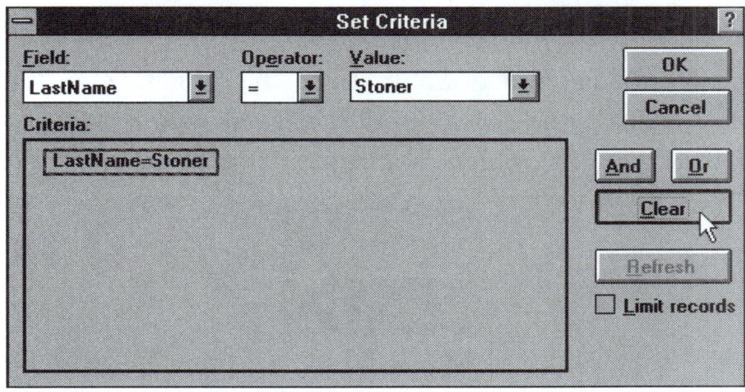

Figure 10.14 *Clear button in the Set Criteria dialog box.*

Using One Criteria

You can set the criteria to search for all records with a 516 area code. To do this, you need to create a criterion that contains the field AreaCode, the value 516, and the operator =.

To select the field for your criteria:

1. Click on the down arrow next to the field box.

   A drop-down list of all of the fields in your selected database appears, as shown in Figure 10.15.

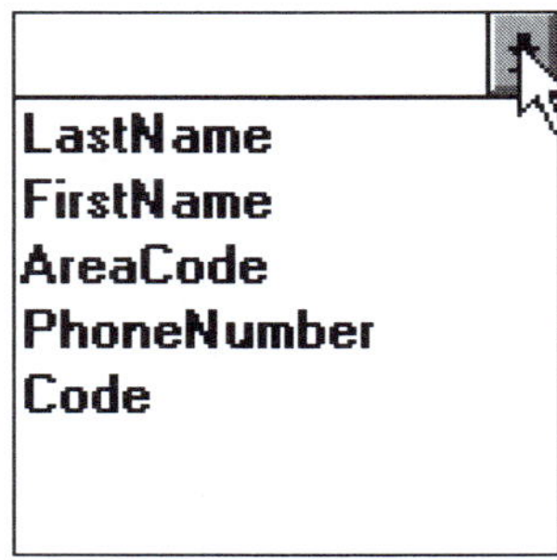

Figure 10.15 *Drop-down list of fields.*

2. Select AreaCode from this list.

When you select the field, 1-2-3, by default, automatically fills in the operator (=)
and the first value in your database for the selected field (in this case, 407).

If you want to change the operator from the = sign, click the down arrow
next to the operator box, and the drop-down list shown in Figure 10.16 appears.
Table 10.2 lists the different operators and their functions.

Figure 10.16 *Operator drop-down list.*

To select the value, as with the other two parts of the criteria, click on the down
arrow and the drop-down list shown in Figure 10.17 appears.

If a substantial number of different values for this particular field appears in
your database, the drop-down list may have a scroll bar. If you need to view a

value that is located further down the list, just click on the down scroll arrow. If you need to scroll back up, click on the up scroll arrow. This list contains every value in your database for the particular field you have selected. Because you want to find all records with the area code 516, select 516 from this list.

Table 10.2 *Operators and Their Functions*

Operator	Function
=	Equal To
<	Less Than
>	Greater Than
<=	Less Than or Equal To
>=	Greater Than or Equal To
< >	Not Equal To

If you know the field, the operator and the value you want, you can type them into their respective boxes immediately without having to use the drop-down lists.

You can type a formula or an @Function in the value box if you want 1-2-3 to look for values that would satisfy that formula. In the example, however, you will not be using this feature.

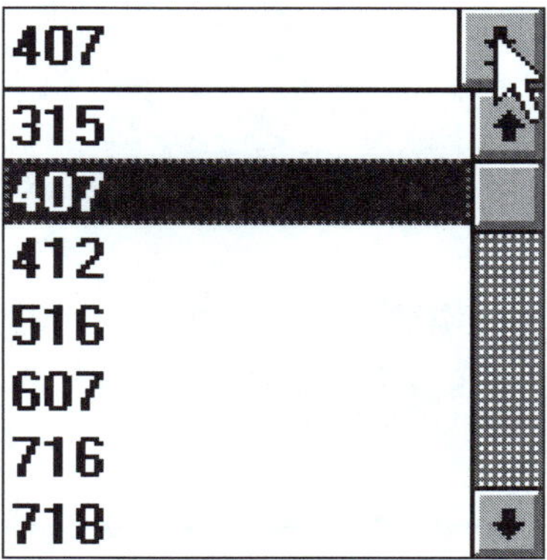

Figure 10.17 *Value drop-down list.*

At the bottom of the Set Criteria box is an outlined area called Criteria in which 1-2-3 displays the search request you have chosen. Naturally, if you change the field, operator, and value, the criteria in this box will change. Now that you have finished the criteria, it should look as shown in Figure 10.18.

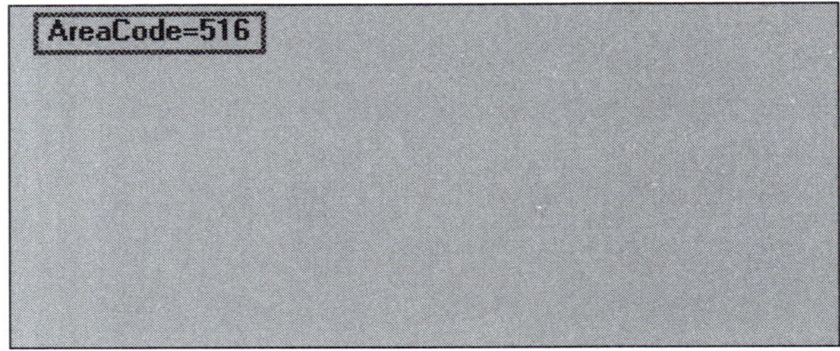

Figure 10.18 *Our search criteria.*

After you review the criteria to see that it is correct, click **OK** and you return to the New Query dialog box. After you set everything else in this dialog box, you can click **OK** and 1-2-3 will create a new query table for you. If, for example, you ran the query for the fields FirstName and LastName on the criteria AreaCode=516, 1-2-3 would create the new query table shown in Figure 10.19.

Sussman	Neil & Leslie	516	555-0126	Family
Cohen	Rebecca	718	555-0626	Family
Zivyak	Irene & Jeff	516	555-1208	Family
Zivyak	Michael & Jenn	516	555-0427	Family
Macharola	Heather & Joe	814	555-0930	Friend
Xiao	Jack	412	555-1016	Friend
Misciagna	Caroline	412	555-0416	Family
Stone	Jen	716	555-0513	Friend
Emens	Shelly	315	555-0309	Friend
Magera	George	412	555-1019	Friend
Fishman	Michael	412	555-1202	Friend

FirstName	LastName
Kenn	Brotman
Neil & Leslie	Sussman
Irene & Jeff	Zivyak
Michael & Jenn	Zivyak

Figure 10.19 *New query table.*

Using Multiple Criteria

Suppose that you want to create a list of all family members in the 516 area code. In this situation, you would need to use multiple criteria in your query table. You can use the logical connectors AND and OR to link multiple criteria in a query search. This process is similar to the embedded @Functions discussed in Chapter 9. You may remember that when you embed @Functions, you can have an @SUM in an @IF statement. Similarly, you can embed multiple criteria in a new query table.

The logical connector AND is used to narrow the search. When you use this connector, the record has to satisfy both criteria in order to satisfy the search request. If, for example, you had the criteria AreaCode=516 and Code=Family connected by AND, this would narrow the search to family members who are also in the 516 area code.

The logical connector OR is used to broaden a search. With this connector, the record has to satisfy either of the criteria in order to satisfy the search request. If, for example, you had the criteria AreaCode=516 and Code=Family connected by OR, the search would be broadened to include anyone who either is a family member or has a 516 area code. The OR connector really signifies either or both. This means that a record will be selected if it is a family member, or if it is a 516 area code, or if it is both a family member and a 516 area code.

To create multiple criteria to find all family members in the 516 area code, follow these steps:

1. Open the **Set Criteria** dialog box.
2. Select **Code** from the Field List.
3. Select = from the Operator List.
4. Select **Family** from the Value List.
5. Click the **And** button.
6. Select **AreaCode** from the Field List.
7. Select = from the Operator List.
8. Select **516** from the Value List.

Now the criteria should look as shown in Figure 10.20.

Suppose that you want to search for those who either are family members or have a 516 area code. In this case you would use the OR connector. To find these records, follow these steps:

1. Open the **Set Criteria** dialog box.
2. Select **Code** from the Field List.

Figure 10.20 *Multiple search criteria with And connector.*

3. Select = from the Operator List.

4. Select **Family** from the Value List.

5. Click the **Or** button.

6. Select **AreaCode** from the Field List.

7. Select = from the Operator List.

8. Select **516** from the Value List.

The Criteria should look as shown in Figure 10.21.

You also can change the criteria from AND to OR without having to go through all of the steps again. When the criteria are linked by AND, they are displayed in the Criteria Box as one block, as shown in Figure 10.20. In contrast, when they are linked by OR, they are displayed as two blocks, as shown in Figure 10.21. If you had linked the criteria with AND and wanted to change it to OR, you could do so by clicking on the AreaCode field that was connected to Code and dragging it to the right, as shown in Figure 10.22.

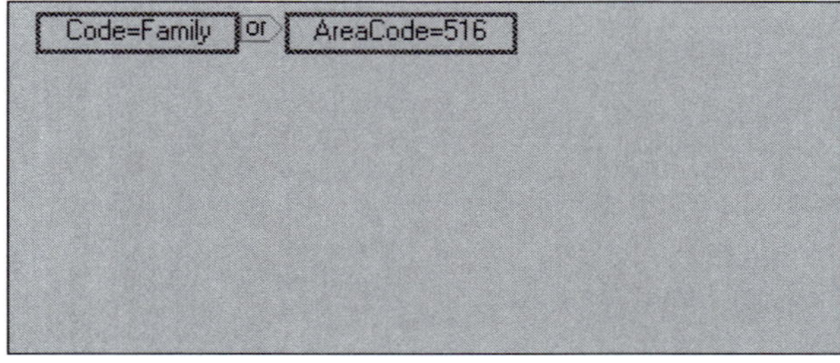

Figure 10.21 *Multiple search criteria with Or connector.*

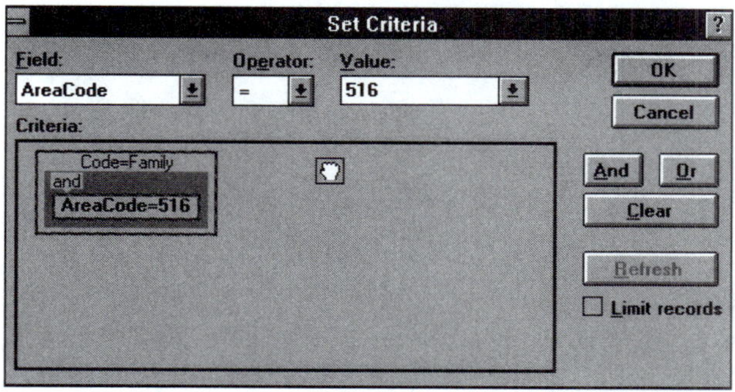

Figure 10.22 *Drag field to the right to change AND to OR.*

If you do this, 1-2-3 changes the connector from AND to OR. Similarly, if you had the OR connector but wanted it to be AND, you could select the criteria that you want to change and drag it to the left. 1-2-3 automatically changes the connector to AND and merges the two blocks so that they are one block (see Figure 10.23).

Depending on the number of fields you have and how complex you want your query to be, you can create extremely long strings of criteria. You are not limited to two criteria as in the example (see Figure 10.24).

Sorting

Another useful feature of the 1-2-3 database table is its capability to sort your records, that is, your rows. For example, the phone list records are not sorted. The list starts with Stoner, and then Smith, and so forth. Suppose that you want to sort this list alphabetically by last name. If you select **Sort** from the Range menu, the Sort dialog box appears (see Figure 10.25).

There are two items to be set in the Sort dialog box. First, you must select the range of cells you want to sort. You can do this before you open the Sort dialog box or you can use the Range Selector after you are in the dialog box.

When you select the range, 1-2-3 sorts the rows, keeping all columns in your range together. Therefore, if you select the range A:A2..A:E16, rows 2 through 16 will be sorted, and for each row, columns A through E will be kept together. If, however, you selected only A:A2..A:D16, column E would not be sorted with columns A through D. If you sort this way, your database table will be incorrect because the values in column E for each record will not be sorted and the cells will no longer be in the row with their corresponding record. Therefore, you must be careful that you select the correct range to be sorted.

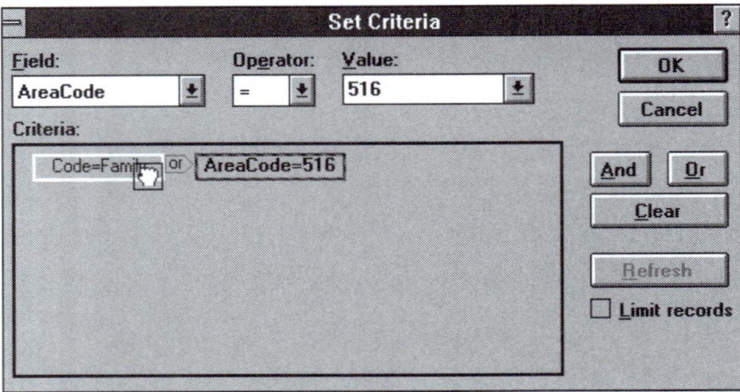

Figure 10.23 *Drag field to the left to change OR to AND.*

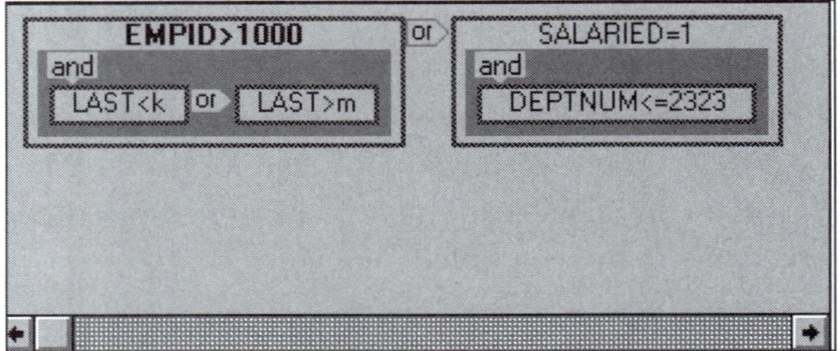

Figure 10.24 *Example of complex criteria.*

If you accidentally omit one or more columns from a sort, you can restore the original order of all the cells by choosing the Undo function, but you must do so immediately.

When you select a range for sorting, do not include the field names. If you do, they will be sorted with your records. Unlike the process that you follow when you are using queries and must select the entire database table, when you are sorting, you should not select the field names or they will get mixed up with your records.

In addition to setting the range in the Sort dialog box, you must also set the Sort By Key. This is the column by which the rows will be sorted. If, for example, you want to sort by last name, your Sort By Key would be column A. When you set a Sort By Key, you need only select the first cell in that column for the range you are sorting. Therefore, in the example, if you want to sort by last name, select cell A:A2 as the Sort By Key. To select the Sort By Key, you can either type it manually in the box or use the Range Selector.

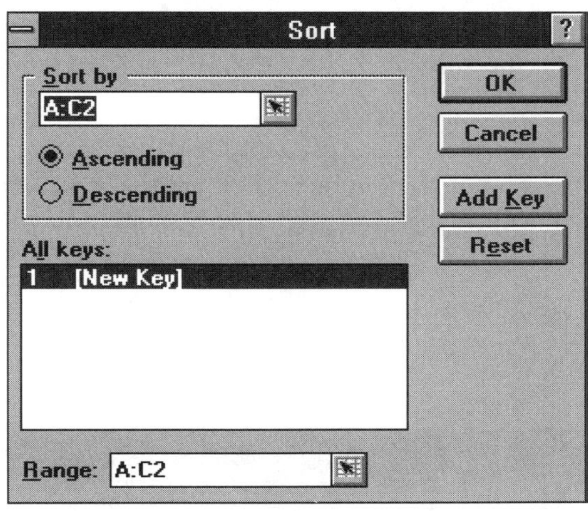

Figure 10.25 *Sort dialog box.*

You must also set the order for 1-2-3 to sort your range on the Sort By Key. You can sort in ascending or descending order. If, for example, you want the phone list to be sorted alphabetically, you would select Ascending. Sometimes you may want to select Descending. If, for example, you had a list of sales for different salespeople, you might want to list them in descending order with the highest sales first.

The database in 1-2-3 also gives you the capability to sort on multiple keys. Suppose, for example, that you want a phone list with all friends listed first, followed by family members. Suppose that in each group, you also want the names to be sorted alphabetically by last name. Moreover, if more than one person has the same last name, you want them sorted alphabetically by first name. To do this, you need to indicate three sort keys.

When you are using multiple sort keys, you have to think about the order in which each item should be sorted. If, for example, you make the first sort key

Code and the second sort key LastName, 1-2-3 will sort the Codes, and then in each code, it will sort the LastName. If, however, you make the first sort key LastName and the second key Code, 1-2-3 would sort the LastNames, and then in each LastName, it would sort the Codes. Think of it as a big outline. The first item you sort is rather broad, and the following items further narrow the search.

In the example, you want the Codes sorted, and in each code, the LastNames sorted, and in each last name, the FirstNames sorted. Accordingly, the first sort key is Code, the second sort key is LastName, and the third sort key is FirstName.

To accomplish this, select cell **A:E2** (the first entry in the Code column) in the Sort By box as your first sort key. Remember, you want this to be in descending order, because you want Friends before Family. To do this, click Descending.

To add a second sort key, click on the **Add Key** button. The first sort key you entered appears in the All Keys box and a new sort key is started, as shown in Figure 10.26.

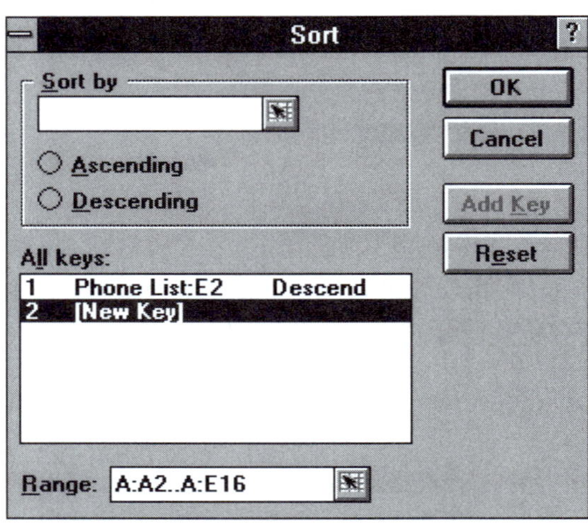

Figure 10.26 *A second sort key has been added.*

For this sort key, select cell **A:A2** (the first entry in the LastName column), and select **Ascending** order.

Because you want to add a third sort key, click on the **Add Key** button again. A third sort key is started as the second one is added to the All Keys list.

This third key is cell A:B2 (the first entry in the FirstName column), and it should be in Ascending order as well.

Click **OK**, and 1-2-3 sorts the records first by Code, then by LastName, and finally by FirstName, as shown in Figure 10.27.

LastName	FirstName	AreaCode	PhoneNumber	Code
Brotman	Kenn	516	555-0611	Friend
Emens	Shelly	315	555-0309	Friend
Fishman	Michael	412	555-1202	Friend
Macharola	Heather & Joe	814	555-0930	Friend
Magera	George	412	555-1019	Friend
Smith	Bruce & Amy	607	555-0428	Friend
Stone	Jen	716	555-0513	Friend
Xiao	Jack	412	555-1016	Friend
Cohen	Rebecca	718	555-0626	Family
Misciagna	Caroline	412	555-0416	Family
Stoner	Ronnie & Jeff	407	555-1130	Family
Sussman	Neil & Leslie	516	555-0126	Family
Young	Marianne	808	555-1208	Family
Zivyak	Irene & Jeff	516	555-1208	Family
Zivyak	Michael & Jenn	516	555-0427	Family

Figure 10.27 *Sorted phone list.*

Notice that all of the friends are listed first, because you sorted Code in descending order. Also notice that where there were two records with the same last name (Zivyak), they were sorted by first name as well (Irene is before Michael).

You are not limited to only three sort keys. You can sort by more keys if you want.

If you sort something by mistake and want to reverse it, select **Undo** from the Edit menu immediately after you sort. The sort must be the most recent command you entered, or else 1-2-3 cannot undo the sort.

To Sum Up

At this point, you can use 1-2-3 for tasks that extend beyond the usual spreadsheet functions. In this chapter, you taught yourself about using 1-2-3 as a database to store information. You learned about the different parts of a database[md]the fields and records[md]and how to insert any data you want. You then moved on to teach yourself how to find specific information in a database by setting queries. Finally, you learned to sort the information you searched in the order you like.

What You Learned

Create a database table:

1. Enter records down the rows of one column of your worksheet.

2. Using text labels, create field names for each field across the columns of your worksheet.

   Use each field name only once, avoid names that look like cell addresses and don't use the following characters: :_ ' ! = < > # . ~ or space.

3. Enter the data.

   The row below your field names must not be left blank.

Name a database table:

1. From the Range menu, select **Name**.

   The field names must be the first row of the range selected.

   The Name dialog box appears.

2. Enter name for range.

   The range name must not be a field name.

Create a query:

1. From the Tools menu, select **Database** and choose **New Query**.

   The New Query dialog box appears.

2. Select the database table by either typing a range, clicking the **Range Selector** button, or clicking the **Navigator** button to select a previously named range.

3. Click **Choose Fields**.

   The Choose Field dialog box appears.

4. By clicking the **Clear All** button, and then the **Add** button, you will be able to see all of the Available Fields and the Selected Fields. The order in which fields appear in the Selected Fields can be controlled by clicking on the up and down arrows at the bottom of the dialog box.

5. Choose the **Selected Fields** and click **OK**.

6. Click **Set Criteria**.

   The Set Criteria dialog box opens.

7. Click on the arrows next to the field box, the operator box and the value box to access drop down menus from which you can select your desired field, operator, and value.

8. Click **OK**.

   If you already know the field, operator and value you want, you can type them into their respective boxes immediately, without using any of the drop-down menus.

9. Select the location of the new query table in the New Query dialog box by typing only the top left cell where the new query table will begin or by selecting a specified range for the new query table.

   If you select a specified range, the program displays only as much of the new query table as will fit in the range.

Create queries with multiple criteria:

1. Open the **Set Criteria** dialog box and select the first field, operator, and value from the respective Field List, Operator List, and Value List.

2. Click on either the **AND** button or the **OR** button.

   The AND connector narrows your search because the record must satisfy both criteria. The OR connector broadens your search because the record may satisfy either or both of the criteria.

3. Select the next field, operator, and value from the respective Field List, Operator List, and Value List, as you did in step 1.

   You can change the linkage of criteria from AND to OR by clicking on the criteria that is to the left and dragging it to the right of the other criteria. Similarly, you could change the linkage from OR to AND by clicking on the criteria that is to the right and dragging it to the left of the other criteria.

Sort your records:

1. From the Tools menu, select **Database** and choose **Range**.

2. Click on **Sort**.

   The Sort dialog box appears.

3. Choose the range to be sorted.

    Do not include field names in the range to be sorted.

4. Choose the type of sorting by setting the **Sort By Key** for the column(s) by which the rows will be sorted.

    To set a Sort By Key, select only the first cell in that column by typing it into the sort box or by using the **Range Selector** button.

5. Set the order of the sort as **Ascending** or **Descending**.

6. Click on the **Add Key** button for multiple sort key operations and repeat the previous steps.

7. Click **OK**.

    If you sort something in error, select **Undo** from the Edit menu immediately after the error is made.

Chapter 11

Using Macros

Many times we have mentioned that *macros* are a function you can use in Lotus 1-2-3 Release 5. But what exactly is a macro?

Macro is a computerese-sounding word that might seem intimidating, but the concept is a simple one. A macro combines a series of commands to automate a task, in this case, a Lotus 1-2-3 Release 5 task. In this chapter, you will learn the basics of macros and their uses. You will teach yourself to:

- Understand basic macro-writing syntax.
- Plan a macro.
- Create a macro in the Transcript Window, a cell, or a macro library.
- Record a macro.
- Analyze and edit a macro.
- Run a macro.
- Name a macro range.
- Create and use the macro button.

Understanding Macros

The way macros work is rather basic: You tell your computer the series of functions that you want to be able to do quickly and easily, and the computer provides you with an automatic way to perform them. When you think about it, Windows may be thought of as a series of macros that make it easy to use DOS. Instead of having to enter a long string of keyboard commands, you can click with the mouse on icons that are programmed to carry out that string of commands. These icons are macros that represent the DOS commands. Let's look at an example of a macro for Lotus 1-2-3 Release 5. Suppose that in your work you often go to the Number & Format dialog box to set the number format to currency. Following this, you go to the Font & Attributes dialog box to set the font to Times Roman, 12 point, bold, and underlined. Instead of following these individual steps over and over again, you can create a macro that will do it all for you. Then, when you run the macro, Lotus 1-2-3 Release 5 will automatically perform these commands for you as one task.

Lotus 1-2-3 Release 5 lets you use more than 200 macro commands to automate your menu choices and your mouse and keyboard actions. Although macros may seem like a confusing and difficult feature at first, they are actually easy to work with once you understand how they operate. Also, once you have learned how to use macros, they will make your life much easier.

NOTE Although many types of programs have macro commands, the macro language is usually different for each program. If you are already familiar with macros for another program, you may find that helpful in understanding Lotus 1-2-3 Release 5 macros, but you will still have to learn how to use the macros specific to Lotus 1-2-3 Release 5.

Creating a Macro

There are many different aspects to creating a macro. Indeed, books have been written which discuss only the macro functions in Lotus 1-2-3. However, here we will provide only the essentials and teach you about certain aspects of macros on a "need to know" basis. To help you understand the need for macros, as well as their structure and execution, we will "dissect" a macro in the context of the steps for creating one. This should help you get the most out of macros in the shortest possible time.

Macro Syntax

Creating a macro is somewhat like creating a Lotus 1-2-3 Release 5 formula. Both require a certain specified string of commands, which are referred to as a *macro syntax*. A distinguishing feature of macros, though, is that they begin and end with brackets,{ and }. Inside these brackets is the macro command name and arguments. As with formulas, there are certain arguments required for a particular command.

Although some arguments are required to run a macro command, others are merely optional.

N O T E

Macro arguments are separated by semi-colons. These arguments are similar, in a way, to @Function arguments. You may remember that there are items that you must provide Lotus 1-2-3 Release 5 in order to perform an @Function. For example, to sum a range of cells, you must provide the range to be summed. The same is true for macro commands. You must provide certain arguments to allow macro commands to automate your tasks.

Suppose we wanted to make a cell entry bold. The command name which will format a cell entry in this way is STYLE-FONT-ATTRIBUTES. This command formats a cell with a font style. After the command name, you must provide two arguments. The first argument tells Lotus 1-2-3 Release 5 which font style to apply. The second argument tells Lotus 1-2-3 Release 5 whether to turn this style on or off. Therefore, if we wanted to format a cell with bold, the macro would look as follows:

```
{STYLE_FONT_ATTRIBUTES BOLD;"ON"}
```

Notice that this macro begins with an open bracket, {, followed by the name of the command, STYLE_FONT_ATTRIBUTES, followed by the first argument BOLD, followed by an argument separator (;), followed by the last argument "ON" (in quotes).

If you are underlining a cell entry, there will be more than two arguments, because you also need to tell Lotus 1-2-3 Release 5 what type of underlining to apply (i.e., single, double, thick single, etc.).

N O T E

Don't feel overwhelmed by the idea of memorizing all the macro commands and their syntax. You don't have to memorize anything! There are different ways to enter macros in Lotus 1-2-3 Release 5. We will learn how to create macros without the need to memorize any of the commands. Although Lotus 1-2-3 Release 5 allows you to create your macro by typing the macro commands manually, you can also have Lotus 1-2-3 Release 5 record the commands that you use and program them as macros. When you use the recording feature, Lotus 1-2-3 Release 5 automatically enters your macro commands for you, thus eliminating the need for you to memorize them.

As you go along, you will learn commands and shortcuts for creating macros. For now, do not concern yourself with memorizing the different macro commands and their syntax. The purpose of this section is simply to become familiar with what Lotus 1-2-3 Release 5 macros look like so you can recognize their usefulness to you and the kinds of mistakes or problems that may arise when you use them.

N O T E

There are eight rules for writing macros.

1. Begin your macro command with an open bracket and end it with a closed bracket.

2. Do not put a space between the open bracket and your macro command keyword.

3. If the macro command keyword is more than one word, separate the words with a hyphen, not an underscore or a space.

4. There should be one space between your keyword and your first argument.

5. The only spaces permitted in a macro command are those between the keyword and the first argument and, if applicable, those spaces that are part of a quoted text entry. That is, text entries are required to be enclosed by quotation marks. For example, the command {GET_LABEL "Type your first name please";FIRST} will display the text on the screen,

"Type your first name please." You can include the spaces between these words and the program will recognize that they are part of a text entry because they are enclosed by quotation marks. Also, there is a space between the keyword and the beginning of the text entry, since the text entry is the first argument. However, there are no spaces between the first argument (the text entry), and the argument separator, or between the argument separator and the second argument (the word FIRST).

6. If there are optional arguments in a macro command and you omit one or more of them, you must still include an argument separator to act as a placeholder for the omitted argument. This will tell Lotus 1-2-3 Release 5 that there is an argument that is part of the command that you have chosen not to include.

This is different than the treatment of optional arguments in @Functions, which are simply omitted in their entirety.

7. All arguments are separated by an argument separator (;).

8. All macros must end with either the command {End} or with a blank cell.

Planning a Macro

As with most multi-step tasks, it is a good idea to plan the steps you will use in your macro before you do anything. Whether you are creating a macro manually or having Lotus 1-2-3 Release 5 create it for you, initial planning will streamline your commands and reduce the number of errors. Remember, the purpose of a macro is to simplify your tasks. If you don't plan, your macro could end up being extremely large and complex, and take longer to execute than the original multi-step task.

Planning is especially crucial when you are manually writing macros to ensure that you do not forget to include any necessary steps. Although we will not be writing a macro manually (instead we will record one), it is still important that we plan our steps first. It will save time and frustration if the commands we select are planned in advance. If not, our macro may contain extraneous steps that will slow down the operation of the macro, or prevent it from working properly.

When you start to create your own macros, take a moment to make a rough draft of what you are going to do. You do not need to create a formal flow diagram to show your steps, although this does help when creating macros manually. Instead, your rough draft, outlining what you want the macro to do, will enable you to think through the steps and reach the most efficient way of accomplishing your task.

Where to Create a Macro

There are three locations where you can create macros in Lotus 1-2-3 Release 5. In all three locations the macros would be the same. However, the way you would access the macros is very different for each place.

Transcript window

First, you can create a macro in the Transcript Window, a "scratch pad" where you can enter data manually. Or you can use the record feature to enter commands for your macro. You can edit, delete, or add to commands in the Transcript Window, or you can copy the contents and paste them elsewhere. The Transcript Window is often the best place to begin your macros, because it is easy to work with and it allows you to manipulate your commands easily. The Transcript Window is shown in Figure 11.1.

The Transcript Window is a window that opens on top of your worksheet. In this window, you would type your macro commands. If you were recording a macro, the recorded commands would appear here. To open the Transcript Window:

1. Go to **Tools**.
2. Select **Macro**.
3. Choose **Show Transcript** from the hierarchical menu.

When you select Show Transcript, the window will open on top of your worksheet. When you are finished using the Transcript Window, there are two ways to close it.

- Double-click the _ sign in the upper left corner.
- Go to **Tools**, select **Macro** and choose **Hide Transcript** from the hierarchical menu.

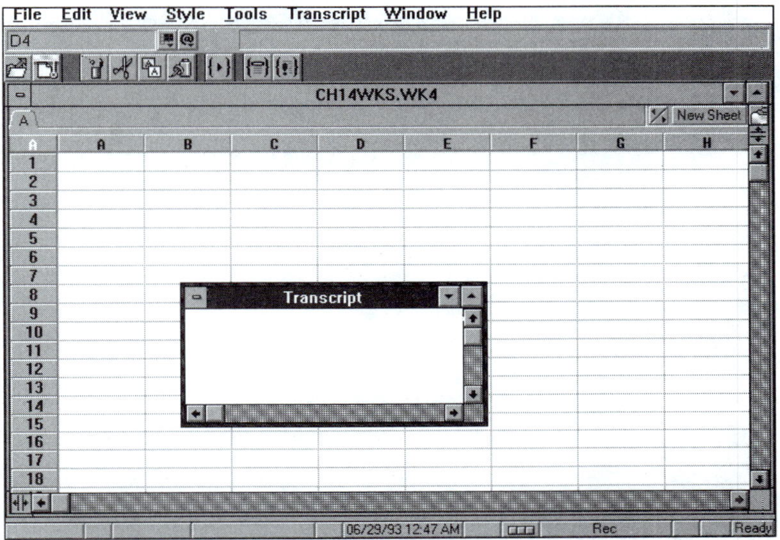

Figure 11.1 *Transcript Window.*

The Hide Transcript command only appears if the window is open. Similarly, Show Transcript is an option in the menu only if the Transcript Window is closed.

N O T E

Since the Transcript Window is a window, like your worksheet, it could disappear if you select your worksheet or something else to be the active window. To prevent this, Lotus 1-2-3 Release 5 shrinks the size of the current window when you open the Transcript window and arranges the two windows so that they overlap. If you select the worksheet window, you'll still be able to see a corner of the Transcript window. But if you do lose sight of the Transcript window, your Transcript Window is not closed; it is merely covered by the active window. Therefore, if you went to Show Transcript, it would not appear as an option. Since the Transcript Window is still open, (but simply not active), you could access it by going to Window and selecting Transcript from the list of open windows, as shown in Figure 11.2.

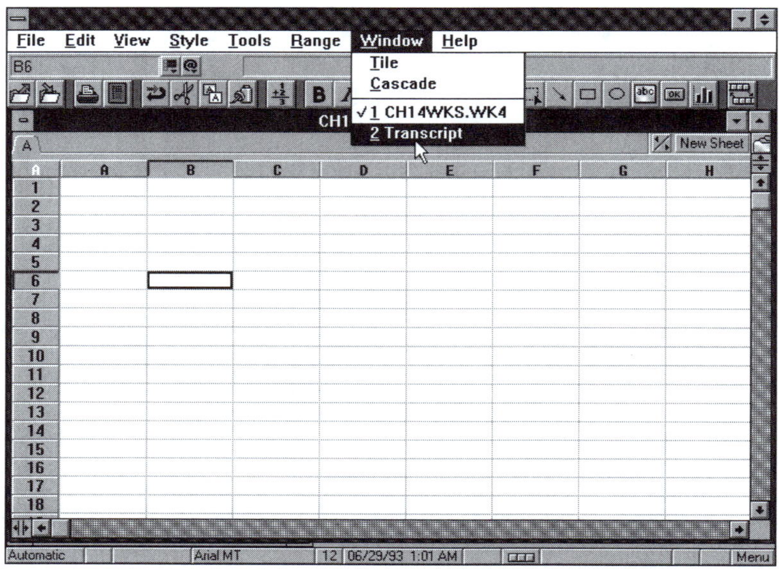

igure 11.2 *Select Transcript Window from the Window menu.*

Worksheet cell

The second place to create a macro is right within your worksheet. When you create a macro in a worksheet, you type the macro commands directly into cells in the worksheet. When you create macros this way, it is important to input the macro commands in cells where you will not be entering data for your worksheet. To accomplish this, it is recommended that you enter macros in the bottom right corner of your worksheet (assuming you start your worksheet in the top left corner), as shown in Figure 11.3.

By putting your macros in the bottom right corner, you can more safely expand your worksheet to the right or down without the risk of overwriting your macros. You will have a problem only if you need to expand both ways to the full extent of the worksheet.

When you enter a macro directly into the worksheet, you can either put all the macro commands in one cell or put each command in its own cell in a column, as shown in Figure 11.4.

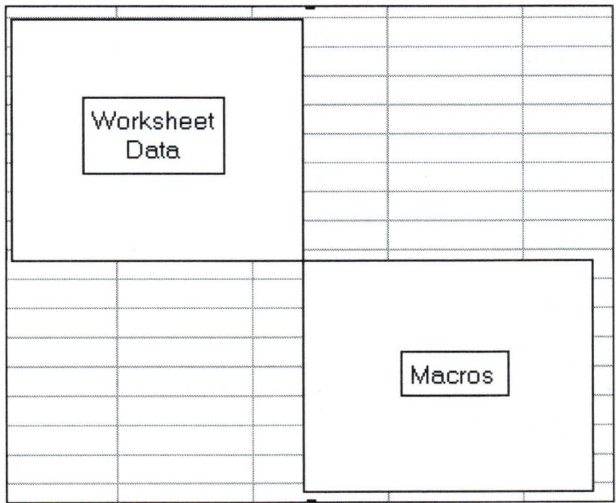

Figure 11.3 *Enter your macros in the bottom right corner.*

It does not matter which way you choose to enter a string of macro commands although, as you can see in Figure 11.4, entering the macro commands in a column of cells often makes it easier to read the commands. If you enter them in one line, they may not fit on the screen and you will have to scroll to see the rest of the formula.

Figure 11.4 You can enter macros in one cell or in a column of cells.

You can enter macros in the Transcript Window and then copy and paste them into your worksheet.

A macro library

The third location available for you to create macros is a macro library—a file that contains only macros. A macro library is a good place to enter macros because you will not need to be concerned that your worksheet data will overwrite your macros. In addition, having a macro library is a way to consolidate all of your macros in one place, making it easier to find the macro that you previously created. By collecting your macros in one file, you can reuse a macro with several different worksheets or use your favorite macros as templates for future macros.

There are a few guidelines for using your macro library files. First, if you store your macros in a file separate from your worksheet, both files must be open in order to run the macro. You must make sure that you open two files—your worksheet file and your macro file—when you go to work on your spreadsheet. Second, macro library files are only useful for macros that you plan to use with more than one worksheet file. If you are using a macro with only one particular file, it is simpler to create a new worksheet in that file and store the macro there. That way you will not run into the problem of overwriting your data, and, since your macros will be part of the worksheet file, they will be available to you when you open that particular file.

If you give your macro worksheet a name such as "Macros," you will be readily reminded of where to find your macro commands. Remember, the purpose of macros is to make your life easier, not more difficult.

How To Create a Macro

There are two main ways to create a macro. You can manually write the macro, step by step, or you can create a macro by recording it, using the Record command. We will not be writing macros step by step. Instead, we will record a macro and then edit it so that it performs exactly as we wish.

To practice recording macros, let's first create a new, blank file, where we can experiment without altering any of our other work. To begin, go to **Tools**, select **Macro** and choose **Show Transcript** from the hierarchical menu. Your screen should look something like the one shown in Figure 11.5.

If your Transcript Window is not clear, clear it now so that there are no extraneous commands in your macro. To clear the Transcript Window:

1. Select the **Transcript Window** so that it is the active window.

2. Go to **Edit**.

3. Choose **Clear All**.

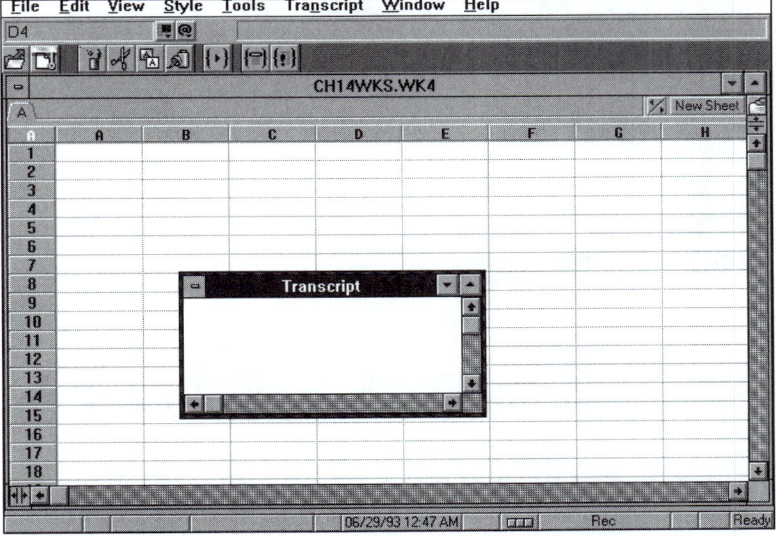

Figure 11.5 *New worksheet with empty Transcript Window.*

NOTE When you select the Transcript Window to make it active, the SmartIcon bar changes icons, as shown in Figure 11.6. The new icons are tools for you to use when you create macros.

Recording a Macro

Lotus 1-2-3 Release 5 makes it easy for you to create macros. The program records your menu choices as well as your mouse and keyboard commands and translates them into macro commands. These commands will be listed in the Transcript Window where each command will appear in its own line. Once the macro command is in the Transcript Window, it can be modified and copied to a cell in your worksheet or applied to a macro button.

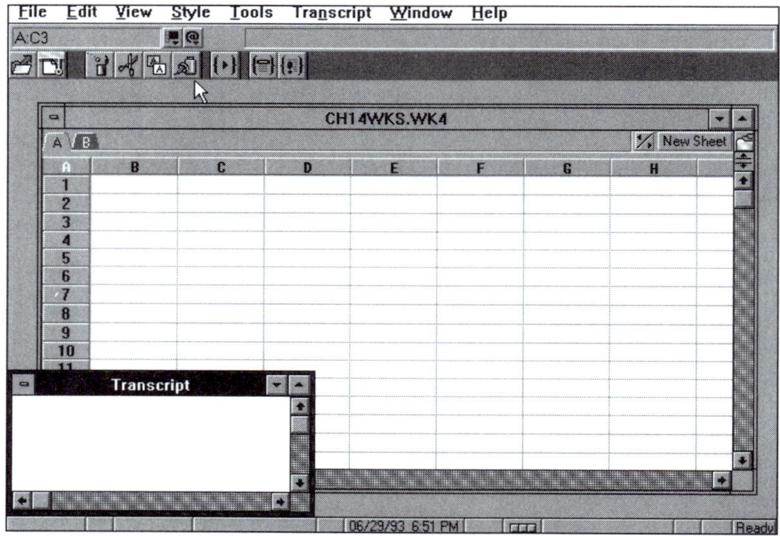

Figure 11.6. *Macro SmartIcon bar.*

It is easy to record a macro. To start, just turn on the Record command. To do so:

1. Go to **Tools**.
2. Select **Macro**.
3. Choose **Record**.

Once Record is turned on, anything you do, even selecting a particular cell, will be recorded in the Transcript Window.

The default setting for Lotus 1-2-3 Release 5 is to turn off the Record button. Once you turn on Record, it will remain on until you turn it back off. Once Record is on in Lotus 1-2-3 Release 5, you will notice a menu choice that says *Stop Recording*. To turn off Record:

N O T E

1. Go to **Tools**.
2. Select **Macro**.
3. Choose **Stop Recording**.

When you turn off Record, Lotus 1-2-3 Release 5 will stop listing your commands in the Transcript Window. You can turn the Record function on and off as you wish. Whenever you turn it on, Lotus 1-2-3 Release 5 will continue to add your commands to the end of the Transcript Window. The Transcript Window will not be erased each time you turn Record on or off. You will need to use the Clear All command to clear the Transcript Window.

Now, let's try to record a macro. To begin, make sure Record is off. Tile your worksheet window and the Transcript Window so that they look as shown in Figure 11.7.

Figure 11.7 *Tile your windows.*

For this exercise we will tile the windows so that you can see Lotus 1-2-3 Release 5 automatically create the macro as it records your commands.

Next, make sure that you have selected your worksheet. If you begin recording before you activate your worksheet file, the macro recorded by Lotus 1-2-3 Release 5 will include a command that selects a window you do not want to be part of the macro. Therefore, the planning you undertake to think through your macro should include making sure that you have already selected your worksheet when you start recording.

Let's begin recording a macro. The macro we will create accomplishes four tasks at once. First, it will change the number formatting to currency with two decimal places; second, it will change the font to Times Roman; third, it will change the style to bold; and fourth, it will include a single underline.

As stated earlier, it is a good idea to plan your steps and put them in order before you begin. Here is our plan:

1. Turn on **Record**.
2. Open the **Number Format** dialog box.
3. Change the number format to currency and leave the decimal places at two.
4. Close the **Number Format** dialog box.
5. Open the **Font & Attributes** dialog box.
6. Change the font to Times Roman.
7. Select bold **On**.
8. Select underlined **On**.
9. Select the type of underline as bold single line.
10. Close the **Font & Attributes** dialog box.
11. Turn off **Record**.

Before you turn on Record, practice steps 2 through 10 to familiarize yourself with the commands. This way, when you actually create your macro, you will be comfortable with the steps, and not accidentally omit some or insert extra ones.

Once you feel comfortable with steps 2 through 10, continue with this exercise.

1. Select your worksheet by clicking on any cell.

2. Go to **Tools**, choose **Macro** and select **Record**.

When you turn Record on, the status bar at the bottom of your screen will say *Rec*, as shown in Figure 11.8.

Figure 11.8 *The Status bar says Rec while Lotus 1-2-3 is recording a macro.*

This will help you confirm whether Lotus 1-2-3 Release 5 is recording your commands.

3. Go to Style and select **Number Format**.

4. You will see the Number Format dialog box shown in Figure 11.9

5. Select **Currency Format** and leave it set at two decimal places, so that your dialog box looks like the one shown in Figure 11.9.

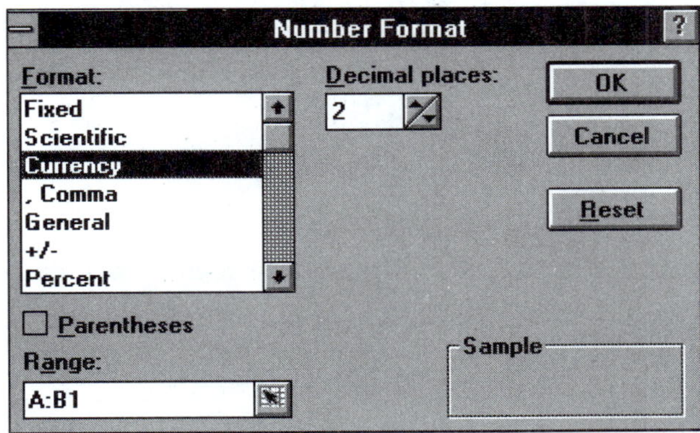

Figure 11.9 *Number Format dialog box.*

6. Click **OK**.

Now if you look at the Transcript Window, you will see that Lotus 1-2-3 Release 5 has begun to record the commands you entered by using the Number Format dialog box, as shown in Figure 11.10.

The macro you have begun to record extends beyond the width of the window, so you cannot see it all. However, you will see the command STYLE_NUMBER_FORMAT, which is the beginning of the macro. Later we will look at these commands in greater detail. For now, simply notice that Lotus 1-2-3 Release 5 has begun to record your macro.

The first macro command recorded in this example is {SELECT A:B1}. This particular command would vary, depending upon which cell you have selected. We do not require a particular cell selection command in the macro and when we edit the macro later, we will erase this command.

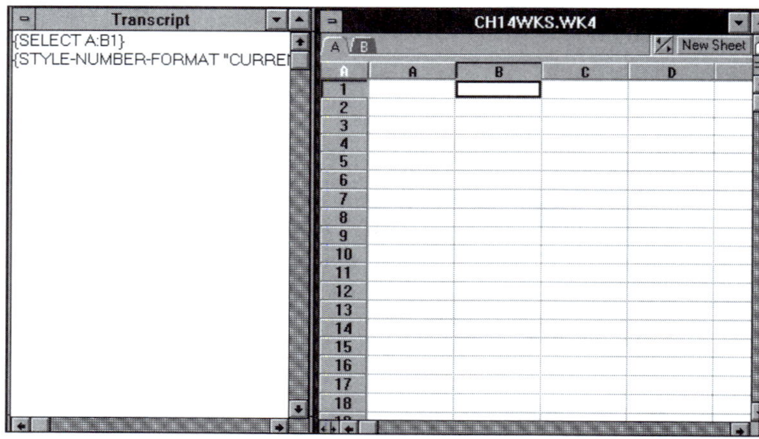

Figure 11.10. *Lotus 1-2-3 has begun to record the macro into the Transcript Window.*

7. Go to Style and select **Font & Attributes**.

8. You will see the Font & Attributes dialog box shown in Figure 11.11.

9. Select **Times New Roman** from the typeface list and make sure it is on 12 point size.

We have used Times New Roman in our example. You may choose any font you wish.

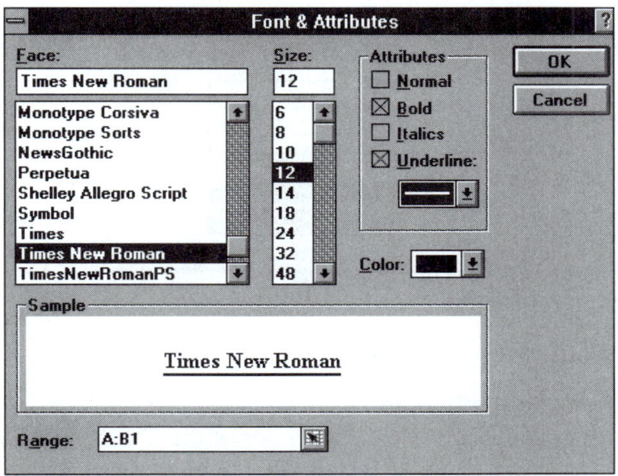

Figure 11.11 *Font & Attributes dialog box.*

10. Click with the mouse in the box next to **Bold**.

11. Click with the mouse in the box next to **Underline**.

12. Select the type of line you want (in our example we chose a bold, single line).

To select the type of underline, click with the mouse on the down arrow and click on the type of line you want from the drop-down list shown in Figure 11.12.

N O T E

13. Click **OK**.

Now if you check the Transcript Window, you will see that Lotus 1-2-3 Release 5 has created new macro commands. There is one for the type of font, one for the style bold, and another for the style underline.

Again, you can ignore the inserted command, {SELECT A:B1}, which we will delete when we edit this macro.

N O T E

Figure 11.12 *Select single bold underline from the drop-down list.*

14.   Go to **Tools**, select **Macro** and choose **Stop Recording**.

Now that we have finished recording the macro, let's look at it. Click with the mouse on the up arrow in the top right corner of the Transcript Window to maximize it, as seen in Figure 11.13. This way we can view the entire recorded macro.

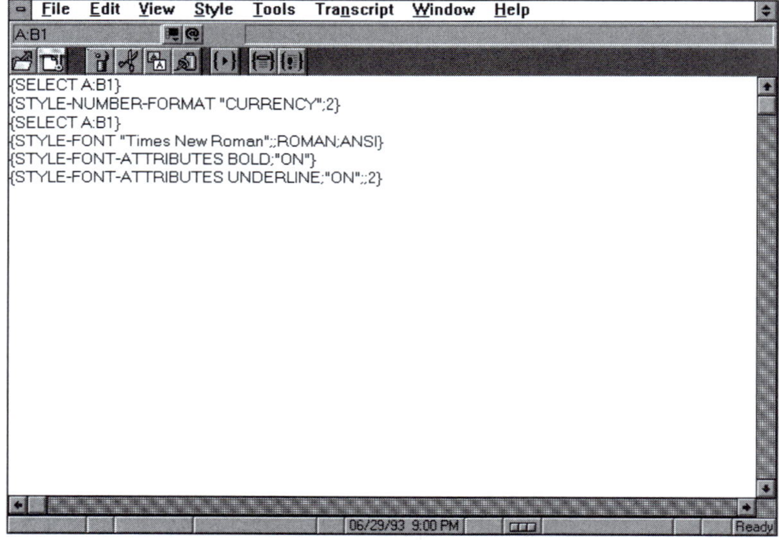

Figure 11.13 *Maximized Transcript Window.*

Analyzing and Editing a Macro

Now that we have recorded the macro, let's analyze what we have recorded. The first step in the macro says,

```
{SELECT A:B1}
```

This command is as simple as it seems. It selects cell A:B1. As mentioned earlier, we do not want this in our macro because it imposes limitations. If there is a command in a macro that selects a particular cell, you will not be able to perform that macro in any other cell. For example, if we selected cell A:C1 and tried to run this macro, we could not do it. Lotus 1-2-3 Release 5 would automatically switch to cell A:B1 as the first step. In order to apply this macro to any cell in the worksheet, we must remove cell-specific commands. We will do so when we edit the macro, as discussed below.

The next command in the macro is:

```
{STYLE_NUMBER_FORMAT "CURRENCY";2;"OFF";;"US
Currency"}
```

This command tells Lotus 1-2-3 Release 5 to apply the number format Currency to the active cell. The second argument in the number format command tells Lotus 1-2-3 Release 5 how many decimal places to include in the format. The third argument turns off parentheses for negative numbers. And the last argument selects US Currency as the type of currency format.

The next command is to select cell A:B1 again. As noted above, we will remove this limitation when we edit the macro.

The next commands sets the font and its style:

```
{STYLE_FONT "Times New Roman";ROMAN;ANSI}
{STYLE_FONT_ATTRIBUTES BOLD;"ON"}
{STYLE_FONT_ATTRIBUTES UNDERLINE;"ON";2}
```

It is worth pointing out that the 2 in the underline command refers to the type of line that we chose for underlining. Note also that the Bold and Underline commands have the argument "ON:" after the first arguments. This tells Lotus 1-2-3 Release 5 to turn this particular style on.

Now that we have analyzed our macro, we can edit it to make changes. The Transcript Window is useful because it lets you edit the macro before applying it to a cell or a macro button. To edit in the Transcript Window, you only have to click the cursor in the window and type your corrections.

Since we want to delete the select cell A:B1 commands from this macro, we must go to the Transcript Window, select the lines for selecting the cell A:B1 and delete them. When you do, your Transcript Window should look like Figure 11.14.

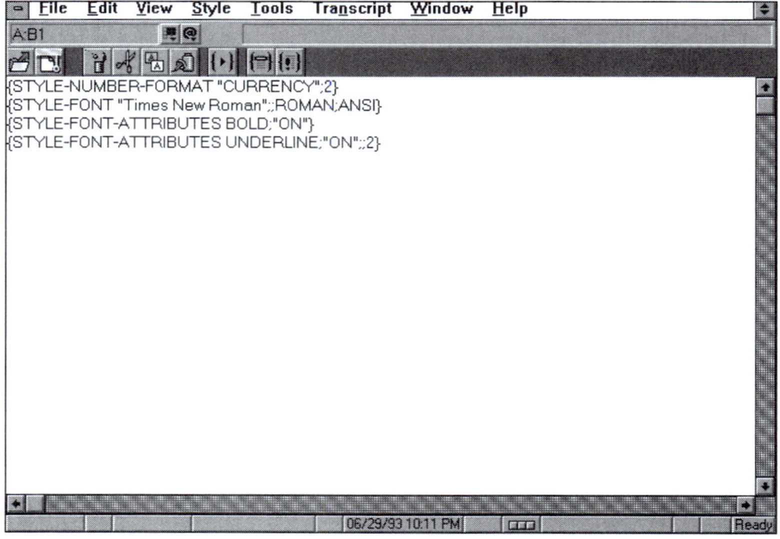

Figure 11.14 *Edited Transcript Window.*

Let's make one more change in our macro. Let's change the number of decimal places from 2 to 0. To do this, select the number 2 in the STYLE_NUMBER_FOR-MAT command, and change it to 0.

If at this time we wanted to add other commands to our macro, we could turn on Record again. Lotus 1-2-3 Release 5 would begin recording our commands and adding them to the Transcript Window. However, in this case, we have finished our macro. To continue, go to the end of the macro in the Transcript Window and type:

{END}

When you are finished, your macro should read as shown in Figure 11.15.

Now that we have completed our macro in the Transcript Window, we can apply it to our worksheet in either of two ways. We can place it into a selected range of cells in our worksheet, or we can assign it to a macro button. We will discuss both of these approaches shortly. In either case, we will need to copy our macro from the Transcript Window. Whenever you finish recording and editing a macro, it is important to select the set of commands and copy it to the clipboard. This way, you can paste it into the worksheet or onto a button. To do this:

```
{STYLE-NUMBER-FORMAT "CURRENCY";0}
{STYLE-FONT "Times New Roman";;ROMAN;ANSI}
{STYLE-FONT-ATTRIBUTES BOLD;"ON"}
{STYLE-FONT-ATTRIBUTES UNDERLINE;"ON";;2}
{END}
```

Figure 11.14 *Edited Transcript Window.*

1. Use the mouse to select the entire macro so that it is highlighted.
2. Go to the **Edit** menu and select **Copy** (or type **Ctrl+C**).
3. When you are ready to paste the macro, go to **Edit** and select **Paste** (or type **Ctrl+V**).

Now that we have completed our macro and copied it to the clipboard, click on the maximize arrow in the Transcript Window so that it returns to normal size. It should be tiled with the worksheet window once again. This way we can see the worksheet in which we will use our new macro.

Running a Macro

We have recorded and edited our macro. Now, let's use it. To run a macro, it must be entered directly into a cell or assigned to a macro button. If it is entered into a cell or a range of cells in your worksheet, you can run this macro by using the RUN command. This command allows you to select a range of cells or a named range and run the macro contained within it. If you assign the macro to a macro button, Lotus 1-2-3 Release 5 will run the macro when you click on the macro button with the mouse. In the following sections we will discuss how to name a macro range and create a macro button so that you can run your macro.

Naming a Macro Range

If you paste your macro into a worksheet cell, it will appear in your worksheet as any entry would. Right now, we will paste the macro we created into cell A:A1. Maximize your worksheet window so you can see the entire macro entry, as shown in Figure 11.16.

If you have many macros pasted into your worksheet, or even a few, it can be difficult to determine which range refers to which macro. Therefore, it is strongly recommended that you name all your macro ranges.

To name a macro, use the **Named Range** command we learned in Chapter 5. However, when you name a macro, it is only necessary to name the first cell of the macro. You can, if you wish, name the entire range, but you are only required to name the first cell. Lotus 1-2-3 Release 5 knows, when it sees the first cell of a macro, to continue executing that macro down a column, until it either sees a blank cell or the command {END}. Since we have entered the command {END} in cell A:A5, if we named the macro based only on cell A:A1, Lotus 1-2-3 Release 5 would continue to execute the macro down through cell A:A5. To name a macro:

1. Select the first cell of the macro or the entire range.
2. Go to **Range** and choose **Name**.
3. You will see the Name dialog box seen in Figure 11.17.
4. Give the range a name and click **Add**.

When you are choosing a name for your macro there is one more item to consider. You can name a macro range with any name you like. It can consist of multiple characters as did other ranges that we named earlier in this book. However, there is an additional feature you can choose when naming macro ranges. It is called a *backslash name*. If you name the macro range with a backslash (\) followed by a single letter, Lotus 1-2-3 Release 5 will allow you to run this macro simply by typing **Ctrl** plus the letter you chose. For example, if you named this macro "\a" and you typed **Ctrl+a**, Lotus 1-2-3 Release 5 would automatically run this macro. We will discuss this in depth shortly, but it is worth mentioning briefly now as you are naming your macro.

For this example, let's give this range two names. One name will be a multi-character name and the other will be a backslash name. This way we can practice with both. In the name box, type **Macro1** and click **Add**. Then, type **\a** and click **Add**. Now your Name dialog box should look like the one shown in Figure 11.18.

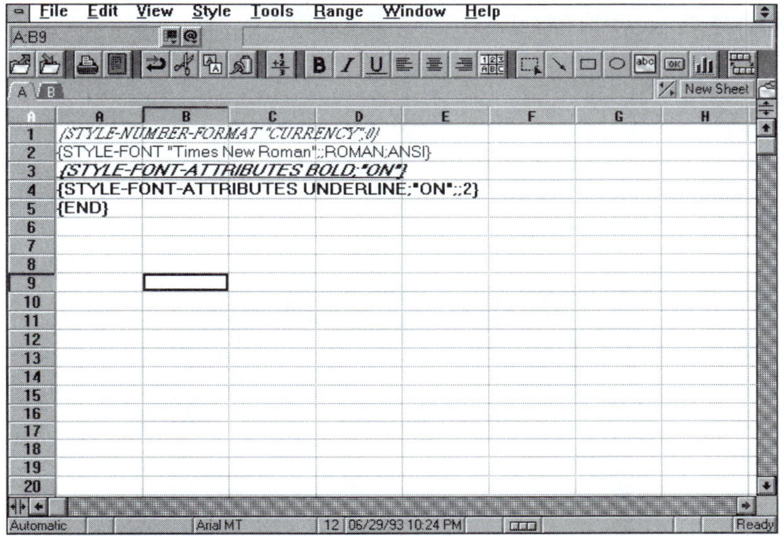

Figure 11.17 *Name dialog box.*

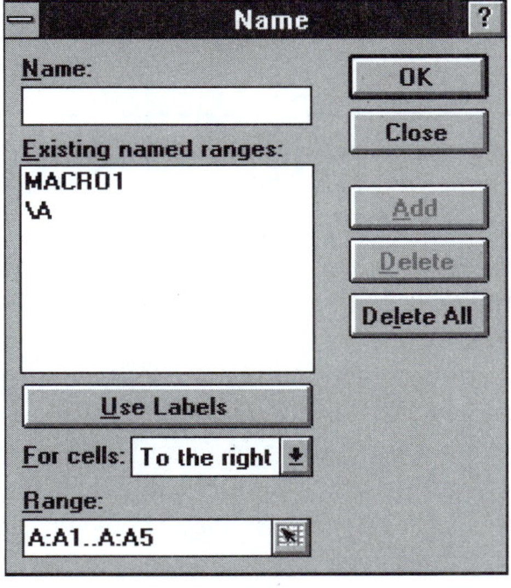

Figure 11.16 *Macro pasted into worksheet cells.*

Running a Named Macro Range

Now that we have named our macro range, we are ready to run the macro. As mentioned earlier, there are two ways to run a named macro range. The easiest way to run a named range is to use the shortcut for macros with backslash names. Since we named our macro \a, if we type **Ctrl+a**, Lotus 1-2-3 Release 5 will automatically run the macro.

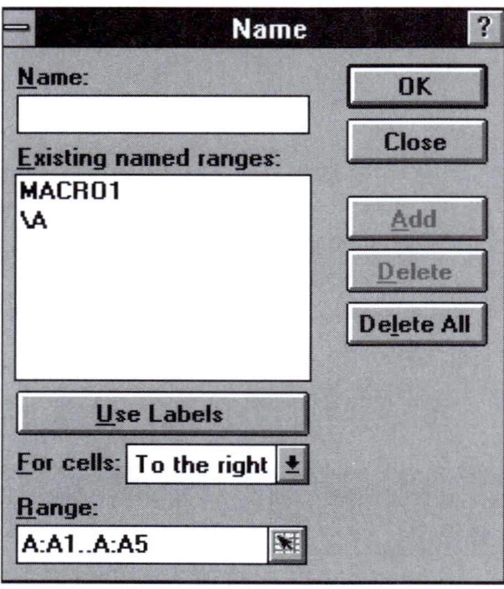

Figure 11.18 *Named macro ranges in the Name dialog box.*

N O T E

If there is already a keyboard command assigned to the **Ctrl**+character command you chose, priority will be given to executing the macro. For example, **Ctrl+S** is the keyboard shortcut for **Save**. However, if we named our macro "\S" and typed **Ctrl+S**, Lotus 1-2-3 Release 5 would run the macro instead of saving the document. This may be worth bearing in mind when you choose a backslash name for your macro. If there is a **Ctrl**+character combination you use often, such as **Save**, you may not want to name a macro with that keyboard combination.

Let's try to run this macro. Go to cell A:B10 and enter the number **1000**. Now, type **Ctrl+a** and watch Lotus 1-2-3 Release 5 format this number for you. Notice that this number now is formatted as $1000.

There is another feature available when you use backslash names. If you name your macro "\0" (zero), Lotus 1-2-3 Release 5 will automatically run the macro when you open the worksheet. This is called an autoexecute macro. For example, suppose we created a macro library file that we wanted to open every time we opened our other worksheets. You could create an autoexecute macro within your worksheet which opened the macro library file. By doing this, every time you opened your file, the library file would open as well.

The other way to run a named macro range is to use the Run command. If you go to **Tools**, select **Macro** and choose **Run**, Lotus 1-2-3 Release 5 opens the Macro Run dialog box shown in Figure 11.19.

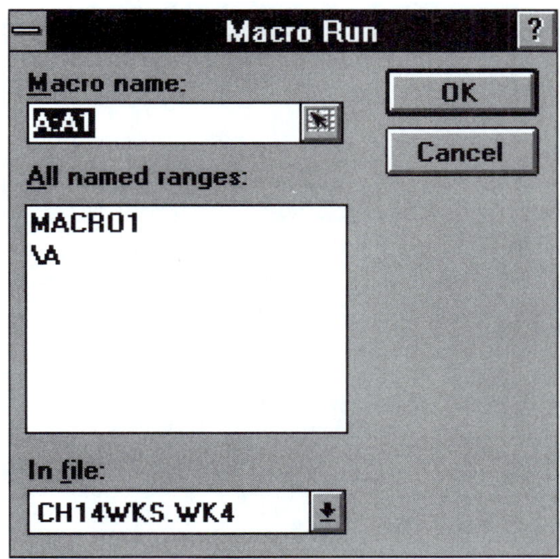

Figure 11.19 *Macro Run dialog box.*

In the Macro Run dialog box, you can either choose a range of cells, using the Range Selector, or you can choose a named range from the All Named Ranges box. Notice that both of our names for the macro appeared in this box. For this exercise, we are going to use the MACRO1 named range to run our macro.

At the bottom of the dialog box is a box where you can select the file in which the macro can be found. However, this will only display open files. It will not search through closed files on your disk. In other words, you must have a file open to run the macro.

N O T E

To run a macro on a cell:

1. Enter **2000** into cell A:C10.

2. Go to **Tools**, select **Macro** and choose **Run**.

3. Select **MACRO1** from the Macro Run dialog box.

4. Click **OK**.

Notice how Lotus 1-2-3 Release 5 automatically formatted your number in currency format, with Times New Roman, Bold, and Single Bold Underline style font as shown in Figure 11.20.

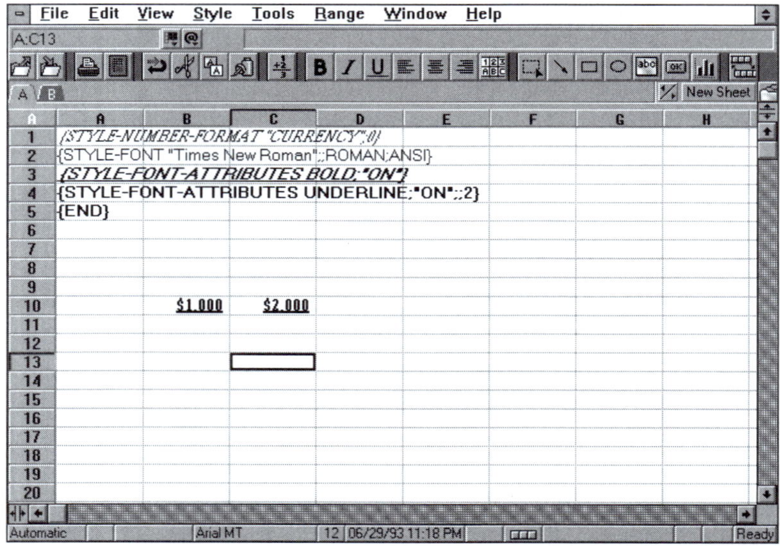

Figure 11.20 *The numbers were automatically formatted using the macro.*

Creating a Macro Button

Lotus 1-2-3 Release 5 has another way to run macros. You can create a button and assign your macro to it. Then, if you click with the mouse on this button, the macro will run automatically. The macro button you create is a graphic image made with the Button command to which you assign a particular macro. Once the button is assigned, pressing it is a shortcut to run the macro.

To create a macro button:

1. Go to **Tools**.
2. Select **Draw**.
3. Choose **Button**.

When you choose the Button command, the cursor changes to a + sign. You use this sign to draw a button, similar to a rectangle, as shown in Figure 11.21.

If you click the + in your worksheet, Lotus 1-2-3 Release 5 automatically creates a standard size button so you don't have to size it yourself.

N O T E

Assigning a Macro to a Button

When you create a macro button, Lotus 1-2-3 Release 5 automatically opens the Assign to Button dialog box, as shown in Figure 11.22.

In this dialog box, you can change the name of the button and assign a particular macro to the button. There are two ways to assign a macro to a button, as shown in Figure 11.23:

*   By range
*   Manually by button

If you choose to enter the macro manually, you can either type the macro into the box that says "Enter Macro Here," or you can paste the macro which you cut out of the Transcript Window by typing **Ctrl+V**. If you do the latter, your dialog box will look like the one shown in Figure 11.24.

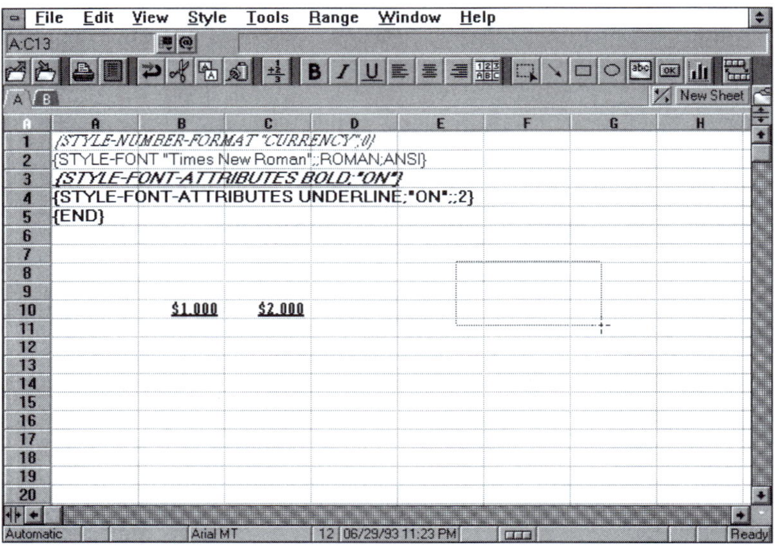

Figure 11.21 *Creating a button.*

Figure 11.22 *Assign to Button dialog box.*

Figure 11.23 *Two ways to assign a macro to a button.*

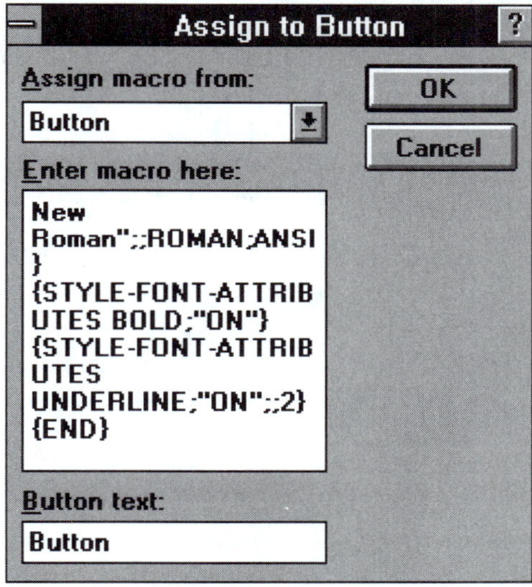

Figure 11.24 Assigning a macro manually.

If you switch to "Assign Macro From a Range," the Assign Button dialog box changes to resemble the one shown in Figure 11.25.

You can either enter a range by using the Range Selector, or you can select the named range MACRO1 which we named earlier. Whichever way you choose to assign your macro to a button will produce the same result.

You can change the name of the button to help you remember what this button does.

N O T E

Suppose you forgot to assign a macro to your button or you forgot to enter a name for the button. To reopen the Assign to Button dialog box, you will need to hold the Shift key while double-clicking with the mouse on the button. When you do this, the cursor changes and placeholders appear around the button, as shown in Figure 11.26.

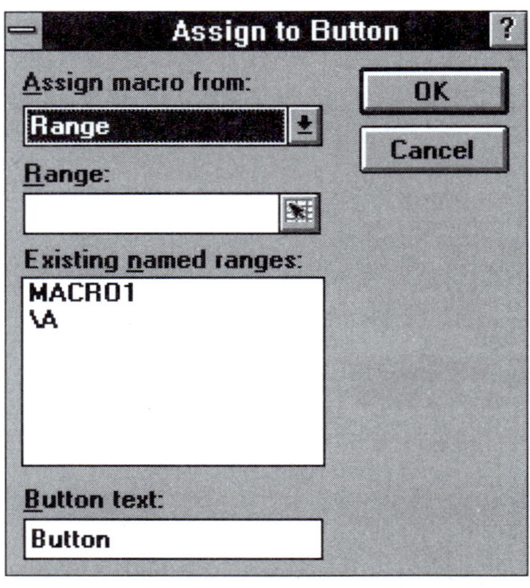

Figure 11.25 *Assigning a macro from a range.*

Running a Macro Button

Running a macro button is probably the easiest way to work with macros. All you have to do to run a macro button is double-click with the mouse on the button without holding the **Shift** key. The cursor will look like a hand pointing to the button, and Lotus 1-2-3 Release 5 will execute the macro, as shown in Figure 11.27.

For example, type **3000** into cell A:D10. Now click the mouse on the macro button with the hand. Notice that the 3000 automatically formats to $3000.

Practice

Now that you have taught yourself the basics of creating, editing, and running macros, it is time to practice what you have learned. Try recording various macros and editing them to remove any cell-specific items that are not useful in the macro. Then try running them by naming a macro range and by using macro buttons. With a little practice, you will be able to automate even the most difficult of tasks.

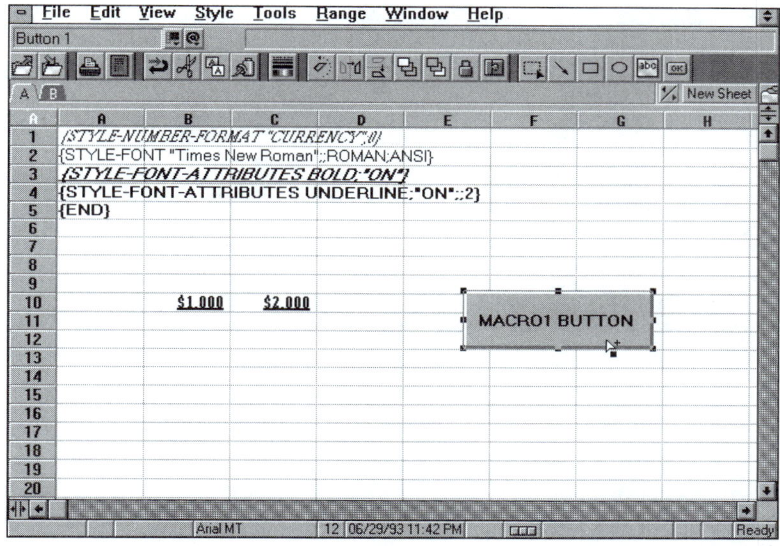

Figure 11.26 *Selecting a button to open the Assign To Button dialog box.*

To Sum Up

In this chapter, you learned about one of the easiest ways to make work on your spreadsheet easier: using macros. You discovered that a macro is a shortcut to perform a task or set of tasks. You learned the guidelines for writing a macro, including the benefits of planning the steps of your macro and finding the right location for it. You learned the three places where you can create a macro: in the Transcript Window, in a worksheet cell, or in a macro library.

Then, you learned the differences between recording macros and writing them. After some practice creating a macro, you learned how to analyze and edit one. Finally, you learned how to name and run a macro and how to create and use a macro button to further simplify your work.

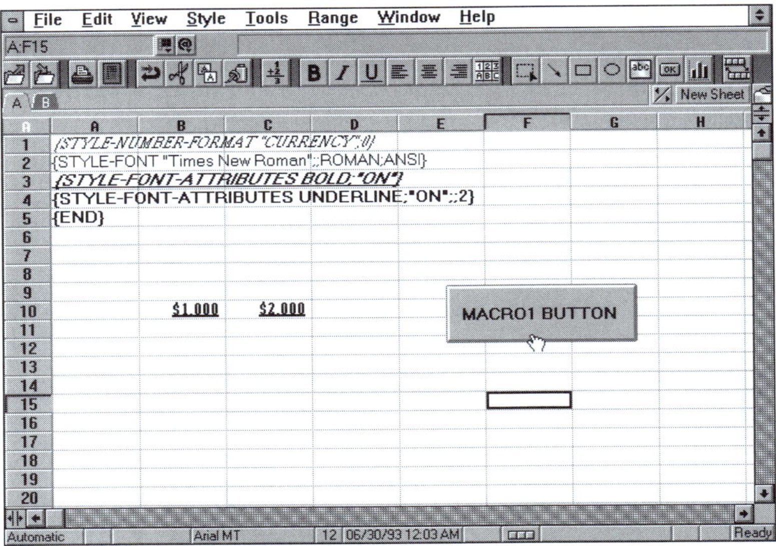

Figure 11.27 Running a macro button.

What You Learned

General rules for creating a macro:

1. Begin with an open bracket ({), and end it with a closed bracket (}).

2. Do not put a space between the open bracket and your macro command keyword.

3. If your macro command keyword is more than one word, separate the words with hyphens, -, not with underscoring, _, or a space.

4. Put one space between your keyword and your first argument.

5. Use a semi-colon as an argument separator.

6. Do not put a space between the first argument and the argument separator or between the argument separator and the second (or subsequent) argument.

When an argument is a text entry, it must be enclosed by quotation marks. Spaces between the words of a text entry that is enclosed by quotation marks are permitted.

7. Optional arguments may be omitted but the argument separator that follows them must be retained as a placeholder.

8. The final command of all macros is {End} or a blank cell.

If you enter a macro command directly into your worksheet, you must be careful not to overwrite your data.

Open (or close) the Transcript Window:

1. Go to **Tools**.
2. Select **Macro**.
3. Choose **Show Transcript** to open window.
4. Choose **Hide Transcript** to close window.

You can also close the window by selecting Close from the drop-down window. HIDE TRANSCRIPT will appear only if the window is open and SHOW TRANSCRIPT will appear only if the window is closed.

Macros entered in the Transcript Window may be copied and posted into your worksheet.

Create a macro library:

1. Open a separate file.
2. Enter and save your macros in this file.

Create a macro by recording it:

1. Go to **Tools**, select **Macro**, choose **Show Transcript**.
2. Select the Transcript Window as your active window.
3. Go to **Edit**, select **Clear All**.
4. Go to **Tools**, select **Macro**, choose **Record**.
5. Enter your macro commands.

It is a good idea to prepare a written list of the order of the commands so that you create your macro accurately.

6. Click the Transcript Window to confirm that the new macro has been properly created.
7. Go to **Tools**, select **Macro**, choose **Stop Recording**.

Copy a macro:

1. Select the entire macro by clicking on it with the mouse.
2. Go to **Edit**, select **Copy** (or type **Ctrl+C**).
3. Go to **Edit**, select **Paste** (or type **Ctrl+V**).

Macros can be pasted into your worksheet or onto a macro button.

Name a macro range:

1. Select the first cell of the macro (or, if you wish, the entire range).

2. Go to **Range** and choose **Name**.

3. The **Name** dialog box appears.

4. Name the range and click **Add**.

Run a named macro range:

- To run a macro with a backslash name, type **Ctrl+** the character name of the macro.

- To run macros that do not have a backslash name:

    1. Select the cell on which you want to run the macro.

    2. Go to **Tools**, select **Macro**, choose **Run**.

    3. The Macro Run dialog box appears.

    4. Select the range of cells that contains the macro you desire.

    5. Click **OK**.

Create a macro button:

1. Go to **Tools**, select **Draw**, choose **Button**.

2. The cursor changes to a + sign.

3. Use the cursor to draw a button, or, click with the mouse on the button to create a default sized button.

Assign a macro button manually:

1. Create a macro button.

2. The Assign to Button dialog box appears.

3. Type the macro into the box that says, "Enter Macro Here," or paste a macro you cut out of the Transcript Window by typing **Ctrl+V**.

Assign a macro from a range:

1. Create a macro button.

2. The Assign to Button dialog box appears.

3. Use the **Range Selector** to choose the current range.

Reopen the Assign to Macro dialog box:

Hold down the **Shift** key while double-clicking with the mouse on the button.

Run a macro button:

Double click with the mouse on that button.

Appendix A

Installing Lotus 1-2-3

System Requirements

Now that you know a bit about the program's intended uses, you are ready to install Lotus 1-2-3 Release 5. To install the program, you must make sure that your computer satisfies the system requirements for running Lotus 1-2-3:

- An IBM-compatible 386 or higher computer

- A VGA or higher monitor

- DOS Release 3.3 or later

- Windows Release 3.1 or later

- At least 4 megabytes of RAM; at least 6 megabytes if you plan to use the Lotus Approach integration feature or Lotus Maps

- At least 11 megabytes of available hard disk space; at least 23 megabytes for the default installation

- A mouse is recommended

If your system satisfies these requirements, you are ready to install Lotus 1-2-3 Release 5. In order to run the Lotus 1-2-3 installer disks, Windows must be currently running on your computer. Following are the steps you will take to install Lotus 1-2-3 Release 5.

Before you do anything, we recommend that you back up your copies of the program disks for your protection. Please note that you are authorized to make copies of these disks for archival purposes only.

Starting the Installation

1. Insert the Install Disk into your disk drive.

Every machine is configured differently. This may be your A drive or your B drive. It is important that you note the drive into which you put the disk, as you will be telling the computer in which drive to look for it..

2. Open the Windows Program Manager.

3. Choose **File** and then **Run**. You will see the following window (see Figure A.1).

4. Type **A:INSTALL** or **B:INSTALL** depending on whether your disk is in the A or B drive.

5. Install takes a few moments to copy its files to your hard disk. Then you will see the following window (see Figure A.2). Install fills in the default name and company name from your computer system, if it can.

6. Fill in the name and company name. If you are installing Lotus 1-2-3 on a network file server, click the box labeled **Install on a File Server**. Then click **Next >** with the mouse. (The **Next >** button won't work until you have filled in a name and a company name.)

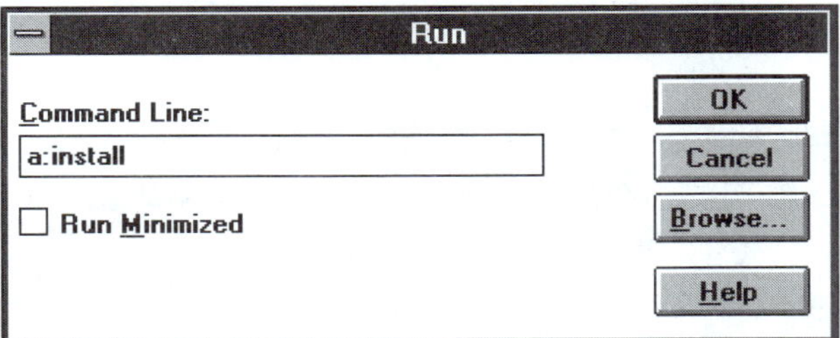

Figure A.1 *Run window.*

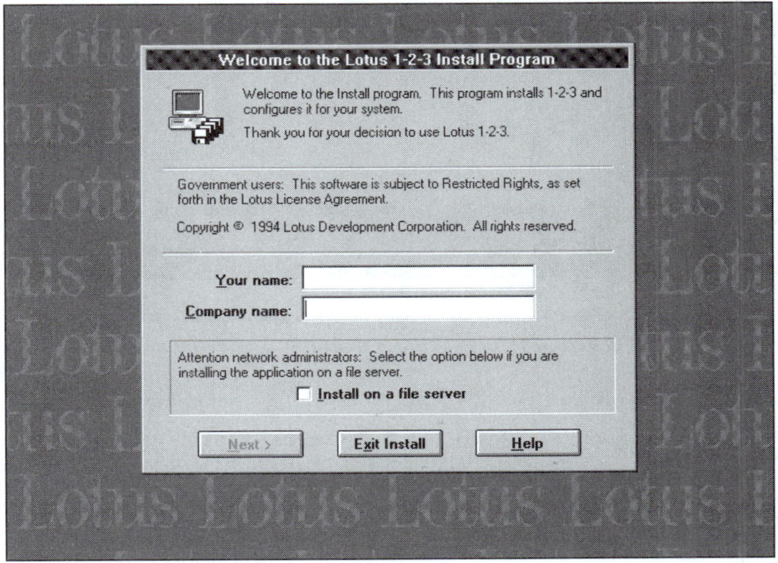

Figure A.2 *Install Welcome Screen*

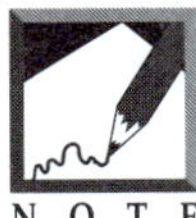

Notice that **Next >** has a darker outline. This means that it is the active button. When a button is active, hitting **Return** on the keyboard performs the same function as clicking the button with the mouse.

7. Install asks you to confirm the name and the company name. Click **Yes** to continue.

8. The Install Options and 1-2-3 Directory appear on your screen (see Figure A.3).

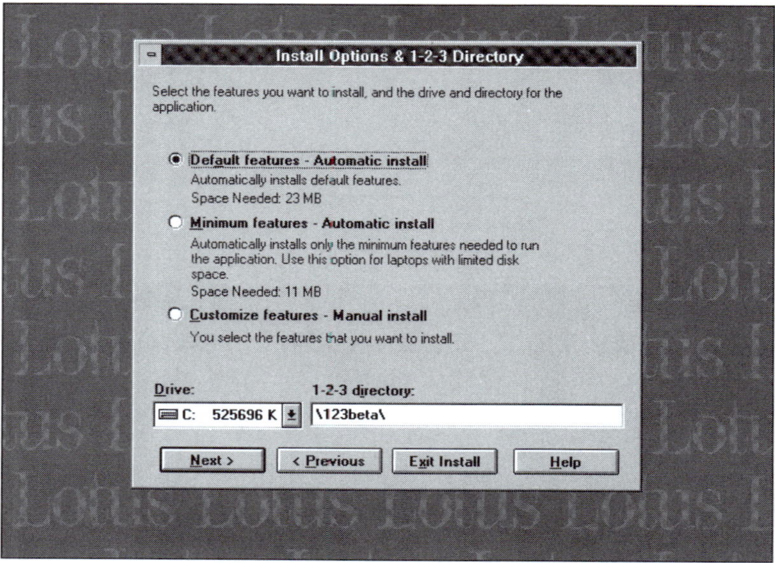

Figure A.3 *Install Options and 1-2-3 Directory.*

9. If you choose the default features, you will automatically install the most popular Lotus 1-2-3 Release 5 features, including Lotus Maps, the Tutorial, the spelling checker, and the ability to access dBASE databases. If you choose the minimum installation, you install only the core of Lotus 1-2-3 Release 5 and none of the special features. If you want to select the features to install, or if you want to install some of the features that are not included in the default installatoin, such as access to Lotus Notes or Paradox databases, choose the Custom installation.

Notice that the default installation requires 23 megabytes of hard disk space. The minimum installation needs 11 megabytes. If you choose a custom installation, the space you need depends on which features you select. The Drive box at the lower left shows how much available space, in kilobytes, is on the currently selected drive. Drop the last three digits for a rough estimate of how many megabytes the drive has. (The drive in the figure, for example, has approximately 525 megabytes available.)

10. You can change to another hard drive by clicking the down arrow next

to the box. A list of your hard drives drops down (see Figure A.4) and you can see the amount of space you have available on each one. Click a drive to select it.

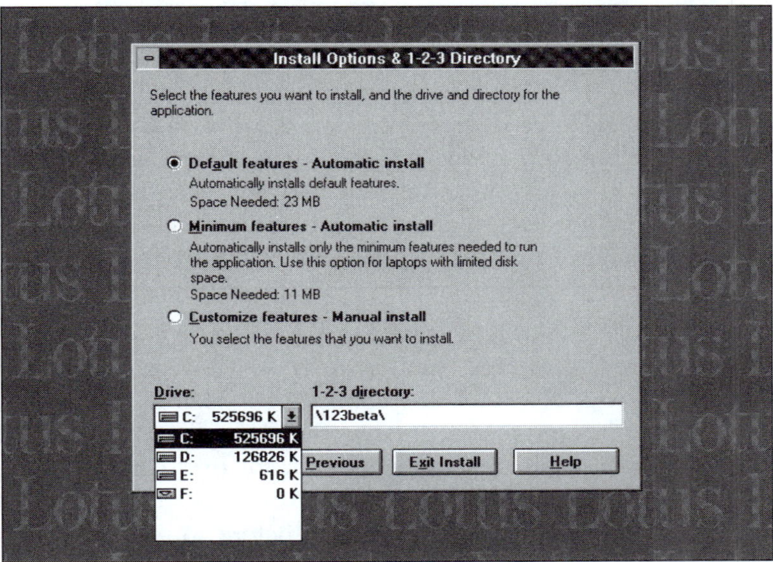

Figure A.4 *Drive list.*

11. Install also suggests a default directory in which to install the Lotus 1-2-3 files on the hard drive. You can change the name of the directory if you wish, but most people don't. (If you change the name, be sure the new name starts with a backslash (\).)

To use the default or minimum installation, continue reading steps 12 through 18. To customize your installation, skip to step 19.

N O T E

If you have an older copy of Lotus 1-2-3 for Windows already installed on your computer, Lotus 1-2-3 Release 5 will allow you to automatically replace the older copy with Release 5. The following instructions assume that you are installing Lotus 1-2-3 Release 5 for the first time or on a hard drive which does not contain an older copy of Lotus 1-2-3. If you are installing over an older copy, the installation screens will be slightly different than the ones which follow, but the general steps are the same.

Default or Minimum Installation

12. Default features is already selected for you. If you want to do a minimum installation instead, click **Minimum Features**. In either case, click **Next >** continue.

Notice that every screen also has a **< Previous** button so that you can return to previous screens if you change your mind about an earlier choice. You can also request on-screen **Help** information by choosing the Help button, or you can exit the installation without completing it by choosing the **Exit Install** button.

13. Install next asks you to name the directory where you want to place the Lotus shared tools files (see Figure A.5). These are features that are shared among all your Lotus applications, such as the spell checker. They must be stored in a directory where every Lotus application can find them. Installer suggests a location for the shared tools files, and most people accept that suggestion. (You might not see this screen if you have installed a Lotus application before so that there already is a shared tools directory.)

14. The next thing to do is select a program group (see Figure A.6). This is where installer will place all your new Lotus 1-2-3 program icons on your Windows desktop. Installer shows you a list of your current groups to select from, but it suggests that you use the Lotus Applications group (which it will create if you don't already have one). Click **Next >** to accept the default suggestion and go on to the next screen.

15. The next screen asks if you are ready to start copying files to your hard disk. Click **Yes** or press **Enter** to continue.

16. While it copies the files, the installer displays useful information on your screen (see Figure A.7). The percentage bar at the bottom lets you know how far along you are in the process. Every so often, you are asked to insert the next disk in the floppy drive.

17. After all the files are copied, the installer must make some entries in your AUTOEXEC.BAT file (see Figure A.8). This is a file of commands that DOS executes during booting. You can choose to let Install change your AUTOEXEC.BAT file or to do it yourself. Unless you know exactly what you are doing, you should let Install do it for you by clicking **Yes**

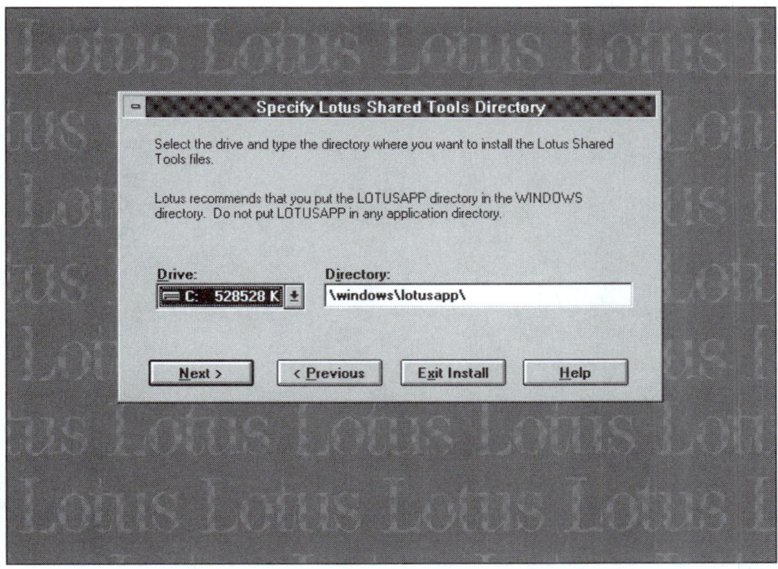

Figure A.5 *Specify Lotus Shared Tools Directory.*

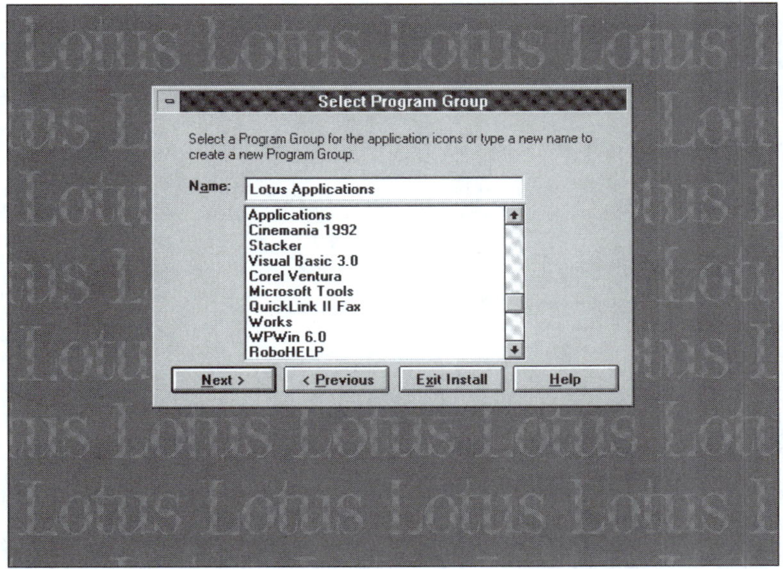

Figure A.6 *Select Program Group.*

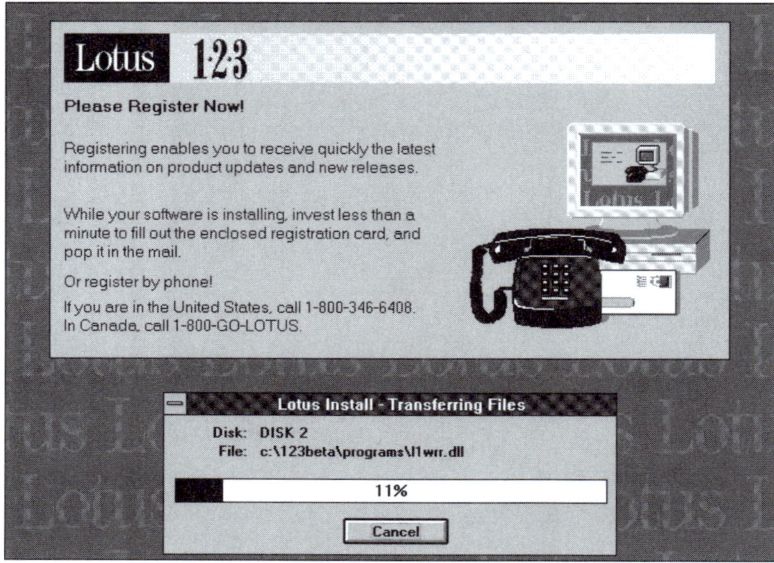

Figure A.7 *Progress screen.*

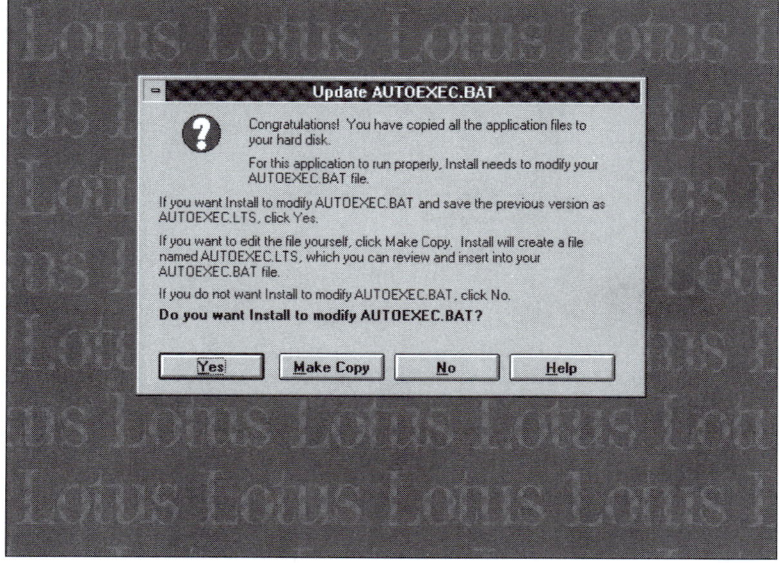

Figure A.8 *Update AUTOEXECBAT.*

N O T E   If you choose to let Install update your AUTOEXEC.BAT file auto-
matically, Install saves your former AUTOEXEC.BAT under the name
AUTOEXEC.LTS. If you find that you have to remove Lotus 1-2-3
from your system for some reason, you can go back to your old
AUTOEXEC.BAT file by copying AUTOEXEC.LTS to
AUTOEXEC.BAT.

18. The final screen tells you that the installation is complete (see Figure
    A.9). You must restart before you can use your new Lotus 1-2-3 Release
    5. You can choose to restart now if you want to try it out immediately.
    Or you can choose to return to Windows without restarting if you don't
    plan to use Lotus 1-2-3 Release 5 now. If you choose not to restart, don't
    forget that you have to restart before you can use the new program.

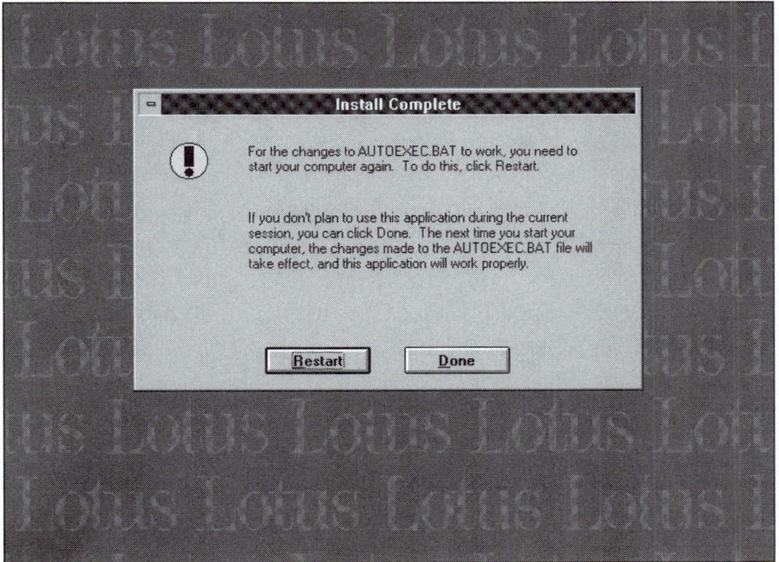

Figure A.9 *Install Complete.*

Customized Installation

19. If you want to customize installation, click the mouse on **Customize
    Features** (see Figure A.10).

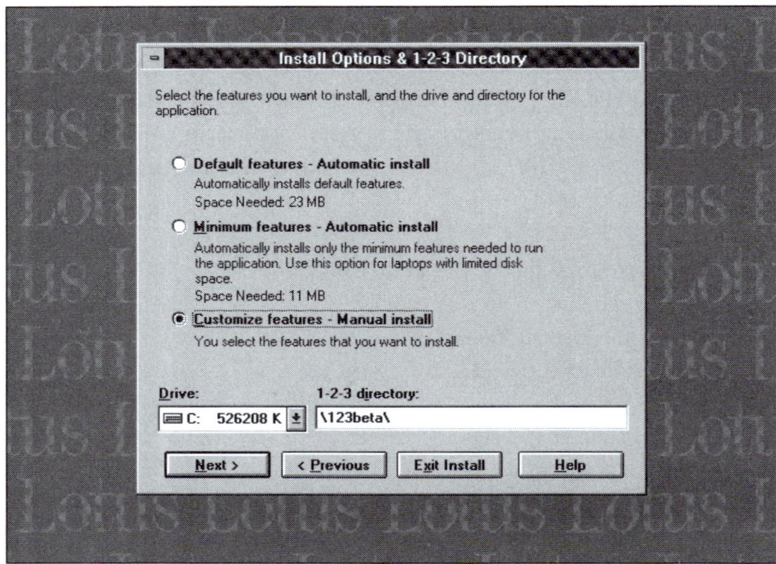

Figure A.10 *Install Options and 1-2-3 Directory.*

20. Install will bring up the Customize window (see Figure A.11). You are asked to select the specific features you want to install. The default features are automatically selected. (Selected features have an X in the box next to them.) You can deselect any feature that you don't want except for 1-2-3 Core, which is the basic 1-2-3 program. Click a feature to select or deselect it.

There are three pages of features, as indicated by the tabs at the top of the box. Figure A.11 shows the first page, which provides general 1-2-3 features. To see the other two pages, click their tabs. Be sure to select and deselect the features on all three pages before going on.

The installer tells you how much space is required for your selected items as well as how much space is available on your disk. This is like being at the grocery store and having the checker ring up each item individually. You can decide which items take priority based on which ones you can "afford." That is, your decision may be made depending on how much disk space you have available.

Even though you selected the drive and directory before, you can change your mind while you are working on selecting features. If you find that the current drive doesn't have enough room for the features you want, for example, you may switch to another hard drive with more room (if you have one).

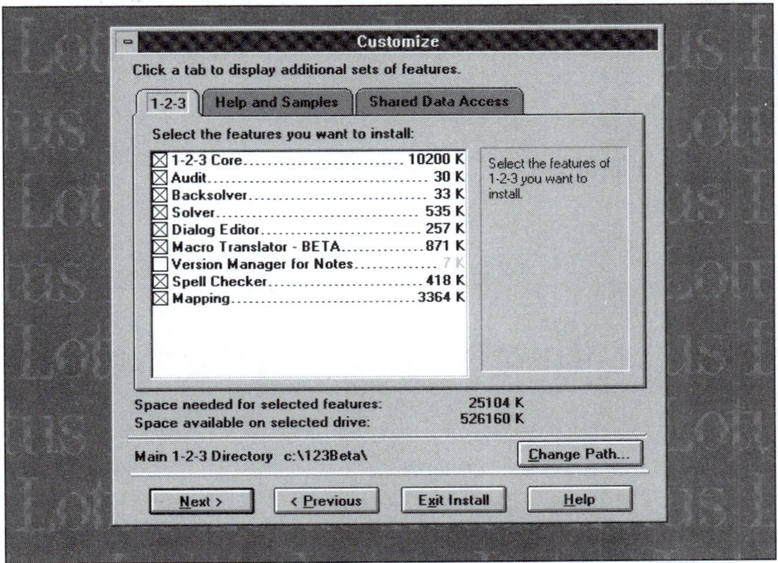

Figure A.11 *Customize window.*

The directory name should have a back slash (\) before its name if you change the default directory name.

N O T E

21. The installer next asks you to name the directory where you want to place the Lotus shared tools files (see Figure A.12). These are features that are shared among all your Lotus applications, such as the spell checker. They must be stored in a directory where every Lotus application can find them. Installer suggests a location for the shared tools files, and most people accept that suggestion. (You might note see this screen if you have installed a Lotus application before so that there already is a shared tools directory.)

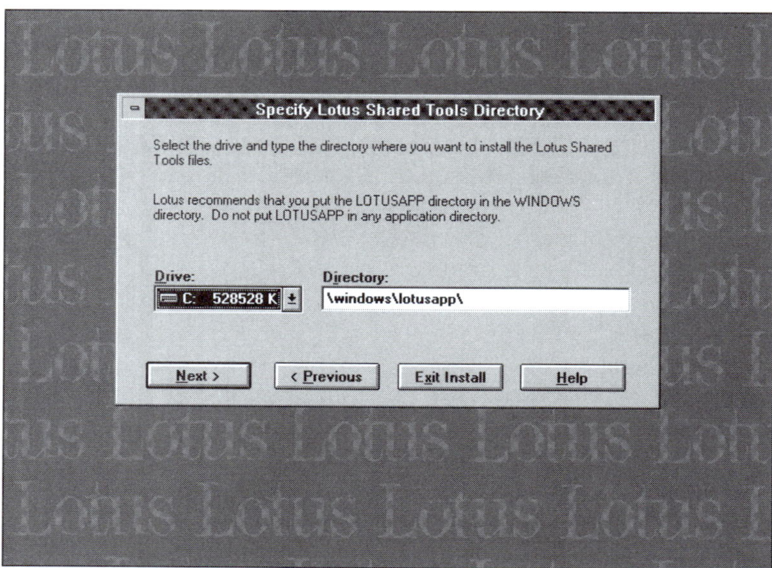

Figure A.12 *Specify Lotus Shared Tools Directory.*

22. The next thing to do is select a program group (see Figure A.13). This is where installer will place all your new Lotus 1-2-3 program icons on your Windows desktop. Installer shows you a list of your current groups to select from, but it suggests that you use the Lotus Applications group (which it will create if you don't already have one). Click **Next >** to accept the default suggestion and go on to the next screen.

23. The next screen asks if you are ready to start copying files to your hard disk. Click **Yes** or press **Enter** to continue.

24. While it copies the files, the installer displays useful information on your screen (see Figure A.14). The percentage bar at the bottom lets you know how far along you are in the process. Every so often, you are asked to insert the next disk in the floppy drive.

25. After all the files are copied, the installer must make some entries in your AUTOEXEC.BAT file (see Figure A.15). This is a file of commands that DOS executes during booting. You can choose to let Install change your AUTOEXEC.BAT file or to do it yourself. Unless you know exactly what you are doing, you should let Install do it for you by clicking Yes.

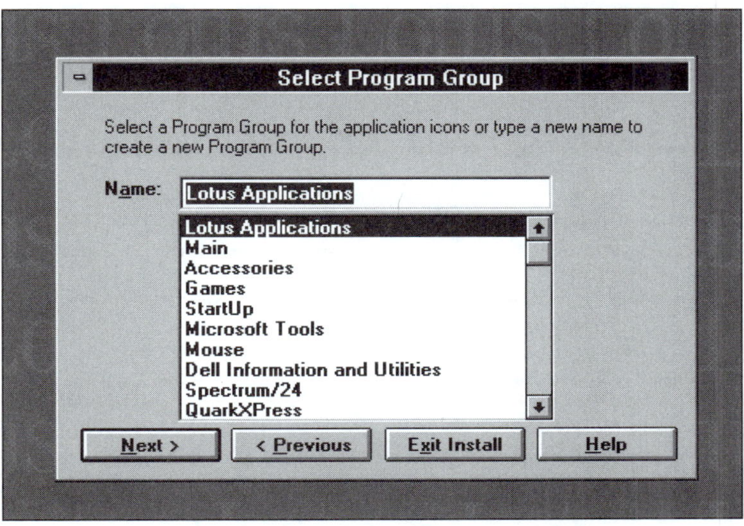

Figure A.13 *Select Program Group.*

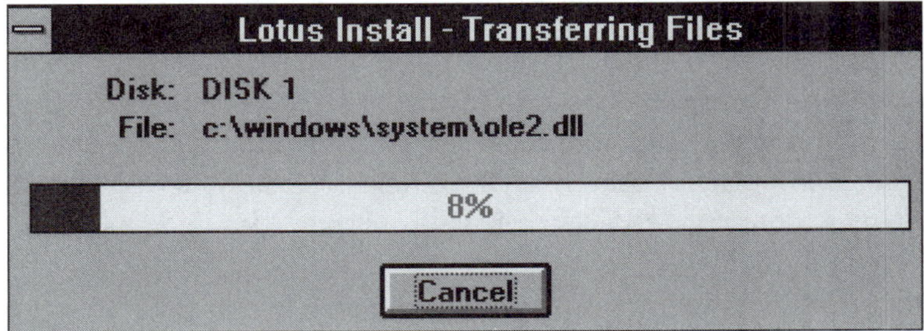

Figure A.14 *Progress screen.*

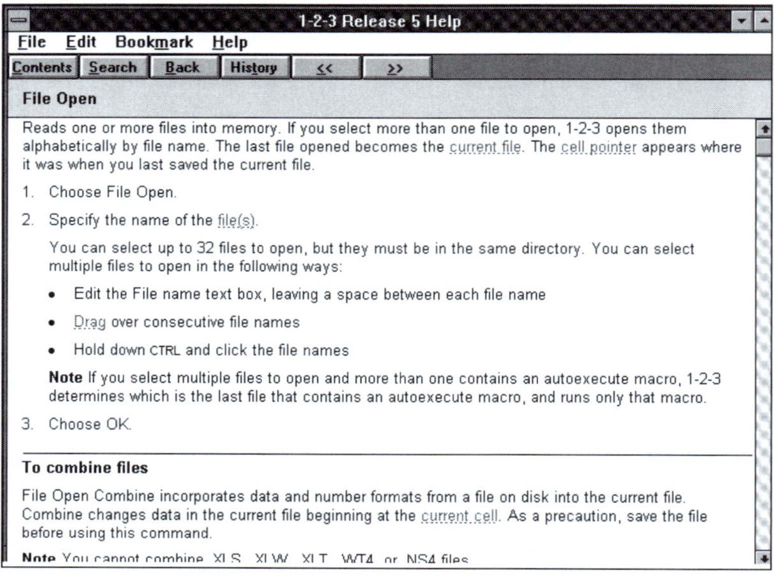

Figure A.15 *Update AUTOEXEC.*

N O T E   If you choose to let Install update your AUTOEXEC.BAT file automatically, Install saves your former AUTOEXEC.BAT under the name AUTOEXEC.LTS. If you find that you have to remove Lotus 1-2-3 from your system for some reason, you can go back to your old AUTOEXEC.BAT file by copying AUTOEXEC.LTS to AUTOEXEC.BAT.

26.   The final screen tells you that the installation is complete (see Figure A.16). You must restart before you can use your new Lotus 1-2-3 Release 5. You can choose to restart now if you want to try it out immediately. Or you can choose to return to Windows without restarting if you don't plan to use Lotus 1-2-3 Release 5 now. If you choose not to restart, don't forget that you have to restart before you can use the new program.

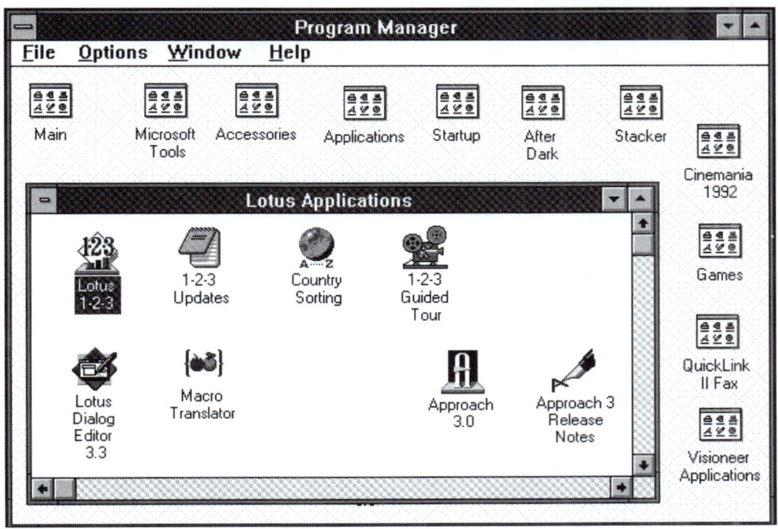

Figure A.16 *Install Complete.*

Appendix B

Customizing Lotus 1-2-3

Once you become more familiar with Lotus 1-2-3 Release 5, you may want to customize certain default settings to suit your personal preference. For example, you may want to change the color of your worksheet, or you may want the File menu to list your most frequently used worksheets.

View Preferences

The first set of preferences which can be customized relates to how you view your worksheet and the Lotus 1-2-3 interface. To change these defaults, go to **View** and select **Set View Preferences**. The Set View Preferences dialog box will appear (see Figure B.1).

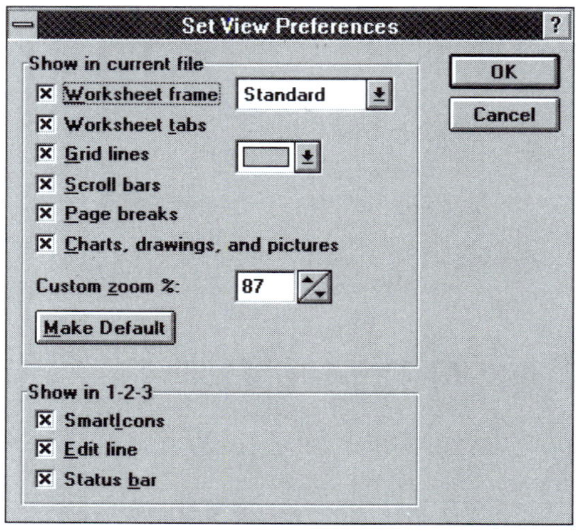

Figure B.1 *Set View Preferences dialog box.*

The first item you can change in this dialog box is Worksheet Frame, the inverted-L that outlines your worksheet. The frame consists of the column and row headings. By default, Lotus 1-2-3 uses a "standard" worksheet frame. This frame has letters for column headings and numbers for row headings. However, you are not limited to this type of worksheet frame. If you click on the down arrow to the right of "standard" in the dialog box, the following drop-down list will appear (see Figure B.2).

The following table explains the different worksheet frame options:

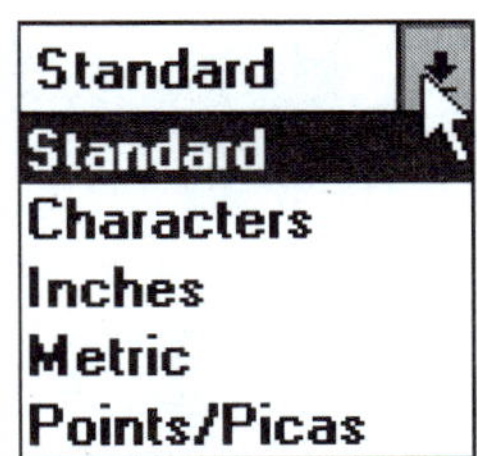

Figure B.2 *Worksheet frame options.*

Table B.1 *Worksheet frame options.*

Standard	This frame uses letters for column headings and numbers for row headings.
Characters	This frame shows how many characters could fit across the column and down the rows.
Inches	This frame shows how many inches could fit across the columns and down the rows.
Metric	This frame shows how many centimeters could fit across the columns and down the rows.
Points/Picas	This frame shows how many points or picas can fit across the columns and down the rows. Figure B.3 is an example of your worksheet frame if you changed the default setting to Inches.

In addition to being able to change the type of worksheet frame, you can tell Lotus 1-2-3 whether to display the worksheet frame at all. If you click the mouse in the box to the left of Worksheet Frame, you can remove the x from the box.

The following information applies to all the items in the customizing dialog boxes. If an x is in the box to the left of an item name, the item will be displayed. If the x is not in the box, the item will not be displayed.

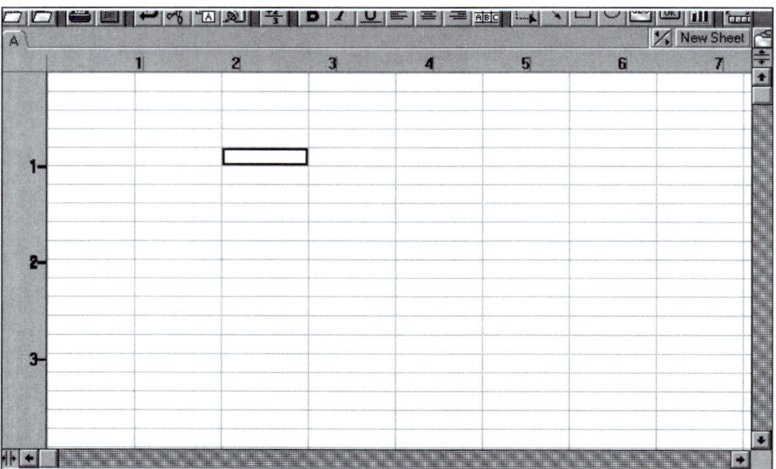

Figure B.3 *Worksheet frame in inches.*

The next item in the Set View Preferences dialog box is Worksheet Tabs. By default, Lotus 1-2-3 displays the tabs for your different worksheets (i.e., Budget, Actual, Difference). If you do not want these tabs displayed, remove the x from the box.

The next item is Grid Lines. By default Lotus 1-2-3 displays grid lines. If you do not want to see your grid lines, remove the x from the box. (Many of the SmartMasters achieve a more sophisticated appearance by suppressing the grid lines.)

N O T E

The Grid Lines option only applies to what is seen on the screen. If you do not want the grid lines to be printed, you can change this option in the Page Setup dialog box. See Chapter 9 for more information.

Next to Grid Lines is a small gray square and a down arrow. If you click on this arrow, a drop-down color palette will appear (see Figure B.4).

With this palette you can change the color of the grid lines displayed by Lotus 1-2-3. Because the default color is very light gray, some people find it easier to see the grid lines when they change the color.

Next, you may opt to hide the scroll bars. By default, Lotus 1-2-3 displays the scroll bars. If you want to hide them, remove the x from the box.

Lotus 1-2-3 also allows you to hide the page breaks. Traditionally, page breaks appear as dotted lines in the worksheet. If you do not want them displayed, remove the x from the box to the left of Page Breaks.

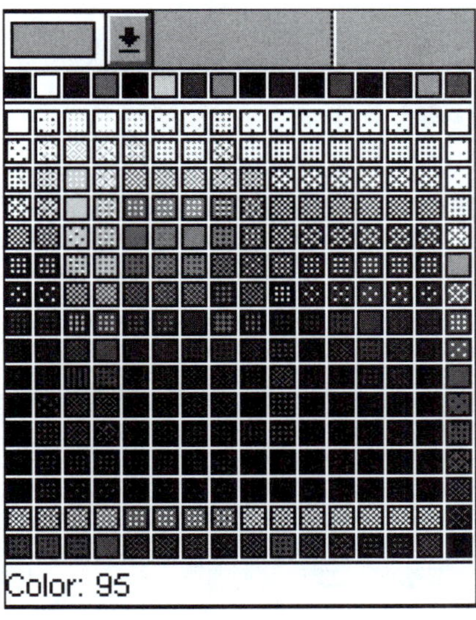

Figure B.4 *Grid line colors.*

The next item in the Set View Preferences dialog box determines whether or not charts, drawings, and pictures should be displayed in your worksheet. If you remove the x from this box, Lotus 1-2-3 will hide all charts and graphics in your worksheet. When you're working on your worksheet, you can move around faster if you suppress charts and graphicsm which take time to display.

Lotus 1-2-3 also allows you to change the Custom Zoom. In Lotus 1-2-3 you can zoom in and out of your worksheet to reduce or enlarge it on your screen. To zoom in or out, go to the **View** menu and select **Zoom In** or **Zoom Out.**

Lotus 1-2-3 also allows you to view the worksheet at a default percentage. The default is 87%. Therefore, if you zoom in and later want to return to the default setting, go to **View** and select **Custom—87%**. If you want to change this default custom setting, enter a new number in the **Custom Zoom %** box in the **Set View Preferences** dialog box.

If you want to make the settings in the group labeled Show in Current File your default settings for all future files, press the **Make Default** button. This affects new files only, not existing files.

Finally, in the Set View Preferences dialog box you can determine whether or not the Lotus 1-2-3 interface should include the SmartIcons, the Edit Line, or the Status bar. Remove the x from the respective box to hide one or more of these items.

Worksheet Defaults

The next set of preferences which can be customized relates to the default styles used in your worksheet. To change these defaults, go to **Style** and select **Worksheet Defaults**. The Worksheet Defaults dialog box will appear (see Figure B.5).

Figure B.5 *Worksheet Defaults dialog box.*

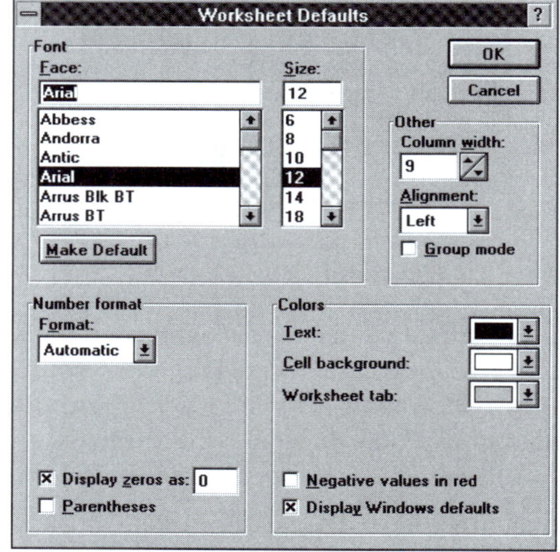

The first items you can change in this dialog box are the worksheet font face and size. You can change these by selecting a font from the list available and by either choosing a size from the list or manually typing a size into the box.

Next, you can change the default column width. Lotus 1-2-3 automatically chooses 9 for the column width, but you can change this by typing a new number in the box or by using the up and down arrows to increase and decrease column width.

You can also alter the default cell alignment used in your worksheet. Lotus

1-2-3 uses left alignment for the cells, but you can change this to right or center alignment by clicking the down arrow and choosing the appropriate alignment from the drop-down list (see Figure B.6).

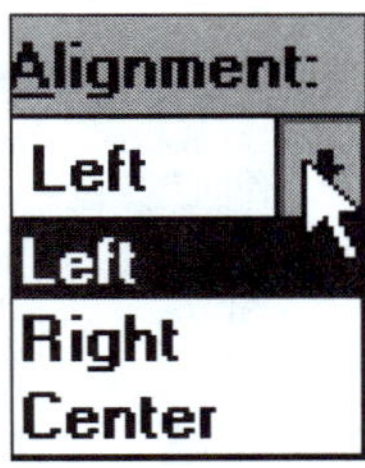

Figure B.6 *Default cell alignment.*

Below Alignment is a box for Group Mode. Earlier, in Chapter 7 we discussed working with multiple worksheets in group mode. If you click in the **Group Mode** box and select it, Lotus 1-2-3 will apply any formatting you do in this worksheet to all your other worksheets as well.

If you select group mode, any changes you make to one worksheet will be applied to all worksheets. Therefore, if you delete a row or column from one worksheet, all worksheets have a row or column deleted.

N O T E

Next you can set the preferences for number format. By default, Lotus 1-2-3 uses automatic formatting for numbers. Therefore, if you type **$150**, Lotus 1-2-3 knows that this is currency, and thus uses the Currency format. Similarly, if you type **50%**, Lotus 1-2-3 knows that this is a percentage, and uses the Percentage format. To change the default format to a specific type, click on the down arrow next to Automatic and select the desired Number format from the drop-down list available (see Figure B.7).

Next, you can tell Lotus 1-2-3 how to display cells which contain zero values in a cell. By default, Lotus 1-2-3 displays them as 0. If, however, you want to change this, you can type a different value into the box for Display Zeros As. For example, suppose you want cells with the value 0 to say "n/a" or to show the value as 0.0. Instead of retyping all those cells, you can tell Lotus 1-2-3 to Display Zeros As n/a or 0.0.

Next, you can determine whether or not Lotus 1-2-3 should display negative values with parentheses. If you click in this box and select it, negative values will appear with parentheses. For example, if you type -100, Lotus 1-2-3 will display (100).

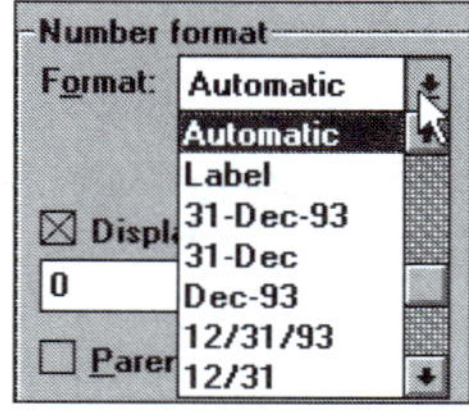

Figure B.7 *Default number format.*

Lotus 1-2-3 also allows you to change the default colors used in your worksheet. By default, 1-2-3 uses whatever colors you have selected for Windows in general. You can select various colors for text and cell background, as well as worksheet tab background, from the color palettes, as we did for grid lines earlier. You can also determine whether or not negative values should be displayed in red by adding or removing an x from the box to the left of Negative Values in Red. Finally, if you want the selected colors to appear in print (and you have a color printer) but the screen colors to be the default Windows colors, select **Display Windows Defaults** so that an x appears in the check box. For more information on the Windows default colors, see the information on the Control Panel in your Windows manual.

User Setup

The final set of defaults which can be customized are in the User Setup dialog box. To open this dialog box, go to **Tools** and select **User Setup** (see Figure B.8).

The first item in this dialog box can be checked to skip the Welcome dialog box that appears each time you start lotus 1-2-3 Release 5. The next item can be checked to skip the New File dialog box that lets you choose between a blank new file and a SmartMaster.

The next item is Drag and Drop Cells. If this option is selected, Lotus 1-2-3 allows you to copy and move cells with the mouse. For more information on this, see Chapter 2. The next item should be checked if you want Lotus 1-2-3

Release 5 to display a confirmation dialog box each time you perform a drag and drop operation.

The next item is Use Automatic Format. If this option is selected, Lotus 1-2-3 will use the Automatic format as the default setting. If it is not selected, the default will be General format.

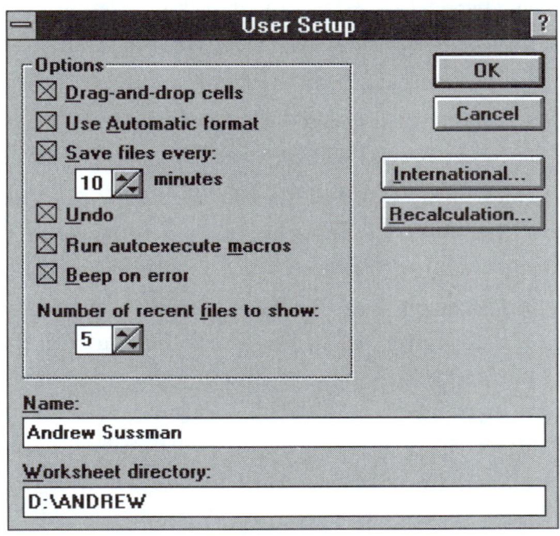

Figure B.8 *User Setup dialog box.*

You can later change this for your worksheet by changing the default format in the Worksheet Defaults dialog box.

N O T E

Next, you can tell Lotus 1-2-3 to automatically save your worksheet and after how many minutes to do so. This is a very useful feature. Once you save your worksheet for the first time, thus giving Lotus 1-2-3 a file name and a location for the file, it will automatically save your file at the selected time interval. You do not have to remember to choose **Save** from the **File** menu when you select this option.

N O T E   If your computer should crash, "autosave" will help to ensure that, at most, you only lose a few minutes of your work. You will be able to recover whatever has been saved. Anything you completed between the last save and the crash will be lost. Therefore, it is recommended that you do not make the autosave time interval too long.

The next item in this dialog box is Undo. If this option is selected, you will be able to undo your last command. If you remove the x from this box, you will not be able to undo it.

Next, you can set whether Lotus 1-2-3 should Run Autoexecute Macros. For more information on Autoexecute Macros, see Chapter 11.

Next, you can determine whether or not Lotus 1-2-3 should beep to signal an error. If this option is selected, Lotus 1-2-3 will cause your computer to beep when you have an error in a formula.

The next item is Refresh File Links Automatically. If you have taken advantage of Windows OLE 2 feature to link a worksheet to another file, such as a database, this option determines when Lotus 1-2-3 copies the linked data from the database to the worksheet. When this option is not checked, Lotus 1-2-3 offers you the option of refreshing the link each time you open the worksheet; you can choose whether or not you want to update the worksheet from the linked file. If this option is checked, Lotus 1-2-3 automatically refreshes the link each time you open the worksheet.

The next item is Number of Recent Files To Show. If this box contains a number greater than zero, your File menu will display recently used files. To determine the number of files displayed, use the up or down arrows to increase or decrease the number of recent files shown. If you set this option to five files, your File menu would include the last five files used in Lotus 1-2-3 (see Figure B.9).

Finally, in the User Setup dialog box, you can enter the name of the user and the default Worksheet Directory used by Lotus 1-2-3 to save and open files. The name that is entered into the Name box is the name that the Version Manager uses for assigning versions to specific users. It also appears in the Document Info for each file, showing who created the worksheet.

The default Worksheet Directory is the location where Lotus 1-2-3 will begin looking to save a file or open existing files. You can always manually change this location in the Save As dialog box or the Open dialog box. This default setting makes your life easier by automatically placing you in the directory where you usually save your work. To change this directory, type the desired path into the box. For example, if you save your work on the C: drive, in the directory 123, in the subdirectory DATA, you would type the following into the Worksheet Directory box:

```
C:\123\DATA.
```

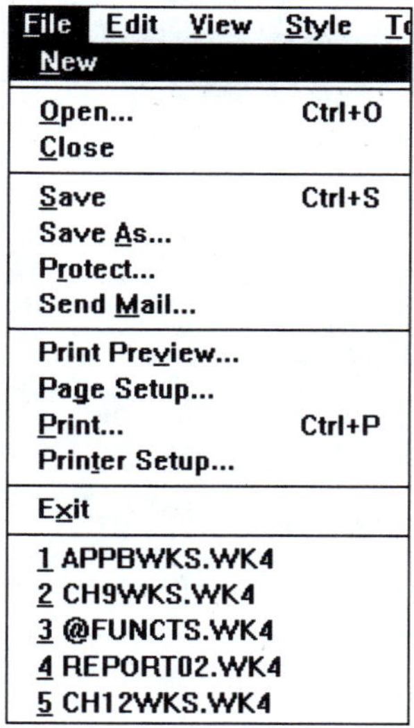

Figure B.9 *File menu with five recent files displayed.*

International Settings

If you click on the **International** button in the **User Setup Dialog Box**, the International Dialog Box will appear (see Figure B.10).

In this dialog box, you can set the defaults for the Date and Time format. If you click the down arrows next to each of these options, you can select the desired format from the drop-down list available. (See Figures B.11 and B.12.)

You can also select the punctuation styles used in Lotus 1-2-3. This feature allows you to determine whether Lotus 1-2-3 should use commas, periods, or semi-colons for different items. For example, you may choose whether numbers should have a comma or a period for separating thousands and decimals. You may also use this option to select whether @ Function arguments are separated by commas or semi-colons. Figure B.13 shows the different options for punctuation styles available in Lotus 1-2-3.

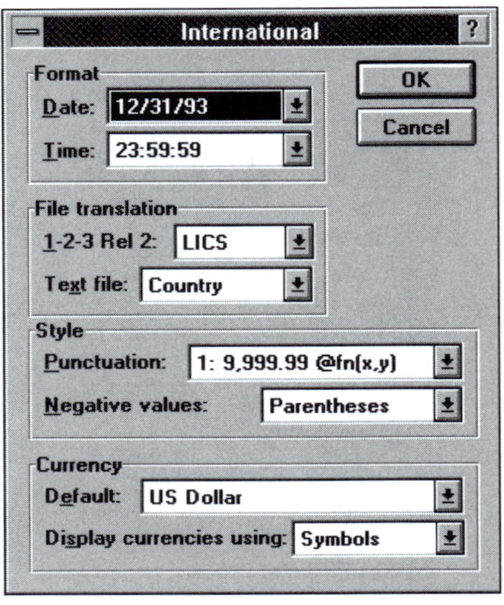

Figure B.10 *International dialog box.*

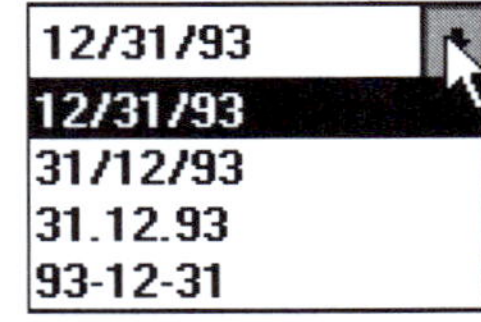

Figure B.11 *Date format options.*

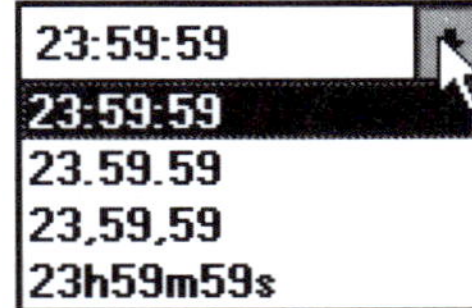

Figure B.12 *Time format options*

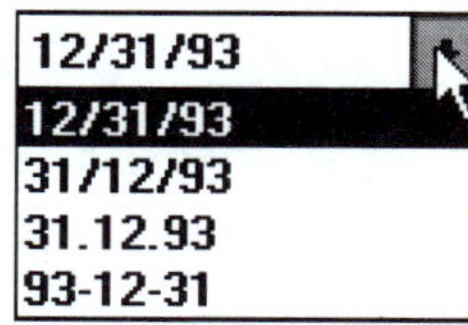

Figure B.13 *Punctuation style options.*

You can also determine how negative values should be formatted by Lotus 1-2-3. If you click on the down arrow next to Parentheses, you can select whether to use parentheses or the negative sign to denote negative numbers (see Figure B.14).

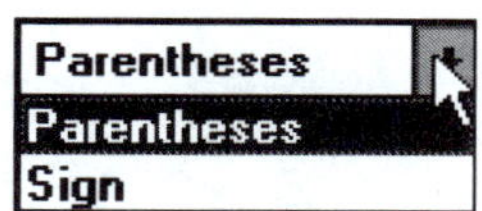

Figure B.14 *Negative values style options.*

Finally, you can select the default styles for Currency. You can select the default currency type (as in US Dollars or Swedish Krona) and choose whether currency symbols (as in $45.23) or the International Standards Organization (ISO) codes (as in USD 45.23) should be displayed in the cells.

Recalculation Settings

If you click on the **Recalculation** button in the **User Setup** dialog box, the Recalculation dialog box will appear (see Figure B.15).

In this dialog box you can select whether Lotus 1-2-3 should automatically recalculate your worksheet or whether you need to manually select this option. Also, you can determine the order of recalculation, whether Lotus 1-2-3 should follow the natural order, or whether it should calculate by row or by column. Table B.2 explains the different orders of recalculation.

In the Recalculation dialog box you can also select the number of iterations used by Lotus 1-2-3. Iterations are used by Lotus 1-2-3 when you have chosen to recalculate by row or by column or when your worksheet has a circular reference. In each of these situations, Lotus 1-2-3 must recalculate the worksheet multiple times to arrive at the correct answer. By selecting the number of iterations, you are telling Lotus 1-2-3 how many times to recalculate the worksheet. For example, suppose cell A1 is equal to 2*B1, but B1 is equal to A1+5. This is a circular reference, because to calculate A1, Lotus 1-2-3 needs to look at B1, which needs to look at A1, and so on. To arrive at an answer, you need to tell Lotus 1-2-3 how many iterations to follow before stopping this circular reference.

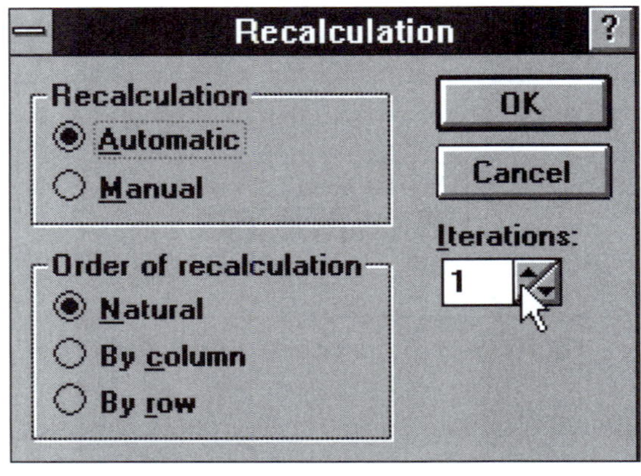

Figure B.15 *Recalculation dialog box.*

Table B.2 *Order of recalculation.*

Natural calculation	Lotus 1-2-3 calculates all formulas that are required by the current formula before recalculating that formula.
By column	Lotus 1-2-3 calculates all formulas from left to right, working across each column.
By row	Lotus 1-2-3 calculates all formulas from top to bottom, working down each row.

Appendix C

Introduction to SmartIcons

What is a SmartIcon? In the beginning of this book, when we looked at the Lotus 1-2-3 interface, we noticed a collection of buttons directly below the Edit Line which make up the SmartIcon Bar. SmartIcons are little buttons which automate tasks in Lotus 1-2-3 to simplify and speed your work. SmartIcons eliminate the need to select commands from the menus and dialog boxes by putting them in buttons which can be clicked with the mouse.

When you start Lotus 1-2-3, it displays a list of SmartIcons in the Button bar. As you select various items in a worksheet, such as a chart or a map, the set of SmartIcons on the Button bar changes so that you always have the most appropriate icons for what you are currently doing. Because there are so many icons (more than 150 of them) and you may have difficulty remembering what they all mean, when you pause your mouse pointer over a SmartIcon, a bubble pops up to explain that icon.

You can move the SmartIcons around on the Button bar to suit your own style. Just hold down **Ctrl** while you drag an icon to another position.

N O T E

If you want to edit the Button bar, select a different set of SmartIcons, or choose a different location for the Button bar, you need to open the SmartIcons dialog box. To open the SmartIcons dialog box, go to **Tools** and select **SmartIcons.** You will see the following dialog box:

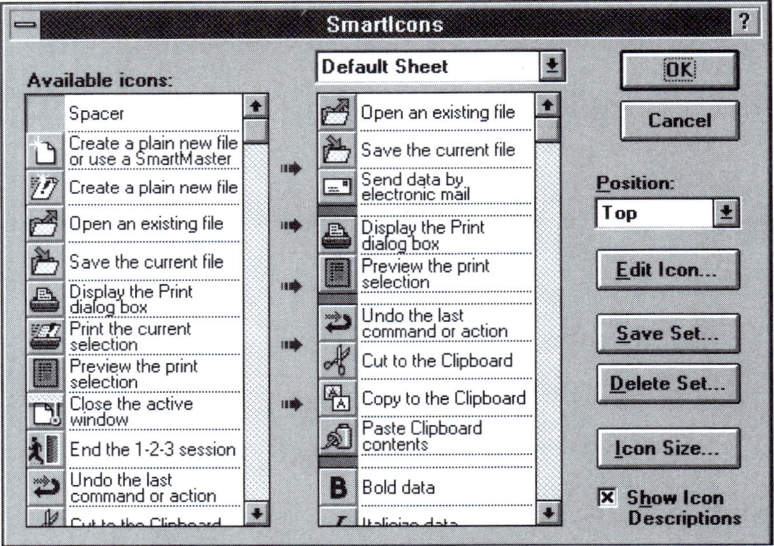

Figure C.1 *SmartIcons dialog box.*

List of SmartIcon Sets

The top of the SmartIcons dialog box says Default Sheet. This tells you which set of SmartIcons Lotus 1-2-3 is currently displaying. If you click on the down arrow with the mouse, a drop-down list will appear, showing you the different sets of SmartIcons currently available (see Figure C.2).

N O T E You can also select the list of SmartIcon sets by clicking on the SmartIcon button on the Status bar at the bottom of your worksheet. The button is the fifth section from the right on the Status bar. If you click on this, a pop-up list of the SmartIcon sets will appear, allowing you to quickly and easily select a different set.

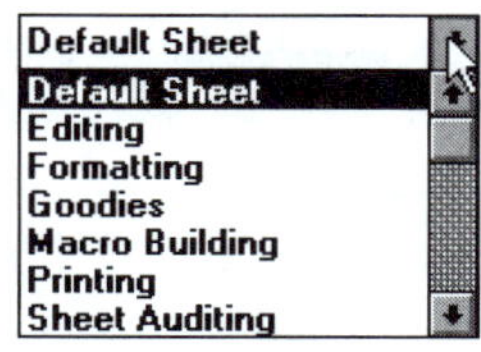

Figure C.2 *SmartIcon sets.*

You will notice that Lotus 1-2-3 comes with a variety of pre-defined SmartIcon sets. It is helpful to use different sets when you are performing different functions. For example, you may want to use the Editing set when you are editing your worksheet. This set contains more SmartIcons for cutting, pasting, inserting, deleting, etc. Similarly, if you are formatting your worksheet, you may want to use the Formatting set, which contains more SmartIcons for font styles, number styles, cell alignment, etc.

N O T E When a cell or range is selected, an easy way to change the active SmartIcon Set is to click on the respective section on the Status Bar (see Figure C.3). A pop-up list will appear and you can select the SmartIcon Set you want to be displayed. The set you choose appears whenever a cell or range is selected, at least until you choose another set. It does not affect the icon set that is displayed when you select a drawing, chart, or map; those sets cannot be changed. However, no matter what type of object is selected, you can hide the Button bar altogether by choosing Hide SmartIcons from the pop-up list.

Creating New SmartIcon Sets

In addition to the pre-defined SmartIcon sets, you may wish to define your own SmartIcons. Below the name of the current set, Lotus 1-2-3 has two lists of

SmartIcons. On the left, Lotus 1-2-3 displays the entire list of available SmartIcons which you may use (Available List). On the right, Lotus 1-2-3 displays the SmartIcons currently used in that set (Set List).

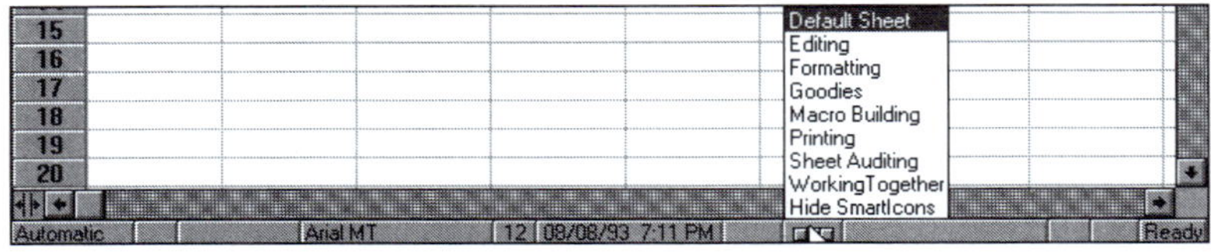

Figure C.3 *Pop-up SmartIcon Set list on the status bar.*

To add a SmartIcon to the set:

1. Find the SmartIcon which you want from the **Available List.**
2. Click and hold the mouse button on the icon you want.
3. Drag the mouse from the **Available List** to the **Set List.**
4. Release the mouse when the icon is over the **Set List.**

Lotus 1-2-3 will insert the SmartIcon into the set where you release the mouse button. For example, if you drag a SmartIcon from the Available List to the Set List so that it is on top of the Open and Save icons, Lotus 1-2-3 will insert the new SmartIcon between these two icons.

N O T E

To remove a SmartIcon from a set:

1. Find the SmartIcon you want to remove from the **Set List.**
2. Click and hold the mouse button down on the icon you want.
3. Drag the mouse from the set list to the **Available List.**
4. Release the mouse when the icon is over the **Available List.**

Unlike adding SmartIcons to a set, when you remove the icon, it does not matter where you are in the Available List when you release the mouse button.

N O T E

Saving a SmartIcon Set

Once you have removed the old SmartIcons and added the new ones you want for your set, save them by clicking on the Save Set button. When you do this, Lotus 1-2-3 will ask you to name this set the file. The set name is the name which Lotus 1-2-3 will display when it lists all available SmartIcon sets. The file name is the name which Lotus 1-2-3 will use to save this icon set to your hard drive. It is often useful to choose a name which is similar to the set name, because this will help you remember which file belongs to which set.

NOTE

Remember that you only have eight characters for the file name. However, you are not limited by the DOS file name structure when you are naming the set. Therefore, the names you use for the set and the file may not be identical, but that is okay.

WARNING

Do not use the same name for your set or file as that of a currently existing set or file.

Position of SmartIcon Bar

We have already noticed that, by default, Lotus 1-2-3 displays the SmartIcon Button bar directly below the Edit Line. However, you are not limited to this location. You may set Lotus 1-2-3 to display the bar at the top, bottom, left, or right of the screen. Also, you may create a floating Button bar which can be placed anywhere on the screen. If you click on the down arrow below Position:, the following drop-down list will appear, (see Figure C.4).

From this list, you can select the location of the SmartIcon Button bar. If you select **Floating,** Lotus 1-2-3 will create a small window which contains your icons. You can drag this window to any location on your screen. If you choose any of the other options, Lotus 1-2-3 will automatically place the Button bar in the specified location.

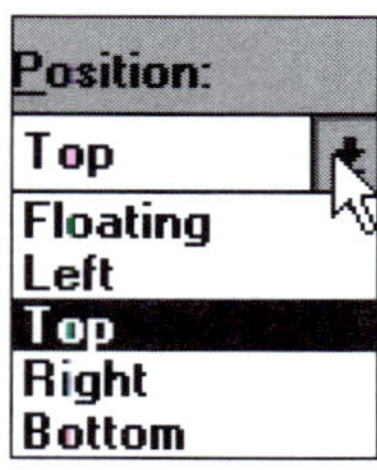

Figure C.4 *Position of SmartIcons.*

Editing Icons

Although each of the icons for the SmartIcons is designed to graphically represent its respective command, you may want to edit the icons which Lotus 1-2-3 uses for your SmartIcons. To edit an icon, click on the **Edit Icon** button and the Edit Icon dialog box will open (see Figure C.5).

In this dialog box you can use the mouse as a paint brush to alter the icons, pixel by pixel. You can change the colors by clicking on a color from the list.

You can select different colors for the left and right mouse buttons by clicking on the desired colors with the respective mouse button.

You can save the icon by clicking on the **Save As** button or create a new icon by clicking on the **New Icon** button. Also, if you create an icon in a different program (i.e., a paint program), you can copy it to the Clipboard, and paste it into Lotus 1-2-3 by clicking on the **Paste Icon** button.

SmartIcons work by assigning macros to these icons. If you are good with macros, you can create your own SmartIcons by editing an icon and adding your desired macro in the Enter Macro Here: box.

Finally, in the Description: box, you can add or change the description associated with the particular icon. This description appears in the list of available SmartIcons as well as in the bubble that pops up when you move the mouse pointer over the icon on the Button bar.

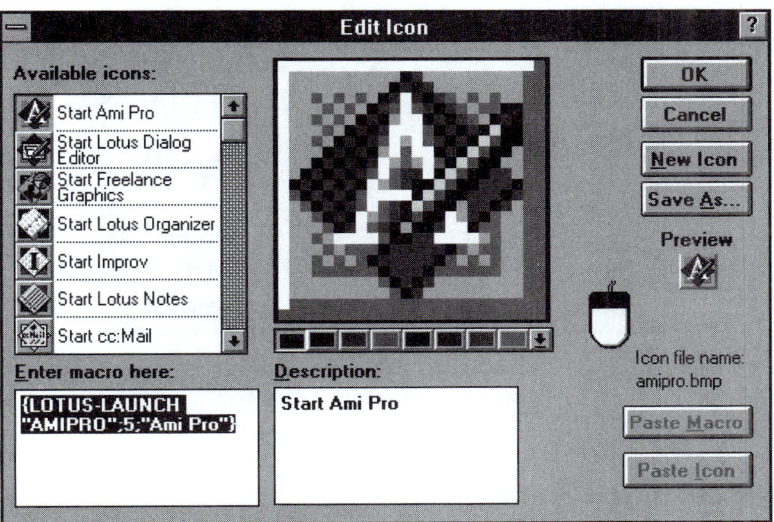

Figure C.5 *Edit Icon dialog box.*

Icon Size

Another option in the SmartIcons dialog box is to change the size of the SmartIcons. In your Button bar, the icons, by default, are displayed at medium size. With the icons at this size, you can have access to more SmartIcons on your Button bar. However, you may find that these icons are too small to work with. If this is the case, you may wish to increase the size of the SmartIcons. To do so, click on the **Icon Size** button in the SmartIcons dialog box. The Icon Size dialog box will open (see Figure C.6).

To change the size of the icon, just click on the radio button to the left of the size you want. When you are finished, click **OK**.

This option will change all the icons in the Button bar. You cannot change individual icons in the bar.

N O T E

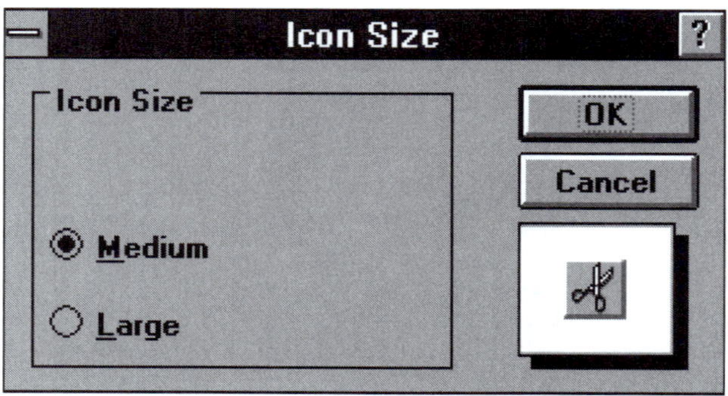

Figure C.6 *Icon Size dialog box.*

List of SmartIcons

The following is a list of the available SmartIcons in Lotus 1-2-3 Release 4 with their respective descriptions.

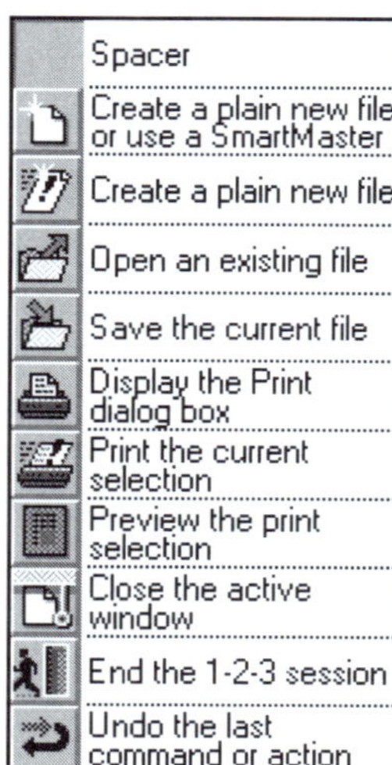
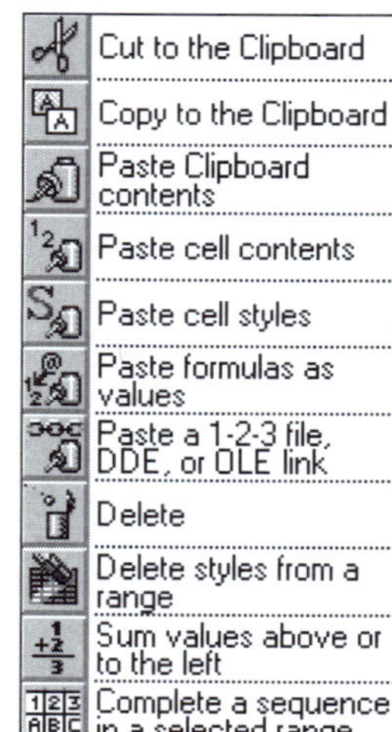
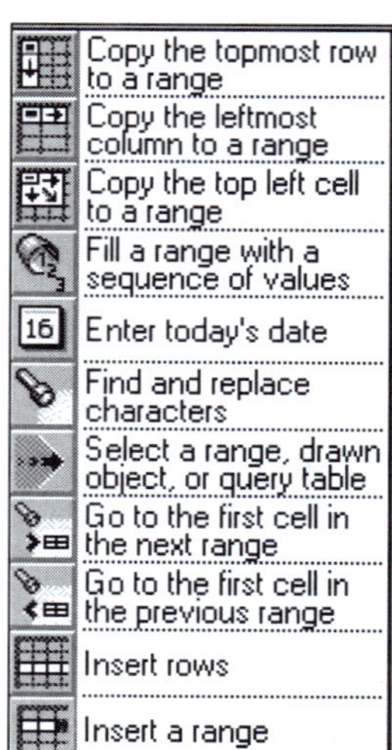

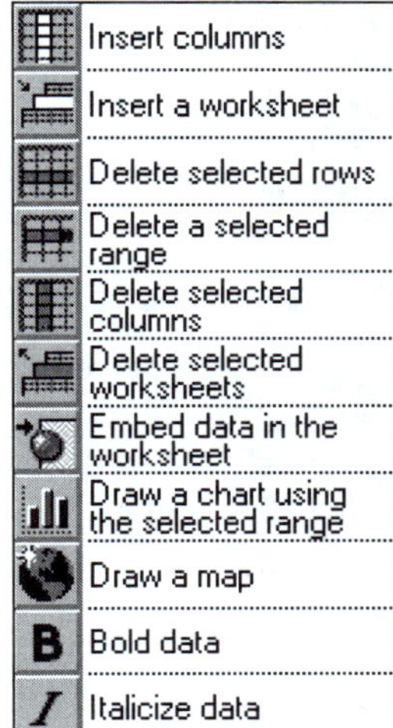

	Insert columns
	Insert a worksheet
	Delete selected rows
	Delete a selected range
	Delete selected columns
	Delete selected worksheets
	Embed data in the worksheet
	Draw a chart using the selected range
	Draw a map
B	Bold data
I	Italicize data

U	Underline data
U	Double underline data
N	Remove bold, italics, and underline
	Change font and attributes
	Select a style template
	Copy a range's styles to other ranges
	Define or apply a named style
	Set color, pattern, border, and frame
	Add a range border and drop shadow
	Add a border to a range
	Align data to the left

	Center data
	Align data to the right
	Space data evenly
	Center text across columns
	Rotate data in a range
	Size columns to fit widest entries
0,0	Display values in Comma format
%	Display values in Percent format
	Display values in the default currency
	Create and delete range names
	Work with versions and scenarios

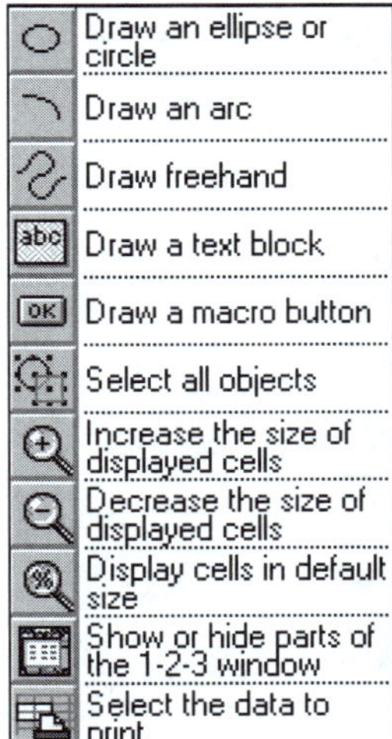

	Transpose a range in place
	Sort in ascending order
	Sort in descending order
	Select several objects
	Draw a forward-pointing arrow
	Draw a double-headed arrow
	Draw a line
	Draw a segmented line
	Draw a polygon
	Draw a rectangle or square
	Draw a rounded rectangle or square

	Draw an ellipse or circle
	Draw an arc
	Draw freehand
abc	Draw a text block
ok	Draw a macro button
	Select all objects
	Increase the size of displayed cells
	Decrease the size of displayed cells
	Display cells in default size
	Show or hide parts of the 1-2-3 window
	Select the data to print

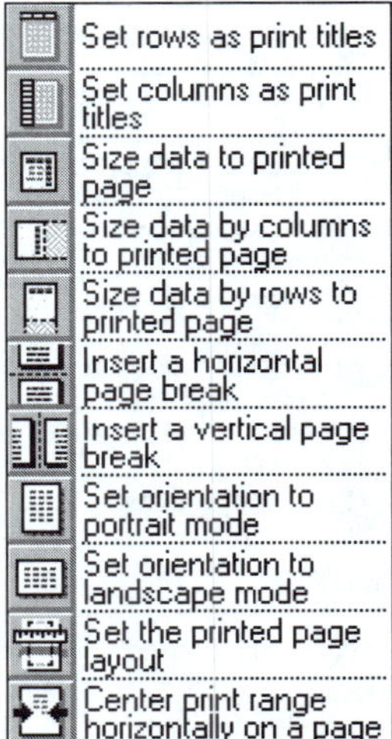

	Set rows as print titles
	Set columns as print titles
	Size data to printed page
	Size data by columns to printed page
	Size data by rows to printed page
	Insert a horizontal page break
	Insert a vertical page break
	Set orientation to portrait mode
	Set orientation to landscape mode
	Set the printed page layout
	Center print range horizontally on a page

	Center print range vertically on a page
	Center print range on a page
	Turn macro recording on or off
	Run a macro
	Select a macro command
	Turn Trace mode on or off
	Turn Step mode on or off
	Show or hide the Transcript window
	Create a query table
	Cross-tabulate values from a database table
?=	Find solutions that meet constraints

ABC	Check spelling
	Send data by electronic mail
	Arrange open windows side by side
	Arrange open windows diagonally
	Go to top left cell
	Find bottom right corner of active area
	Find next cell up adjoining blank cell
	Find next cell down adjoining blank cell
	Find next cell right adjoining blank cell
	Find next cell left adjoining blank cell
	Go to the next worksheet

	Go to the previous worksheet
	Display contiguous worksheets
	Recalculate the worksheet
	Audit cells
	Find formulas
	Find cell dependents
	Find formula precedents
	Find DDE links
	Find links to 1-2-3 files
	Customize SmartIcons
	Select the next set of SmartIcons

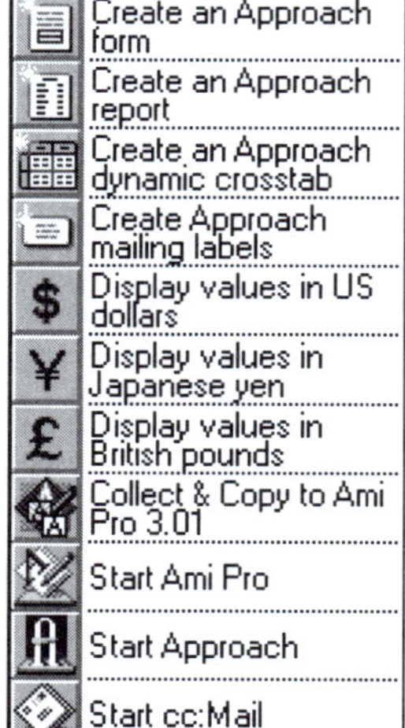

	Create an Approach form
	Create an Approach report
	Create an Approach dynamic crosstab
	Create Approach mailing labels
$	Display values in US dollars
¥	Display values in Japanese yen
£	Display values in British pounds
	Collect & Copy to Ami Pro 3.01
	Start Ami Pro
	Start Approach
	Start cc:Mail

	Start Lotus Dialog Editor
	Display the DOS prompt
	Start File Manager
	Start Freelance Graphics
	Start Improv
	Start the Macro Translator
	Start Lotus Notes
	Start Lotus Organizer
	Start SmartPics
	Set map redraw for this file to automatic
	Set map redraw for this file to manual

	Start Lotus ScreenCam
	Redraw all maps in this file

Appendix D

Common @ Functions

There are over 200 @ Functions available in Lotus 1-2-3 Release 5. This appendix contains a list of 66 of the more commonly used @ Functions. After each @Function name is a brief description of the purpose of the @Function and an example using that @ Function.

We will only look at the required arguments. The optional arguments have been listed but are not discussed. For more information about these or any other @ Functions, refer to Lotus 1-2-3's built-in **NOTE** Help feature.

@ABS(X)

@ABS calculates the absolute value of X. X can be a data value entered into the @ Function or it can be a cell reference. For example, suppose you want cell C1 to contain the absolute value of the result of the formula in cell B1. Your @Function would look as follows:

```
@ABS(B1)
```

437

@AVG(List)

@AVG calculates the average or the mean of a range of cells. For example, suppose you want cell B10 to average the values in B1—B9. Your @Function would look as follows:

```
@AVG(B1—B9)
```

@BINOMIAL(Trials;Successes;Probability;[Type])

@BINOMIAL calculates the binomial probability of getting a certain number of successes in a certain number of trials where you know the probability of getting a success. Trials can be any integer. Success can be any integer less than or equal to Trials. Probability is a number between zero and one. For example, suppose you want to get the binomial probability of three successes in ten trials where the probability of getting a success is 25%. Your @Function would look as follows:

```
@BINOMIAL(10,3,.25)
```

@COLS(Range)

@COLS counts the number of columns in a range. For example, suppose you want to know the number of columns included in your worksheet, which spans A1—BY15. Your @Function would look as follows:

```
@COLS(A1—BY15)
```

@COUNT(List)

@COUNT counts the number of non-blank cells in a range. For example, suppose you want to know the number of cells which contain values of some kind in the range A1—BY15. Your @Function would look as follows:

```
@COUNT(A1—BY15)
```

@DATE(Year;Month;Day)

@DATE calculates the respective date number for a given date. Year is an integer between zero (1990) and 199 (2099). Month is an integer between one and 12. Day is an integer between one and 31 (or as many days in the month, i.e. 28, 29, or 30) For example, suppose you want to know the number which corresponds to April 16, 1968. Your @Function would look as follows:

```
@DATE(68;4;16)
```

@DATEDIF(Start_Date;End_Date;Format)

@DATEDIF calculates the number of years, months or days between two date numbers. To get the date numbers, use @DATE (above). The different formats are as follows: Y returns the number of years; M returns the number of months; D returns the number of days). For example, suppose you want to know the number of days between April 16, 1968 and November 9, 1970. Your @Function would look as follows:

```
@DATEDIF(@DATE(68;4;16);@DATE(70;11;9);ÒDÓ)
```

@DATEVALUE(Text)

@DATEVALUE calculates the number value for a date if the date was entered as a text label instead of a number. For example, suppose you want to calculate the date number for April 16, 1968. Your @Function would look as follows:

```
@DATEVALUE(April 16, 1968)
```

@DB(Cost;Salvage;Life;Period)

@DB calculates the depreciation allowance of an asset using the fixed-declining balance method. Cost is the cost of the asset. Salvage estimates the value of the asset at the end of its useful life. Life is the number of periods it takes to depreciate the asset to its salvage value. Period is the time period for which you want to find the depreciation allowance. Life and Period must be expressed in the same units. For example, suppose you want to find the depreciation allowance for a car in the third year of a five-year useful life, where the cost of the car was $15,000 and the salvage value is $5,000. Your @Function would look as follows:

```
@DB(15000;5000;5;3)
```

@DDB(Cost;Salvage;Life;Period)

@DDB calculates the depreciation allowance of an asset using the double-declining balance method. Cost is the cost of the asset. Salvage estimates the value of the asset at the end of its useful life. Life is the number of periods it takes to depreciate the asset to its salvage value. Period is the time period for which you want to find the depreciation allowance. Life and Period must be expressed in the same units. For example, suppose you want to find the depreciation allowance for a car in the third year of a five-year useful life, where the cost of the car was $15,000 and the salvage value is $5,000. Your @Function would look as follows:

```
@DDB(15000;5000;5;3)
```

@EVEN(X)

@EVEN rounds the value X away from zero to the nearest even integer. For example, suppose you want to round the value in B1 up to the nearest even integer. Your @Function would look as follows:

```
@EVEN(B1)
```

@EXACT(Text1;Text2)

@EXACT compares two sets of text to see whether they are identical. If the texts match exactly, Lotus 1-2-3 returns a "1." If they do not match exactly, it returns a "0." For example, suppose you want to determine whether the value in B1 is the same as "Balance." Your @Function would look as follows:

```
@EXACT("Balance";B1)
```

@EXP(X)

@EXP calculates the constant e raised to the power X. For example, suppose you want to calculate e^2. Your @Function would look as follows:

```
@EXP(2)
```

@FACT(N)

@FACT calculates the factorial of N. For example, suppose you want to calculate 8! Your @Function would look as follows:

```
@FACT(8)
```

@FV(Payments;Interest;Term)

@FV calculates the future value of a series of equal payments earning a specific interest rate over a period of time. The unit of time used to calculate the term and interest must be the same. For example, suppose you want to know the future value of $1000 paid monthly for ten years at an interest rate of 5% per year. Your @Function would look as follows:

```
@FV(1000;.05/12;10*12)
```

@GRANDTOTAL(List)

@GRANDTOTAL sums the cells in a range which contain @SUBTOTAL. For example, suppose you want to find the net total for your worksheet in range A1—H25 and there are @SUBTOTAL formulas in cells A10—H10 and A25—H25. Your @Function would look as follows:

```
@GRANDTOTAL(A1—H25)
```

@IF(Condition;X;Y)

@IF evaluates a condition and returns X if the condition is true and Y if the condition is false. For example, suppose you want the cell to be 10% if B1 is less than $10,000 or 5% if B1 is greater than or equal to $10,000. Your @Function would look as follows:

```
@IF(B1<10000;.1;.05)
```

@INT(X)

@INT returns the integer portion of a value. For example, suppose you want the cell to equal the integer of the value in B3. Your @Function would look as follows:

```
@INT(B3)
```

@ISERR(X)

@ISERR tests for the value ERR. Lotus 1-2-3 returns the value "1" if X is the value ERR, or it returns "0" if X is not the value ERR. For example, suppose you want to know if there is an error in cell B3. Your @Function would look as follows:

```
@ISERR(B3)
```

@ISNA(X)

@ISNA tests for the value NA. Lotus 1-2-3 returns the value "1" if X is the value NA, or "0" if X is not the value NA. For example, suppose you want to know if there is the value NA in cell B3. Your @Function would look as follows:

```
@ISNA(B3)
```

@ISNUMBER(X)

@ISNUMBER tests for a value, NA, ERR, or a blank cell. Lotus 1-2-3 returns the value "1" if X is one of the above, or it returns "0" if X is text. For example, suppose you want to know if there is a number in cell B3. Your @Function would look as follows:

    @ISNUMBER(B3)

@ISSTRING(X)

@ISSTRING tests for text or a label. Lotus 1-2-3 returns the value "1" if X is text or a label, or "0" if X is a value, NA, ERR, or a blank cell. For example, suppose you want to know if there is a label in cell B3. Your @Function would look as follows:

    @ISSTRING(B3)

@LARGE(Range;N)

@LARGE finds the Nth largest value in a range. For example, suppose you want to find the eighth largest number in the range A1—C30. Your @Function would look as follows:

    @LARGE(A1—C30;8)

@LEFT(Text;N)

@LEFT copies a designated number of characters, N, beginning with the left-most character, into another cell. For example, suppose you want to have the first five characters of the text in cell B2 repeated in cell C2. Your @Function would look as follows:

    @LEFT(B2;5)

@LENGTH(Text)

@LENGTH counts the number of characters in a string of text. For example, suppose you want to know how many characters of text are in cell B2. Your @Function would look as follows:

```
@LENGTH(B2)
```

@LN(X)

@LN calculates the natural logarithm, base e, of X, any number greater than zero. For example, suppose you want to calculate the natural logarithm of two. Your @Function would look as follows:

```
@LN(2)
```

@LOG(X)

@LOG calculates the common logarithm, base ten, of X, any number greater than zero. For example, suppose you want to calculate the common logarithm of two. Your @Function would look as follows:

```
@LOG(2)
```

@LOWER(Text)

@LOWER converts all characters in a text string to lower case. For example, suppose you want to change the text in cell B2 to lower case. Your @Function would look as follows:

```
@LOWER(B2)
```

@MAX(List)

@MAX finds the largest value in a selected range. For example, suppose you want to find the largest value in B2—C3. Your @Function would look as follows:

```
@MAX(B2—C3)
```

@MEDIAN(List)

@MEDIAN finds the median value in a selected range. For example, suppose you want to find the median value in B2—C3. Your @Function would look as follows:

```
@MEDIAN(B2—C3)
```

@MID(Text;Start_Number;N)

@MID copies a designated number of characters, N, from one cell into another, beginning with a specified character. For example, suppose you want to copy the fifth through 12th characters from cell B2 into cell C3. Your @Function would look as follows:

```
@MID(B2;5;8)
```

@MIN(List)

@MIN finds the smallest value in a selected range. For example, suppose you want to find the smallest value in B2—C3. Your @Function would look as follows:

```
@MIN(B2—C3)
```

@NOW

@NOW returns the date and time which corresponds to your computers clock. Your @Function would look as follows:

```
@NOW
```

@NPV(Interest;Range)

@NPV calculates the net present value of future cash flows given a fixed interest rate. Suppose that you want to determine the value today of the salaries you will receive for the next 15 years, which are listed in the range A10—A24, at an interest rate of 5% per year. Your @Function would look as follows:

```
@NPV(.05;A10—A24)
```

@ODD(X)

@ODD rounds the value X away from zero to the nearest odd integer. For example, suppose you want to round the value in B1 up to the nearest odd integer. Your @Function would look as follows:

```
@ODD(B1)
```

@PI

@PI returns the value for the constant pi. Your @Function would look as follows:

```
@PI
```

@PMT(Principal;Interest;Term)

@PMT calculates the payment of a loan, given a specified interest rate and a specified number of payment periods. For example, suppose you want to calculate the monthly payment for a 15-year, $80,000 mortgage at 10% interest per year. Your @Function would look as follows:

```
@PMT(80000;.1/12;15*12)
```

@PRODUCT(List)

@PRODUCT multiplies the values in a specified range. For example, suppose you want to know the product of cells B2—C3. Your @Function would look as follows:

```
@PRODUCT(B2—C3)
```

@PROPER(Text)

@PROPER capitalizes the first letter of each word in a selected cell and converts the remainder of the letters to lower case. For example, suppose you want the first letter of each word in cells B2 and B3 capitalized and combined in cell C2. Your @Function in C2 would look as follows:

```
@PROPER(B2&" "&B3)
```

@PV(Payments;Interest;Term)

@PV calculates the present value of an investment based on a series of equal payments, discounted at a specified interest rate for a given period of time. For example, suppose you want to know the value today of $25,000 paid yearly for 15 years when the interest rate is 8%. Your @Function would look as follows:

```
@PV(25000;.08;15)
```

@QUOTIENT(X;Y)

@QUOTIENT calculates the result of X divided by Y. The result is truncated to an integer. For example, suppose you want to know the quotient of 395 divided by 4. Your @Function would look as follows:

```
@QUOTIENT(395;4)
```

@RAND

@RAND generates a random number between zero and one. Your @Function would look as follows:

```
@RAND
```

@RANGENAME(Cell)

@RANGENAME returns the name of the range in which the cell is located. For example, suppose you want to know the name you used for the range containing cell B2. Your @Function would look as follows:

```
@RANGENAME(B2)
```

@RATE(Future_Value;Present_Value;Term)

@RATE calculates the interest rate necessary for an investment today to grow to a specified future value over a certain time period. For example, suppose you want to know at what interest rate you need to invest $10,000 to yield $12,200 in two years. Your @Function would look as follows:

```
@RATE(12200;10000;2)
```

@REPEAT(Text;N)

@REPEAT duplicates selected text N times. For example, suppose you want the text in cell B2 repeated five times in cell C2. Your @Function would look as follows:

```
@REPEAT(B2;5)
```

@REPLACE(Original_Text;Start_Number;N; New_Text;TR8)

@REPLACE replaces N characters in original text with new text beginning at a specified character number. For example, suppose you wanted to replace the fifth through tenth characters in cell B2 with the word ÒIncome.Ó Your @Function would look as follows:

```
@REPLACE(B2;5;6;ÒIncomeÓ)
```

@RIGHT(Text;N)

@RIGHT copies a designated number of characters, N, beginning with the right-most character, into another cell. For example, suppose you want to have the last five characters of the text in cell B2 repeated in cell C2. Your @Function would look as follows:

```
@RIGHT(B2;5)
```

@ROUND(X;N)

@ROUND rounds the value X to the nearest power of ten specified by N. If N is positive, Lotus 1-2-3 rounds the decimal portion of the number. If N is negative, Lotus 1-2-3 rounds the integer portion of the number. If N is zero, Lotus 1-2-3 rounds to the nearest integer. For example, if you wanted to round the value in cell B2 to the nearest integer, your @Function would look as follows:

```
@ROUND(B2;0)
```

@ROUNDDOWN(X;[N;Direction])

@ROUNDDOWN rounds the value X down to the nearest power of ten specified by N. If N is positive, Lotus 1-2-3 rounds the decimal portion of the number. If N is negative, Lotus 1-2-3 rounds the integer portion of the number. If N is zero,

Lotus 1-2-3 rounds to the nearest integer. For example, if you wanted to round the value in cell B2 down to the nearest hundredth, your @Function would look as follows:

```
@ROUNDDOWN(B2;2)
```

@ROUNDUP(X;[N;Direction])

@ROUNDUP rounds the value X up to the nearest power of ten specified by N. If N is positive, Lotus 1-2-3 rounds the decimal portion of the number. If N is negative, Lotus 1-2-3 rounds the integer portion of the number. If N is zero, Lotus 1-2-3 rounds to the nearest integer. For example, if you wanted to round the value in cell B2 up to the nearest hundred, your @Function would look as follows:

```
@ROUND(B2;-2)
```

@ROWS(Range)

@ROWS counts the number of rows in a range. For example, you want to know the number of rows included in your worksheet which spans A1—BY15. Your @Function would look as follows:

```
@ROWS(A1—BY15)
```

@SIGN(X)

@SIGN returns a "1" if X is positive, "0" if X is zero, and "-1" if X is negative. Your @Function would look as follows:

```
@SIGN(B2)
```

@SLN(Cost;Salvage;Life)

@SLN calculates the depreciation allowance of an asset using the straight line method. Cost is the cost of the asset. Salvage estimates the value of the asset at the end of its useful life. Life is the number of periods it takes to depreciate the asset to its salvage value. For example, suppose you want to find the depreciation allowance for a car with a five-year useful life, where the cost of the car was $15,000 and the salvage value is $5,000. Your @Function would look as follows:

```
@SLN(15000;5000;5)
```

@SMALL(Range;N)

@SMALL finds the Nth smallest value in a range. For example, suppose you want to find the fifth smallest number in the range A1—C30. Your @Function would look as follows:

```
@SMALL(A1—C30;5)
```

@SQRT(X)

@SQRT returns the positive square root of X. Your @Function would look as follows:

```
@SQRT(B2)
```

@STD(List)

@STD calculates the standard deviation of a specified range. For example, suppose you want to find the standard deviation of the range B1—B9. Your @Function would look as follows:

```
@STD(B1—B9)
```

@STRING(X;N)

@STRING converts the data value to a text label with N decimal places. For example, suppose you want to place the number in cell B2 into cell C2 as a text label with two decimal places. Your @Function would look as follows:

```
@STRING(B2;2)
```

@SUBTOTAL(List)

@SUBTOTAL sums the values in a range of cells. @SUBTOTALs can later be added using @GRANDTOTAL. For example, suppose you want to sum the range A1—A9. Your @Function would look as follows:

```
@SUBTOTAL(A1—A9)
```

@SUM(List)

@SUM adds the values in a specified range. For example, suppose you want to sum the values in B1—B9. Your @Function would look as follows:

```
@SUM(B1—B9)
```

@SUMSQ(List)

@SUMSQ calculates the sum of the squares of the values in a specified range. For example, suppose you want the values in C1—C9 squared and then added together. Your @Function would look as follows:

```
@SUMSQ(C1—C9)
```

@SUMXMY2(Range1;Range2)

@SUMXMY2 subtracts the values in Range 2 from the values in Range 1, squares the differences, and then sums those results. Your @Function would look as follows:

```
@SUMXMY2(B1—B9;C1—C9)
```

@TERM(Payments;Interest;Future_Value)

@TERM calculates the number of periods required for a series of equal payments to yield a specified future value at a given interest rate. For example, suppose you want to know how many years it will take for $1,000 paid yearly to equal $12,200 if the interest rate is 8%. Your @Function would look as follows:

```
@TERM(1000;.08;12200)
```

@TRUNC(X;[N])

@TRUNC truncates the value X to N decimal places. If N is positive, Lotus 1-2-3 truncates the decimal portion of the number. If N is negative, Lotus 1-2-3 truncates the integer portion of the number. If N is zero, Lotus 1-2-3 truncates to the nearest integer. For example, suppose you want to truncate the value in B2 to the nearest hundredth. Your @Function would look as follows:

```
@TRUNC(B2;2)
```

@UPPER(Text)

@UPPER converts all characters in a text string to upper case. For example, suppose you want to change the text in cell B2 to upper case. Your @Function would look as follows:

```
@UPPER(B2)
```

@VALUE(Text)

@VALUE converts a number entered as text to its corresponding data value. For example, suppose B2 contained a label which was a number and you want to convert it into a data value. Your @Function would look as follows:

```
@VALUE(B2)
```

@VAR(List)

@VAR calculates the variance of a specified range. For example, suppose you want to find the variance of the range B1—B9. Your @Function would look as follows:

```
@VAR(B1—B9)
```

Appendix E

Working with Windows

In this appendix we will discuss Windows, an operating environment that makes DOS user-friendly. We will cover the components of Windows and how to move or change the size of a window to suit your preference.

Window Components

Windows is an operating environment that runs on top of DOS. It creates what is called a user-friendly graphical interface. In layman's terms, that means it is easy to use because all the commands and functions are right on the screen. Instead of being required to memorize a series of keyboard commands, Windows lets you see what you are doing in a picture form that makes sense. And you can use a mouse to interact with and control it.

To start Windows, enter the command **WIN** at the DOS command prompt. You will see a title screen first. After a pause while Windows loads your data, your electronic desktop appears. On the desktop, you see windows and icons that represent the various applications you have installed.

Using Your Mouse

Since your mouse is your most important way of interacting with Windows, you should be familiar with the four primary mouse actions. When you work with the mouse, there is a small drawing on your screen, called the mouse pointer, that shows you where you are. The mouse pointer frequently looks like an outlined arrow, but it might take other shapes as well, depending on what you're working on. To click an object, you move the mouse so that the pointer is positioned over the object, then you click the left button once. Just tap the button to click it. You should press hard or hold it down.

If you prefer to use your mouse with your left hand, Windows lets you swap your mouse buttons so that you click with the right button instead of the left. See your Windows manuals for details.

N O T E

Sometimes you are instructed to *double-click* an object. You do this by positioning the pointer over the object and clicking twice in rapid succession. Again, you don't have to press hard. A couple of light taps on the button should do it.

Occasionally, you are asked to click with the right button instead of the left. In Lotus 1-2-3 Release 5, you click the right mouse button to pop up quick menus anywhere on the screen.

Many functions can be accomplished by *dragging*. To drag an item, position the pointer over it, **press** *and hold* the left mouse button down, and move the pointer. As long as you hold the mouse button down, the item moves with the pointer. Usually, you see an outline or a shadow move rather than the item itself. When you reach the place where you want to drop the item, just release the mouse button.

Window Features

Your data and programs in a Windows program appear on the screen in the form of a Window. Let's examine Windows so that you can begin to navigate your way around a Windows program (see Figure E.1).

Before we discuss Windows functions, you should be familiar with how to adjust the shape and size of your window.

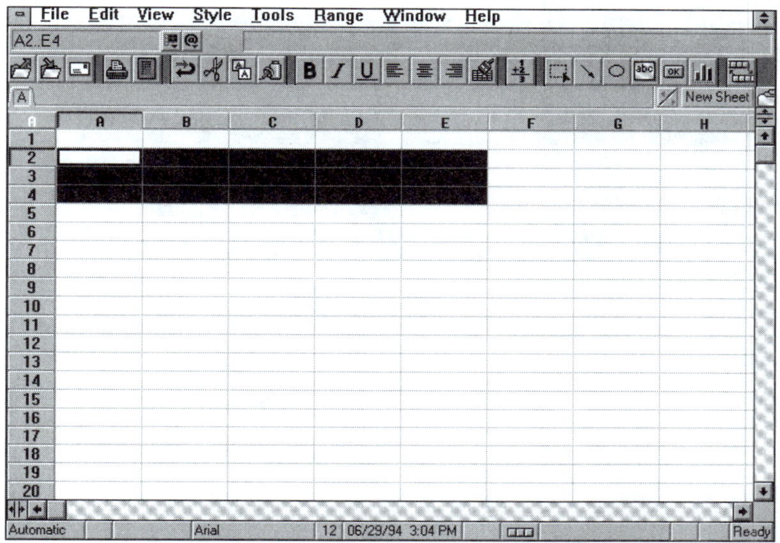

Figure E.1 *A window.*

In the top left corner of any window is a dash (—) called the *control-menu box*. If you click the dash, a menu appears with commands that let you control the window's size, location, and so on. A quick way to close most windows is to double-click the control-menu box.

In the top right corner of a window are two arrows. They also control the size of the window; clicking on the up arrow can maximize the window size, while clicking on the down arrow can minimize it. *Maximizing* a window expands it so that it takes up the entire area. You won't be able to see any other windows simultaneously, but you'll be able to see the largest amount of data possible in the maximized window. When you're working on a large spreadsheet, for example, it makes sense to maximize the window so you can see as many cells as possible. When you maximize a window, the Up arrow becomes a double arrow; click the double arrow to restore the window to its unmaximized size.

Minimizing a window reduces it to an icon and parks it in the lower left corner of your screen. This gets the window out of the way for a while while you work on something else. To restore the window to its former size, double-click the icon.

You can also manually change a window's size and shape. There are three ways of doing this. First, you can use the mouse to move the pointer to the border on the side of the window. Notice that the pointer changes shape (see Figure E.2). Dragging the border makes the window wider or narrower.

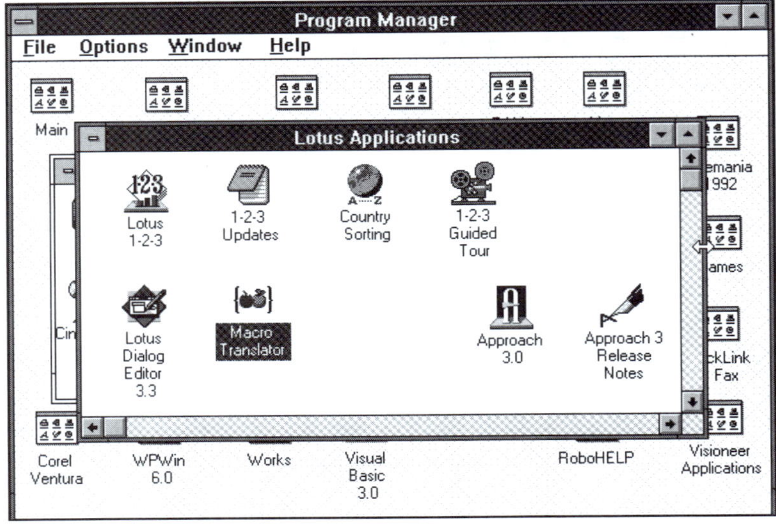

Figure E.2 *Making a window wider or narrower.*

Another way to change the shape of your window is to move the pointer to the top or bottom edge of the window. Again, the pointer changes (see Figure E.3), and dragging the border makes the window taller or shorter.

Finally, you can move the pointer any corner of the window. Once more, you should notice how the cursor changes shape (see Figure E.4). Dragging a corner makes both dimensions of the window larger or smaller while retaining their proportions. You can make your window small or large, rectangular or square, depending on your preference.

You can also move your windows. To do this, position the pointer over the title bar of a window—the very top bar on the window, which gives a name to the window. Next, click the left button of the mouse, hold it down, and drag the window to the desired location.

You can have many windows open at once on your desktop, but only one at a time can be active. The active window contains the cursor, and this is where you are currently working. To make a window active, just click it. It moves to the top of the pile of windows, perhaps covering over some other windows. If you want to get back to a hidden window, drag the active window out of the way so that you can see the windows that are underneath it.

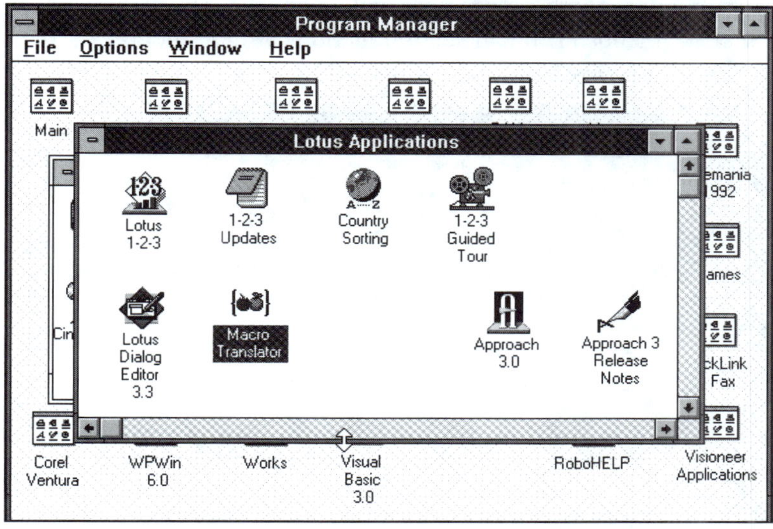

Figure E.3 *Making a window taller or shorter.*

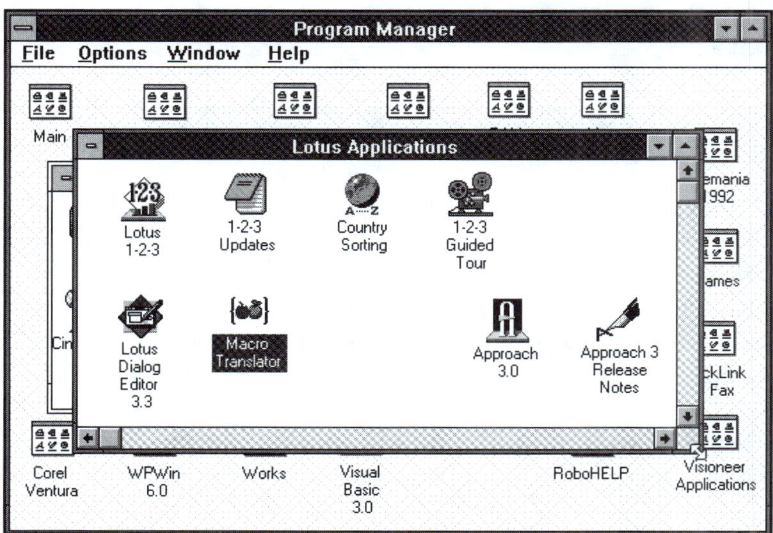

Figure E.4 *Making a window proportionally bigger or smaller.*

Menus

When you're working with a program such as Lotus 1-2-3, its window probably contains a set of menus. You can see the menu bar right underneath the title bar in Figure E.5; it contains eight menus named File, Edit, View, Style, and so on. These are Lotus 1-2-3's menus; another program probably has different menus.

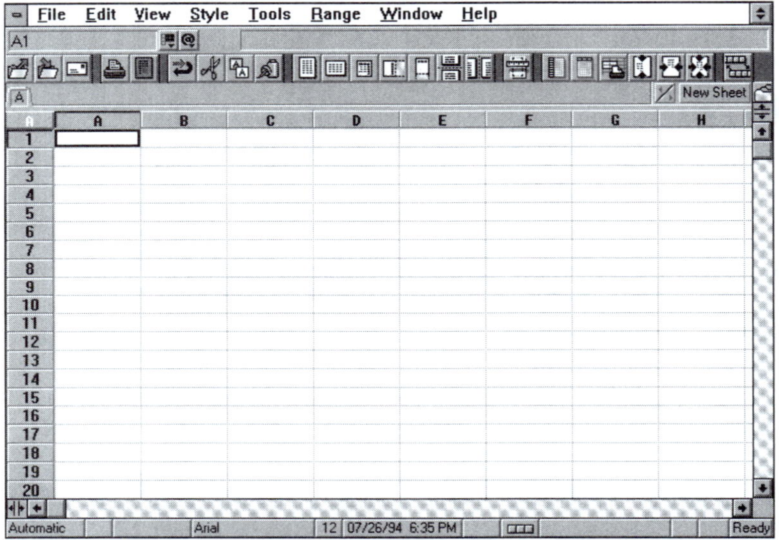

Figure E.5 *Lotus 1-2-3's menu bar.*

You must pull down a menu to see the commands it contains. Click the name in the menu bar to pull it down. Figure E.6 shows the Edit menu pulled down. You click a command to select it.

On the Edit menu, you can see that some commands have key combinations written next to them. These are keyboard shortcuts for those commands. For example, you can execute the Cut command by pressing **Ctrl+X**. (That is, hold down the **Ctrl** key and press the **X** key. Then release both keys.) They are shortcut keys because you don't have to pull down the menu to use them. Just press **Ctrl+X** anywhere in the Lotus 1-2-3 window to execute the Cut command.

Sometimes a command is printed in lighter color on a menu. This means the command is not available at this time. In Figure E.6, Paste Link, Arrange, Copy Down, and Copy Right are not currently available. These commands are not available because they require some condition that is currently not true. For example, Copy Down requires a range to be selected, and there is no range selected currently.

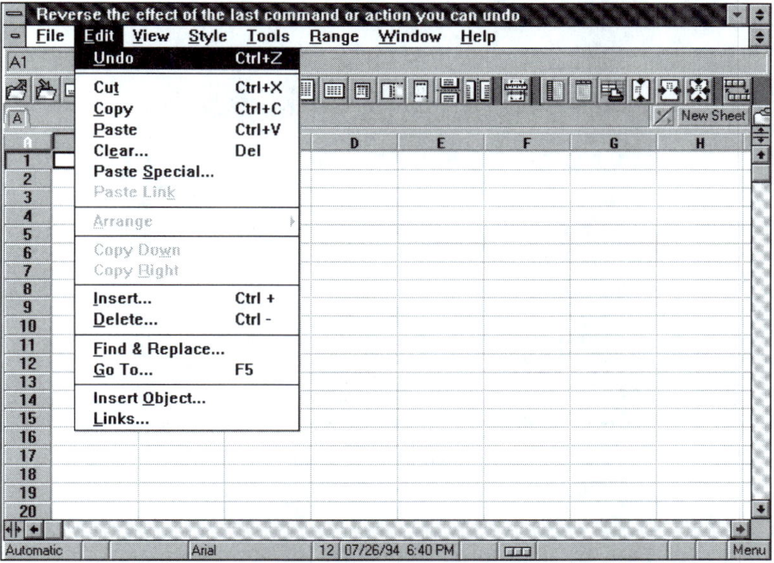

Figure E.6 *Lotus 1-2-3's Edit menu.*

Dialog Boxes

Commands that end in three dots lead to dialog boxes. Figure E.7 shows an example of a dialog box. The purpose of most dialog boxes is to tell you something or to collect information from you. The dialog box in the figure appears when you select the Delete command from the Edit menu. In the dialog box, you must tell Lotus 1-2-3 what you want to delete. You'll learn how to use dialog boxes throughout this book as you learn how to accomplish your worksheet tasks.

Scrolling

A window or box often isn't big enough to display everything it is holding. Then you must scroll to see the entire contents. You scroll with your mouse using a scroll bar. You can see scroll bars at the right side and bottom of the window in Figure E.6. The small square inside the bar is called the scroll box. It shows you where you are within the entire set of information to be displayed. In Figure E.6, you are looking at the top and left portion of the entire worksheet. In other words, you are looking at the beginning of the worksheet.

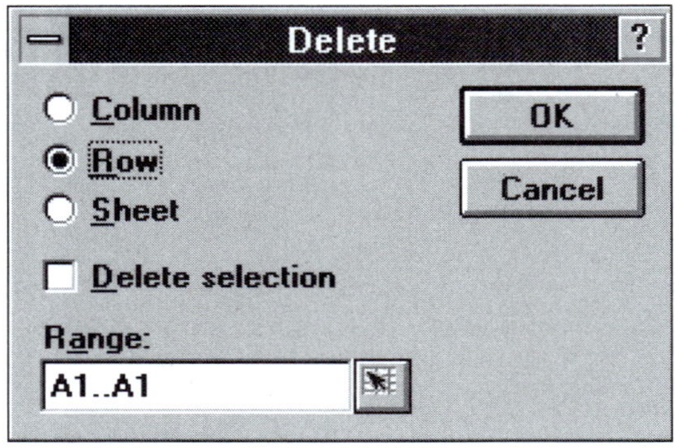

Figure E.7 *Lotus 1-2-3's Delete dialog box*

To scroll down one line at a time, you click the Down arrow at the bottom of the vertical bar. To scroll down one window at a time, click anywhere on the bar below the scroll box. The scroll box moves in the bar as you scroll. To scroll back up again, click the Up arrow or the bar above the scroll box. To scroll longer distances, drag the box up or down.

Use the horizontal scroll bar to scroll left and right in the same manner.

Undo

Many Windows applications include an Undo feature. If you make a mistake or change your mind, you can undo the *last action only* by choosing the **Undo** command. In most applications, Undo is the first command on the Edit menu. In Lotus 1-2-3, for example, if you accidentally delete the data in a cell, you can choose Undo to restore it—but you must do so before you do anything else.

The Help System

Almost all Windows applications include an on-screen Help feature. You can ask for help for a specific task or browse through the Help library in search of information. To ask for help with the task you are working on, just press the **F1** key. Lotus 1-2-3 opens the Help window (see Figure E.8) and selects a help topic for you, depending on where the cursor is. To browse through the Help library on your own, pull down the Help menu and select one of its commands.

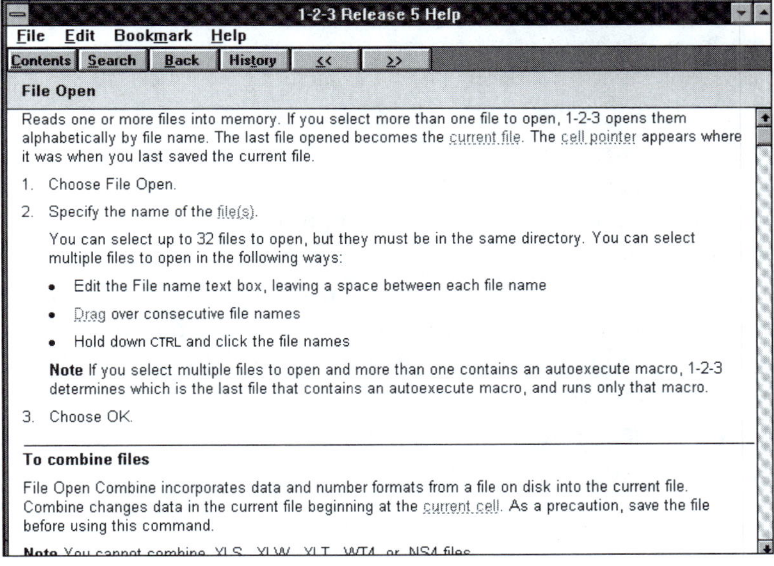

Figure E.8 *The Help window.*

In the Help window, you often have to scroll to read the entire topic. Phrases displayed in a contrasting color are jumps to other topics. If they are underlined in dashes, as you can see in Figure E.8, they pop up a little definition box instead of jumping to another topic. When you're done reading the definition, click anywhere to close the box.

The Help window's menu bar provides such facilities as printing the topic (the File Print command), adding your own notes to the topic (the Edit Annotate command), and marking the topic with an electronic bookmark so you can get back to it easily (the Bookmark Define command).

Directly below the menu bar is a button bar. The Contents button takes you to the table of contents for the application's Help library. From the table of contents, you can choose any topic in the library. The Search button lets you search for topics by contents. For example, if you wanted to find out more about how to resize a window, you might search for any topic about "window size."

The Back button takes you back to the previous topic you viewed. It is common in the Help system to use the jumps, the contents, and the search facility to view several topics in one session. The Help facility remembers all the topics you view, in order. Press the **Back** button to return to previously-viewed topics.

The History button displays your entire list of topics so that you can select a former one to see again. After you have looked at several topics, it is sometimes easier and faster to get back to an earlier one from the History list than by pressing **Back** several times.

The buttons marked << and >> moved backward and forward in the Help library one topic at a time. The order of the topics is determined by the way the library is stored. The program designers usually try to establish a logical order for the topics so that you can move to a related topic by pressing the << or >> button.

To close the Help window, choose the **Exit** command from the File menu or double-click its control-menu box.

Program Manager

The Program Manager contains all your Windows applications. As its name indicates, it manages or organizes all the programs you have installed. Within the Program Manager there are two elements, Program Groups and Program Items. In Figure E.9 the icons in the Program Manager window (which all use the same picture) represent Program Groups. Only one Program Group window is open—the Lotus Applications group. You can see that it contains several Program Items.

When you start up Windows, the Program Manager window is open on your desktop. You will see all your Program Groups. You can double-click a Program Group icon to open its window, where you can see the Program Items it contains. You can think of Program Items as links to programs that you have installed. When you double-click on the icon of a Program Item, it automatically starts up the program associated with that item. For example, to start Lotus 1-2-3 Release 5, you would double-click the icon labeled Lotus 1-2-3.

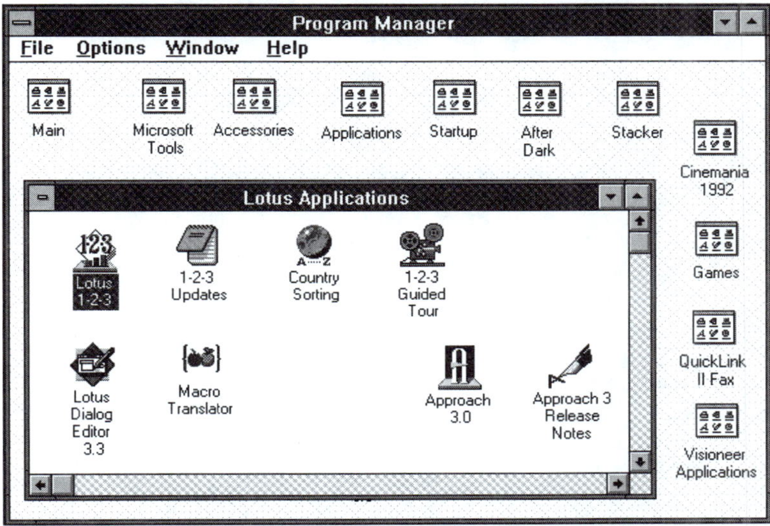

Figure E.9 *Program Groups and Program Items.*

For more information on Program Groups and Items, or about configuring your version of Windows, refer to your Windows manual.

NOTE

Index

Symbols and Numerics

$ (dollar sign), 165-166
& (ampersand), 152
* (asterisk)
  file extension
    wildcards, 20
  as formula result, 155
  as multiplication
    operator, 151
+ (plus sign) addition
  operator, 151
3D area charts
  appearance of, 214
  vs. area charts, 218
3D bar charts
  appearance of, 214
  vs. bar charts, 218
3D line charts
  appearance of, 214
  vs. line charts, 218
3D pie charts
  appearance of, 214
  vs. pie charts, 218
3D ranges, selecting, 57-
  58, 106
; (semicolon), 363, 392
<= (lesser than or equal
  to) operator
  database queries, 349
  logical conditions, 152
<> (not equal to)
  operator
  database queries, 349
  logical conditions, 152
< (less than) operator
  database queries, 349
  logical conditions, 152
= (equal sign)
  beginning formulas
    with, 153, 156
  database query criteria,
    347, 348, 349
  as logical condition,
    152

>= (greater than or equal
  to) operator
  database queries, 349
  logical conditions, 152
> (greater than)
  operator, logical
  conditions, 152
( ) (parentheses)
  @Function arguments,
    169
  negative values in, 419-
    420
  in numeric formulas,
    154
' (apostrophe)
  as alignment character,
    78
  in headers and footers,
    200-201
\ (backslash), 78
{ } (brackets), 363, 392
^ (caret), 78, 151

" (double quotation marks)
  as alignment character, 78
  macro arguments, 393
... (ellipses), 17
- (minus sign)
  subtraction operator, 151
/ (slash) division operator, 151
@ABS(X) function, 437
@AVG function, 438
@BINOMIAL function, 438
@COLS function, 438
@COUNT function, 438
@DATE function, 439
@DATEDIF function, 439
@DATEVALUE function, 439
@DB function, 439-440
@DDB functio, 440
@EVEN function, 440
@EXACT function, 440-441
@EXP function, 441
@FACT function, 441
@Function List, 172-175
@Function Selector feature
  changing @Function categories, 179-180
  edit line, 171-172
  overview, 9
@Functions
  changing categories of, 179-180
  described, 167-171
  list of commonly used, 437-454
  nested, 175

@FV function, 441
@GRANDTOTAL function, 441
@IF function, 442
@IF functions, 175, 424
@INT function, 442
@ISERR function, 442
@ISNA function, 442
@ISNUMBER function, 443
@ISSTRING function, 443
@LARGE function, 443
@LEFT function, 443
@LENGTH function, 444
@LN function, 444
@LOG function, 444
@LOWER function, 444
@MAX function, 445
@MEDIAN function, 445
@MID function, 445
@MIN function, 445
@NOW function, 446
@NPV function, 446
@ODD function, 446
@PI function, 446
@PMT function, 446-447
@PRODUCT function, 447
@PROPER function, 447
@PV function, 447
@QUOTIENT function, 447-448
@RAND function, 448
@RANGENAME function, 448
@RATE function, 448
@REPEAT function, 448
@REPLACE function, 449
@RIGHT function, 449
@ROUND function, 449
@ROUNDDOWN function, 449-450

@ROUNDUP function, 450
@ROWS function, 450
@SIGN function, 450
@SLN function, 450-451
@SMALL function, 451
@SQRT function, 451
@STD function, 451
@STRING function, 451-452
@SUBTOTAL function, 452
@SUM function, 452
@SUMSQ function, 452
@SUMXMY2 function, 452
@TERM function, 453
@TRUNC function, 453
@UPPER function, 453
@VALUE function, 453
@VAR function, 454

A

absolute references, 164-166
activating windows, 458-459
adding. *See also* combining; creating; inserting
  borders, 134-137, 146
  comments to versions, 290
  headings to charts, 229-230
  SmartIcons to sets, 430
  words to user dictionary, 97, 99
addition operator, 151
addresses, cell, 48-49
aligning cell data

customizing default,
418-419
described, 127-131
text, 78
alignment characters, 78
Alignment (Style menu)
command, 128, 145
altering. *See* changing;
editing
ampersand (&), 152
Analyze (Range menu)
command
Backsolver, 317, 331
What-if Table, 320, 332
analyzing data
Backsolver, 317-319,
331-332
scenarios, 309-314
Version Manager, 283-
299
Version Manager Index,
299-305
version reports, 305-
309, 330-331
What-If tables, 320-328
what-if's, 314-317
#AND# logical formula
connector
creating formulas, 153
database queries, 351-
353
apostrophe (')
as alignment character,
78
in headers and footers,
200-201
applying
gallery templates, 142,
148
named styles, 140, 147-
148

arcs, drawing, 251-252,
276
area charts
appearance of, 213
type of data
represented by, 215
arguments
@Function, 169, 316
macro, 363, 392
arithmetic operators, 151
Arrange (Edit menu)
command
fastening drawn objects
to cells, 267, 280
flipping drawn objects,
273, 282
grouping drawn
objects, 269, 280
locking drawn objects,
269, 280
moving drawn objects,
265
rotating objects, 274,
282
arranging drawn objects,
264-266, 279-280
Arrow (Tools menu)
command, 250
arrows
changing, 81, 270-271
drawing, 249-251
assigning macros to
buttons, 387-390, 395
asterisk (*)
file extension
wildcards, 20
as formula result, 155
as multiplication
operator, 151
@ABS(X) function, 437
@AVG function, 438

@BINOMIAL function,
438
@COLS function, 438
@COUNT function, 438
@DATE function, 439
@DATEDIF function, 439
@DATEVALUE function,
439
@DB function, 439-440
@DDB functio, 440
@EVEN function, 440
@EXACT function, 440-
441
@EXP function, 441
@FACT function, 441
@Function List, 172-175
@Function Selector
feature
changing @Function
categories, 179-180
edit line, 171-172
overview, 9
@Functions
changing categories of,
179-180
described, 167-171
list of commonly used,
437-454
nested, 175
@FV function, 441
@GRANDTOTAL
function, 441
@IF function, 442
@IF functions, 175, 424
@INT function, 442
@ISERR function, 442
@ISNA function, 442
@ISNUMBER function,
443
@ISSTRING function, 443
@LARGE function, 443
@LEFT function, 443

@LENGTH function, 444
@LN function, 444
@LOG function, 444
@LOWER function, 444
@MAX function, 445
@MEDIAN function, 445
@MID function, 445
@MIN function, 445
@NOW function, 446
@NPV function, 446
@ODD function, 446
@PI function, 446
@PMT function, 446-447
@PRODUCT function, 447
@PROPER function, 447
@PV function, 447
@QUOTIENT function, 447-448
@RAND function, 448
@RANGENAME function, 448
@RATE function, 448
@REPEAT function, 448
@REPLACE function, 449
@RIGHT function, 449
@ROUND function, 449
@ROUNDDOWN function, 449-450
@ROUNDUP function, 450
@ROWS function, 450
@SIGN function, 450
@SLN function, 450-451
@SMALL function, 451
@SQRT function, 451
@STD function, 451
@STRING function, 451-452
@SUBTOTAL function, 452
@SUM function, 452

@SUMSQ function, 452
@SUMXMY2 function, 452
@TERM function, 453
@TRUNC function, 453
@UPPER function, 453
@VALUE function, 453
@VAR function, 454
Auto Format feature, entering numbers and, 78, 421
AUTOEXEC.BAT file, 402, 405, 408, 410
autoexecute macros, 385, 422
axes, chart X-Y
labels, changing, 232
overview, 212-213
units, changing, 233-234

B

backslash (\), 78
backslash names, 382, 384
Backsolver, 317-319
balloons, SmartIcon help, xxi, 11, 427
bar charts
appearance of, 213
as default Quick Chart type, 226-227
type of data represented by, 216
boldface text. *See* font attributes
borders, 134-137, 146. *See also* Designer Frames
brackets { }, 363, 392
Button bar, SmartIcon

editing, 428
positioning, 431
SmartIcons, xxi
buttons
active, 399
header and footer insert, 199-201
macro, 387-390
Tutorial window, 4

C

calculations
to achieve desired results, 317-319, 320-328
formulas, 150-167
what-if versions, 314-315
canceling. *See also* Undo (Edit menu) command; undoing
data entries, 75-76
edits, 86
range selection function, 53
caret (^)
as alignment character, 78
as exponentiation operator, 151
Cascade (Window menu) command, 35-36
cell addresses,48-49
cell grid lines
customizing display of, 416
hiding, 201-202
cells. *See also* collections of cells; ranges
aligning data within, 78-79, 127-131

behind drawn objects, 261-262

centering data in, 128-129

creating macros in, 368-370

data exceeding width of, 74, 129

fastening drawn objects to, 266-267, 280

formats of, 81

formula results too large for, 155

going to, 61

hiding, 142

moving, 86-88

referencing, in different files, 163-164

row/column references to, 13

running macros on, 386

selecting, 49-58

selection indicator and, 9

value of empty referenced, 154, 157

what-if table input, 320

wrapping text in, 129, 257

centering cell data, 128-129

changing. *See also* editing; resizing

@Function categories, 174, 179

background colors/patterns, 137-138, 147

cell alignment, 127-131, 145, 418-419

chart axes labels, 232, 241

chart legends, 230-231, 241

chart orientation, 227-228

chart types, 226-229, 240

column widths, 131-134, 145-146, 418

Custom Zoom settings, 417

data series colors, 236, 242

date formats, 80-81, 145

drawn objects, 270-273

fonts/font attributes, 116-122, 143-144

label-prefixes, 78

multiple variables, 319, 332

number formats, 124-127, 145, 419

page margins, 197-199, 209

page setups for printing, 194-196, 208

print orientation, 197, 209

printer settings, 182-183

row height, 131-134, 145, 146

scale of chart axes, 234, 241

screen split size, 66

version sorting options, 303

worksheet names, 27

characters

label-prefix, 78

prohibited from field names, 337

chart headings, 229-231, 240

chart notes, creating, 230, 240

Chart (Tools menu) command, 221, 222, 239

Data Labels command, 235, 242

Headings command, 229, 240

Legend command, 230, 241

Name command, 224, 225, 239

Range menu and, 224

Type command, 227, 240

charts. *See also* Quick Chart

changing types of, 226-229, 240

creating, 219-224

Designer Frames, 236-237, 242

finding by name, 226, 239

formatting, 229, 229-234

naming, 224-225, 239

overview, 212-213

printing, 237-238, 242-243

types of, 213-219

Clear All (Edit menu) command, 371, 394

Clear Split (View menu) command, 33, 66, 107

Clear Styles Only (Style menu) command, 142

Clear Titles (View menu) command, 71, 107

clearing. *See also*
deleting; removing
gallery templates, 142
splits from windows,
66, 107
Transcript Window,
371
clipboard
copying data to, 89,
109
moving data using, 87,
109
closing
Transcript window,
366, 393
Version Manager, 286
collections of cells,
selecting, 53-56, 105
colors
background, 137-138,
147
border, 134-135, 146
data series, 236, 242
drawn object, 273
font, 119-120
grid line, 416
worksheet, 420
column headings
customizing, 414-415
described, 13
freezing, 67-71, 107
hiding, 201-202
printing on multiple
pages, 204-205, 210
Column Width (Style
menu) command, 132,
146
columns
aligning data across,
128, 145
chart categories vs.
series, 219-220

deleting, 91, 110-111
inserting, 90-91, 110
page breaks, 192-193
selecting, 51
sorting database
records, 353
width of, changing,
131-134, 145-146,
418
combining
different chart types in
one, 218
files, 101-103, 113
labels, 151
comma number format,
125
comments, version, 290
conditions, logical, 152-
153
confirming data entries,
75-76, 77
Contents Box, edit line,
10
Contents page,
SmartMaster, 39
control-menu box, 457
conventions, xxv
Copy Down (Edit menu)
command, 90, 110
Copy (Edit menu)
command, 89, 109, 260,
381
Copy Right (Edit menu)
command, 89, 110
copying
cells, 164-165
data, 88-90, 109
drawn objects, 263, 279
Lotus 1-2-3 distribution
disks, 398
macros from Transcript
window, 381

creating. *See also* adding;
combining; drawing;
inserting
absolute references,
165-166
chart notes, 230, 240
charts, 219-224, 239
database queries, 339,
358
database tables, 336,
358
drawn objects, 247-257
field names, 336-337
files, 16, 43
formulas, 153-155, 178
macro buttons, 387,
395
macros, 362-363, 370-
371
named styles, 139-140,
147
one-variable tables,
320-323
scenarios, 310-312, 331
SmartIcon sets, 429-431
spreadsheet versions,
284-285, 288-291,
329
symmetrical objects,
273
text blocks, 257-259
three-variable tables,
326-328
two-variable tables,
323-325
version reports, 305-
309, 330-331
worksheets, 28, 44
criteria, database query,
346-357
multiple criteria, 350-
353, 359

overview, 346-347
single criterion, 347-350
Ctrl key
  collections of cells,
    selecting, 56, 105
  copying data, 89, 109
  freehand line segments,
    drawing, 254, 255
  multiple versions
    simultaneously,
    selecting, 302, 330
  running macros, 382,
    384
currency number format,
  125, 425
customizing
  international settings,
    423-425
  Lotus 1-2-3 installation,
    405-411
  recalculation settings,
    425-426
  user setup, 420-423
  view preferences, 414-
    418
  worksheet defaults,
    418-420
Cut (Edit) menu
  command, 86-87

D

data. *See also* analyzing
  data; entering data;
  series, data
  centering in cells, 128-
    129
  charting, 211-243
  combining files, 101-
    103, 113
  copying, 88-90, 109
  exchanged between

applications, xxiv
  finding, 93-97, 111
  moving, 86-88, 109
  sharing with work
    groups, xxiii-xxiv
  values vs. labels, 72
Data Labels (Chart
  submenu) command,
  235, 242
database tables. *See also*
  query tables
  creating, 336, 358
  maximum fields and
    records, 336
  naming, 338-339, 358
  selecting, 340
Database (Tools menu)
  command
  New Query command,
    339, 358
  Sort command, 353
databases
  described, 334
  fields, 335-336
  queries, 336
  records, 335
dates
  changing format of, 145
  customizing default
    formats of, 423-424
  entering as data, 80-81
  filling ranges with
    series of, 82, 107
  formatting, 126-127
  sorting versions by, 304
DDE (Dynamic Data
  Exchange) standard,
  xxiv
decimal places, 125
default Lotus 1-2-3
  installation, 400-401,
  402-405

Delete (Edit menu)
  command
  columns and rows, 91,
    110-111
  ranges of cells, 92, 110-
    111
  worksheets, 30
Delete key, editing data
  using, 86
deleting
  cell-specific macro
    commands, 379
  columns, 91, 110-111
  data from cells or
    ranges, 91-93, 108-
    109, 110-111
  drawn objects, 270, 281
  rows, 91, 110-111
  Version Manager
    entries, 286, 290
  words from user
    dictionary, 97
  worksheets, 29-30, 44
Designer Frames
  cells, 147
  charts, 236-237, 242
  described, 136-137
  drawn objects, 271-272,
    281
dialog boxes, 461
dictionaries, user, 97-99
directories
  installing Lotus 1-2-3,
    407
  opening files, 18-19
  saving files, 23
discontiguous ranges.
  See collections of cells
displaying. *See also*
  viewing
  database field values,
    348-349

hidden cells, 148
multiple worksheets, 32-33
negative values in red, 138
scenario data values, 313-314, 331
SmartIcon set lists, 428-429
versions in Version Manager Index, 301
worksheet frame, 415
worksheet tabs, 416
division operator, 151
dollar sign ($), 165-166
double quotation marks (")
as alignment character, 78
macro arguments, 393
dragging mouse
arrows, drawing, 250
copying data by, 89, 109, 420-421
described, 456
filling ranges by example, 83-84, 108
hiding cells by, 142
moving data by, 87, 109, 420-421
polylines and polygons, drawing, 254, 255, 277
positioning SmartIcon Button bars, 431
rectangles and ellipses, drawing, 252
resizing windows, 457-458
rotating drawn objects by, 274-275, 282
selecting ranges, 49-50,

104
text boxes, drawing, 258
Draw (Tools menu) command
Arc command, 252, 276
Arrow command, 250, 276
Freehand command, 257, 277
Line command, 247
Polygon command, 255, 277
Polylines command, 254, 277
Rectangle, Rounded Rectangle, or Ellipse commands, 252, 276-277
Text command, 258
drawing
arcs, 251-252, 276
arrows, 249-251, 276
freehand objects, 256-257, 277
lines, 247-249
polylines and polygons, 253-256, 277
rectangles and ellipses, 252-253, 276-277
drawn objects
arranging, 264-266, 279
changing, 270-273
copying, 263, 279
deleting, 270, 281
fastening, to cells, 266-267, 280
flipping, 273, 282
grouping, 268-269, 280
locking, 269, 280
moving, 264, 279

overview, 246-247, 260-261
resizing, 262-263, 279
rotating, 273-275, 282
selecting, 261-262
drives, selecting, 19-20
Dynamic Data Exchange (DDE) standard, xxiv

E

e-mail features, xiii
edit line
@Function Selector feature, 171-172
described, 7-10
displaying/hiding, 418
editing data on, 108
entering data using, 74-75, 107
Edit menu. *See also* Arrange (Edit menu) command; Paste (Edit menu) command; Undo (Edit menu) command
Clear All command, 371, 394
Copy command, 89, 109, 260, 381
Copy Down command, 90
Copy Right command, 89
Cut command, 86-87
Delete command, 30, 91, 111
Find & Replace command, 94, 95, 111-112
Go To command, 60-62, 106, 226

Insert command, 90
editing
  Button bar, 428
  cells, 74, 85-86, 108
  macros, 378-381
  SmartIcons, 432-433
  text blocks, 259, 278
  user dictionaries, 97
ellipses (...), 17
ellipses (drawn objects),
  252-253, 276-277
embedded @Functions,
  175
entering
  @Functions, 169-171
  chart headings, 230,
    240
  data, in database
    tables, 337-338
  formulas, 155-164, 178
  macro commands into
    worksheets, 368-370,
    393
entering data. *See also*
  filling ranges
  confirming/canceling
    entries, 75-76
  dates and times, 80-81
  numbers, 76-78
  overview, 71
  procedures, 72-75, 107
  in SmartMaster
    worksheets, 40-42
  text, 78-79
equal sign (=)
  beginning formulas
    with, 153, 156
  database query criteria,
    347, 348
  as logical operator, 152
equations. *See* formulas
ERR result, 155

errors in formulas, 155,
  422
Esc key
  ranges selection
    function, canceling,
    53
  retrieving old data
    values, 86
exploded pie charts,
  234-235, 241-242
exponentiation operator,
  151

F

fastening drawn objects,
  266-267, 280
fields, database record
  described, 335-336
  naming, 336-337
  query criteria, 347-350
  selecting, 341, 342-346
file extensions, opening
  files and, 20
File menu
  New command, 16, 38
  Open command, 17,
    43, 103
  Page Setup command,
    195, 208, 209
  Print command, 183,
    185, 186
  Print Preview
    command, 189, 208
  Printer Setup
    command, 182
  Save As command, 25,
    100
  Save command, 22, 26,
    43
file names
  described, 16

saving files, 23
files. *See also* creating;
  saving
  combining, 101-103,
    113
  created by
    SmartMasters, 37-42
  creating new, 16, 43
  display of recently
    opened, 21
  importing pictures into
    worksheets, 260, 278
  macro library, 370, 393-
    394
  opening, 17-21
  password protection of,
    23-26, 43
  printing all worksheets
    in, 185-186
  ranges as separate, 100-
    101
  referencing cells in
    different, 163-164,
    178-179
  using multiple,
    simultaneously, 34-
    37
Fill by Example (Range
  menu) command, 83,
  108
Fill (Range menu)
  command, 82-83, 107
filling ranges
  by example, 83-84, 108
  with series, 81-83, 107
Find & Replace (Edit
  menu) command, 94,
  95, 111-112
finding. *See also* Go To
  (Edit menu) command
  charts by name, 226,
    239

data, 93-97, 111
files to open, 20-21
fixed number format,
125
flipping drawn objects,
273, 282
floating SmartIcon
Button bars, 431
Font & Attributes dialog
box, 118-121, 144
Font & Attributes (Style
menu) command, 52,
144, 260
font attributes, 116-122,
143-144. *See also*
underlining
fonts, changing, 52, 116-
122, 143-144
footers, 199-201
formats
cell, 81
customizing default
international, 423
date and time, 80-81,
145, 423-424
number, 124-127, 145,
419
formatting. *See also* Auto
Format feature
applying, in group
mode, 122-124, 144
charts, 229-234
text blocks, 259-260,
278
text in cells, 78
worksheets, 115-148
formulas
creating, 153-155, 178
database query
calculations, 345
entering, 155-164, 178
errors in, 155

logical, 152-153
moving, 166-167
numeric, 151
one-variable tables,
320-321
overview, 150
relative vs. absolute
references, 164-166
searching for, 94
spaces and, 154
text, 151-152
three-variable tables,
326
too large results of, 155
two-variable tables,
323-325
types of, 150
in what-if tables, 320
frames. *See* Designer
Frames
freehand drawing, 256-
257, 277
Freeze Titles (View
menu) command, 68,
107
freezing worksheet
views, 67-71, 107

G

Gallery feature, 140-142
gallery templates,
installing, 140-142
Go To (Edit menu)
command
described, 60-62, 106
finding charts by name,
226, 239
graphics
drawn objects, 246-257,
260-275
importing pictures, 260,

278
text blocks, 257-260,
278
graphs. *See* charts
greater than (>) operator
database queries, 349
logical conditions, 152
greater than or equal to
(>=) operator
database queries, 349
logical conditions, 152
grid lines, cell
customizing display of,
416
hiding, 201-202
group mode
applying formatting,
122-124, 144
customizing worksheet
defaults, 419
Group Mode (Style
menu) command, 123,
144
grouping drawn objects,
268-269, 280
Guided Tour, launching,
2

H

hard disk space
requirements, 400-401,
406-407
headers, 199-201, 209
headings. *See* chart
headings; column
headings; row headings
Headings (Chart
submenu) command,
229, 240
Help menu, 4
Help, Windows, 463-464

Hide (Style menu)
  command, 142, 148
Hide Transcript
  command, 366, 393
hiding
  cells, 142, 148
  page breaks, 417
  row and column
      headings, 201-202
  scroll bars, 416
  Transcript window,
      366-367
horizontal cell
  alignment, 127, 128

I

icons. *See* SmartIcons
importing pictures, 260,
  278
input cells and values,
  what-if table, 320
Insert (Edit menu)
  command, 90, 110
inserting
  new worksheets, 28-29
  page breaks, 192-194,
      208
  ranges, 91, 110
  rows and columns, 90-
      91, 110
insertion marker, 74
installing Lotus 1-2-3
  Release 5
  customized installation,
      405-411
  default installation, 400-
      401, 402-405
  overview, 397-398
  procedure, 398-402
  system requirements,
      397-398

international settings,
  customizing, 423-425
italics. *See* font attributes

K

Key, Sort By, 354-357
keyboard commands.
  See also macros
  menus and menu
      items, 7, 460
  selecting ranges, 50,
      104
keywords, macro
  command, syntax, 364,
  392

L

label-prefix characters
  described, 78
  storing numerical dates
      as labels, 81
labels
  chart axes, 213, 232,
      241
  combining, 151
  data series, 231
  dates and times as, 80
  described, 72
  searching for, 94
landscape print
  orientation, 196-197,
  209
learning aids, xx
Legend (Chart submenu)
  command, 230, 241
legends, chart, 213, 229,
  230-231, 241
less than (<) operator
  database queries, 349
  logical conditions, 152

lesser than or equal to
  (<=) operator
  database queries, 349
  logical conditions, 152
line charts
  appearance of, 213
  type of data
      represented by, 214-
      215
lines
  changing, 270-271, 281
  drawing, 247-249, 276
Lines & Color (Style
  menu) command
  background
      colors/patterns, 137,
      147
  borders, 134, 146
  Designer Frames, 136,
      147, 237, 242
  drawn object
      colors/patterns, 273,
      281
  lines and arrows, 270,
      271, 281
  pie charts, 236
locking drawn objects,
  269, 280
logical formulas, 152-153
Lotus 1-2-3 Release 5
  customizing, 413-426
  database functions,
      333-360
  installing, 397-411
  macros, 361-396
  overview, xix-xxiv
  program group, 2
  Working Together
      strategy, xxiv
Lotus 1-2-3 window
  features, 6-14
  overview, 4-6

M

macro commands
   entering into
      worksheets, 368-370,
      393
   removing cell-specific,
      379
   syntax, 363-365
macro libraries, 370, 393-
   394
Macro (Tools menu)
   command
   Hide Transcript
      command, 366-367,
      393
   Record command, 372,
      375
   Run command, 385
   Show Transcript
      command, 366, 393
   Stop Recording
      command, 373, 378
macros
   autoexecute, 385, 422
   creating, 362-363, 370-
      371
   editing, 378-381
   naming ranges, 382-
      384, 394-395
   overview, 362
   planning, 365-366
   running, 381, 384-386,
      395
   SmartIcons and, 432
   syntax, 363-365
margins, page, 197-199,
   209
maximizing windows,
   457
menu bar, Lotus 1-2-3, 7
menu commands
   conventions, xxv

dimmed, 460-461
menu names, underlined
   letters in, 7
menus. *See also entries
   for specific menus*
   @Function Selector, 171
   described, 460-461
Microsoft Windows. *See*
   Windows, Microsoft
minimizing windows, 36-
   37, 457
minimum Lotus 1-2-3
   installation, 401-405
minus sign (-)
   subtraction operator,
   151
Minute interval, 82
mixed charts, 214
mouse, 456. *See also*
   dragging mouse
mouse pointer
   described, 456
   resizing windows, 457-
      458
   screen response to, xxi-
      xxii
moving
   chart headings, 230,
      240
   charts in chart boxes,
      228
   data, 86-88, 109
   drawn objects, 264, 279
   formulas, 166-167
   windows, 458
multiplication operator,
   151

N

Name (Chart submenu)
   command, 224, 225

Name (Range menu)
   command, 59, 106
   database tables, 338,
      358
   macros, 382
Named Style (Style
   menu) command, 140,
   147
naming
   charts, 224-225, 239
   database record fields,
      336-337
   database tables, 338-
      339, 358
   legend labels, 231
   macro ranges, 382-384,
      394-395
   ranges, 59-60
   scenarios, 312
   styles, 138-142, 147
   worksheet tabs, 27, 44
Navigator
   going to named ranges,
      62, 106
   overview, 9
nested @Functions, 175
networks, installing
   Lotus 1-2-3 Release 5
   on, 398
New (File) menu
   command, 16, 38
New Query (Database
   submenu) command,
   339, 358
New Sheet button, 12, 28
#NOT# logical formula
   connector, 153
not equal to (<>)
   operator
   database queries, 349
   logical conditions, 152

Number Format dialog box, 124-127

Number Format (Style menu) command, 126, 145

numeric formulas, 151, 154

numerical data
changing format of, 124, 145
default cell alignment, 127
entering, 76-78, 107
values as, 72

O

Object Linking and Embedding (OLE) 2.0 standard, xxiv

objects, drawn. *See* drawn objects

ODBC (Open Database Connectivity) standard, xxiv

OLE 2.0 (Object Linking and Embedding) standard, xxiv

one-variable tables, 320-323

Open Database Connectivity (ODBC) standard, xxiv

Open File dialog box, 18

Open (File menu) command, 17, 103

opening
existing files, 17-21
Lotus 1-2-3 Release 5 group window, 2
Transcript window, 366, 393

#OR# logical formula connector
creating formulas, 153
database queries, 351-353

outlines, cell. *See* borders

P

Page Break (Style menu) command, 193, 194, 208

page breaks
hiding, 417
inserting, 192-194, 208
printing, 192-194

Page Setup (File menu) command, 195, 208, 209

pages
headers and footers on, 199-201, 209
inserting breaks in, 192-194, 208
margins, 197-199, 209
print orientation, 196-197, 209
setting up for printing, 194-196
viewing before printing, 189-192

parentheses ( )
@Function arguments, 169
negative values in, 419-420
in numeric formulas, 154

passwords
described, 23-26
removing, 44

saving files with, 43-44

Paste (Edit menu) command
copying data, 89, 109
importing pictures into worksheets, 260, 278
inserting macros into worksheets, 381
moving data, 86, 109

patterns, background, 137-138, 147, 273

percent number format, 125

perspective mode
3D range selection, 57, 106
viewing multiple worksheets, 32

pictures, importing, 260, 278

pie charts
appearance of, 214
enhancing, 234-236
exploding, 234-235, 241-242
type of data represented by, 217

placeholders
grouping drawn objects, 268
resizing drawn objects, 262, 279

planning macros, 365-366

plus sign (+) addition operator, 151

polygons and polylines, drawing, 253-256, 277

pop-up menus
charting commands, 229
font lists, 121

right mouse button, 138

status bar, 14

portrait print orientation, 196, 209

positioning

graphs in chart box, 228

legends, 231, 241

SmartIcon Button bar, 431

previewing printing, 189-192, 207-208

Print (File menu) command, 183, 185, 186

Print menu

Selected Chart command, 237, 243

Selected Drawn Objects command, 238, 243

print orientation, 196-197, 209

Print Preview (File menu) command, 189, 208

Print Titles option, 204-205, 210

Printer Setup (File menu) command, 182

printing

charts, 237-238, 242-243

headers and footers, 199-201, 209

hiding row and column headings, 201-202

page breaks, 192-194

preventing cells from, 142

previewing, 189-192, 207-208

print orientation, 196-197, 209

Print Titles option, 204-205, 210

quick, 182-185

saving settings, 205-206, 210

selected ranges, 186-189

setting page margins, 197-199, 209

setting up pages for, 194-196

SmartMaster topics, 39

SmartMaster-created worksheets, 42

worksheets, 183-186, 207

productivity features

macros, 361-396

overview, xxii-xxiii

Program Manager, Windows

described, 464-465

Lotus 1-2-3 Release 5 program group, 2, 408

Q

queries, database

creating, 339, 358

described, 336

selecting fields for, 342-346

setting criteria for, 346-357

query tables, selecting locations for, 341

Quick Chart

changing chart types, 226-229

creating charts using, 222-224, 239

plotting ranges, 221

quick menus, xxi-xxii

quick printing, 182-185

QuickStart tutorial, 3-4

quotation marks. *See* apostrophe ('); double quotation marks (")

R

range cursor, 52

Range menu

Analyze command, 317

Chart submenu and, 224

Fill by Example command, 83, 108

Fill command, 82-83, 107

Name command, 59, 106, 338

Version command, 284, 288, 292, 300

ranges. *See also* filling ranges; table ranges, what-if

centering data across, 128

combining selected, 101-103, 113

containing named versions, 287-288

defined, 48

deleting, 91-93, 110-111

fonts in, formatting, 118

going to, 60-64

inserting, 91, 110

macro, 382-383, 384-386

moving, 86-88, 109

naming, 59-60
naming database tables
as, 338-339
numbers in, formatting,
124
performing functions
on, 52
plotting in charts, 221
printing selected, 186-
189, 207
referencing named,
159-161
saving as separate files,
100-101
selecting, 49-53, 104-
105
separating with
borders, 135, 146
sorting database
records, 353-354
switching between
multiple versions of,
290
recalculation settings,
customizing, 425-426
Record command, 372,
375, 394
recording macros
procedure, 372-378,
394
vs. typing commands,
364
records, database
described, 335
selecting, 341
setting criteria for
queries, 346-357, 359
sorting, 353-357
rectangles
applying Designer
Frames to, 271, 281
drawing, 252-253, 276

references
moving formulas and,
167
relative vs. absolute,
164-166
referencing
across worksheets, 33,
161-163, 178-179
cells
in different files, 163-164
empty, 154, 157
in what-if calculations,
316
named ranges, 159-161
relative references, 164-
166
removing. *See also*
clearing; deleting
frozen titles, 71
gallery templates, 141-
142
passwords, 25-26, 44
SmartIcons from sets,
430
renaming. *See also*
naming
charts, 224-225
worksheet tabs, 27, 44
replacing. *See also*
combining
data, 93-97, 111-112
misspelled words, 98-
99, 112
reports, version, 305-309,
330-331
resizing. *See also* scaling
columns, 131-134
drawn objects, 262-263,
279
fonts, 119
rows, 131-134
SmartIcons, 433-434

windows, 457-458
worksheets, 7, 202-204,
209
retrieving
old data values, 86
print settings, 205-206,
210
rotating drawn objects,
273-275, 282
row headings
customizing, 414-415
described, 13
freezing, 67-71, 107
hiding, 201-202
printing on multiple
pages, 204-205, 210
Row Height (Style
menu) command, 133,
146
rows. *See also* records,
database
chart categories vs.
series, 219-220
deleting, 91, 110-111
height of, changing,
131-134, 145, 146
inserting, 90-91, 110
inserting page breaks
along, 193-194, 208
selecting, 51
Run command, 385, 395
running
macro buttons, 390,
396
macros, 381, 384-386,
395

S

sans serif fonts
defined, 116
numbers in

spreadsheets, 117
Save As (File menu)
  command, 100
  ranges, saving, 112-113
  removing passwords,
    25
Save (File menu)
  command, 22, 26
saving
  additional copies of
    files, 26-27, 44
  customizing automatic
    file, 421-422
  existing files, 26, 43, 44
  newly created files, 21-
    23
  password protected
    files, 23-26, 43
  print settings, 205-206,
    210
  ranges as separate files,
    100-101, 112-113
  SmartIcon sets, 431
  SmartIcons, 432
  SmartMaster-created
    files, 40
scaling. *See also* resizing
  chart axes, 234, 241
  worksheets, 202-204,
    209
scenarios
  described, 309-314
  sorting versions by,
    304-305
scientific number format,
  125
scroll bars
  described, 461-462
  hiding, 416
scrolling
  database field values,
    348-349

frozen views, 69-70
synchronized, 66
windows and dialog
  boxes, 461-462
worksheet tabs, 31
Selected Chart (Print
  menu) command, 237,
  243
Selected Drawn Objects
  (Print menu)
  command, 238, 243
selecting
  3D ranges, 57-58, 106
  appropriate chart types
    for data, 214-215
  collections of cells, 53-
    56, 105
  database fields and
    records, 341, 342-
    346
  database tables, 340
  directories in Open File
    dialog box, 18
  drawn objects, 261-262,
    279
  drives in Open File
    dialog box, 19-20
  font attributes, 119
  font colors, 119-120
  fonts, 118-119
  Lotus 1-2-3 program
    group, 408
  multiple versions
    simultaneously, 301-
    302, 330
  query table locations,
    341
  ranges, 49-53
  rows and columns, 51
  SmartIcon set lists, 429
  worksheet areas, 48-49
  worksheet versions,

285
selection indicator, edit
  line, 9
semicolon (;), 363, 392
series, data
  changing color of, 236,
    242
  chart Y-axes displaying,
    213
  formatted by rows vs.
    columns, 219-220
  labels, 231
serif fonts, 116
Set View Preferences
  (View menu)
  command, 414
sharing data, xxiii-xxiv.
  See also Version
  Manager
Shift key
  arrows, drawing, 250
  extending range
    selections, 51, 104
  polylines and
    polygons, drawing,
    254, 255
  rotating drawn objects,
    275, 282
  selecting objects for
    grouping, 269
  squares or circles,
    drawing, 253
  text boxes, drawing,
    258
shifting cells, 164. *See
  also* moving
shortcut keys, 7, 460
Show Transcript
  command, 366, 393
sizing. *See* resizing;
  scaling

slash (/) division operator, 151

SmartIcon sets
  adding SmartIcons to, 430
  lists of currently available, 428-429
  removing SmartIcons from, 430
  saving, 431

SmartIcon (Tools menu) command, 428

SmartIcons
  currently available, 434-436
  displaying/hiding, 418
  editing, 432-433
  Lotus 1-2-3 window, 11
  overview, xxi, 427-428
  resizing, 433-434

SmartMasters
  creating files using, 37-42, 45
  overview, xx

Sort By Key, 354-357

Sort (Database submenu) command, 353

sorting
  database records, 353-357, 359-360
  worksheet versions, 302-305, 330

space character, macro syntax, 364, 392

space characters, 154

Spell Check (Tools menu) command, 98, 112

spell checking, 97-99, 112

Split (View menu) command, 32, 64, 106

splitting worksheet views, 64-67

spreadsheets. *See also* Version Manager
  calculations, 149-180
  creating versions of, 288-291
  fonts, 117
  overview, 1-2

stacked bar charts
  appearance of, 213
  type of data represented by, 216

status bar
  changing font faces/sizes, 121
  described, 14
  displaying/hiding, 418
  e-mail notification, xxiii
  group mode indication, 123
  recording macro indication, 375
  values vs. labels, 72

Stop Recording command, 373, 378, 394

Style menu
  Alignment command, 128, 145
  Clear Styles Only command, 142
  Column Width command, 132, 146
  Font & Attributes command, 52, 144, 260
  Group Mode command, 123, 144
  Hide command, 142, 148
  Lines & Color command, 134, 136, 137, 236
  Named Style command, 140, 147
  Number Format command, 126, 145
  Page Break command, 193, 194, 208
  Row Height command, 133, 146
  Worksheet Defaults command, 418

styles, font. *See* font attributes

styles, named, 138-142, 147

subtraction operator, 151

synchronized scrolling, 66

syntax, macro, 363-365

system requirements, 397-398

T

table ranges, what-if
  defined, 320
  one-variable tables, 321, 332
  three-variable tables, 326

tables. *See* database tables; query tables, selecting locations for; what-if tables

tabs. *See* worksheet tabs

templates, gallery, 140-142, 148

text
  attaching with lines, 247
  customizing colors, 420

entering into cells, 78-79

in headers and footers, 199-201, 209

wrapping in cells, 129, 257

text blocks

creating, 257-259, 278

editing, 259, 278

formatting, 259-260, 278

rotating, 273-274, 282

text formulas, 151-152, 154

three-variable tables, 326-328

3D area charts

appearance of, 214

vs. area charts, 218

3D bar charts

appearance of, 214

vs. bar charts, 218

3D line charts

appearance of, 214

vs. line charts, 218

3D pie charts

appearance of, 214

vs. pie charts, 218

3D ranges, selecting, 57-58, 106

Tile (Window menu) command, 36

times

customizing default formats for, 423-424

entering as data, 80-81

filling ranges with series of, 82

formatting, 127

title bar, Lotus 1-2-3 window, 6

ToIndex button, 287

Tools menu. *See also* Draw (Tools menu) command

Arrow command, 250, 276

Chart command, 221, 222

Database command, 339

Macro command, 366-367, 372, 375, 393

SmartIcon command, 428

Spell Check command, 98, 112

User Setup command, 420

Tracking button, 288

Transcript window

clearing, 371

creating macros in, 366-367

editing macros in, 379-380

opening/closing, 366, 393

Tutorial (Help menu) command, 4

Tutorial window, 3-4

two-variable tables, 323-325

Type (Chart submenu) command, 227, 240

typefaces. *See* fonts

underlining. *See also* font attributes

macro arguments and, 364, 392

selecting types of, 119

Undo (Edit menu) command

combining files, 102

deleting entries, 91

editing data, 86

enabling/disabling, 422

moving data, 88, 109

uninstalling gallery templates, 141

undoing

database record sorts, 354, 357, 360

described, 462

drawn object deletions, 270, 281

menu selections, 7

unlocking drawn objects, 269, 280

updating worksheet versions, 286, 293, 329

User Setup (Tools menu) command, 420

values. *See also* series, data

combining across files, 101-103, 113

customizing display of negative, 425

dates and times as, 80-81

described, 72

displaying negative, in red, 138

incrementing in ranges, 82

numeric formulas and, 151

referenced empty cells, 154, 157

U

V

selecting database field, 348-349

tables of, in charts, 228-229

what-if table input, 320

variables

changing multiple, 319

in multiple worksheet versions, 296

one-variable tables, 320-323

three-variable tables, 326-328

two-variable tables, 323-325

Version Manager

creating versions, 288-291, 329

described, 283-288

multiple versions, working with, 291-299

overview, xxii

Version Manager Index

described, 299-305

overview, 287

Version (Range menu) command

creating new versions, 292, 329

naming versions, 288

opening Version Manager, 284, 329

Version Manager Index, 300

version reports, 305-309, 330-331

vertical cell alignment, 129

View menu

Clear Split command, 33, 66, 107

Clear Titles command, 71, 107

Freeze Titles command, 68, 107

Set View Preferences command, 414

Split command, 32, 64, 106

Zoon In/Out commands, 417

view preferences, customizing, 414-418

viewing. *See also* displaying

@Function List, 172-175

formulas inserted by Lotus 1-2-3, 166

multiple worksheets, 32-33, 45

pages before printing, 189-192

scenario lists, 312, 331

SmartMaster topics, 39

worksheet tabs, 31

worksheet version information, 286

views, worksheet

freezing, 67-71, 107

multiple, 32-33, 45

splitting, 64-67, 106

W

Week interval, 82

what-if tables

one-variable, 320-323, 332

three-variable, 326-328

two-variable, 323-325

what-ifs, 314-316

wildcards, DOS, 20

Window menu

accessing hidden Transcript window, 367

described, 34-36

windows

cascading, 35-36

Lotus 1-2-3, 4-6, 6-14

manipulating, 456-459

minimizing, 36-37

splitting, 64-67

tiling, 36

Transcript, 366-367, 393

Tutorial, 3-4

Windows, Microsoft. *See also* clipboard; Program Manager, Windows

components of, 455

default screen colors, 420

features, 456-459

Help feature, 463-464

Lotus 1-2-3 installation and, 405, 410

mouse actions, 456

Program Manager, 2, 408, 464-465

standards supported by, xxiv

.wk* file extension, opening files, 20, 21

Working Together strategy, xxiv

Worksheet Defaults (View menu) command, 418

worksheet frame, customizing, 414-415

worksheet names

selection indicator, 9

window title bar, 6

worksheet tabs

displaying, 416

Lotus 1-2-3 window, 11-12
viewing multiple, 31
worksheet window, 12. *See also* Lotus 1-2-3 window
worksheets. *See also* Version Manager; views, worksheet
activating group mode, 123, 144
creating, 28
customizing default styles, 418-420
deleting, 29-30, 44
entering macro commands into, 368-370
formatting, 115-148
identifying current, 11-12

importing pictures into, 260, 278
Lotus 1-2-3 window, 4-6, 6-14
maximum database table size in, 336
naming, 27, 106
pasting macros into, 381
printing, 183-186
recalculation settings, 425-426
referencing across, 33, 161-163, 178-179
renaming, 27, 44
scaling for printing, 202-204, 209
selecting areas in, 48-49
spell checking, 97-99, 112

wrapping text in cells, 129, 257

X 

X-axis, 212-213
XY charts
appearance of, 214
type of data represented by, 218-219

Y 

Y-axis, 213

Z

zero value, 154, 157, 419
Zoom In/Out (View menu) commands, 417